# THE GUIDE TO ANSWERING ISLAM

## What Every Christian Needs to Know About Islam and the Rise of Radical Islam

Daniel Janosik

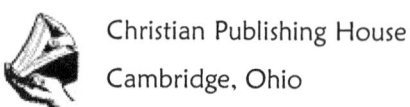
Christian Publishing House
Cambridge, Ohio

Copyright © 2019 Daniel Janosik

All rights reserved. Except for brief quotations in articles, other publications, book reviews, and blogs, no part of this book may be reproduced in any manner without prior written permission from the publishers. For information, write, support@christianpublishers.org

Unless otherwise stated, Scripture quotations are from English Standard Version (ESV) The Holy Bible, English Standard Version. ESV® Text Edition: 2016. Copyright © 2001 by Crossway Bibles, a publishing ministry of Good News Publishers

*THE GUIDE TO ANSWERING ISLAM: What Every Christian Needs to Know About Islam and the Rise of Radical Islam* by Daniel Janosik

ISBN-13: **978-1-949586-76-3**

ISBN-10: **1-949586-76-6**

The Guide to Answering Islam by Daniel Janosik

# Table of Contents

Dedication .................................................................................. 7

INTRODUCTION ..................................................................... 8

PART 1: CONTROVERSIES ABOUT THE DEVELOPMENT OF ISLAM ............................................................................................. 11

    CHAPTER 1 Pre-Islamic Overview: Paganism or Heretical Monotheism? ............................................................................ 12

    CHAPTER 2 Muhammad: Final Prophet or Apocalyptic Preacher? .................................................................................. 22

    CHAPTER 3 Qur'an: Divine Authorship or Authored by Men? ... 40

    CHAPTER 4 The Origin of Islam: New Path to God or a Jewish-Christian Heresy? ..................................................................... 52

    CHAPTER 5 Theological Development of Islam: The Opening of the Gates of Heaven or the "Closing of the Muslim Mind"? ..................... 68

    CHAPTER 6 Islamic Golden Age and Expansion: Path of Peace or Trail of Blood? ........................................................................... 79

PART 2: BELIEFS AND PRACTICES .................................................. 96

    CHAPTER 7 Islamic Doctrine: Five versus Three Equals One? ..... 97

    CHAPTER 8 Sharia Law: External Laws or Internal Sanctification 116

    CHAPTER 9 Sin and Salvation in Islam: Works Alone or Grace Alone? ....................................................................................... 141

    CHAPTER 10 Eschatology: Waiting for the Mahdi or the Messiah? .................................................................................... 158

    CHAPTER 11 Sects and Schools: What is the Real Agenda? ......... 183

PART 3: JIHAD, CRUSADES, AND ISIS ............................................ 200

    CHAPTER 12 History and Meaning of Jihad: A Struggle Against Violence or a Violent Struggle? ................................................. 201

    CHAPTER 13 Crusades: Christian Holy War or Delayed Response? .................................................................................. 221

    CHAPTER 14 Radical Islam: What is ISIS and What do they Want? ......................................................................................... 242

PART 4: APPROACHES TO REACHING MUSLIMS WITH THE GOSPEL .................................................................................... 264

CHAPTER 15 Do Muslims and Christians Worship the Same God? ................................................................................................ 265

CHAPTER 16 How Do You Answer Muslim Objections? .......... 275

CHAPTER 17 What is God Doing in the Muslim World?........... 294

CHAPTER 18 How Do You Reach Muslims with Both Truth and Love?................................................................................................ 310

Epilogue ................................................................................ 324

Glossary for The Guide to Answering Islam .............................. 328

Subject Index ........................................................................ 335

Bibliography .......................................................................... 349

# Dedication

This book is dedicated to the memory of Nabeel Qureshi (1983-2017). His example of presenting the truth of Islam while demonstrating the love of Christ toward Muslims has been a continual guiding light to me. May his books continue to bring Muslims to Christ through their clear presentation of Christ as God the Son, and their excellent modeling of how Christians should love Muslims with the love of Christ.

# INTRODUCTION

## The Dilemma

Our world has changed greatly in the last few decades. However, the struggles we have are still fundamentally the same. As Ephesians 6:12 reminds us, "We do not struggle against flesh and blood, but against the rulers, the authorities, the powers of this dark world, and the forces of evil in the heavenly realms." Perhaps the greatest challenge to Christianity in the West is the growth of Islam and its ever-growing influence in our daily lives. Christians need to understand what Islam teaches in order to defend their own beliefs against Islamic ones. Christians also need to be able to refute heretical doctrine. Understanding, defending and refuting beliefs together form the heart of Apologetics. They are also what this book is about.

## The Problem

What if Muhammad of traditional Islam was an invention of a later Arab leader; or the Qur'an was not collected and written down until the early 8th century — and actually came from many sources, including Christian and Jewish liturgy? What if it turned out that the city of Petra in Northern Arabia was the birthplace of Islam, not Mecca, and that Mecca was only established as a city after the death of Muhammad? Perhaps the even greater question is, "how would Muslims react to these claims?" These questions are startling because they each suggest in some way that Islam had a very different origin than the one detailed by the earliest Muslim sources, and that the original Muhammad of Islam is not the man the Muslims revere today. If such claims are true, and enough evidence and solid facts can be presented to support them, then much of what we have been taught about the origins of Islam may actually be erroneous. This book seeks to examine those claims and the evidence that may support them. If Islam did start as a heretical Christian sect, then through its denial of the deity of Christ it has led billions of people away from the truth of orthodox Christianity. This book, therefore, addresses a topic which should be of interest to all Christians. If the foundation and beliefs of a religion are faulty, then the consequences are either based on deceit or fear, and force is often advocated to keep the religious culture intact. Both the foundation and beliefs of Islam are examined in this book, which seeks to expose historical inaccuracies and closely examine its teachings for errors.

## The Plan

There are four main sections in the book. In the first section, the **historical critique**, I discuss the Muslim's traditional view concerning various subject areas using primarily Muslim sources. I will then give a historical perspective of this subject based on the most recent discoveries and interpretations, as well as a critique of the traditional view based on a Christian perspective. Finally, I explain how the biblical or historical view can be used to witness to Muslims in order to "build bridges" to the gospel. The second section is a **theological critique** of Islam. Again, I give the Muslim view using primarily their own sources. I then contrast the Muslim beliefs with Christian positions and counter-beliefs. Again, I follow this up with an explanation of how the Christian counter-view can be used to build bridges. The third section is a **critique of radical Islam**. I first demonstrate how this **is** about Islam! I then demonstrate how a faulty foundation (part 1) and false religious teachings (part 2), inevitably lead to dysfunctional religious practices that often are propagated through deceit or by coercion. This section examines how Jihad is necessary to propel Islam; without force, Islam would probably have been relegated to the "heresy bins" of the past. Thus, the traditional three choices (convert, pay, or die) have been necessary to force Islam upon others. Seen in this light, the Crusades were a delayed response to this force, and Islamic radicalism today demonstrates the continuation of the original need for force. The only way to end this cycle is to win Muslims over to Christ. Finally, in the fourth part, the book discusses several approaches to reaching Muslims with the gospel of Jesus Christ. First, it explains how the typical Muslim views Christianity. This helps us gain a fresh perspective from the other side. The book then reviews ways that do not work well when Christians try to reach out to Muslims. It also reviews the best ways that Christians can answer the core questions that Muslims bring up. Finally, the most effective ways that Christians can witness to Muslims are discussed. Through all of these approaches, the goal is for Christians to use reason in order to remove the obstacles to faith so that Muslims can see the truth about Christianity and the preeminence of Christ, the Son of God, who is the lover of their souls.

There are also study questions at the end of each chapter to help readers reflect on the material. These would be helpful discussion starters in a small group or Sunday school class. In addition, a Glossary at the end of the book should aid in defining words that may not be familiar. There are also charts showing the differences between Christianity and Islam. These will be helpful for discussions focused on demonstrating the core beliefs that separate the two religions.

It is my hope and prayer that this book will serve the Christian Church so that they will understand more about what they believe as well as what Muslims believe. Then Christians will be better able to defend the truth of Christianity and refute the errors of Islam, not in a spirit of fear, hatred or condemnation, but in the spirit of love and respect.

This apologetic approach is summed up by 1 Peter 3:15, which states, "Always be prepared to give an answer to everyone who asks you to give the reason for the hope that you have. But do this with gentleness and respect." I pray that this book will indeed prepare you to give an answer to any Christian or Muslim who asks you to give an answer for the hope that we have in Christ, and that they might, in turn, receive that same true hope in the only one who can give them eternal life.

Finally, I have many Muslim friends whom I respect and greatly enjoy. We have had lively discussions about our beliefs, and I have learned a lot about Islam from them. When I consider these relationships, I am reminded that **our critique is against Islam, not Muslims**. We are commanded to love Muslims, for they are made in the image of God and need to know who Jesus Christ really is. In addition, Ephesians 6:12 tells us that "we do not struggle against flesh and blood, but against the rulers, against the authorities, against the powers of darkness, and against the spiritual forces in the heavenly realms." Therefore, let us stand firm in His mighty power and bring light, and love, and truth to this conversation.

# PART 1: CONTROVERSIES ABOUT THE DEVELOPMENT OF ISLAM

# CHAPTER 1 Pre-Islamic Overview: Paganism or Heretical Monotheism?

## Introduction

The traditional accounts describe Arabs before the time of Muhammad as being in a state of confusion, which Muslims refer to as "Jahiliyyah." This term means that the Arabs were spiritually lost, and their practices were strongly opposed to Allah's ways – they did not know the truth and were always fighting among themselves. Culturally they are depicted as morally decadent and perverse, illiterate, animistic, disobedient to the laws of Allah, idolatrous, and cruel to the point of burying baby girls alive.[1] Muhammad's revelations of Allah are therefore believed to have changed the Arabic world both dramatically and permanently. This chapter studies the traditional representation of the pre-Islamic period in detail, and then considers the evidence and arguments for a more complex religious, cultural, and political picture of pre-7th century Arabia. The chapter concludes with apologetic considerations about how the factual details of this historical setting matter in discussing the role of Muhammad and the founding of Islam.

## The Traditional Muslim View

Muslims traditionally consider the period of approximately 300-610 AD as one when most people in Arabia were pagan idol worshippers, though they also note traces of monotheism in a group called the Hanifs, who had rejected idolatry and retained some form of beliefs based on an Abrahamic concept of "submission to God." The Qur'an uses the term Jahiliyyah in several places when it refers to this pagan, pre-Islamic time. Arabic life before Muhammad is described as:

- An age in which false thoughts of Allah were widespread (Q. 3:154)[2]
- A time of paganism when laws were not from Allah (Q. 5:50)
- A time of general lawlessness or lack of rule (Q. 48:26)

---

[1] Mohd Shukri Hanapi, "From Jahiliyyah to Islamic Worldview: In a Search of an Islamic Educational Philosophy," International Journal of Humanities and Social Science, Vol. 3 No. 2, January, 2013, 214-15.

[2] This refers to the Qur'an, surah (chapter) 3, verse 154.

- A barbaric age marked by women displaying the adornments of their dress and ornaments before others (Q. 33:33)

These specific verses paint a picture of a culture that was dominated by tribalism and ignorance. There was chaos between the clans, constant warfare, rivalry, and continual pagan practices – such as the abominable worship of fertility gods, which were among the 360 gods housed at the Ka'aba. Hubal, the moon god was worshiped there,[3] as well as three female deities who were known as the "daughters of Allah": al-Lat, "the Goddess," al-Uzzah, "the Mighty," and Manat, the "Goddess of Destiny."[4] The Hadith[5] expressly describes this type of pagan adulation in the following account:

> We used to worship stones, and when we found a better stone than the first one, we would throw the first one and take the latter, but if we could not get a stone then we would collect some earth (i.e. soil) and then bring a sheep and milk that sheep over it, and perform the Tawaf around it. When the month of Rajab came, we used (to stop the military actions), calling this month the iron remover, for we used to remove and throw away the iron parts of every spear and arrow in the month of Rajab.[6]

The primary emphasis in the traditional Muslim view of this period is the utter lack of any knowledge of Allah's law, but the overall culture of ignorance is also significant to the concept of Jahiliyyah. As one prominent Muslim writer explains:

> No one seemed interested in the cultivation and advancement of knowledge. The few who were literate were not educated enough to understand the existing arts and sciences. Although they did possess a highly developed language capable of expressing the finest shades of human thought in a remarkable manner, a study of the remnants of their literature reveals how limited was their knowledge, how low was their standard of culture and civilization, how saturated were their minds with superstitions, how barbarous and ferocious were their thoughts and customs, and how decadent were their moral standards ... As regards their religious beliefs, they suffered from the same evils which were playing havoc with the rest of the world. They

---

[3] Ibn Hisham 1/151-155; Rahmat-ul-lil'alameen 2/89, 90.

[4] Reza Aslan, *No God but God: The Origins, Evolution, and Future of Islam* (New York: Random House, 2006), 7.

[5] The Hadith are the traditional sayings of Muhammad written down around 200 years after the death of Muhammad.

[6] Sahih al-Bukhari, Vol 5, #661 (Narrated Abu Raja Al-Utaridi)

worshipped stones, trees, idols, stars and spirits; in short, everything conceivable except God.[7]

This lack of learning, government structure, or civilizing influences made Arabia truly a dark place – but some Muslims see this very ignorance and *tabula rasa* (blank slate) quality as making Arabia the perfect place for Allah's truth to shine forth in a final, uncorrupted revelation (since Muslims believe that all previous revelations had been corrupted after the deaths of the prophets Abraham, Moses, Jesus Christ, etc.). Many Muslims believe that this pagan past was completely rejected after Muhammad brought the truth of Allah's word and law into Arabia.[8]

However, there are a number of Jahiliyyah practices that were not discarded. As one Muslim scholar explains, a few of these practices were accepted in Islam, though with obvious reforms.[9] For example, the Tawaf, or circumambulation of the Ka'aba,[10] remained obligatory, but with the body covered (Q. 7:31). In marriage, during the former time, a man could marry as many women as he pleased. However, the Qur'an now specifies that a man can only marry up to four wives at a time (Q. 4:3). Retaliation for the murder of a clan member is still in place, but now only the proven murderer faces the death penalty instead of random members of the murderer's clan also becoming subject to possible execution (Q. 6:51). During the Jahiliyyah, women did not receive any inheritance from their husband or family's estate, but with the advent of Islam, a woman would have the rights of inheritance of her husband's or family's estate (Q. 4:11, 12, 176). In addition, in the earlier time conducting war was considered a noble profession and the expected outcome of a man's pride, but after Muhammad, safeguards were put in place in order to ensure that the innocent were protected and that war was conducted according to the will of Allah (Q. 2:190, 193, 224). Also, in business, the sale and purchase of goods were filled with usury and fraud, but the Qur'an forbids usury, and the conduct of business is expected to be fair and accurate (Q. 2:275). Finally, in the "times of ignorance" slavery was rampant and full of "oppression, humiliation, and exploitation," but now the Qur'an forbids the exploitation of slaves, and laws have been put in place to preserve the

---

[7] Abu al-Ala Maududi, *Towards Understanding Islam* (U.K.I.M Dawah Centre), 31.

[8] Tom Holland, *In the Shadow of the Sword: The Birth of Islam and the Rise of the Global Arab Empire*, (Anchor, 2013), 50.

[9] Hanapi, "From Jahiliyyah to Islamic Worldview," 217-19.

[10] Even today Muslims walk around the Ka'aba seven times during their hajj, or pilgrimage, just as the pagans did before Muhammad.

dignity of the slave as one who shares the intrinsic nature of the free man (Q. 24:33).[11]

This traditional view of religious and cultural practices before Muhammad, however, does not seem to be a study of priority among Muslims. More traditionally-inclined histories of Islam by non-Muslims, such as the one by Karen Armstrong, place the Muslim concept of Jahiliyyah (the pagan years) into a more complex social and religious context, but still, accept the central idea of widespread barbarism and poverty in both an economic and cultural setting.[12] More commonly, however, traditional Muslim writers do not typically examine Jahiliyyah as a historical concept. Instead, Muslim scholars often use Jahiliyyah as a theological concept to describe the secular chaos which not only preceded Islam but which also describes any society or any person that rejects the sacred truth and way of life Islam teaches. Thus, a number of Muslim writers argue that the modern western culture is also Jahiliyyah, or corrupt, degenerate, and lacking knowledge of the true God, which the faithful Muslim must strive to escape in order to remain on what is known as the straight path.[13]

For example, Sayyid Qutb, one of the most influential 20th-century Muslim thinkers, says that Jahiliyyah is an antithesis of Islam, the opposite of Allah's plan for the human race in religion, politics, philosophy, and law. Thus, since even the Muslims of his day (1960s) were living without the laws of God, or Sharia, Qutb believed that the Muslim community did not actually exist at that time, for even those who called themselves Muslims did not live in an Islamic world, but rather in Jahiliyyah, or pre-Islamic ignorance.[14] Qutb argues, then, that, "Our whole environment, people's beliefs, and ideas, habits and art, rules and laws -- is *Jahiliyyah*, even to the extent that what we consider to be Islamic culture, Islamic sources, Islamic philosophy and Islamic thought are also constructs of *Jahiliyyah*!"[15] Thus, for many Muslim leaders today, anything that is contrary to the rule of Allah through Sharia is considered Jahiliyyah, whether it depicts the situation before the time of Muhammad or the present age. For the Muslim traditionalist, then, the teachings of Muhammad were crucial in bringing his followers out of the darkness and into the light of Islam.

---

[11] Hanapi, "From Jahiliyyah to Islamic Worldview," 217-219.

[12] Karen Armstrong, *Islam: A Short History* (New York: Random House, 2002), 4.

[13] Abu al-Ala Mawdudi (see Asyraf Rahman, The Influence of Al-Mawdudi and the Jama'at Al Islami Movement on Sayid Qutb Writings, World Journal of Islamic History and Civilization, 2 (4): 232-236, 2012) ; Sayyid Qutb, Milestones (Birmingham, UK: Maktabah, 2006).

[14] Sayyid Qutb, Milestones (Birmingham, UK: Maktabah, 2006), 9.

[15] Sayyid Qutb, Milestones, 20.

## Scholarly Views Which Support the Jahiliyyah or Traditional View

A number of historians and other scholars who study the Middle East, and accept much of the traditional Muslim view based almost exclusively on the Muslim sources, generally agree with the overall depiction of this pre-Islamic Arabia as being one of "moral depravity and religious discord," as one writer puts it.[16] However, these historians also present evidence of a more complex set of circumstances that casts doubt on the simplistic idea of Jahiliyyah. Pre-Islamic society and politics are generally seen as being a mixed bag: while Bedouins or desert nomads (ruled by Shaykhs or elders and renowned for their bravery) probably made up the majority of the population, more advanced agricultural and trading economies abounded in the more fertile parts of the peninsula. These groups were, however, still bound together by common economy, culture, and the ties of family and clans.[17]

One Jewish scholar, Yehuda Nevo, acknowledges that in the present a number of traditional Muslim scholars promote the idea that "many nomadic tribes inhabited the pre-Islamic Arabian Peninsula, and an extensive trade network, whose hub was Mecca, resulted in the rise of the peninsula as a political power."[18] These Muslims further believe that Muhammad was able to merge this political power together with his religious message to bring about a paradigm shift that transformed this pagan area from a dry place of ignorance to a fount of knowledge in the one God of the universe.

## Non-Muslim Counter View

On the other hand, a number of non-Muslim scholars point to specific historical records and scholarly studies that strongly indicate that the situation was much more complex than Muslim traditional accounts portray. These non-traditional scholars argue that this Muslim view is overly simplistic in regard to the picture it paints of Arabic religious groups and practices before the 7th century. They point to evidence that there were some established monotheistic religions already existing in pre-Islamic Arabia. While barbaric practices doubtless did occur, they conclude, overall there were too many different religious elements to accept the story of

---

[16] Aslan, *No God but God*, 5.

[17] Jonathan Berkey, *The Formation of Islam: Religion and Society in the Near East, 600–1800* (Cambridge: Cambridge University Press, 2003), 40.

[18] Yehuda Nevo, and Judith Koren, *Crossroads to Islam: The Origins of the Arab Religion and the Arab State* (Amherst, New York: Prometheus, 2003), 1.

tribes wallowing in pagan ignorance and yearning for cultural unity and sophistication. These mixed religious groups mean that Muhammad's message and subsequent military conquest did not liberate the entire continent from theological and cultural ignorance. These scholars thus agree that pagan idolatry was rampant, but some highlight evidence that semi-heretical Christian beliefs were prominent as well. Monophysitism, Nestorianism, Arianism, and Ebionism – interpretations which all deny some aspect of Christ's divinity as it is understood in orthodox Christianity – may all have mixed with the pagan religions around them. There even seem to have been a number of Arabs who had converted to Judaism and prospered in clans as farmers, camel-breeders, and merchants.[19]

Fred Donner, an expert in early Islamic history, has documented the existence of Jews in certain parts of Arabia as early as the 1st century AD, and suggests that there may also have been some communities of Jewish Christians called Nazoreans, who recognized Jesus as Messiah and accepted some Christian doctrine, but continued to practice their own legal code. In addition, he concludes that while Christianity was found in eastern Arabia, in northern border areas with Syria and Iraq, as well as in Yemen, it is harder to show any significant Christian presence in the Hijaz, where Mecca and Medina are located.[20] Another scholar, Jonathan Berkey, points out that religious practices varied widely among various Arabic groups. Many gods were recognized (as at the Ka'aba), and the supernatural was an important element of daily life, but the moral order of society was based on social needs rather than theological standards. "Religion was something immediate and real – could some deity help you find a lost camel? – rather than a matter of abstract doctrine and principle," he explains.[21] It seems logical to assume that the religious life of Bedouins was ancestor-based and had all the trappings of supernatural paganism that traditional accounts credit it with, but that at the same time certain settled regions of the Arabic peninsula had more sophisticated religious beliefs that could focus on issues like the afterlife.[22]

Scholars Sidney Griffith and Yehuda Nevo specifically point to evidence of Jews and Christians (as well as their scriptures) during the time

---

[19] Jonathan Berkey, *The Formation of Islam*, 39-49.

[20] Fred Donner, *Muhammad and the Believers: At the Origins of Islam* (Cambridge, MA: Harvard University Press, 2010), 30-31. This may be an indication that Islam did not develop in the Hijaz, but rather in the northern regions of Arabia around Petra. This is the premise of Dan Gibson's new book, *Qur'anic Geography* (Independent Scholars Press, 2011).

[21] Berkey, *The Formation of Islam*, 41.

[22] Aslan, *No God but God*, 12.

of the Qur'an's formation.[23] This argument is supported by the fact that the Qur'an itself mentions them and their scriptures specifically, indicating that Arabic-speaking Jews and Christians lived in the time and vicinity of early Islam. At the very least, the fact that the Qur'an clearly describes Old Testament figures and cites the Prophets, Psalms, and Gospels indicates that these older monotheistic religions were prevalent and influential. Some scholars take this argument further and use the above evidence to suggest that Islam developed out of heretical Christianity, Judaism, and even Zoroastrianism. They hypothesize an intermediate monotheism developing early in the 7th century A.D. and ultimately culminating in an early form of Islam.[24] Other scholars suggest that this intermediate monotheism developed from an earlier Jewish-Christianity, which, in turn, was derived from 2nd-century heretical views of Jesus Christ held by the Nestorians, Monophysites, and Ebionites – all of whom have non-orthodox views of Jesus' divine and human natures.[25] Interestingly, this theory of Islam having evolved from a mixture of heretical Christianity and paganism was introduced in the 8th century by the Byzantine scholar John of Damascus (whose influential writings will be discussed in a later chapter).[26] The time before Muhammad, at any rate, would have been marked not so much by ignorant paganism but rather as a mixed society in which paganism rubbed shoulders with Christianity and Judaism, possibly providing religious elements that would later be absorbed into the new religion of Islam.

## Conclusion

The traditional Muslim view of pre-Islamic times, drawn primarily from the Qur'an, is that there was very little good happening in Arabia either in terms of right living or knowledge of the true God. There appear to have been, however, a number of Christians, Jews, and Zoroastrians who contributed to a mixed culture. They may have also contributed to a new monotheistic belief system which held strongly to Jewish legalism and apocalyptic trends, as well as claiming that Jesus was a sinless prophet without divine status.

While most historians and scholars who accept the traditional Muslim view generally agree with the Qur'an's description of a lawless and pagan

---

[23] Sydney Griffith, *The Church in the Shadow of the Mosque*, 6; Nevo, *Crossroads to Islam*, 190-194.

[24] Nevo, *Crossroads to Islam*, 195-6.

[25] Karl-Heinz Ohlig, Gerd Puin, Volker Popp, Yehuda Nevo, Fred Donner, Patricia Crone, Gerald Hawting, Jonathan Berkey, and Andrew Rippin.

[26] John of Damascus, *Heresy of the Ishmaelites*. Found in Daniel Janosik, *John of Damascus, First Apologist to the Muslims* (Wipf & Stock, 2016), Appendix C, 260-268.

lifestyle in the pre-Islamic Arabian Peninsula, they now have to admit that modern historical discoveries reveal that these practices were limited to certain areas and among certain groups. The idea of a widespread dark age which Muhammad gloriously interrupted in the 7th century is a concept that has been shown to be somewhat simplistic in scope.

From an apologetic stance, the historical and archaeological evidence demonstrates that the simplistic picture painted by traditional Islamic sources do not take into account the complexity of the religious, political, and cultural aspects of Arabia in pre-Islamic times. Thus, even the small details about what the "age of ignorance" really looked like can be very important. The version that one accepts will have significant implications as to what a person believes Muhammad and the founding leaders of Islam really accomplished: did they unite a struggling pagan continent? Or did they simply weave together existing strands of monotheism and political instability into a new militant religion? It is important for Christians to understand the complexities of this historical setting so that the explanations given by Muslims of Muhammad being a prophet who initiated a glorious civilization are not accepted without due critical consideration.

## Further Implications

Implications about this pre-history will play an important role in later chapters in two ways. First, noting these heretical Christian sects and the political situation of the 7th century – with Arabian border guards taking over as Byzantine forces abandoned the area – is key to understanding the argument that some non-Muslim scholars advance regarding the possibility of Islam evolving out of Jewish-Christian heresies. Such a complex theological situation in early Arabia is not one acknowledged by traditional Muslim accounts. Second, the historical evidence presented in this section argues that the Islamic forces were able to rapidly conquer the Arabian Peninsula, not necessarily because Allah was on their side, but probably because the retreating Byzantine armies left a vacuum in their military defenses. Also, the fact that many people regarded the Muslims as merely a sect of Jewish-Christianity, and therefore not a real threat, may have lulled Christians into a passive acceptance of the new regime. Clearly, then, what one believes about the state of Arabia before Muhammad is very important in interpreting Islam's development both theologically and militarily. These arguments will be discussed in detail in later chapters.

## Apologetic Conclusions

Apologetically, it is important to note that evidence demonstrating a vibrant Christian and Jewish influence in pre-Islamic Arabia not only counters the Muslim assumptions that Arabia was pagan and chaotic, a "time of ignorance," but specifically clashes with some of the statements made by the Qur'an about Muhammad and the reasons for Allah sending his revelations. This brings up the issue of external evidence supporting a scriptural text, which is a key apologetic issue to examine. Does the historical evidence support the Qur'an's account of Arabia before the time of Muhammad? A number of scholars have presented detailed reasons to believe that the concept of Jahiliyyah is a limited perspective that does not take into account a complex religious and political state of affairs in early Arabia. If this argument is accurate, then the Qur'an's explanation cannot be corroborated with external evidence, and a certain amount of doubt must be thrown on the truth of its own explanation of the origins of Islam.

Another apologetic point to consider from this section is why some of the practices that Muslims still follow today are borrowed directly from the pre-Islamic days or the time of Jahiliyyah. If the time of ignorance is to be repudiated, why should certain customs from that very time, such as circumambulating the Ka'aba and throwing stones at pillars representing Satan, still be practiced? This creates a degree of confusion that can give Christians an opportunity to discuss these theological and practical issues with Muslim friends.

## Building Bridges to Understand

Applying these apologetic points and historical evidences to our Christian witness underscores the importance of why Christians should trust in their worldview and their Scriptures. Muslims generally accept the concept of Jahiliyyah and its dark contrast with Allah's perfect revelation to Muhammad without considering any evidence outside of the Qur'an. In fact, examining the actual historical details of Jahiliyyah has not appeared to be of much importance to Muslim scholars. Yet Christians historically have had the opposite approach to determining the truth of the Bible: external evidences have been strenuously examined, and the wealth of written and archeological records around the time of Christ, in particular, have been studied diligently by scholars. In the end, these external sources have shown remarkable support of the Biblical narrative, with cities and military campaigns and even the existence of biblical persons being confirmed through historical sources. This gives Christians confidence in trusting the Bible, and particularly in knowing that the life of Christ is documented more thoroughly than that of any other person from the 1st century.

Christians can reach out to their Muslim friends by sharing that they, as Christians, trust the Bible's account of the 1st century AD, and thus also trust the identity of Jesus as the person whom the Bible claims that he is. This important role of verification gives Christians confidence to delve into the historical record. Why don't Muslims do the same to confirm the accuracy of the Qur'an? This can lead to important conversations about worldviews and the role of reason in one's religious faith.

### Study Questions

1. What are the main characteristics of Jahiliyyah according to the traditional Muslim view?
2. How do some modern Muslim scholars interpret Jahiliyyah for today's world? Who are the leading proponents of these ideas?
3. How does the non-Muslim view counter the traditional view?
4. What seems to be the most likely religious situation in pre-Islamic Arabia?
5. Discuss in Groups: What are some of the Apologetic conclusions that should be considered in relation to the Muslim concept of Jahiliyyah, especially in regard to the formation of Islam and the Qur'an?
6. Discuss in Groups: How can you apply these Apologetic points and historical evidences to reaching out to your Muslim friends? What is the most significant thing that they need to know about this material?

# CHAPTER 2 Muhammad: Final Prophet or Apocalyptic Preacher?

Who was Muhammad? Is every word and action attributed to him verifiable, or were some biographical details added in the years following his death? This is a question that must be asked when examining the records of almost any historical figure, and the issue is as complex as it is significant. The life of Muhammad is obviously an essential part of Islam —not just for understanding its origins but also because his life serves as the foundation for Islam's legal code (Sharia law).

This chapter recounts the traditional view of Muhammad's life, as it would be told by most Muslims or found in a general book on Islam, which would emphasize both Muhammad's actions and his character. It then examines the historical record as it stands today and highlights arguments of both Muslim and non-Muslim scholars on the identity of the historical Muhammad. The chapter concludes with discussion questions for a group study as well as suggestions about how to approach a conversation between a Christian and a Muslim.

## The Traditional View of Muhammad's Life

The following pages recount the view of Muhammad as accepted by Muslims in general. According to this traditional view, Muhammad was born in the year 570 AD in the city of Mecca. His parents were 'Abdu'llah ibn 'Abdu'l-Muttalib and Amina bint Wahab of the Quraysh, the tribe that served as caretakers for the Kaaba shrine. Muslims believe that this was a very important responsibility because Mecca relied on trade for survival, and veneration of the purported 360 gods housed in the shrine was its primary attraction. According to the Muslim sources, Abdullah died before Muhammad was born, and his mother died when he was six. Muhammad then lived with his uncle Talib and his cousins, and he was said to be an honest boy and a hard worker. Later he accompanied his uncle on some caravan journeys where he learned about other beliefs and traditions. It was during one of these journeys that a Nestorian monk named Bahira told Muhammad that he was chosen by God to be a prophet (which the monk deduced from an unusual mole on Muhammad's back). In the years to follow, Muhammad became known for his integrity, honesty, and wisdom, which earned him the title *Al Amin*, or "the trustworthy one."[27]

These qualities enabled him to be employed as a camel driver for a wealthy widow, named Khadija, who was Muhammad's cousin and 15 years his senior. In time his exemplary character won over Khadija, and they were married in 595 AD when Muhammad was 25. Relieved of financial pressure, Muhammad had time to go up into the mountains near his home and contemplate the injustices that he saw around him, such as widespread paganism, the live burial of infant girls, discrimination (especially in regard to women), and fighting among the different tribes. In 610 AD, as he sat in a mountain cave called *Hira*, where he often had dreams, an angel came and stood before him with writing on a piece of cloth and commanded him to read. However, Muhammad, like most of the people at that time, did not know how to read. When Muhammad said that he could not read, the angel embraced him and forced the air out of his lungs, and then commanded him again to read. Again, Muhammad said he did not know how to read. This sequence occurred three times before the angel finally told him what the words were on the cloth.

> "Proclaim! (or read!) in the name of thy Lord and
> Cherisher, Who created-
> Created man, out of a (mere) clot of congealed blood:
> Proclaim! And thy Lord is Most Bountiful,
> Who taught (the use of) the pen,
> Taught man that which he knew not." (Qur'an 96:1-5)

This passage was the first revelation of what has become known as the Qur'an, which is a term related to the command *to read*, or *to recite*.

Muhammad was initially terrified by this vision —even to the point of contemplating suicide, some accounts say —but his wife Khadija recognized his experience as being from Allah. She encouraged him to visit her cousin Waraqah ibn Newfal, who some believe may have been a Christian. Upon hearing of Muhammad's experience, Waraqah concluded that it was a genuine experience from God and testified that Muhammad must be a prophet from God.

Muhammad eventually accepted this call and began preaching against paganism, discrimination, and injustice (613 AD). His main message was that there was only one God, named Allah and that all people should submit to this God. Initially, Muhammad faced much resistance and persecution. His first convert was his wife, followed soon thereafter by a

---

[27] Ziauddin Sardar and Zafar Abbas Malik, *Introducing Islam* (Cambridge: Icon Books, 2001), 9.

merchant and trusted friend, Abu Bakr. Through the next 20 years Muhammad continued receiving revelation from Allah through the angel Gabriel, sometimes in visions, sometimes while in a trance, and sometimes from a man claiming to be Gabriel. Muhammad faithfully proclaimed the message he received, but the people of Mecca strongly opposed his teachings. The major reason for this was that the concept of submission to one God struck at the very heart of the city's economy. If the Kaaba's gods were no longer revered, the flourishing trade in Mecca would be jeopardized. The resistance grew to the point that even his own relatives decided that Muhammad needed to be dealt with.

However, Muhammad was warned about the impending treachery and escaped to a city 200 miles north of Mecca called Yathrib (later called Medina), where some of the city leaders had invited him to become the chief arbiter between the Arabs and the Jews. This "emigration" to Medina is known as the "Hijrah," and marked the beginning of Islam and the Islamic calendar (622 AD). Various conflicts had been raging in Medina for decades, but the five main tribes were finally unified when they assented to a series of articles that Muhammad drew up. This agreement was called the *Constitution of Medina*, and it served as the blueprint for later treaties that would stipulate the roles of believers and non-believers, especially for Muslims with the "People of the Book" (Jews and Christians).

Although the agreement at Medina initially procured peace, Jewish scholars soon began to criticize Muhammad for plagiarizing his messages from other sources. Ridicule followed by animosity arose between the Jews and the Muslims, and over the years, as Muhammad and his followers gained more power, the Muslims eventually banished two of the three largest Jewish tribes from the city and seized the vacated properties for themselves.

In addition to these tribal contests of power in Medina, Muhammad and his followers simultaneously became involved in skirmishes with tribes of other cities. During the flight to Medina, when the Muslims were essentially defenseless fugitives, Allah had given Muhammad permission to lead offensive battles in times of need. Soon, Muhammad and his men expanded the application of this message to allow raiding Meccan caravans, justifying their actions with the words from Allah.[28] The raids allowed the

---

[28] Q22.39: "To those against whom war is made, permission is given (to fight), because they are wronged; and verily, Allah is most powerful for their aid." Q2:217: "They ask you concerning fighting in the sacred months (i.e. 1st, 7th, 11th and 12th months of the Islamic calendar). Say, 'Fighting therein is a great (transgression) but a greater (transgression) with Allah is to prevent mankind from following the way of Allah, to disbelieve in Him, to prevent access to Al-Masjid-Al-Haram (at Makkah), and to drive out its inhabitants, and Al-Fitnah is worse than killing."

Muslims to acquire wealth and power, but they also initiated conflict between the Quraysh tribe of Mecca and the Muslims of Medina. In time this led to armed battles between the two groups.

During this period in Medina, Muhammad ordered at least 87 raids, although he himself was only personally involved in 27 of them.[29] These raids brought in needed funds for the believers as well as helping them to increase the ranks and were used as a measure of faithfulness to Allah. Over the 10 years Muhammad was in Medina, these raids, also known as *maghazi*, increased revenue greatly, and Muhammad's leadership and his role as a prophet were solidified. Of the many maghazi raids and battles, there were four that became an integral part of the story of Muhammad's life, as not only the growth of his nascent religion but also his political and religious leadership was demonstrated in all of them.

The first took place in the spring of 624 near the town of Badr when a group of Meccans attacked Muhammad and 300 of his men in retaliation for an earlier caravan raid. Though the Muslims were outnumbered 3:1, they soundly defeated the Meccans, killing 70 and taking 70 prisoners for ransom, while only losing 14 of their own.[30] This victory was interpreted as confirmation of Allah's favor, and it strengthened Muhammad and his followers' position over the Jews in Medina, especially when the Jewish Banu Qaynuqa tribe was accused of violating the Constitution of Medina. The tribe was promptly banished from the city and their property was confiscated.[31]

The second military encounter between the Meccans and the followers of Muhammad took place the following March of 625, outside of Medina on the slopes of Mount Uhud. This battle was a deliberate attempt by the Meccans to destroy Muhammad and his followers, and though the Muslims had an initial tactical advantage, they suffered defeat due to poor discipline. Only a false rumor of Muhammad's death kept the Muslim army from being decimated by the Meccan generals, who considered Muhammad's death to be sufficient victory. Once Muhammad had revived from his wounds, he explained to his demoralized army that disobedience and a desire for loot had led them out of Allah's will and protection. This became a standard theme or doctrine: fighting for Allah's glory brought victory while fighting for selfish gain would be divinely punished by defeat. A further example of Muhammad's combined role of prophet and warrior occurred a few months after this when Muhammad received a revelation from Gabriel that a certain Jewish tribe (the Banu Nadir) was plotting to

---

[29] David Cook, *Understanding Jihad* (University of California Press, 2005), 6.
[30] Sahih Bukhari 4:52:276.
[31] Tabari, vol. VII, 86.

assassinate him. The Muslim army besieged the tribe, which surrendered two weeks later, and the Banu Nadir were subsequently banished and their lands and goods were seized.

The third notable conflict occurred in March of 627 when the Meccans called for a "rematch" and Abu Sufyan, the leader of the Meccan army, set out for Medina with 10,000 men. When the Muslims heard about the threat, they began to make preparations. However, they could only muster 3,000 men. Fortunately, a Persian convert suggested that the Muslims dig a trench between the two mountains near the entrance to the city. In a short time, with Muhammad working beside his men, the Muslims dug a trench nearly 2 kilometers in length. When the Meccans arrived, the ditch was too wide for their horses, and they could only pitch volleys of arrows and engage in small skirmishes outside the city. After 27 days, the confederacy gave up this inglorious battle and left abruptly in the morning. The Muslims were left to rejoice in what they considered a victory. Hearing a rumor that some of the Jews of the Banu Qurayza tribe had plotted with these enemies, Muhammad acted quickly to remove this last tribe of Jews from the city.[32]

These conflicts moved toward resolution beginning in 628 when Muhammad and 1,400 of his men marched to Mecca for the annual pilgrimage and negotiated a peace agreement with the city leaders that would allow them to attend the *hajj* rituals. This agreement, called the *Treaty of Hudaybiyyah*, called for a 10-year truce between the two cities beginning the following year, at which point each party would agree to peaceful relations with each other conducted with honesty and honor. Although some of the Muslims were initially angry at Muhammad's leniency in the agreement, since they felt it brought humiliation upon the prophet, Muhammad assured them in private that it would bring them victory in the end. Indeed, the treaty was only active for two years and actually benefited the Muslims. This benefit arose in 630 AD when a Quraysh-allied tribe violated the terms by attacking a tribe allied with the Muslims. In a response justified by the treaty, Muhammad marched on Mecca at the time of the next hajj with an army of 10,000 Muslims and local allies. The Meccans capitulated without a fight, and Muhammad then demonstrated his mercy by having only a small number of his opponents killed and sparing the remaining inhabitants of the city. He also destroyed the idols in the Kaaba and rededicated it to Allah alone. Muhammad did not force anyone to convert, but many did, since it had become apparent

---

[32] Muhammad Ibn Ishaq, *The Life of Muhammad*, ed. Alfred Guillaume (Karachi: Oxford University Press, 1955), 450-469.

to even Muhammad's staunchest opponents, such as Abu Sufyan, that the power had shifted over to the Muslims.

For the next two years, Muhammad led his followers in a campaign to unite all the Arabian tribes in a universal tribe, or *ummah*. By the time of his death in 632, most of the tribes in Arabia had sworn their allegiance to Muhammad and converted to Islam. The many conflicts, of which the three described above are some of the most famous, are said to demonstrate Muhammad's prestige in battle as well as his merciful conduct toward his adversaries and his devotion to the cause of Allah. The Hadith is said to attest to Muhammad's life as being marked by generosity, his elevation of the status of women, his ability to unify people with a vision that reached beyond the divisions of tribe or region, and his ability to motivate his followers to victory in battle. By the end of his life, Muhammad had realized his dream of bringing peace to his war-torn people, and even more importantly, he was used to initiate the true path of Allah that would grow to be the second largest religion in the world. Turning now from the traditional story of Muhammad's life, the next section examines scholar's views and critical arguments on the subject.

## The Counterview According to Historical Documents and Archeological Evidence

The traditional view of Muhammad, summarized above, is the account that almost every Muslim knows by heart. Most Muslims would also sincerely believe that there is overwhelming evidence for Muhammad's life. One modern author presents the most common Muslim understanding of the historical documents of Muhammad's time:

> "The life of Muhammad is known as the Sira and was lived in the full light of history. Everything he did and said was recorded. Because he could not read and write himself, he was constantly served by a group of 45 scribes who wrote down his sayings, instructions and his activities. Muhammad himself insisted on documenting his important decisions. Nearly three hundred of his documents have come down to us, including political treaties, military enlistments, assignments of officials and state correspondence written on tanned leather.... Within a few decades of his death, accounts of the life of Muhammad were available to the Muslim community in written form. One of the earliest and the most famous biographies of Muhammad, written

less than [sic.] hundred years after his death, is Sirat Rasul Allah by ibn Ishaq."³³

The issue, then, that must be considered is whether the documents that describe the life of Muhammad are complete and authentic in comparison to other ancient documents, or whether the written record overall is too unreliable to make categorical claims of validity. Muslims and many modern non-Muslim scholars argue for the former, while others —including Christian scholars —have made a case for the latter. The arguments generally revolve around historical records penned by Muslims, records penned by non-Muslims, and archeological evidence in the form of coins and inscriptions.

## Historical Documents Written by Muslims

The first major issue that should be considered in evaluating the historical identity of Muhammad is the strength or weakness of documents from his time. Four types of historical documents that have been written by Muslims are used to support the traditional view: early biographies of Muhammad, the Hadith, the Qur'an, and copies of the treaties made during Muhammad's lifetime. Muslims and other traditional scholars see these sources as being trustworthy and argue that any chronological gaps can be explained by an oral culture and the effects of time. Scholars who take the opposite side claim that too many discrepancies and unknown factors exist to accept all the claims about Muhammad's actual life or even his true identity.

Early biographies of Muhammad's life support the traditional view of Muhammad and the early days of Islam by providing information outside of the accounts in the Qur'an and Hadith, which are not chronological or narrative works. The very first biography of Muhammad is attributed to ibn Ishaq (d. 767), but this significant work only survives in a shortened version written down by another author, ibn Hisham, before his own death in 827 AD. Although this biography provides invaluable supporting evidence about the life of Muhammad, non-traditional scholars point out several flaws in this source. First, the actual copy of this work that can be studied today was not penned until almost 200 years after Muhammad's death. Patricia Crone remarks that this is comparable to "reconstructing the origins of Christianity on the basis of the writings of Clement or Justin

---

³³ Ziauddin Sardar, *Introducing Islam*, 30.

Martyr in a recension[34] by Origen."[35] Second, the Muslim historians who wrote after this date — including the eminent chroniclers Ibn Sa'ad (d. 845), Baladhuri (d. 892), al-Tabari (d. 923), and Ibn Khaldun (d. 1406) — used this early work as the basis for much of their own material. This situation places a heavy weight on the accuracy of not merely the work of ibn Ishaq, but also of his copier ibn Hisham.

In writing the first biography of the prophet, ibn Ishaq (Ibn Hisham), interestingly presents a rather different version of Muhammad than that of the standard narrative. While today Muhammad is considered the most perfect man who has ever lived,[36] it was not until the 13th century that this idea actually arose. The idea originated with Ibn Arabi, a Sufi mystic, who said that Muhammad was "Al-Insan al-kamil," or the perfect man. Ibn Ishaq (through ibn Hisham), however, presented a much different picture of the prophet. Seeking to give context to the Qur'an and some of the traditions circulating at that time, ibn Ishaq's biography, according to historical scholar D.S. Margoliouth, summarized Muhammad as follows:

> The character attributed to Muhammad in the biography of Ibn Ishaq is exceedingly unfavorable. In order to gain his ends he recoils from no expedient, and he approves of similar unscrupulousness on the part of his adherents, when exercised in his interest. He profits to the utmost from the chivalry of the Meccans, but rarely requites it with the like. He organizes assassinations and wholesale massacres. His career as tyrant of Medina is that of a robber chief, whose political economy consists in securing and dividing plunder, the distribution of the latter being at times carried out on principles which fail to satisfy his follower's ideas of justice.
>
> He [the prophet Muhammad] is himself an unbridled libertine and encourages the same passion in his followers. For whatever he does, he is prepared to plead the express authorization of the deity. It is, however, impossible to find any doctrine that he is not prepared to abandon in order to secure a political end ... This is a disagreeable picture for the founder of a

---

[34] *Recension*: a revised edition of a text; parts of an earlier text adapted and included in a later one.

[35] Patricia Crone, *Slaves On Horses: The Evolution of the Islamic Polity* (Cambridge: Cambridge University Press, 1980), 202.

[36] Maududi calls Muhammad the "greatest revolutionary," and goes on to say of Muhammad that, "In the cavalcade of world history, the sublime figure of this wonderful person towers so high above all the great men of all times that they appear to be dwarfs when contrasted to him." A.A. Maududi, Towards Understanding Islam (U.K.I.M Dawah Centre).

religion, and it cannot be pleaded that it is a picture drawn by an enemy.[37]

A key example of Muhammad's unscrupulous actions presented by ibn Ishaq involved the aftermath of the Battle of the Trench when some of the Jews in the tribe of the Banu Qurayza were accused of treason. Muhammad chose to follow the advice of one of the non-Jewish tribal leaders and have all of the Banu Qurayza punished. The men were taken out to a newly dug trench in the middle of the city and beheaded, eight at a time. When it was all over 600-800 men filled the trench. The women and the children were then sold into slavery or exchanged for weapons.[38] Apparently, in the time of ibn Ishaq, these kinds of actions were considered proper and praiseworthy. However, there is evidence to show that today these kinds of stories of Muhammad are often marginalized in order to uphold the preferred image of the perfect man.[39]

The second type of historical documents that inform and support the traditional view are the Hadith or the collected sayings of Muhammad. Neither Muhammad nor any of his close associates are known to have recorded any of the prophet's words, but, according to some Muslim scholars, a group of scribes is believed to have traveled with him and written down everything he said.[40] However, the earliest copies of Hadith available are included in collections by scholars such as al-Bukhari, Sahih Muslim, and abu-Da'ud, and date from the end of the 9th century or later. Again, this creates a gap of over 200 years between the times that Muhammad allegedly spoke the words and the first copies that are currently known.

Treaties are the third type of historical documentation. According to the traditional view, the *Treaty of Hudaybiyyah* and the *Constitution of Medina* represent significant events in the development of Islam and Muhammad's life. Written copies of these exist, but unfortunately, the earliest of them does not pre-date ibn Hisham's mention of these documents in the early 9th century. In other words, there is no mention of these documents until the biography itself. This makes it difficult to

---

[37] D.S. Margoliuth, *Encyclopedia of Religion and Ethics*, volume 8, Ed. James Hastings (Edinburgh: T&T Clark, 1915), 878.

[38] Muhammad Ibn Ishaq, *The Life of Muhammad*, ed. Alfred Guillaume (Karachi: Oxford University Press, 1955), 450-469.

[39] See W.N. Arafat, "New Light on the Story of Banu Qurayza and the Jews of Medina" (Journal of the Royal Asiatic Society of Great Britain and Ireland, 1976), 100-107; and Ahmad Barakat, *Muhammad and the Jews* (New Delhi: Vikas Publishing House, 1979); Daniel Janosik, "The Real Story Behind the Massacre of the Banu Qurayza" (CSIOF Occasional Papers, No. 3, 2012).

[40] Sardar, *Introducing Islam*, 30.

determine with any accuracy whether the copies changed in content or form at any time, and theoretically makes it possible that ibn Hisham could have gotten many or most of the details wrong in his account, and then the later copies would have reflected those errors. At any rate, the historical strength of the major treaties as corroborative documentation is lessened because of this two-century gap.

Finally, the Qur'an itself, which Muslims claim was written down within 20 years of Muhammad's death, is said to support the traditional view to some extent because it includes Muhammad's name and certain events that are linked to the life of the prophet. Non-traditional scholars point out, however, that the name "Muhammad" only occurs four times in the text, and three of those times could just as easily refer to a position or title as to an actual person.[41] The events linked to the life of the prophet mentioned in the Qur'an are also somewhat vaguely identified and have no known contemporary supporting evidence. Because of this, it has been suggested that the Hadith (sayings of Muhammad) were actually derived from early commentaries on the Qur'ān, beginning sometime in the latter half of the 8th century, as believers tried to make sense of various passages in the Qur'ān; and then this material was used to write the *Sira* (history of the Prophet's life), as well as explain the Qur'an in a more sustained narrative form.[42]

A number of these Muslim documents, therefore, exhibit a common feature — a chronological gap of at least 100 years between the time in which they should have been created and the date of the earliest known copy. Should this be considered a serious flaw in the historical reliability of Muhammad's life and the origins of Islam? Several considerations must be noted. First, traditional scholars point out that the Arabic culture of the 7th century was an oral one, and writing functioned mainly as a way to validate what a person should remember from oral communication. People were expected to memorize rather than to read, and much of the education process was carried out through rote memory. Thus, these scholars conclude, it is perfectly reasonable to assume an accurate passing on of knowledge orally until the time that it could be set down on paper. A 100-200-year gap is thus not only understandable but perhaps the most logical outcome.

However, an additional consideration which Christian and non-traditional scholars emphasize is that an oral culture only addresses the issue of a lack of written documentation. It does not answer the question of how

---

[41] Q. 3:144; 33:40; 47:2, 48:29.

[42] Fred Donner, *Narratives of Islamic Origins: The Beginnings of Islamic Historical Writing*, (New Jersey: The Darwin Press, 1998), 24-25.

reliable the transmission was originally or what kinds of adaptations it underwent as it was passed on. Written versions of texts permit a better analysis, allowing scholars to study alterations and gauge how much the text really changed over years of being re-told and passed on to different peoples and places. The closer to the date of origin a copy can be dated, then, the more likely it is to be the authentic version. Ultimately, therefore, it is certainly possible that many of these stories concerning Muhammad circulated orally for a long time, but the lack of seventh-century documents makes it very difficult to validate many of the claims made by ninth-century Muslim sources.

## Archeological Evidence of Muhammad

Archaeological evidence reveals that the earliest reference to Muhammad by Muslims[43] is in the form of inscriptions on coins.[44] Around 687 AD, fifty-five years after Muhammad's death, a rival of the caliph Abd al-Malik named ibn Zubayr minted a coin bearing the phrase "Muhammad is the messenger of Allah." After defeating Zubayr, Abd al-Malik began minting his own coins in 691 with the same phrase.[45] Looking more closely at these early Arabic coins mentioning Muhammad, a curious detail is that a number of them feature figures holding crosses, which would seem to indicate a Christian influence. Later coins dispense with both the figures and the crosses. This has caused some scholars to wonder if there was a conscious effort to erase any traces of Christianity from these later coins, indicating a deliberate transition to Islam.[46]

The other early evidence of Muhammad's existence is in an inscription on a building. In the late 7th-century, around the same time as the coins were minted, Abd al-Malik had the Dome of the Rock built and prominently inscribed on the walls what is known as the *Shahada*, or the basic Islamic creed, "There is no God but Allah, and Muhammad is his messenger." This inscription is considered by many to be an exceptionally solid piece of evidence that verifies that a specific person named

---

[43] Note: Muslims were not known by this name at this time. For the first 100 years they were called Saracens, Ishmaelites, Hagarenes by others. They referred to themselves as "mum'nin" (believers), and sometimes the "Muhajirun" (emigrants, or those on pilgrimage). They did not refer to themselves as "Muslims" until the middle of the 8th century.

[44] The specific field of Archaeology that studies coins is called "numismatics."

[45] Karl-Heinz Ohlig, ed., *Early Islam: A Critical Reconstruction Based on Contemporary Sources* (NY: Prometheus Books, 2013), 72-75.

[46] Karl-Heinz Ohlig and Gerd-R. Puin, eds., *The Hidden Origins of Islam: New Research into its Early History* (NY: Prometheus Books, 2010); Volker Popp in Ohlig, *Early Islam*, 68-87.

Muhammad not only existed but was also the acknowledged prophet of the new religion of Islam.

The traditional Muslim view is that when "Muhammad" appears in any historical documents or inscriptions, it is the name of an actual person. However, specialists in the fields of historical documents, epigraphy (inscriptions), and numismatics (study of coins) have expressed concern over this traditional interpretation. They argue that the evidence strongly suggests that the Arabic word "Muhammad" in these inscriptions, both on the early coins and the walls of the Dome of the Rock, is actually a title that may refer to Jesus Christ and not the prophet of Islam. This is because the root of the term "mu-hammad" is "Ahmad," which means, "praise." Therefore, "Muhammad" could be translated as "the one (mu-) who is praised (Ahmad)," or the "chosen one."[47] Thus, when the Dome of the Rock inscriptions proclaimed that "there is no God but Allah, and Muhammad is the messenger of Allah," the inscription could be referring to someone besides Muhammad the prophet. Taking this a step further, some scholars have even argued that these inscriptions may very well be evidence of a transitional phase in the development of Islam, in which elements of Judaism and Arian Christianity held sway. In this case, the inscriptions would refer to Jesus as the "praised one" of God.[48]

Traditional and Muslim scholars object to this view by pointing out that many of the inscriptions on the walls of the Dome of the Rock reflect a rejection of Jesus as the Son of God (Allah "has no associate") as well as a strong refutation of the Christian concept of the Trinity ("say not three"). They argue that the term "Muhammad" could not refer to Jesus as the "chosen one," or "praised one" because of this clear rejection of the Trinity. However, this argument only refutes the idea of the inscriptions referring to an orthodox understanding of Jesus. Heretical Christian views of Christ would actually agree with such rejections of the Trinity. Thus, this "Jesus" may not be referring to the Jesus Christ of orthodox Christianity, nor the later Isa of Islam, but rather the Jesus of an intermediate monotheism where

---

[47] Ohlig, *The Hidden Origins of Islam*, 63-64; Robert Spencer, *Did Muhammad Exist? An Inquiry into Islam's Obscure Origins* (Wilmington, Delaware: ISI Books, 2012), 45-46, 55-56.

[48] This transition may be reflected in the Qur'an as well. There is a difference between the first three times when the term "Muhammad" is mentioned as a title (Q. 3:144; 33:40; 47:2), and the final time when "Muhammad" is used in reference to a particular person (Q. 48.29). Yehuda Nevo, a Jewish Archaeologist, believes that this reference to Muhammad as a person may have been written in the 8th century, and therefore documents a transition from a time when the title "Muhammad" was used in reference to Jesus as the "chosen one," and a later time when the term "Muhammad" is used in reference to the prophet of a new religion.

"Jesus" is praised as the chosen messiah but not the Son of God.[49] Robert Spencer concurs and concludes, "It is therefore possible that the Dome of the Rock inscription is a surviving expression of the theology of a heretical Christian group that viewed Jesus solely as a divine messenger, not as the Son of God or Savior of the world."[50]

Whatever the origins of these inscriptions, within five years (696 AD), the removal of figures and crosses from the coins seems to indicate that Abd al-Malik consciously began transforming the title referring to Jesus into a proper name for the prophet of a new religion. Thus, while the material evidence supports Muhammad as the acknowledged prophet of Islam, it also leaves room for questions concerning the development of Islam and the exact origins of historical references to the name "Muhammad."

## Historical Documents by Non-Muslim Sources

While historical documents written by Muslims before the time of Abd al-Malik are scarce, there are a number of extant documents from the 7th century written by non-Muslims that DO provide early information concerning Muhammad and the origin of Islam. However, these documents often give a very different view of events and chronologies compared to the Muslim traditional account. For example, a document dated around 634 AD, called the *Doctrina Jacobi*,[51] mentions a prophet among the Saracens, riding on a horse leading his men, proclaiming the advent of the anointed one, the Christ who was to come, and preaching an apocalyptic message based on Jewish legalism. However, he is unnamed, and if this refers to Muhammad, then the date would indicate that he was still alive two years after the traditional date of his death. This prophet also claimed to have keys to the kingdom, which Muhammad never mentioned. Some scholars believe this is probably a different prophet or this may hint that the true origin of the Muslim prophet began as an apocalyptic leader of a Jewish-Christian heretical religion that promoted Jesus Christ as the Messiah but not as the Son of God.[52] Robert Spencer even speculates that the unnamed prophet of the *Doctrina Jacobi* may have been one of several religious figures later subsumed into a single figure under the name of Muhammad.[53]

---

[49] Yehuda Nevo, and Judith Koren, *Crossroads to Islam: The Origins of the Arab Religion and the Arab State* (NY: Prometheus Books, 2003), 258-267.

[50] Robert Spencer, *Did Muhammad Exist?*, 56.

[51] Robert Hoyland, *Seeing Islam as Others Saw It* (Princeton, NJ: Darwin Press, 1997), 55-60.

[52] Yehuda Nevo, *Crossroads to Islam*, 208-209.

[53] Spencer, *Did Muhammad Exist?*, 22-23.

Another account, attributed to Thomas the Presbyter[54] (written about 640 AD in Syriac), tells how nomadic Arabs, or "*tayyaye d-Mhmt*," invaded and took Syria in 635-636, storming monasteries and even killing a number of monks. If the Syriac word "Mhmt" refers to Muhammad, then Thomas could be the first to mention Muhammad by name. However, there is evidence that this document was revised in the 8th century, and since we do not have the original manuscript, the name of Muhammad could have been inserted in later copies of the document.[55] It is also possible that these early references to a "Muhammad" may be references to the Jesus of an intermediate monotheism who was worshiped as the Messiah of the Old Testament but not as the Son of God of the New Testament.

In addition, around 687, a Christian named John bar Penkaye wrote that Muhammad was a guide and teacher for those who followed him. Though he does not use the word "prophet," this reference to "Muhammad" fits well with what we know of the rise of Abd al-Malik during this time and his proclamation of Muhammad as the prophet after 691. As noted above, the name "Muhammad" was unknown in any of the writings of the Arabs. In addition, there was no mention of a book called the "Qur'an" or a religion known as "Islam."[56] Thus, the written testimony of the non-Muslims seems to corroborate the view that Muhammad as a person and prophet developed in the time of Abd al-Malik, perhaps from a composite drawn from some of the earlier religious figures mentioned, or perhaps from a deliberate effort to transform the "Jesus" of an intermediate monotheism into a distinct prophet of a new Arab religion.

One of the Christian eyewitnesses of these events was John of Damascus, who served as the chief tax collector for Abd al-Malik around 700 AD. Writing several decades later (743 AD) in a treatise called the *Heresy of the Ishmaelites*, John indicates that he is aware of Muhammad ("Mahmed") as a person, though he refers to him as a "false prophet" leading the "coercive religion of the Ishmaelites." He also indicates that this false prophet "fabricated his own heresy" after conversing with an Arian monk.[57] This assessment corresponds well with the view that Islam developed from a heretical monotheism of a Jewish-Christian cult, and that by the time John wrote his treatise Muhammad had been fully transformed

---

[54] Hoyland, *Seeing Islam as Others Saw It*, 118-120.

[55] This apparently became a common practice, as we shall see with other examples. This would be understandable since it would be easy for us to discuss the Muslims in Medina with Muhammad when actual history demonstrates that the early followers of Muhammad were not called "Muslims" until after 691 AD.

[56] Spencer, *Did Muhammad Exist?*, 25.

[57] Bonifatius Kotter, Die Schriften Des Johannes Von Damaskos, II, translation by author (NY: Walter De Gruyter, 1981).

from a title representing Jesus Christ as the "praised one" in an intermediate monotheism to a full-blown prophet of a new Arab religion.

## Implications

What difference do these critical arguments make? First of all, the traditional narrative is not an inerrant record, as many modern summaries often imply. Documents purportedly written during the time of Muhammad do not, as far as can be discovered, exist today, and the documents we do have – copies from at least a century later – offer fragmentary accounts that can contradict the traditional narrative as well as support it. Also, the archeological evidence of the 7th century that refers to Muhammad is limited, and the inscriptions can be interpreted in several ways. Thus, reliable evidence that Muhammad really did live when and how the Sira and the Hadith claim that he did is not nearly as plentiful as most people assume that it must be. In fact, there is enough evidence to reasonably question numerous details about the traditional account of Muhammad. Some would even go so far as to reject entirely the traditional narrative on the basis of flawed information.

Depending on how strongly the evidence is questioned, other issues must, in turn, be raised for consideration: Where did the traditions all come from? How much of Muhammad's teaching can be historically verified? Is the basis for the Qur'an really revelation to a single person? This opens up the door to considerations that the Qur'an came instead from many sources over a long period of time, undermining the authority of Islam and precluding any claims of divine origin.

## Apologetic Conclusions

What is the overall conclusion here for our apologetic approach with Muslims? No one can know perfectly all the answers about Muhammad's exact identity or whether Islam as a religion was still developing from a transitional monotheism decades after Muhammad's death. However, it is known that there are good arguments based on real evidence that Muhammad's life and teachings are not what is commonly believed. As Christians, we want to take that evidence and use it first to consider the various implications of a different origin of Islam, and second to apply those implications to how we view the life of Muhammad and how we view our role in engaging Muslims.

# Building Bridges to Understand

When discussing Muhammad, it is important for a Christian to not speak disrespectfully of him or of Islam. This prevents the conversation (and maybe the relationship) from being rejected. Thus, try to couch your discussion firmly in the more neutral realm of evidence – saying something like, "This is what the traditional view states, but other evidence suggests something else." Let the evidence raise good questions rather than trying to force them yourself.

A good way to reach out to Muslim friends and colleagues in regard to Muhammad is to compare him to Jesus Christ. Discussing the differences between evidence for the life of Jesus and the life of Muhammad is a good conversation to have but should be done respectfully and carefully. (The chart below highlights some of the major differences and should help you focus your discussion.) This comparison should not be done to denigrate Muhammad, but rather to demonstrate that the Jesus Christ of the Bible is a much greater person than the "Isa" described in the Qur'an. This bridge toward understanding – using evidence to discuss the differences between Jesus and Muhammad – should always be used with the goal of showing Muslims the personal nature of Jesus in Christianity. Muslims need to know how Jesus Christ should be our focal point because he is the only one who can teach us the truth and lead us to the Father (John 14:6). Christians, on the other hand, need to understand what Muslims believe about Muhammad, as well as what details historical records do and do not support, in order to wisely discuss the life of Muhammad. This allows us to defend what we believe by answering the questions that Muslims ask as well as offer piercing questions that will help Muslim friends realize that their assumptions are not always true. Keep in mind that at the end of the conversation you want to leave them with a clearer understanding of Jesus Christ.

### Study Questions:

1. What are the major sources Muslims use in order to learn about the life of Muhammad? What is problematic about these sources?

2. What are some of the points of evidence you would use in discussing the life of Muhammad with your Muslim friends?

3. Read an online article concerning the life of Muhammad from a Muslim perspective. What are some of the things that are mentioned that would be difficult to support historically?

4. Muslims hold Muhammad in high esteem, and many are offended when non-Muslims are critical of their prophet. How would you be

able to balance Truth and Love in a discussion with them concerning Muhammad?

5. **Class Activity:** After reviewing the Comparison Chart between Muhammad and Jesus Christ, how would you use this information in your witness to Muslims? If you are in a class setting, break up into partners and practice what you would say to a Muslim. Critique each other and then share your results with the rest of the class.

## Comparison between Jesus and Muhammad

| Jesus | Muhammad |
|---|---|
| 1. Born of a virgin (Mt. 1:18-25, S. 19:20) | 1. Born normally from a mother and father (Ibn Hisham, 68-69) |
| 2. Read the Scriptures (Lk. 4:16-21?) | 2. Was illiterate (S. 7:157) |
| 3. Fulfilled over 300 prophecies from the Old Testament | 3. Was not mentioned in any prophecy in the Old Testament |
| 4. Prophecies of Jesus are recorded in the Bible (Matt. 24) | 4. Gave no prophecies in the Qur'an |
| 5. Performed miracles (Mk. 3:9-10; S. 3:49) | 5. Never did miracles (S. 29:50) |
| 6. Jesus is the Word of God (Jn. 1:1; S. 4:171) | 6. The Qur'an was considered the word of Allah and Muhammad was only a messenger (S. 3:144) |
| 7. Jesus is the Son of God, the second person of the Trinity (Lk. 9:35; Rom. 1:4; 2 Cor. 1:19) | 7. Muhammad is only considered a messenger of Allah (S. 3:144) |
| 8. Jesus said, "For all who take the sword will perish by the sword." (Matt. 26:52) | 8. Muhammad was a warrior; involved in at least 27 battles (Ibn Hisham, Sirat Rasul Allah) |
| 9. Jesus received and heard the direct voice of God (Mk. 1:10-11) | 9. Muhammad heard only from the angel Gabriel (note: Galatians 1:8) |
| 10. Mentioned by name in the Qur'an 25 times in over 90 verses. | 10. The word "Muhammad" is found only 4 times in the |

| | |
|---|---|
| 11. Mentioned in the Bible hundreds of times. | Qur'an. (Q. 3:144; 33:40; 47:2; 48.29)<br>11. Muhammad is not mentioned in the Bible (contrary to S. 7:157; S. 61:6) |
| 12. Jesus was a prophet according to Deuteronomy 18:14-22 | 12. Muhammad was not a prophet according to Deuteronomy 18:14-22 |
| 13. The message of Jesus supported the Old Testament (Matt. 5:18) | 13. The message of Muhammad often contradicted the Old and New Testament |
| 14. Was sinless (Jn. 8:46; S. 19:19) | 14. Was sinful (S. 40:55; 47:19; 48:1-2) |
| 15. Died to save sinners (Jn. 1:29; 10:18) | 15. Could not save himself (S. 46:8-9) |
| 16. Rose from the dead on the third day just as he predicted (Mk. 8:31-38; Lk. 23-24) | 16. Died and was buried in Medina (al-Tabari 9:208) |
| 17. Jesus is the King of Kings and Lord of Lords (Rev. 19:16), and is coming again for his followers (Matt. 24:27) | 17. Muhammad was the prophet of Islam and cannot save any of his followers (S. 46:9) |
| 18. Jesus is the only way to the Father (Jn. 14:7) and the only one who can save (Acts 4:12) | 18. Muhammad denied the Father, and he denied that Jesus is the Son of God. (See 1 John 2:22) |

# CHAPTER 3 Qur'an: Divine Authorship or Authored by Men?

## Introduction

As is true of any scripture, the Qur'an is a vital part of understanding Islam both as it is practiced today and as its origins are described. Since most non-Muslims have never read the Qur'an, a brief introduction is in order. The word "Qur'an" means "recitation" in Arabic and is thought to be derived from the Syriac word "Quryana," which refers to "lectionary, or liturgical, readings."[58] As the holy scripture of Islam, the Qur'an is the main source of guidance for Muslims, though much of the sharia law is derived from other sources (namely the *Hadith*, which records the traditional sayings of Muhammad, the *Sira*, which contains biographical material on Muhammad, the *Tafsir,* which contains commentaries on the Qur'an, and *Fiqh*, which is Islamic Jurisprudence).[59] The 114 chapters, or Surahs, in the Qur'an contain instruction on a variety of topics, including the greatness of Allah, relationships with Jews and Christians, interactions with non-Muslims, and how Muslims ought to conduct themselves in everything from prayer and alms to marriage and military conflicts. Unlike the Christian or Jewish scriptures, the Qur'an is organized by chapter length rather than chronology. It also contains a number of stories about Old Testament figures such as Moses, David, and Abraham, as well as narratives about Jesus (known as "Isa" in the Qur'an) and his mother, Mary.

This chapter will examine several key concepts that must be understood about the Qur'an, with an emphasis on how Muslims believe it establishes itself as trustworthy and divinely inspired. First, this chapter records the traditional view of what the Qur'an is and where it came from; second, it explains how Muslims defend the truth and accuracy of the Qur'an; and finally, it considers the various arguments from non-Muslim scholars who use historical and manuscript evidence to challenge the traditional view about the origins of the Qur'an. In closing, a section on how these various claims and arguments affect Christians and their witness to Muslims is included for discussion and further reflection.

---

[58] Christoph Luxenberg, *The Syro-Aramaic Reading of the Koran: A Contribution to the Decoding of the Language of the Koran (Berlin: Verlag Hans Schiler, 2007),* 70-72.

[59] Arthur W. Diamond Law Library Research Guides. Retrieved from "http://web.law.columbia.edu/sites/default/files/microsites/library/files/guides/islamic_law_research_guide.pdf"

## Traditional Muslim View

The Qur'an is the most important and often the only book Muslims will have. It not only prescribes how they view and worship God, but it also instructs them on how they should treat other Muslims as well as those who reject Islam. A number of key details about the Qur'an are important to understand. First, Muslims claim that the Qur'an is the most perfect book of all time. They maintain that it was revealed to Muhammad by the angel Gabriel, and then shortly after Muhammad's death scribes wrote it down. This is believed to be the very version that has been passed on to us today. As God's final revelation, Muslims argue that it supersedes and corrects previous scriptures, such as the Bible, all of which they contend have been corrupted by men. Second, Muhammad's direct experience in the process of receiving the Qur'an is foundational to the whole religion of Islam. This section recounts what Muslims affirm regarding the nature of the Qur'an and the reasons they declare that it can be trusted as the infallible and uncorrupted word of Allah.

The traditional account of the Qur'an's transmission from Allah to man is as follows: Muhammad received revelations from Gabriel over a 23-year period (between the years 610 and his death in 632).[60] Unlike the Bible, which was written by men who were inspired by God, the Qur'an is considered a word-for-word dictation to Muhammad and an original message from God. Muhammad, who was unable to read or write, began receiving revelations through the angel Gabriel in a cave outside Mecca. He was forced to memorize the words and then recite them to the people in the city. After his death, his successors realized that they would need to record the oral recitations in a book in order to preserve the exact wording of God's message. At this point, they began to collect whatever portions had been written down on scraps of bone, leaves, and cloth and to combine these verses with those recorded from the ones who had memorized portions of the Qur'an. Muslims believe this was completed around 650 AD during the time of Uthman, who was the third Caliph, or successor of Muhammad.[61] Tradition asserts that copies of this final compilation were then made and sent out to the various new centers of the growing Islamic sphere of influence.[62] Through all of these transitional

---

[60] See Ali Dashti, *Twenty Three Years: A Study of the Prophetic Career of Mohammad*, (Mazda, 1994), 47-58.

[61] A religious successor to Muhammad who was also the leader of the entire Muslim community.

[62] Muslims also claim that the earliest copy of the Qur'an was written out by Muhammad's secretary, Zayd ibn Thabit, who collated the Qur'an from various written and oral sources during the time of Abu Bakr, the first Caliph who served from 632-634. After this volume was completed Umar, the second caliph, left the book with his daughter Hafsah, who stored the

phases —from Muhammad to Muhammad's followers, to their transmission to the scribes, to the scribes' various compilations, to the final compilation by one single scribe — Muslims believe that the exact words of Allah have been faithfully recorded in the Qur'an that we have today.

Muslims present several beliefs that they feel support the authenticity and divine origin of the Qur'an. First, they point out several verses within the Qur'an itself which attest to the nature of the revelation as being gradual, perfect in both its original form and its preservation, and the final word of Allah to man. Three elements of this internal evidence should be noted.

1. *The Qur'an is literally "sent down from heaven"*

Muslims believe that the original Qur'an is written on a tablet that is eternally kept in heaven. In Surah 39:41, the text describes how the revelation was sent down and why it was given: "Verily, We have sent down to you (O Muhammad) the Book for mankind in truth. So whosoever accepts the guidance, it is only for his own self; and whosoever goes astray, he goes astray only for his own loss." This emphasizes the sacred purpose of the Qur'an. Another verse reiterates the unique nature of the revelation: "And this Qur'an is not such as could ever be produced by other than Allah" (Qur'an 10:37).

2. *The Qur'an is the final revelation*

One essential aspect of Islamic beliefs is that the revelation from Allah is the last word of God, and thus is the corrected version of truth. All other "scriptures" from other religions should defer to it whenever there is a conflict. In Surah 4:47 of the Qur'an, the text specifically warns: "O you who have been given the Scripture! Believe in what We [sic] have revealed confirming what is (already) with you…"

3. *Allah will preserve the Qur'an*

The Qur'an today is believed to be the actual word of Allah because he promised to preserve it intact – and he will certainly be able to do so in his power. The verse which addresses this is Surah 15:9 - "We have, without doubt, sent down the Message; and We will certainly guard it (from corruption)."

Secondly, the writing process itself of the Qur'an is believed to further ensure its authenticity. Although the finalization of the Qur'an did not occur until several decades after Muhammad's death, Muslims still consider

---

Qur'an under her bed. Then, under the guidance of Uthman (644-656), Zayd ibn Thabit was summoned again to take the earlier Qur'an and, together with some other companions, make copies to deliver to the other provinces.

Uthman's collection to be a faithful rendition of the eternal revelation. Muslims believe that some verses were written down during Muhammad's lifetime but that the majority of them were never recorded until after his death.[63] However, as mentioned earlier, the traditional account holds that the full version of the Qur'an was carefully written down about 20 years after Muhammad's death under the guidance of Uthman (by 650 AD).[64] During his reign, many of the warriors who had memorized the Qur'an were killed in battle, and Uthman realized that preserving the Qur'an in an oral form alone was a dangerous prospect. He took it upon himself to order all the portions and testimonies of all who memorized the words of Muhammad to be sent to him so that he could collect and preserve the perfect and original words of Allah's revelation. Afterward, Uthman is said to have destroyed all other manuscripts, as he considered them to be defective. Thus, his work and the resulting version of the Qur'an are considered to be a perfect recollection of the words of Muhammad, exactly as the prophet first uttered them to his followers during his lifetime.[65]

In addition to the internal evidence and the careful compilation process, the Qur'an is considered to be above all error because it is the latest and the most correct of all scriptures. Its basic message was given to various peoples in the past, but it was always corrupted in some way. Therefore, Allah gave this message to Muhammad in order to preserve the true explanation of his law and his nature. Although Muslims believe that the Jews and Christians had once received the same revelation, over time their carelessness and even deliberate alterations changed the true words of Allah, substituting them with man's words. For example, the Qur'an holds Jesus up as an example of a true messenger of Allah but describes him as a prophet who supported the Law of Moses and foretold the coming of a messenger who would be named Ahmed (a form of Muhammad). All other claims about Jesus Christ, especially regarding any claims to divinity, are considered to be falsehoods added by Christians who wanted to create superior beliefs of their own. This action by people in the past is explained in the Qur'an as a "knowing perversion" of the word of Allah in writing. Surah 2:75, 79 says that men "deliberately twist [the words of Allah], even when they understood them" and declares: "woe to those who write

---

[63] Some Muslims believe instead that 40 scribes followed Muhammad during his life and recorded all of his words from Allah, but this is not generally accepted.

[64] Muslims also claim that an earlier copy of the Qur'an was written out by Muhammad's secretary, Zayd ibn Thabit, who collated the Qur'an from various written and oral sources during the time of Abu Bakr, the first Caliph who served from 632-634. After this volume was completed Umar, the second caliph, left the book with his daughter Hafsah, who stored the Qur'an under her bed.

[65] Peter Riddell and Peter Cotterell, *Islam in Context: Past, Present, and Future* (Grand Rapids, MI: Baker, 2003), 58-9.

something down with their own hands and then claim, 'this is from Allah,' in order to make some small gain." A final revelation was needed to correct these corruptions, and Muslims believe that the Qur'an, which calls its words "a universal message" to all people, fulfills this purpose (Q. 80:11).

A fourth reason Muslims give for the perfect authenticity of the Qur'an is the special status of Muhammad. He was the last prophet, giving the final word of Allah, and because of his trustworthiness, he was the only one who could faithfully convey this revelation. The Qur'an describes Muhammad as "the seal of the prophets," referring to the fact that he has given the most perfect and complete copy of Allah's message, and therefore is raised above the status of all other messengers (Q. 33:40).

Finally, the Qur'an's authenticity is defended on the basis of the unsurpassable beauty of its writing. When the Jews in Medina criticized Muhammad for saying his revelation was from God, his defense was that the beauty of the verses verified that only God could author it. One scholar, Karen Armstrong, comments that the Qur'an was "a masterpiece of Arab prose and poetry" which marked the beginning of a new genre of Arabic literature and that many were converted simply through an overpowering sense of wonder and admiration of the text.[66] According to this view, the Qur'an was not only intellectually riveting, but its aesthetic content was also captivating. In fact, the Qur'an several times challenges unbelievers to create something as elegant as its own Surahs. It is believed that no one has ever been able to meet that challenge and offer a Surah equal to the original (Q. 10:38, 11:13, 17:88). Since man cannot produce these words, it is therefore considered evident that the Qur'an must have had a divine origin.

According to Muslims, then, the Qur'an's perfect nature and divine origin are supported in the traditional Muslim view by what the Qur'an says about Allah's role in its revelation, the divine beauty of that revelation, the unique role of Muhammad, and the careful way its final version was compiled. For Muslims, this creates a strong defense for the superiority of the Islamic scriptures over and against any other holy book, regardless of the similarities of certain elements among those scriptures. This is why Muslims believe that the Qur'an is clearly the correction for all other messages, and Muhammad is his final messenger.

## Counterview from Revisionist and Neo-Revisionist Scholars

Since the Qur'an is a work of literature, most of the arguments presented against its authenticity as a divinely revealed 7th-century

---

[66] Karen Armstrong, *Islam: A Short History*, 5.

document are literary critiques. A few historical arguments against its authenticity should also be considered. Revisionist scholars who question the date of its true creation usually highlight the slow development of the Arabic script, the developmental nature of the written language itself, the lack of specificity in early manuscripts, and the possibility of many different sources. Each of these criticisms will be examined in the following sections.

The first argument that revisionist scholars bring up is the precise appearance of the Arabic script in the 7th-century. Andrew Rippin, a scholar of Islam, for example, argues that "the emergence of a fixed and explicit script for the Arabic language"[67] would most likely have still been in its intermediate stage of development. He points to a large body of evidence that Arabic was largely only a spoken language in the 7th century. It would thus have also been too much in flux to have been used only twenty years after Muhammad's death when Caliph Uthman would have been gathering and compiling his final version of the revelations. This is because, as a written language, Arabic is a consonantal language. Some of the letters used were still not specific to any one sound,[68] and the vowel markings had not yet been invented.[69] For an oral culture, this type of writing worked more as a reminder to the reader of content that had already been memorized or at least was very familiar. Fixed or formal correlations between speech and writing did not develop until much later, in the 8th century.[70] Thus, these scholars express doubt that the Qur'an could have existed in any format – much less a complete and perfect form – at the date, it claims to originate from (648 AD).

A similar issue is the literary language of the Qur'an. The Qur'an uses a type of Arabic known as classical Arabic, and scholars argue that this advanced literary form of Arabic developed from an earlier "chancery" or business Arabic. The late 8th century would have been the first time that the more basic version of the language developed the sophistication needed for fine literature and poetry – not merely for basic communication and trade. The classical Arabic of the Qur'an, these scholars argue, would, therefore, have culminated from an artistic flowering of Arabic literary forms, which fits with the rise of the caliphate culture in the late 8th and early 9th centuries. This, as scholar John Wansbrough points out, would be

---

[67] John Wansbrough, *Quranic Studies: Sources and Methods of Scriptural Interpretation* (New York: Prometheus Books, 2004), xv.

[68] For example, the five distinct letters in medial form, ـبـ, ـتـ, ـثـ, ـنـ, ـيـ (Bā' Tā' Ṯā' Nūn Yā') are indistinguishable when all the dots are omitted. Without the dotting, which developed later, it was difficult to discern which letter was being referenced.

[69] This was probably accomplished by al-Hujjaj, the governor of Iraq under Abd al-Malik, during the last decade of the seventh century or the early eighth century.

[70] Wansbrough, *Qur'anic Studies*, 85-91.

a logical explanation for why no Arabic source material from the 7th century has been located: "it never existed in the first place."[71] Since the date of Wansbrough's writing (1977), Arabic manuscripts such as the "Birmingham Qur'an" and some of the early fragments from a mosque in Sana'a, Yemen, have been dated to the late 6th or early 7th century AD. Although this at first seems to contradict Wansbrough's theory, upon closer inspection the dating could indicate that these manuscripts contain material that pre-dates Muhammad's life and was later incorporated into the Qur'an.

Physical evidence from the time of the Qur'an's traditional date of origin also casts doubt on the veracity of its claims. Where exactly did the early manuscripts that scholars study today -- assumed to be from early copies of the Qur'an -- originally come from? The manuscripts do not say who wrote them or when or where. Scholars argue, then, that these first copies are not adequate for proving whether the Qur'an's current meaning is derived from these texts or whether instead, the texts had a separate context that was later woven into the Qur'an. The incomplete form of these documents means that they could have originally been part of a larger work that was not the Qur'an. There is not enough specificity to definitely attach them to the Qur'an. Without context, it is only possible to conclude that the early manuscripts praise, describe, or comment on some type of monotheistic faith. These manuscripts could very well have been some other religious texts that were later incorporated into the final version of the Qur'an. As some scholars point out, even when early fragments do match a part of the established Qur'an, this does not mean that it is known where or through what process the early text originated.[72]

The sources of these fragments are thus a topic of significant scholarly discussion. Revisionist and Neo-Revisionist scholars have brought a textual-critical approach to studying the first two centuries of Islam, which involves the study of archeological sites, epigraphic and numismatic material,[73] and 7th-century non-Muslim eyewitness written accounts. These sources suggest several ways that the Qur'an could have been developed gradually and as a compilation of a variety of religious texts (primarily Jewish, Christian, and Zoroastrian). Yehuda Nevo, a Middle Eastern archaeologist, for example, concludes from an exhaustive study of early inscriptions and seventh-century historical documents that the Qur'an is an amalgamation of various literary texts and scriptures, created around the early 8th or even 9th centuries.[74] John Wansbrough agrees, adding that sectarian controversies in

---

[71] Ibid., 85-91.

[72] See Andrew Rippin in Wansbrough, *Quranic Studies*, xvii.

[73] epigraphic refers to writing on stone, metal or wood, and numismatic refers to the study of ancient coins.

[74] Nevo, *Crossroads to Islam*, 10.

this same time period could have spurred the creation of Islamic literature (including the Qur'an). Eighth and ninth century Muslim leaders who sought to justify an earlier date for authenticity would then have later attributed these eighth and ninth century documents to the seventh century.[75]

Another likely scenario has been put forth by the scholar Reuven Firestone, who suggests that much of the Islamic literature, including the Qur'an, may have evolved as "hybrid stories" as the legends of pre-Islamic Arabia merged with biblical stories from a Jewish and Christian context. These may have been further transformed by the emerging Islamic vision, which found its way into the Qur'an, the Tafsir (commentary) and the Hadith. According to Firestone, this means that,

> [M]any of the legends in the Medieval Islamic exegetical literature that treat Qur'anic material parallel to the Bible derive from Jewish and Christian, orthodox or heterodox religious traditions. Originating in an oral milieu, the legends continually changed as they incorporated motifs and ideas reflecting the changes taking place in the cultures in and for which the legends themselves evolved. Those legends which were brought into the Arabian Peninsula by Biblicists gradually acculturated to pre-Islamic Arabia as they were repeatedly told and retold in that environment. They became partially "Arabized" as they took on some of the motifs and structures of indigenous Arabian legend, but also retained features of their Biblicist past as well.[76]

Thus, according to Firestone's comparisons of early Christian and Jewish literature present in pre-Islamic Arabia, the Hadith, Sirat, Tafsir, and even the Qur'an may have been derived, at least in part, from non-Islamic sources, and later changed by the Arabs in order to come up with their own similar, but unique stories. This argument thus presents Arabic literature in a more complex literary context, and questions the purity of traditional Muslim literature as well as some of the stories that are found in the Qur'an.

Even the inscriptions at the Dome of the Rock, these scholars argue, only attest to material similar to Qur'anic verses; they cannot prove that the verses already existed in a completed Qur'an.[77] Revisionist scholars have suggested a number of possible sources of the written material. One is that the fragmentary manuscripts were originally from earlier Christian liturgy,

---

[75] Ibn Warraq, Introduction: *What the Koran Really Says: Language, Text, and Commentary* (New York: Prometheus Books, 2002), 24.

[76] Ibid., 17–18.

[77] Patricia Cone, and Michael Cook, *Hagarism; The Making of the Islamic World* (Cambridge University Press, 1977), 3, 18.

which had been translated into an early Arabic script by Christian missionaries. Some may have been translations of the Jewish Psalms and commentaries into Arabic from a Syriac text (an older Middle Eastern language commonly in use during this time, especially for religious works), or simply bits of early poetry to a general monotheistic deity. One scholar has even suggested in a controversial argument that certain Qur'anic manuscripts may have come from a Syriac form of the Diatessaron, an early Greek compilation of a harmony of the Christian gospels.[78] For example, part of Surah 48:29 resembles the combined stories of Mark 4:26-7 and Matthew 13:23 as they are in the Diatessaron.

Gerd Puin, a leading scholar in this field of Arabic manuscript study, summarized the general direction of these arguments in his own words: "My idea," he wrote,

> [I]s that the Koran is a kind of cocktail of texts that were not all understood even at the time of Muhammad. Many of them may even be a hundred years older than Islam itself. Even within the Islamic traditions there is a huge body of contradictory information, including a significant Christian substrate; one can derive a whole Islamic anti-history from them if one wants."[79]

His point demonstrates that considerations regarding these more dubious points can lead to a general wariness of taking the traditional account of the Qur'an's accuracy seriously.

## Conclusion of the Counterview

In summary, there are a number of reasons to doubt the idea that the Qur'an was written all at once and compiled in its final form only a few years after Muhammad's death. Only fragments and portions of manuscripts of what is now the Qur'an are known to exist before the late 8th century, and there is inadequate evidence of where those fragmentary manuscripts came from. The text of the fragments does bear witness overall to a clear monotheistic faith, but that does not necessarily mean that they are Islamic texts. There are also literary considerations to bear in mind, as Arabic as a written language was developing in key ways during the 7th and 8th centuries. This casts doubt on the truth of the Qur'an being such a literary marvel, and instead supports the gradual culmination theory. Finally, the

---

[78] Claude Gilliot, "Reconsidering the Authorship of the Qur'an: Is the Qur'an Partly the Fruit of a Progressive and Collective Work?" in *Towards a New Reading of the Qur'an*, Gabriel Said Reynolds, ed. (Indiana: Notre Dame, 2005), 99.

[79] Gerd Puin, *"What Is the Koran?"* Chapter in Ibn Warraq, *What the Koran Really Says: Language, Text, and Commentary (New York: Prometheus Books, 2002)*, 109-110.

fact that only fragmented source material exists from the century in which the Qur'an was supposed to have been written suggests that the traditional date may be inaccurate. One plausible explanation is that the Qur'an is made up of many different texts, some Christian and Jewish, that were gradually transliterated into Arabic as the script and alphabet developed. Later, after Muhammad's death, scholars working under the caliph Abd al-Malik, around 700 AD, could have compiled these documents. There are indications that corrections continued to be made until a final version was completed somewhere around the latter half of the 8th century.[80]

## Implications of the Historical Development of the Qur'an

A significant number of textual scholars have questioned the divine origin of the Qur'an, and they have closely studied the currently existing manuscript fragments to discover more concrete details on the Qur'an's origins. However, the task of accurately dating the Qur'anic manuscripts which survive today is a complex and difficult one, as was demonstrated in a recent effort to date the manuscript known as the Birmingham Qur'an. A radiocarbon dating of the parchment (the physical page material, not the ink) using the Oxford Radiocarbon lab dated the pages to 568-645 AD, within a 95% range of accuracy. Since parchments are generally used soon after their manufacture, these results suggest a possibility that the content of this manuscript could have predated Muhammad himself. However, Saudi Arabian scholars argue that the ink and calligraphy used on the parchment date to the late 600's or early 700's, which would support either the idea of the manuscript being made in Muhammad's lifetime or the idea of the manuscript being a later revision decades after Muhammad's death!

Thus, even interpreting a clear piece of textual evidence is a thorny issue and can often suggest support for more than one viewpoint. It is important to note, though, that such sources can trigger as many questions as they answer. This should sound a clear note of caution to scholars and readers alike not to accept traditional accounts of the facts unquestioningly since such accounts do not by any means have ironclad support from physical, scholarly evidence. Multiple possibilities must be considered. The weightiest of these possibilities is that the Qur'an that is read today is unverifiable or perhaps even a mere collection of poetry, commentary, Arabized narratives, and liturgical texts. Steven Humphreys, a professor of Islamic Studies, emphasized that the Qur'an is the document that gives Islam its reason for existence. If the Qur'an is not directly from God, Humphreys

---

[80] Wansbrough, *Quranic Studies*, xv; Yehuda Nevo, *Crossroads*, 11.

points out, then it is by logical necessity a human document — and since it claims a perfect, divine source, any human authorship would undercut its authority.[81] At any rate, the lack of definitive answers on these issues makes a strong case for Christians not to accept the Qur'an as the final word of God, even though it is a more recent religious text than the Jewish and Christian scriptures.

## Apologetic Conclusions

Discussing the origins of the Qur'an with a Muslim is a conversation which is both delicate and important. It should be remembered that the actual dates for the manuscripts (especially the late date for their canonization) opens the door to scholarly arguments that much of the Qur'an was borrowed from other religious sources, and that historical evidence from 8th-century writers and Qur'anic manuscripts offers support for this view. Christians should be concerned about these dates and the evidence of late canonization because it throws the historicity of the Qur'an into doubt: if it came from other sources, then it cannot be assumed to be from God. In the Christian view, this makes Islam a fallacious religion, presenting a false picture of Christ, which encourages Muslims to view Jesus Christ differently from the way that he is portrayed in the Bible and first century sources. Since understanding Jesus' identity as the source of man's salvation is integral to Christianity, the true apologetic implication of the Qur'an's origin is that the Qur'an cannot be trusted to give an accurate account of Jesus Christ's nature and mission. This different portrayal confuses the central message of Christianity for Muslims — a confusion which can be addressed by discussing the origins of both the Qur'an and the Bible.

## Building Bridges to Understand

Creating a bridge where Christians can discuss the true identity of Jesus would involve a discussion of the Christian scriptures. Christians can show that the tests of scholarship — the internal and external consistency tests, as well as the reliability of the earliest manuscripts — have long demonstrated that the Bible has distinct marks of authenticity and truth. Based on how well the Bible has passed these types of historical and literary tests, Christians can demonstrate to Muslims why the Bible's account of Jesus Christ, and especially its claim that he is God the Son, can be trusted and followed.

---

[81] Toby Lester, "What Is the Koran?" Chapter in Ibn Warraq, *What the Koran Really Says: Language, Text, and Commentary* (New York: Prometheus Books, 2002), 110.

A particularly helpful way to demonstrate to Muslims the differences between the Bible and the Qur'an is to initiate a "Book Study" where the two texts can be compared. Then, the Christian can first use the Qur'an to highlight the verses that refer to Jesus, or Isa, as well as his mother Mary. Next, upon the invitation to view what the Bible says about Jesus, the Christian can go through various parts of the Gospels in order to contrast the biblical Jesus with the Isa of the Qur'an. These differences can then be used to demonstrate that the God of Muhammad is not the Father of Jesus.

This is a good approach because the Qur'an itself allows such comparison between scriptures. In Sura 10:94, the Qur'an tells Muslims that if they are in doubt about anything in the Scriptures, they should ask those who have received the book that was given before, such as the Tauret (the books of Moses), the Zabur (the psalms of David), and the Injil (the Gospels). If Muslims should reply that they cannot read those books because they have been corrupted, then show them Sura 10:64, which reminds Muslims "there is no change in the word of God." Therefore, if God can preserve the Qur'an, then he certainly can preserve the Bible as well. The goal of this Bible study, as well as most apologetic bridges illustrated in this book, is to help our Muslim friends encounter the historical and risen Lord. He is the one who will bring them home.

### Study Questions

1. How can both the Bible and the Qur'an be true if they give conflicting messages?

2. Muslims believe that the Qur'an is the most perfect book of all time. What are some of the arguments Muslims use to defend this position?

3. What are some arguments Christian scholars bring up that indicate that the Qur'an is a man-made book?

4. In a number of Suras, the Qur'an tells Muslims to ask the Christians and Jews about their scriptures, the Old and New Testaments (5:36-38; 35:31; 3:3; 12:111; 29:46; 20:37; 5:66; and 10:94). How can these verses from the Qur'an be used to form a bridge between Christians and Muslims? (Would Allah command people to obey a corrupted Scripture)?

5. How would you witness to a Muslim who says, "We believe that the Qur'an is the pure Word of God and teaches us the truth from God? Since the Qur'an rejects the Bible, how can we trust the Bible?"

# CHAPTER 4 The Origin of Islam: New Path to God or a Jewish-Christian Heresy?

## Introduction

The first 60 years of Islam after the death of Muhammad are not only interesting to study but vital for a thorough understanding of Islam's origin story. How and when did Islam become a fully developed religion? There is a significant controversy over whether it was a perfect and complete faith at the time of Muhammad's death, or whether decades more were required for the various movements and religious elements to come together into a cohesive religion. While traditional Muslim accounts explain these 60 to 70 years as a time in which faithful Muslims spread their new faith militarily, a number of scholars have objected to this view and believe that the historical evidence fits better with a mixed military-religious series of raids and a religion that was still being finalized during this period in regard to leadership, central creeds, and policy toward non-Muslims. Here both sides of this debate will be considered, first recounting the accepted Muslim beliefs about the transition from prophet to empire, and then examining some of the main counter-arguments from scholars who do not accept this traditional account.

## The Traditional Muslim View of Transition from Prophet to Empire

For Muslims, Muhammad's death in 632 AD marked the beginning of a gradual transition of Islam from a localized movement to a global vision. By the time of his death, according to the traditional view, all of Arabia had converted to the new religion of Islam and formed a universal "ummah," or brotherhood. However, the prophet's death, which was rather sudden, also created an immediate need for his followers to appoint a new leader, as he had not named anyone to succeed him.

His close friend and colleague Abu Bakr were chosen to be the first successor, known as the "caliph." Since a number of Muslims fell away or revolted during this transition, the need to bring them back to the fold resulted in the Wars of Apostasy, also called the "Ridda" wars. Abu Bakr was able to subdue this revolt and reunite all the tribes of Arabia. After his short leadership of two years, the next caliph, Umar, had the Muslim forces invade Iraq, Syria, and Egypt with the purpose of spreading the message of

Allah to all people – as the Qur'an commands.[82] In 635 AD, Damascus fell, and in 638 Jerusalem surrendered to the Muslims.[83] The next 100 years saw the forces of Islam conduct a series of successful military campaigns throughout the Middle East and North Africa, reaching up to the very borders of Europe and the Byzantine Empire. This long period of military victories was hailed as a sure sign of Allah's favor.

Despite this overall success, internal strife among the Muslim forces themselves also marked this period. The most enduring part of the struggle was a significant division between two groups who disagreed over whether the succession of Muhammad would be decided by community consensus or by family ties. The group called the Sunnis (followers of tradition) gained the upper hand from the beginning, and the first three "rightly-guided" caliphs — Abu Bakr, Umar, and Uthman — distinguished themselves in their leadership on the battlefields and in their devotion to Allah. After an opponent assassinated Uthman, the prophet's son-in-law Ali was chosen to succeed him. This brought hope to Ali's followers, called the Shia (followers of Ali), but not all Muslims were in favor of this decision. Muawiyah, a strong Sunni leader, criticized Ali for not avenging Uthman's murder and refused to recognize him as caliph. This discontent led to a battle between the forces of Muawiyah and Ali at a place named Siffin in 657.[84]

Though their dispute was resolved by arbitration, Ali was seen as weak, and in time some of his followers, known as the Kharijites ("those who leave"), abandoned him. This led to another rebellion against Ali's forces by the Kharijites, which Ali won. However, shortly after this Ali was wounded by a poisoned sword wielded by a Kharajite assassin and died. Ali's eldest son Hassan was voted in as the next caliph, but Muawiyah brought his army against Hassan and convinced him to make peace and yield the caliphate to Muawiyah in 661. Muawiyah was a shrewd leader and ended up founding the Umayyad Empire, which lasted until 750. The traditional accounts relate how, under the Umayyad rule much of the Middle East, North Africa, and Spain was conquered by forces that believed their success was a reward for faithfully following Allah, for wherever they went they declared "there is one God and Muhammad is his messenger."

One of the most powerful leaders of this new empire was the fifth Umayyad Caliph, Abd al-Malik, the son of Marwan I. It was during his reign

---

[82] Q. 8:38-39; 2:193: "And fight them until persecution is no more, and religion be only for Allah." Also in the Hadith, Sahih Muslim 1:33: The Messenger of Allah said: "I have been commanded to fight against people till they testify that there is no god but Allah, that Muhammad is the messenger of Allah, and they establish prayer and pay zakat."

[83] Fred Donner, *Early Islamic Conquests*, (Princeton University Press, 1981), 130-132; 151-2.

[84] Muhammad ibn Jarir al-Tabari, *Tabari* volume 5, 243; Karim M. S. Al-Zubaidi, *Iraq, a Complicated State: Iraq's Freedom War*, (UK: AuthorHouse, 2010) 254.

(685-705) that Islam gained widespread control of former Byzantine territories in the Middle East. He initiated the building of the Dome of the Rock and was the first one to mint coins inscribed with the *Shahada*, which is the central creed of Islam ("There is no God but Allah"). These inscriptions also proclaimed Muhammad's preeminence as the last and greatest prophet of Allah. Muslims thus believe that Abd al-Malik was instrumentally used by Allah to solidify the hegemony of Islam in the Middle East and North Africa. According to this view, he was especially motivated by a desire to carry out the mandates of the Qur'an in practical terms: to unify the people, to create order in government, and to ensure the flourishing of the one true religion. During his reign, Abd al-Malik also began the process of making Arabic the official language of the empire. All of this brought a new level of prominence to Islam.[85]

Muslims view the military exploits under the reigns of these caliphs not as an arbitrary expansion, but rather as the working out of commands that Muhammad's successors and their followers identified in the Qur'an. As Donner explains, "The Islamic community itself ... saw the conquest as the result of religious zeal for the new faith, and as a truly miraculous demonstration of the divine favor that Islam is supposed to enjoy."[86] For example, Surah 9:33 predicts the conquest of Islam over all religions through the means of Jihad, or a struggle that brings the infidel under the will of Allah. In addition, Surah 9:29 allowed the Muslims to subdue Christians and Jews because they did not acknowledge the truth of Islam. They were given three choices: convert to Islam, pay a head tax called the *Jizyah*, or be killed. Muslims believed that these harsh measures were necessary since a rejection of Islam would mean an eternal sentence in hell. Therefore, it would be much better for everyone to submit to Allah and live under his mercy and compassion.

This first 100 years of Islam after Muhammad's death, therefore, saw the rise not only of internal conflict but ultimately an impressive array of military victories and a new empire that spread the religion and culture of Islam over a vast territory. These remarkable achievements clearly conveyed to Muslims the approval and guidance of Allah in this critical time of growth.

---

[85] Nevo, *Crossroads to Islam*, 255-6. G.E. Von Grunebaum, *Classical Islam: A History 600-1258* (Aldine, 1970), 75.

[86] Donner, *Early Islamic Conquests*, 3.

## Counterview of the Transition from Prophet to Empire

Revisionist scholars, as might be expected, disagree that the Muslims' early military success was the simple outcome of a holy mission, which Muslims were compelled to undertake out of devotion to Allah. Although the conquest was inarguably successful militarily, revisionist scholars question both the nature and motivation for these exploits. Their arguments usually center around two main points: an alternate explanation for Islamic military success, and an argument for the evolutionary development of Islam as a religion, which only reached its final form during the days of Abd al-Malik.

First, while the traditional Muslim accounts portray hordes of faithful Muslim soldiers overpowering formidable forces, scholars give an alternate explanation by arguing that the military exploits of this early period were actually a series of raids and a gradual migration of Arabs into the borderlands of the Byzantine Empire between Arabia and Mesopotamia.[87] These areas had recently been left open to invasion by the retreating Byzantine army in the mid-7th century, and much of the early takeover was accomplished with little bloodshed since the towns and cities were quite vulnerable. For example, Damascus was surrendered to the Arab forces in 635 after a siege lasting several months,[88] and two years later the bishop of Jerusalem capitulated in a similar manner.[89] According to the testimony of certain non-Muslim chroniclers, the elite leaders of the Arab forces were motivated by a simple form of monotheism inspired by an apocalyptic message that mixed together elements of Christian and Jewish beliefs.[90]

In contrast, some modern scholars provide evidence that the Arab soldiers were still mostly pagan, and their forces were even mixed with Christian, Persian, and other foreign soldiers (who, if they were not involved for the sake of financial reward, had been captured and forced to fight as slaves).[91] According to this view, this wave of skirmishes was more of a migratory movement than a conquest, and these scholars have pointed to several details to support this. For instance, it is questionable as to whether Muawiyah's reign, thirty years after the death of Muhammad, was over anything other than a "loose confederation of Arab tribes" or

---

[87] Crone, *Hagarism*, 9.
[88] Donner, *Early Islamic Conquests*, 130-132.
[89] Ibid., 151-52.
[90] Nevo, *Crossroads to Islam*, 219-220.
[91] Ibid., 89, 220-221.

"politically independent communities of mu'minun (believers)."[92] In addition, at the time of the original "invasions," the invading forces actually lived in garrison towns outside the population centers, with the real interest being in collecting taxes rather than converting anyone to their religion.[93] It was only later in the time of Abd al-Malik (685-705) that a "centralized administrative and fiscal apparatus" capable of managing a stable government was present.[94] This contrasts with the traditional account of a determined campaign on the part of the Muslims to convert the local regions to Islam in the early years after the death of their prophet.

The second main point of revisionist thought is an alternate explanation for the beginnings of Islam. It basically supposes that the Middle East in the late 7th and early 8th centuries was marked by a religious trend of Jewish and sectarian Christian influences, and that a leader such as Abd al-Malik took advantage of these trends and mixed them with Arabized elements – especially regarding stories of a historical but vague figure similar to the traditional Muhammad – to create a new, formalized religion. Non-Muslim chronicles refer to a religious and military leader around the same time that Muhammad was supposed to have lived, but there is no way to verify if these accounts describe the Muhammad of Islam. These fragmentary references describe similar events but do not include details that are specific characteristics of Islam. Instead, they describe a local leader who, within a Jewish apocalyptic tradition, was seeking to establish a religious dominance in the region. In addition, some scholars assert that the Arabs who emigrated into Palestine and Syria during the latter half of the 7th century were Ishmaelites who wanted to lay claim to Jerusalem under the rule of a new type of Christianity where Jesus was the Messiah and the "chosen one," but not the divine Son of God.[95] This would certainly fit with the viewpoint of John of Damascus, who was an eyewitness to many of these developments. He even named his apologetic treatise documenting the beliefs of the new rulers as the "Heresy of the Ishmaelites."[96] The revisionist argument, then, suggests a missing element in the origin story of Islam: a person who deliberately tied together the various developing threads of folklore and theological content to create the real beginnings of Islam. This argument is supported by evidence for late

---

[92] Jeremy Johns, "Archaeology and the History of Early Islam: The First Seventy Years" (Journal of the Economic and Social History of the Orient, Vol. 46, 4, 2003), 411–418.

[93] Nevo, *Crossroads to Islam*, 17.

[94] Johns, "Archeology and the History of Early Islam," 418.

[95] Spencer, *Did Muhammad Exist?*, 208. Karl-Heinz Ohlig, *Early Islam*, 251-271. See also Crone, *Hagarism*.

[96] see Janosik, *John of Damascus*.

7th-century religious developments in the Middle East and the actions of the Caliph, Abd al-Malik.

These religious developments center on a concept which scholars have called "intermediate monotheism."[97] They essentially argue that early Arabs believed in a mixture of various religious elements drawn from monotheistic religions – primarily Christianity and Judaism – but that gradually these elements naturally or deliberately were re-shaped into a new monotheistic religion that focused on the Arab people. The final outcome of this process would have been Islam in its final form.

Several key aspects of the intermediate monotheism should be noted. First, the religious beliefs that these early Arabs are believed to have followed were probably developed from several sources. One possible source consisted of 7th-century Jewish and non-orthodox Christian influences.[98] Scholars have also identified evidence of Jewish-Christians called Nazoreans living in Arabia at this time; they believed in Jesus as the messiah but continued to follow Jewish ceremonial laws.[99] As a result of these various influential beliefs, scholars argue that the Arabs from that region picked up the general tenets of these faiths and believed in a "very simple form of monotheism with Judeo-Christian overtones."[100] It is this stage that is referred to as "intermediate monotheism," since it is halfway between Judeo-Christian beliefs and a new faith altogether. However, since the Christians and Jews in that area did not always hold orthodox beliefs, this composite religion is argued to have created a distorted version of Christianity among the Arabs. For instance, they thought that the Trinity included Mary rather than the Holy Spirit. They also rejected the historicity of the crucifixion and the resurrection and viewed Jesus as a political messiah rather than a savior. They also believed this messiah would be the "chosen one" who would lead them back to Jerusalem, which would become the "restored" kingdom on earth, and there they would follow the true religion that would unite all the followers of Abraham.[101]

Another intriguing aspect of the intermediate monotheism theory is addressed by David Cook, a scholar who argues persuasively that this apocalyptic/political messiah movement was highly influential, claiming

---

[97] Nevo, *Crossroads to Islam*, 195-99, 222-29, 243-44. Donner, *Muhammad and the Believers* (though Donner refers to this development as the "Believer's Movement"). Other scholars, such as Patricia Crone, Karl-Heinz Ohlig, and Volker Popp also refer to the same phenomenon by other names.

[98] Berkey, *Formation of Islam*, 61, 65.

[99] Donner, *Muhammad and the Believers*, 31.

[100] Nevo, *Crossroads*, 11.

[101] Spencer, *Did Muhammad Exist?*, 208. Ohlig, *Early Islam*, 251-271. See also Crone, *Hagarism*.

that it may have significantly shaped the eventual development of Islam. He explains,

> The Koran is filled with predictions about the end of the world. The prophet Mohammed envisioned the End as being very close, within a few years after receiving his revelation. My own personal belief is that Islam was started as an apocalyptic movement, not necessarily a millennial movement. An apocalyptic movement is one that feels the end of the world is imminent, whereas a millenarian movement seeks to bring about a messianic otherworldly kingdom.[102]

Ibn Warraq, a scholar, and critic of Islam, agrees with this assessment, writing that the impact of messianic sects was so crucial that "Islam emerged only when it came into contact with and under the influence of Rabbinic Judaism."[103]

A final point of the intermediate monotheism argument is that scholars suggest, based on the evidence discussed above, that this intermediate monotheism formatively shaped Islam as it developed into the religion as we know it today. In a practical sense, it has been argued that non-Orthodox Christian groups, such as the Nestorians and the Monophysites, had a distinct political impact by initially favoring the rule of the Intermediate Monotheist leaders, believing that it was less stringent than the Byzantine rule.[104] This political favor would have enabled the early "Muslims" to take control of large swaths of the Arabian Peninsula with little military conflict, setting up circumstances for the eventual rise of the Umayyad Empire.[105] More specifically, however, scholars suggest that over a period of decades or even centuries certain Arab leaders took material from these monotheistic sources (and even from some pagan ones) and molded the stories into their own Arabized narratives, where Arabs became central to the story.[106]

---

[102] David Cook, 2001 CBN interview: http://www1.cbn.com/onlinediscipleship/islam's-apocalypse

[103] Ibn Warraq, "Introduction," in *The Origins of the Koran: Classic Essays on Islam's Holy Book*, Ibn Warraq, ed. (New York: Prometheus Books, 1998), 24. Warraq cites R. Stephen Humphreys, who adds, 'that Islamic doctrine generally, and even the figure of Muhammad, were molded on Rabbinic Jewish prototypes.' See Stephen Humphreys, *Islamic History: A Framework for Inquiry* (Princeton, 1991), 84.

[104] Nevo, *Crossroads*, 89, 97-98.

[105] Ibid., 89, 97-98.

[106] Nevo, *Crossroads*, 11. Berkey, *Formation of Islam*, 75.

# It All Started with Abd al-Malik

Finally, revisionist scholars offer evidence to argue that this "intermediate monotheism" was codified and formalized by Abd al-Malik by the end of the 7th century. Scholars suggest that this caliph understood the need for legitimacy within his government, which had only been founded decades earlier by Muawiyah and was still becoming established. They offer this explanation because of the evidence of a sharp change in policy during Abd al-Malik's reign that made it unique from that of Muawiyah. Jeremy Johns, the Director of the Khalili Research Center at Oxford University, for instance, argues that there is no evidence of a Muslim state before Abd al-Malik's reign. Muawiyah's empire functioned under a status quo approach with Byzantine administrators continuing their work and "believers" mostly living in garrison towns.[107] Abd al-Malik, however, both expanded and formalized his control over the region, squelching the rebellions of rival leaders such as Ibn al-Zabayr. It is logical to deduce that some kind of unifying factor was needed at this point, and the evidence from coins, inscriptions, and non-Muslim chroniclers all point to a new emphasis on a religion that is clearly Islamic rather than vaguely Christian or just monotheistic. Scholar Robert Hoyland explains "it was pressure from rebel factions that induced Abd al-Malik to proclaim Islam publically as the ideological basis of the Arab state."[108] In this case, the evidence of the coins and inscriptions gives testimony to a government claiming divine authority, religious writings that proclaim dominion over all other religions, and a prophet who claims to be the "seal" of all other prophets. All these things would have brought legitimacy to a new empire while honoring the Arab people.

In addition, the necessity of having a credible government with a formalized religion, a holy book, and a prophet, combined with the first real evidences of an identifiable Islamic agenda, has led scholars to suspect that Islam only took on its first complete form during Abd al-Malik's reign. Thus, if Islam initially took on this formalized position at this time, it was most likely for the purpose of strengthening or legitimizing the reign. According to this view, the minting of coins under Abd al-Malik was used to solidify his position as "Commander of the believers" and to also produce a new Arab identity. It is after all from Abd al-Malik's reign, in 691 AD, that the first Muslim historical reference to Muhammad dates (in the first of his new Arabic coins).

---

[107] Johns, "Archeology and the History of Early Islam," 418.

[108] Hoyland, "New Documentary Texts and the Early Islamic State," (Bulletin of the School of Oriental and African Studies, Volume 69, Issue 3, October 2006), 397.

Scholars who make these arguments, therefore, generally interpret the available historical and archaeological evidence as supporting the theory that Islam only existed in fragmentary form before the creation of the Islamic empire. In fact, they argue that its very cohesion is due to the political and ideological strength which an Arabized state religion would have brought to the caliphate. Intermediate monotheism would have provided the mixture of religious elements necessary for Islam's foundational beliefs, but most likely would not have developed into the form of Islam known today without secular forces playing such an important role. Scholars thus believe that while this mixture was initially adapted as a general monotheistic culture in early Arabia, it later developed into a new, all-encompassing religion that became a primary tool for political hegemony.

## Implications of the Counterview Regarding the Transitional Period

If these scholars are correct and Islam developed from gradually assembled collections of monotheistic thought, and only came into its first recognizable form at the end of the 7th-century, during the reign of Abd al-Malik, then the majority of the traditional origin stories for Islam are inaccurate. In particular, the belief that Islam developed in a relatively short period of time during Muhammad's life is thrown into doubt, since neither the time period nor the finalized version of a divine revelation can logically fit with the points which intermediate monotheistic scholars advocate. The implications of this would include the reduction of Islam to a man-made religion and one that has neither a special message from the true God nor any substantive reason to reject Jesus Christ as God.

In addition, these scholars conclude that the religion of Islam may well have developed out of Abd al-Malik's deliberate effort to synthesize elements from previous religions, including Christianity and Judaism, in order to create a unique religion that would favor the Arab people (or more specifically, the Arabs who also identified as Ishmaelites). If this were the case, then this Arabization of biblical stories would have resulted in a manmade, not divine, revision of earlier so-called "corrupted" scriptures. In fact, the Muslim versions of these narratives would thus have lost any convincing reasons for belief or acceptance. This possible synthesis would also indicate that many narratives in the traditional account would have been fabricated or that later events would have been "retro-fitted" to an earlier time. For example, the traditional account relates that the third caliph, Uthman, burned all the other manuscripts that did not coincide with the official one, but this event is not documented in any written account from the time it supposedly occurred. However, there is documented evidence that the governor of Iraq, al-Hajjaj, who served under Abd al-Malik in the early 8th-century, was known for burning defective manuscripts.[109] This latter story could have been retrofitted to an earlier time in order to build a more credible case for the finalization of the Qur'an half a century earlier. Such examples demonstrate why it is important for Christians to understand the historical background of the origin of the Qur'an as well as the origin of Islam. The evidence will help discern the truth. After all, it is important for Christians to know the truth and also help others find the truth that will set them free.

## Implications of Archaeology, Linguistics, and Geography

An entire additional problematic issue with the traditional story of Islam is the historicity of Mecca itself. This concern has increasingly arisen in recent research, which suggests that Mecca as a city did not exist in the time of Muhammad, and therefore could not have actually been the locus of early Islam

### Primary Source Material

There are a number of scholars who claim that Islam could not have originated in Mecca or even in the Hijaz region of Arabia. For example, Peter Townsend, the author of *The Mecca Mystery*, writes, "To put it as bluntly as possible: there is not a single shred of uncontested primary source evidence confirming the existence of an ancient city at the spot where the modern city of Mecca is located."[110] Instead, Townsend goes on to list numerous reasons that Mecca could not be the birthplace of Muhammad, or the Qur'an, or even Islam. First of all, he points out that there is no primary source evidence of the existence of an ancient city in the present location of Mecca.[111] There are numerous mentions of Taif, just 70 miles away, as well as Najran, Sana'a, Medina, and Petra – but no Mecca. There is even an absence of the name of Mecca in any of the ancient inscriptions found in the records of cities that occupied the Arabian peninsula.[112] If Mecca was known as the "mother of all cities," then surely there would be documents from the 7th century, or earlier, that would mention the city as well as the people. However, there is nothing in the literature that even alludes to a city called Mecca until the middle of the 8th century, when the

---

[109] Ibn Warraq, *Origins of the Koran*, 108-109.

[110] Peter Townsend, *The Mecca Mystery: Probing the Black Hole at the Heart of Muslim History* (Peter Townsend), 48.

[111] Townsend, *The Mecca Mystery*, 48.

[112] Ibid., 49.

city is mentioned in the *Continuatio Byzantia Arabica*, written around 741AD.[113] In addition, it is not found on a map until around 900 AD,[114] and any reference to trade with Mecca is absent in the records of that time.[115] Even Patricia Crone, former professor of Islamic History at Princeton University, in *Meccan Trade and the Rise of Islam*, was dubious of the claim that Mecca was a major center of trade and worship due to the barren landscape and the absence of any reference to historical sources.[116]

In summary of all the evidence that fails to mention the city of Mecca in any of the primary source material surviving from the time Islam came into existence, Townsend writes, "To put it as simply as possible: If Mecca existed in ancient times, the scribes and kings of Arabia and Northeast Africa would have noticed. They clearly did not. It is entirely absent from the historical record and implications of this should be abundantly obvious."[117] On the other hand, Petra was at the crossroads of trade between Arabia and the rest of the Middle East, and it was very well known in the literature of that time as well as for hundreds of years earlier. This is why some scholars are considering the city of Petra as the real birthplace of Islam instead of Mecca.

## Physical Features

In addition, Townsend gives evidence that the physical and geographical features of Mecca do not line up with the Qur'an or the Hadith.[118] For example, the mountains of Safa and Marwah, which mark the journey of Hagar in her quest for water, do not fit with the description in the Hadith. They are too small and close to each other. Also, the Hadith references to Mecca describe a place where the soil is suitable to grow fields of grain, trees, and grapevines. However, Mecca does not have olive trees, and it cannot even support the growth of food for camels and sheep. The Hadith also talks about two parallel valleys with a stream in between, but Mecca does not have these features.[119] However, all of these features are found in the ancient city of Petra.

---

[113] Hoyland, *Seeing Islam*, 43-44.

[114] Townsend, *The Mecca Mystery*, 48.

[115] Ibid., 53.

[116] Patricia Crone, *Meccan Trade and the Rise of Islam* (Gorgias press, 1987), 7. See also Tom Holland, *In the Shadow of the Sword* (Little, Brown, 2012), 303.

[117] Townsend, *The Mecca Mystery*, 54.

[118] Ibid., 50.

[119] Ibid., 110-13.

## Geographical and Archaeological Features

It is also noteworthy that the scant geographic references to the people groups in the Qur'an are concentrated in Northern Arabia near the city of Petra. Of the 65 references, 54 refer to three people groups which did not reside in the Hijaz area of South Western Arabia where Mecca is situated.[120] The people of 'Ad (Uz or Ud), were allies of the tribes led by Edomites living in the land. These could have been the Hyksos, or shepherd kings, who invaded Egypt from Arabia in the time of Moses. The second group of people mentioned was the Midianites, who were descendants of Abraham through his second wife Keturah. Like the people of 'Ad, the Midianites once controlled Northern Arabia and united the Arabian tribes throughout the region. The Thamuds referred to the people "after 'Ud ('Ad)" who united the tribes of Ishmael and were also known as the Nabataeans.[121] These were the ones who settled in a canyon area that became known as Petra. Thus, the majority of the people groups and the geographical places mentioned in the Qur'an centered in Northern Arabia around the city of Petra, and not the Southwestern city of Mecca.

Another major discrepancy, made known by Middle Eastern archaeologist Dan Gibson, is that recent archaeological examinations of the mosques from the first 100 years of Islam indicate that the *qibla*, or the direction of prayer, did not face toward Mecca, but rather to a more northern location, the Nabataean area around Petra where the people of 'Ad, Midian, and Thamud all resided. Due to this archaeological evidence, Gibson does not support Mecca as the birthplace of Islam. Instead, based on his research Gibson concludes that "Islam was founded in northern Arabia in the city of Petra. It was there that the first parts of the Qur'an were revealed before the faithful were forced to flee to Medina. Thus, the prophet Muhammad never visited Mecca, nor did any of the first four rightly guided caliphs. Mecca was never a center of worship in ancient times, and was not part of the ancient trade routes in Arabia."[122] In addition, Gibson mentions that at a 2002 conference on Nabataean Studies held in Petra he had the opportunity to speak to several Jordanian and Saudi archaeologists who admitted that the archeological record at Mecca was basically non-existent before 900 AD."[123] This may be why the Saudi government is destroying most of the ancient buildings and sites in

---

[120] Ibid., 104.

[121] Dan Gibson, *Qur'anic Geography: A Survey and Evaluation of the Geographical References in the Qur'an with Suggested Solutions for Various Problems and Issues*, (Canada: Independent Scholars Press, 2011), 137.

[122] Gibson, *Qur'anic Geography*, 379.

[123] Ibid., 223.

Mecca.[124] They may be trying to cover over something that was "not there" before the 9th century.

## Linguistic Evidence

The final link to Petra can be found through a linguistic study of the Qur'an itself. Robert M. Kerr, a professor of Comparative Semitic Linguistics at Waterloo University, suggests that the language of the Qur'an places it in the context of North Arabia, 600 miles north of Mecca, centered around the city of Petra.[125] He bases his evidence on the fact that the script used in the Qur'an is from the North Arabian Nabataeans and not the South-Arabian alphabet that was used in the Hijaz where Medina and Mecca were located. He also suggests that since the Qur'an's vocabulary is "largely borrowed from Aramaic, especially Syriac, the liturgical language of the local churches," this further indicates that the Classical Arabic used in the Qur'an had its origin in the *Arabia Patraea* of Syro-Palestine with its capital in the city of Petra. He points out that if the Qur'an had been written in Mecca or Medina, it would have been in "a different Semitic language and written in a different script."[126] Based on these linguistics differences, Kerr concludes that "all of the contemporary epigraphical, literary and linguistic evidence points to Islam being a product of Arabs living in Syro-Palestine."[127]

Mark Durie, who has a Ph.D. in Linguistics and a Th.D. in Islamic Studies, agrees with Kerr and points out that there are a number of linguistical features that demonstrate that the Arabic of the Qur'an was not a Meccan dialect, but rather developed in the Southern Levant (the area around Petra) as a Nabataean dialect. Durie concludes that the orthographic and phonological features of the Qur'anic *rasm* (root consonants) provide clear evidence that what became the Classical Arabic of the Qur'an was never the native dialect of Mecca, but rather reflects the Nabataean Arabic dialect of the region surrounding Petra.[128] If these assertions are correct, then it will be necessary to revisit the question of not only the origin of the Qur'an, but also the origin of Muhammad and Islam

---

[124] "Destruction of early Islamic heritage sites in Saudi Arabia," https://en.wikipedia.org/wiki/Destruction_of_early_Islamic_heritage_sites_in_Saudi_Arabia

[125] Robert Kerr, "The Language of the Koran," *Tingis Magazine*, February 18, 2013. https://www.tingismagazine.com/articles/the-language-of-the-koran/

[126] Ibid.

[127] Ibid.

[128] See Mark Durie, *The Qur'an and its Biblical reflexes: Investigations into the Genesis of a Religion* (Rowman and Littlefield, 2018).

itself, for if Mecca did not exist at the time of Muhammad, then he could not have lived there. Also, it would be much more possible for the Qur'an to reflect the beliefs of the Nabataeans who were familiar with the Jewish-Christian heresies and perhaps responsible for creating the greatest Christian heresy of all time.

## Apologetic Conclusions

Ultimately, Christians can gain valuable insight from this discussion about the early years of Islamic expansion. Muslim accounts claim that the empire building which occurred in the decades after Muhammad's death originated from a burst of religious enthusiasm and the desire to fulfill the will of Allah. However, if the arguments discussed above cast any doubts worth considering on the truth of this explanation, then the only other logical option is that the empire was not truly driven by religion. Rather, men like Abd al-Malik used Islam as a tool to unify, motivate, and justify those actively involved in building and controlling the new empire. The thoughtful Christian should immediately compare the early years of Christianity (which, as has been mentioned earlier, are well documented) with the early period of Islam. Did Christianity burst into a period of conquest and expansion in the name of Jesus? The very opposite reality of intense persecution, the early Christians' general separation from government and politics, and the emphasis on poverty and suffering being a natural part of missionary work paint a stark contrast to the Islamic expansion. Thus, a significant apologetic point that Christians should include in their witness is this dramatic difference between how Christianity and Islam saw their respective missions to spread their new faiths. "Why such a difference?" should be the question that naturally arises. This is a great subject to explore, as it includes not only issues of historical evidence but also key differences in the underlying assumptions that each religion has about the world and the role of believers in that world.

## Building Bridges to Understand

To apply these implications and apologetic points, Christians can first build a bridge by sharing how the Christian Scriptures are trustworthy, and that abundant historical sources testify to the traditional view of the development of Christianity, even from the first century AD. Islam claims to have developed in the "full light of history," but in reality, its sources are questioned by a number of scholars for a variety of reasons.

It is likely that Muslim friends will reject any reinterpretation of the origins of Islam, especially if it does not favor their understanding of the events from the past. However, one of the best ways to get someone thinking about the validity of their own belief system is to demonstrate that what they have come to accept may not be accurate. Discussing these points must be done with gentleness and respect, but Christians must also remember that it is difficult to begin building a new foundation when the old one is still in the way. Since Islam's origins have been obscured in darkness, the true light of the gospel can bring redemption and truth to the many Muslims who truly want to know the "true path" to God.

A second "bridge" that can be established between Muslims and Christians is one which addresses the concept of conquest and forced conversions. Several verses in the Qur'an call specifically for world domination:

> Q. 8:38-39; 2:193: *"And fight them until persecution is no more, and religion be only for Allah."* Also in the Hadith, Sahih Muslim 1:33: The Messenger of Allah said: *"I have been commanded to fight against people till they testify that there is no god but Allah, that Muhammad is the messenger of Allah, and they establish prayer and pay zakat."*

Surah 8:38-39 is, therefore, telling Muslims that they need to fight against the non-believers (Jews, Christians, pagans) until everyone follows Islam. In Surah 2:193, Muslims are to fight until "religion be only for Allah." Although liberal Muslims today argue that fighting and forced conversions were only for the time of Muhammad, these verses contradict that view because they emphasize that the only endpoint is when all people in the world follow Islam.

Although there are other verses in the Qur'an that say there is "no compulsion in religion" (Q. 2:256) indicating that Muslims should not try to coerce people to follow Islam, the practice of "abrogation" negates this, stating that whenever there are contradictory statements in the Qur'an, the chronologically later verses replace or nullify the earlier verses. The plea for "no compulsion in religion," then, is abrogated by verses revealed later that call for all the non-believers to face one of three choices: either to convert to Islam, submit to being a "protected" 2nd class citizen, or be executed. This really does not leave non-Muslims much choice about their conversion.

Knowing these verses as well as the practice of abrogation presents a great opportunity for Christians to contrast the dictates of the Qur'an to those of the Bible. Christians can tell their Muslim friends that in Christianity there is no compulsion at all, but rather salvation is a "free gift" provided by Jesus Christ who loves every person so much that he took their sin upon himself and died in their place so that they would not have to face the wrath of God, which will be their destiny if it were not for God's grace. It is still a choice, but one that is guided by love rather than fear. Hopefully, this will open up the door to share the full gospel with Muslim friends.

**Questions for Study**

1. Putting traditional theories as well as revisionist theories aside, list at least five basic historical facts involving the conquest of the Middle East by the Arabs in the 7th century.

2. What are the strongest arguments for the traditional Muslim view of the rise of Islam?

3. What are the strongest arguments for the Revisionist view of the rise of Islam?

4. Explain the main points of "Intermediate Monotheism." What role does the leader Abd al-Malik play in developing the religion of Islam?

5. Explain how you would use the verses in the Qur'an that deal with contradictory views, such as "no compulsion in religion" compared with the call for world religious domination. Be sure that you explain the concept of abrogation. Finally, how would you use this information to transition into talking about the "free gift" of salvation and the hope that we have in Jesus Christ?

# CHAPTER 5 Theological Development of Islam: The Opening of the Gates of Heaven or the "Closing of the Muslim Mind"?

## Introduction

After a religion is introduced to a culture or to an empire, often a period of theological debates will follow, fine-tuning the details and implications of general religious tenets. Certainly, this was the case during the decades following Muhammad's death and the establishment of Islam as a political force. Both secular and theological changes rapidly followed the days of desert warfare and initial conversions, as has been demonstrated in the previous chapter. However, within the context of the new Islamic centers of power in the Middle East, more subtle debates and deeper study of the religion quickly sprang up among certain learned groups of the population. This chapter focuses on three of the most important theological debates among Muslim factions in the early days of the Islamic world (mostly in Persia during the Abbasid empire in the 800 and 900's AD). What did the debates mean to the people participating in them, and what do they mean to Muslims today? The chapter then examines several views by non-Muslim scholars about the long-term impact of these debates and concludes with implications and apologetic conclusions that can be drawn from this fascinating time of theological controversy.

## Factual Overview of the Three Theological Debates in Early Islam[129]

As the new religion developed there were adjustments that needed to be made since the new beliefs confronted the traditional religious views of the area. Although there is disagreement about what the debates signify, the basic facts of the arguments are well documented by both non-Muslim and Muslim sources. The first debate occurred between 661 and 700 AD and centered on the role of works versus faith in the practice of religion. One side, called the Kharijites, argued that sin invalidates faith, and people are saved by what they do. Thus, unrepentant sinners were no longer considered true Muslims and were believed to go to hell. The other side, known as the Murji'ites, refused to judge other people's actions (especially those of leaders) because they believed that only Allah can judge a person's heart. They also maintained that sinners were still true Muslims and part of

---

[129] Refer to the Theological Chart at the end of the chapter for a visual representation of these debates.

the mosque, rather than being infidels and apostates. Interestingly, a third view, proposed by Abu Hanifah[130] and known as the "compromise," also circulated an argument that works must follow faith. Ultimately this third view was accepted, as it appealed to both sides and thus captured a broad swath of support.

The second debate began very shortly after the first one had concluded and continued for a long time (700-870 AD). This concerned the issue of predestination versus free will. One group, known as the Mu'tazilites, believed that everybody has been given power by Allah to make choices regarding how to live (the doctrine of free will). As a result, this group believed that all are responsible for their own eternal destiny, as each person has the right to embrace or reject salvation in Allah. The traditionalists who opposed this view argued that this doctrine limits Allah because all things are predestined by him, including the actions of individuals. The latter side won this debate in the end because most people agreed that Allah would not have true control if he allowed people to act as they desired. If Allah can do anything, they reasoned, he could not be disobeyed or rejected.

The third debate began in the 8th-century but has actually never been fully resolved. This debate is over the nature of the Qur'an itself. Traditionalist Muslim scholars argue that its words are so perfectly given by Allah that those words themselves are essentially an attribute of Allah. They are, in other words, infallible, eternal, and uncreated. In fact, during the mid-800's AD under the caliph al-Ma'mum, the Qur'an almost became an object of worship due to this portrayal. The Mu'tazilites, who disagreed with this view, argued instead that the Qur'an is a created object and therefore cannot be an attribute of Allah. It may be from him, but this does not make it equal to him or represent his eternal will. The entirety of this debate flowed out of the 2nd debate about free will versus predestination. Since reason supported the side of a Qur'an passed down from men, the Mu'tazilite position was weakened when the non-reason group (who argued for predestination and no free agency) won the second debate in the 9th century. Thus, the "eternal word of Allah" defeated the Mu'tazilites, who posited a more representational or created view of the Qur'an, but many of the finer points of the argument were never actually answered. This "winning" view is therefore accepted on the basis of faith and not of logical persuasion.

---

[130] Imam Abu Hanifah (699-767) was the founder of the Sunni Hanafi school of Islamic jurisprudence, and the first of the major Islamic jurists.

## Modern Muslim View of the Debates

How then do Muslims today interpret these theological conflicts? They view them as belonging to a time when the core of Islamic theology, established by the Qur'an and Hadith, began to be eroded by continuous questioning of Islam's tenets. In the 12th century, one of the most famous philosophers of that period, al-Ghazali, rejected the adequacy of human reason to comprehend God because of its inadequacy to understand the will of Allah. Only by placing unquestioning faith and blind obedience over and above reason, he claimed, could one really achieve such an understanding.[131] Muslims now believe that al-Ghazali's brave stand helped to resolve the disputes, which in turn allowed Muslims from then on to freely follow the will of Allah in full obedience and unimpeded by heretical notions. According to many Muslims, the debates took place at a time in which philosophers like al-Ghazali fortuitously eradicated external and false ideas about the nature of faith and Allah himself so that Muslims could return to a pure faith, as it was first preached by Muhammad. This, of course, is a retrospective judgment on the events of many centuries ago, and mostly came into being during the 11th and 12th centuries but has continued to be the explanation that most Muslims accept today.[132]

## Modern Counterview of the Theological Debates

Critics of this retrospective Muslim view see the debates not as a dangerous toying with heresy but as a natural reaction to inherent problems in Islam itself. These exist because of a core instability that could be identified in Islam from its earliest days. Scholars who press this point argue that Islam began as a political religion, created to be beneficial to effective government but not necessarily to be a perfectly thought-out religion. A large body of revisionist literature, therefore, presses the point that Muslim understandings or explanations of doctrine developed out of political needs rather than theological ones.[133] Some of the issues in the debates may have

---

[131] Al-Ghazali, *The Revival of the Religious Sciences*, quoted in Robert Reilly, *The Closing of the Muslim Mind*, 115.

[132] Robert Reilly, *The Closing of the Muslim Mind: How Intellectual Suicide Created the Modern Islamist Crisis* (Wilmington, Delaware: ISI Books, 2010), 119.

[133] See J.W. Sweetman, *Islam and Christian Theology: A Study of the Interpretation of Theological Ideas in the Two Religions*, Part I: Volume 1 (Origins Lutterworth Press, London, 1945); A.J. Wensinck, *The Muslim Creed: Its Genesis and Historical Development* (Cambridge: Cambridge University Press, 1932); A.S. Tritton, *Muslim Theology* (Connecticut: Hyperion Press, 1947); Duncan MacDonald, *Development of Muslim Theology Jurisprudance and constitutional Theory* (New York: Charles Scribner, 1903); Harry Wolfson, *Philosophy of the Kalām* (Cambridge, MA: Harvard University Press, 1976); and

had their origins in objections from Jews and Christians regarding the Islamic doctrines, but these issues overall were problematic because they were internal flaws in not only Islamic theology but also the monotheism and the sectarian Jewish-Christian beliefs that had existed long before. In the past, logical implications about the finer theological details had never been politically or socially important enough to be closely considered. However, current revisionist scholars see the pressures of the empire and the need to centralize Islam as a national religion under Abd al-Malik as bringing a new level of urgency to the need to resolve these internal weaknesses. Ultimately, Muslim scholars addressing these three theological disputes were unable to resolve the inherent flaws that were foundational in the early years of the religion. Revisionist scholars conclude that this failure was due to the fact that they began with a distorted view or premise of how God works in this world. Thus, not only was their theology flawed, but their ability to deal with those flaws was similarly inadequate.

## Implications

Islam is different today than it was in the 9th to 12th centuries. Among modern Muslims general distrust of reason and a resolve to focus on faith and the Qur'an instead have resulted from these three theological debates. One specific outcome of these debates today is that many Muslims believe in predestination to the point that fatalism is prevalent (especially in folk Islam), with a sense of futility and resignation about life. Additionally, as a result of the second debate regarding the nature of the Qur'an, Muslims hold fast to the idea that it is the very word of Allah. Because of this, they believe that they open themselves up to possible disbelief when anything challenges the historicity of parts of the Qur'an. Even a minor discrepancy would challenge their entire view of the Qur'an. These debates, therefore, represent to Muslims a time of dangerous questioning. However, to critics and revisionist scholars, the debates instead recall a lost opportunity to see the inherent flaws of Muslim theology and use reason to deal with them.

The consequences of these foundational flaws are arguably profound. This is because the emphasis on right practice (Orthopraxy) over right doctrine (Orthodoxy) and intuition over reason tends to lead Muslims to a dead end theologically. Subsequently, this provides not only personal but also cultural implications. For example, in *The Closing of the Muslim Mind*, Robert Reilly concludes that the root of the modern day crisis in Islam –

---

Telford Work, *Sharpening the Doctrine of God* Theology between Orthodox Christianity and Early Islam," (November 25, 2002), Orthodox Theology Group, American Academy of Religion, Unpublished manuscript, 14. Accessed at www.westmont.edu/~work (TelfordWork.net), 6-11-2010.

which he defines as the inability to engage with the modern world while staying true to Islam – all stems from the rejection of reason and its eventual result of "intellectual suicide."[134] Interestingly, he emphasizes that this rejection was not encouraged by the Qur'an itself but by the development of early Islamic theology.[135] He explains:

> The closure of the Muslim mind ... is the key to unlocking such puzzles as why the Arab world stands near the bottom of every measure of human development; why scientific inquiry is nearly moribund in the Islamic world; why Spain translates more books in a single year than the entire Arab world has in the past thousand years; why some people in Saudi Arabia still refuse to believe man has been to the moon; and why some Muslim media present natural disasters like Hurricane Katrina as God's direct retribution. Without understanding this story, we cannot grasp what is taking place in the Islamic world today, or the potential paths to recovery – paths many Muslims are pointing to with their rejection of the idea of God that produced this crisis in the first place.[136]

However, there is a deeper consequence that Christians need to be prepared to confront. The "fatal disconnect" in Islamic theology between reason and faith may lead to the belief that nothing can be known for certain, and ultimately to a denial of reality. In that case, as al-Ghazali concluded, "blind obedience" becomes the only valid test of true faith.[137] It is for this reason that Robert Reilly warns that the closing of the Muslim mind has resulted in intellectual suicide and has created the modern Islamist crisis. Reilly concludes, "The closing of the Muslim mind is the direct if somewhat distant antecedent of today's radical Islamist ideology, and this ideology cannot be understood without divining its roots in that closing."[138] Thus, in order to understand the root of Islamism in today's world, it must be realized that the closing of the Muslim mind, which led to modern radical Islamist theology, began when beliefs were divorced from reason. Unfortunately, this rejection of reason often results in irrational behavior where power is used in order to resolve disputes, and this removes the basis on which opposing parties can "reason together."

---

[134] Reilly, *Closing of the Muslim Mind*, 197.

[135] Ibid., 2-4.

[136] Ibid., 6-7.

[137] Al-Ghazali, *The Revival of the Religious Sciences*, quoted in Robert Reilly, *The Closing of the Muslim Mind*, 115.

[138] Reilly, *The Closing of the Muslim Mind*, 6.

Furthermore, on a theological basis, the Islamists view God as pure will and power rather than reason and justice. This conception of God tends to remove all theological barriers to the endorsement of violence in the spread of faith. This may be why violence has been the primary way that Islam spread historically. During an interview, Robert Reilly stated that "Benedict XVI made this point in his Regensburg talk – that not only is violence in spreading faith unreasonable, but that a conception of God without reason leads to this very violence." Reilly then explained, "Once the primacy of force is posited, terrorism becomes the next logical step to power, as it did in Nazism and Marxism-Leninism." Reilly then went on to relate how Osama bin Laden fit this same profile when he stated in a video pertaining to the 9/11 attack that "terrorism is an obligation in Allah's religion." Reilly's response to this is that "this can only be true—that violence in spreading faith is an obligation—if God is without reason and therefore acting unreasonably is not against his nature."[139]

Ultimately, then, the development of Islam was permanently affected by the outcomes of these three debates. Revisionist scholars believe that after some initial success during the 9th and 10th centuries on the part of those who advocated for reason and faith, the Islamic understanding of the nature of God prevented a realistic theology from developing. They feel, therefore, that Muslim thinkers were then, and continue now, to be doomed to accept the ultimate fatalism that a god of pure will dictates.[140] In addition, Muslims who attempt to think through these issues via this worldview must struggle with a consequent deep distrust of anything that has to do with reason or any theology that puts reason above the Qur'an.

## Apologetic Conclusions

As these implications indicate, from the time of al-Ghazali to the present, any theology or philosophy in Islam that raised reason above the Qur'an was ultimately rejected. There are, of course, consequences for this practice. This is why Reilly raises the question, "If one's theological assumptions about reality are incorrect, can one recover from them if these assumptions have been dogmatized and made pillars of one's faith?"[141] While it would never be appropriate to bring up these issues to degrade or ridicule Muslims about their beliefs, it is important for the Christian apologist to explain how Christianity is different and that reason and faith

---

[139] http://www.catholicnewsagency.com/column/ten-questions-with-the-closing-of-the-muslim-mind-author-robert-r-reilly-1328/
[140] Reilly, *Closing of the Muslim Mind*, 114-16.
[141] Ibid., 4.

can both be used in order to develop a theological understanding of God and his creation.

The three theological struggles during the early centuries of Islam demonstrated that some Muslims were seeking to reconcile several core doctrinal issues with Islamic practices dominated by political factions. However, since Islam stresses orthopraxy (right practice), there is an emphasis on obedience to the will of Allah rather than on doctrine. This emphasis tends to lead Muslims to a dead end theologically, or at least to a place where they will no longer question beliefs but will emphasize actions instead.

Christianity, on the other hand, emphasizes orthodoxy (right doctrine). Right doctrine encourages Christian believers to think and use reason to "think God's thoughts after him." This emphasis on linking reason and faith allows Christians to successfully adjust to a changing world. It is important for the reader to understand these theological struggles because when we understand the outcome of these debates, we will be able to better grasp why the Islamic world is struggling with reality today.

A good example of how the different emphases result in different outcomes can be seen in the way that Muslims and Christians view God and power. Since Allah is considered to be totally "other," most Muslims do not believe that they can have a personal relationship with the God of the universe, so the role of mankind is to follow the will of God through blind obedience. This stress on right practice, however, can easily lead to an external faith that only measures devotion through actions. When this motivation is linked to the view that God is a god of power, exerting the will of God over others becomes the dominant goal.

On the other hand, Christians believe that they can have a personal relationship with the God of the universe, who proclaims himself to be the God of Love. Thus, according to this worldview, the role of man is to seek to know God personally and follow his commands freely because God is seen as good and desirous of our wellbeing. This means Christianity emphasizes that God's power is displayed through his love and not his will. This results in the possibility that God's love for man could even manifest itself in the incarnation, death and resurrection of the Son of God for our sakes. This could never happen with the God of Islam. Thus, Christians need to understand the theological differences between Islam and Christianity so that they will be able to explain how the different concepts of the nature of God determine not only the way that people will respond to God and understand his relationship with them, but also how they will treat others.

# Building Bridges to Understand

In building a bridge to connect with Muslim friends, it would be helpful for Christians to use one of the doctrinal areas in order to demonstrate that there is great freedom in Christ and that Christians are encouraged to use their rational minds to explore the nature of God and of their faith.

There are three significant areas of conversation that can be discussed in regard to the theological development of Islam: a comparison of the Christian and Muslim understandings of the basis for salvation, the role of faith in understanding God, and the personal actions and responsibilities of believers to spread their faith. The relationship between reason and faith is a dominant theme in all three of these topics. Therefore, a good bridge in conversation would be to use specific verses to demonstrate how reason can free us from the bondage of blindly following certain interpretations that may be harmful. This practice would also allow us to explore the reasons for the faith that we have. Each of these three topics can be beneficially discussed using verses from both the Qur'an and the Bible to carefully compare the contrasting theologies and draw helpful conclusions about the implications of both Christianity and Islam.

The topic of free will versus the predetermined world of Islam is a key discussion to bring up since it concerns how a believer views his or her personal actions in relation to a sovereign deity. Muslims generally believe Allah has given humans free will, but that the outcomes of all human actions are governed by the will of Allah. If Allah does not will for something to take place, it will not happen, and if he wills for something to happen, then it will occur no matter what is done to stop it. This can be seen in Surah 9:51: "Say, '*Only what God has decreed will happen to us. He is our Master: let the believers put their trust in God.*'" As a result of the historic debates, this type of teaching is now interpreted with an aspect of fatalism. While it still brings comfort to Muslim readers that they can trust that Allah is in control of events, it can also cause these readers to simply be resigned to fate, since the teaching now states that nothing they do can make a difference to their lives.

This strong view against any level of human free will can be contrasted with the Christian teachings of God's will and man's will. Ephesians 1:4 speaks of God choosing his people for redemption, but this is balanced with the free choice of the individual to follow or not follow God in daily life. This lends a greater aspect of freedom in one's personal actions. As Galatians 5:13 explains, "You were called to freedom, brothers. Only do not use your freedom as an opportunity for the flesh, but through love serve one another." I Corinthians 6:12 also points to this balance: "All things are lawful for me, but not all things are helpful. All things are lawful for me, but I will not be enslaved by anything." Thus, in Christianity, there is a balance between God's will (which is sovereign and cannot be ultimately thwarted) and the daily choices of humans, made out of their free will. Because Christians are in Christ, they are given free will so that they can choose to follow Christ daily out of love rather than simply obedience or fear. It also demonstrates that God loves us and dignifies our choices, even if we rebel against him. He will not force us to do something against our will. This brings assurance as well as hope.

Works versus faith as the basis of salvation, which was the subject of the first Islamic theological debate, is also understood very differently by Muslims and Christians. Every known religion in the world has one of two methods for finding favor in the eyes of the deity: good works that earn merit, or a free gift of grace (unmerited favor) from the deity to the human. Islam holds more of the former belief while Christianity holds only the latter. Surah 5:9 explains, "To those who believe and do deeds of righteousness hath Allah promised forgiveness and a great reward." This highlights well the combination of Allah's grace and the believer's works, which together save the Muslim from punishment in hell and reward him or her with divine favor. In fact, technically a Muslim's good works must outweigh his evil deeds to earn him entrance to heaven, but Allah can will the Muslim's entrance despite a negative balance if he, Allah, so wills it. This makes salvation ultimately more of a reward than the free gift the Bible teaches that it is. Ephesians 2:8-9 is a good verse to help explain this concept: "For by grace through faith you have been saved, not by works, so that no one can boast." Christians, therefore, believe that works flow out of a true believer in gratitude and obedience to God, but that those works cannot lend even the slightest benefit to their actual salvation since that is the free gift of God alone and is 100% reliant on him. Such a contrasting view of salvation can give a Christian the opportunity to point out God's gracious love and mercy.

Finally, while the closing of the Muslim mind has made it more difficult to use a reasoned approach to the gospel when reaching out to Muslims, discussing the theological debates of Islam can still lead to a good opportunity to explore the differences between what Islam and Christianity teach about using reason to understand God. This is also an important point for prayer since an opening of the Muslim mind is needed in order for more Muslims to respond to the reasonable evidence for the God of Christianity and the truth about Jesus Christ.

In discussing the theological debates, the Christian must bear in mind that in Islam, since the second and third theological debates established such a strong precedent of not using reason to decide theological points, the emphasis instead is on the nature of Allah being pure Will. This has created the tendency for a strong disconnect between reason and faith in Muslims' lives. Such a gulf helps to strengthen the fatalism discussed above, and can even lead to a denial of reality. Muslims may, therefore, deny the generally accepted cause and effect relationship in the world and claim instead that all things happen only due to the direct intervention of Allah.

Christianity, on the other hand, teaches that God is a reasonable creator who set all things in motion but allows the natural laws of the world to determine basic cause-and-effect outcomes in daily life. This view promotes an understanding among Christians about the need for men and women to exercise wisdom and discipline in their lives, fostering a sense of both responsibility and hope that one's actions can truly make a difference in the world. This difference in our understanding of God's nature, pure Will versus a loving creator who uses reason and logic in the very fabric of the universe, should be highlighted by Christians in conversations with Muslim friends. This is perhaps most important in sharing with them the Christian belief that one must choose to follow Christ, and that there is a balance between faith and reason as well as between God's will and the free will of an individual. Reasonable faith is a difficult goal to achieve, but it avoids the dangers of both reason without faith (the Western secular fallacy) and faith without reason (the Islamic fallacy). Some verses that can be used to discuss the concept of employing reason to explore and defend faith, as well as to better understand God's nature, are: 1 Peter 3:15; 2 Corinthians 10:5; Colossians 2:8; Colossians 4:5-6; Titus 1:9; and Jude 1:3

In all of these discussions, it is important to keep in mind the method by which Islam and Christianity have traditionally been spread. While the Qur'an urges military conquest and emphasizes dominating the world (see Q. 2:193, 9:33), the Great Commission given by Jesus in the gospels (see Matt. 28:19-20) instead focuses on making disciples. This was ultimately achieved through poverty, suffering, and loving others, not military or even political means. Christian evangelism has also traditionally placed a strong emphasis on using reason to both understand and share faith. Early missionaries in the book of Acts can be seen most often appealing to men's reason and understanding of the scriptures before conversion, and once converts did profess faith, these new believers were expected to spend several years learning theology and doctrine before their actual baptism. Although the Crusades may well come up in conversation, the point still remains that Islam has promoted empire-building for nearly 1400 years and has done so from its earliest years. Christianity has not merely a different means of spreading its beliefs but has a different and ultimately non-political goal in spreading them. Keeping these differences in mind while discussing the more technical issues of reason, faith, and works can help steer the conversation along profitable lines while avoiding misunderstandings.

## Questions for Study

1. In the first theological debate between works and faith, why did the Kharijites believe that people are only saved by what they do? How did the Murji'ites counter this view? Why did the compromise view appeal to both sides?

2. Considering the second debate involving free will and predestination, why have most Muslims continued to conclude that everything must be predestined by Allah, including the actions of individuals? What does this say about their view of the nature of Allah? How can Christians bring hope to Muslim friends who are caught in the trap of fatalism?

3. In the third debate, why do the traditionalists believe that the Qur'an must be eternal? Would this mean that there are two eternal entities in the universe, Allah and the Qur'an? How does this debate demonstrate the "fatal disconnect" between faith and reason?

4. Robert Reilly, in his book *The Closing of the Muslim Mind*, concludes that the root of the modern day crisis in Islam stems from the rejection of reason and its eventual result of "intellectual suicide." What are some of the developments that led to this viewpoint? What is the fatal flaw in al-Ghazali's assessment of what he believes is the inadequacy of reason in regard to understanding the will of Allah?

5. Do you think that the Christian emphasis on orthodoxy (right doctrine) is more productive than the Muslim emphasis on orthopraxy (right practice)? What are the strengths of each view? What are the weaknesses? Is there a way to emphasize both orthodoxy and orthopraxy? What would this look like?

# CHAPTER 6 Islamic Golden Age and Expansion: Path of Peace or Trail of Blood?

## Introduction

In a traditional history of Islam, one major chapter is usually dedicated to the Islamic empires, which lasted from the early medieval period to, technically, the fall of the Ottoman Empire after World War I. The details of the rapid conquests, the general trend of expansion over the centuries, and, most of all, the legendary accounts of fabulous wealth, art, and learning that modern readers automatically associate with the Islamic world, are probably the most celebrated aspects of Islamic culture. Each of these aspects gives a significant reason to admire the Islamic empires, especially as it is a generally accepted view that Islamic scholars preserved the learning of the Greeks through Arabic translations of the great works, which were lost in the West for centuries, and thus provided the foundation for the Renaissance and its rediscovery of classical Greek knowledge. Such knowledge was the source of the inventions and innovations that ushered in the scientific advances that began in the 16th-century and flowered in the Industrial Revolutions of the 18th and 19th centuries and also brought about revolutionary gains in medicine.

If these accounts are true, then the world is greatly indebted to the Islamic empires, which allowed centers of learning and culture to flourish while the Western world lay overshadowed by the so-called Dark Ages. However, history is rarely so simplistic. This chapter will consider the historical evidence available regarding these cultural legacies and their potential impact on the world, including some brief counter-arguments from controversial revisionary theorists. If evidence does in fact point to a different interpretation of the Islamic culture's impact in history, especially regarding its claim to be a religion of peace, then some important implications and potential conclusions must be considered.

## Traditional Account of Islamic Expansion and Empire

Islamic expansion is traditionally understood to have been rapid and unexpected: within only 2 years of the prophet Muhammad's death, all of Arabia was conquered. Within 40 years of his death, parts of North Africa, Syria, Iraq, Iran, and Egypt were included in the Islamic territory; within 100 years, all of North Africa, Spain, and parts of Portugal and Afghanistan were included, extending the empire to the borders of India. It has been calculated that by the end of that time, over 50% of lands that had been claimed by Christians in the east was controlled by Islamic forces. As one scholar explains, the Arabs simply "took possession of whole sections of the crumbling Empire [of Byzantium]."[142] What happened to all of that land? To very briefly summarize a long and complex history, these eastern territories became part of four major caliphates and five major empires (all of which overlap with each other to some extent).

## The Caliphates and Their Empires

A caliphate is simply the area of territory under the jurisdiction of the caliph, or religious successor to Muhammad. The caliph is also known as the "Commander of Believers." According to Muslim sources, the first of these great caliphates was the Rashidun Caliphate (632-661) which was centered in Mecca, Saudi Arabia, and primarily made up of Sunni or "orthodox" Muslims (who believe that the caliph should be chosen by community consensus). The second caliphate was the Umayyad Caliphate (661-750). This caliphate was centered in Damascus, Syria, but continued a "capital in exile" in Cordoba, Spain, until the 11th century. The third caliphate was the Abbasid (750-1258), which was established in Baghdad. Interestingly, after Mongols destroyed this capital, the Mamluk rulers in Egypt tried to re-establish the Abbasid caliphate in Cairo. Although this derivative caliphate continued until 1517 (under several dynasties), these Egyptian caliphs had little political power and essentially were only authorities in religious matters. The fourth and final caliphate was the Ottoman Caliphate (1517-1922), which was especially influential in World War I.[143]

These caliphates existed between 661 and 1922 AD and were usually connected to a significant Islamic empire. A few points on each will be sufficient to sketch the main details of these empires' history and influence. The Umayyad Empire (661-750) was established by Muawiya after the First Muslim Civil War (661 AD), and its territory extended from India to Spain to North Africa, making it the largest Arab Muslim state in history.[144] Continued civil wars and power struggles eventually weakened the empire, which was more interested in power than in religion by the end of its existence. The second empire, the Abbasid empire (750-1258), essentially

---

[142] Henri Pirenne, *Mohammed and Charlemagne* (New York: Meridian Books, 1957), 149.

[143] Donald Quataert, *The Ottoman Empire, 1700-1922* (Cambridge University Press, 2005), 3-5.

[144] Blankinship, Khalid Yahya, *The End of the Jihad State, the Reign of Hisham Ibn 'Abd-al Malik and the collapse of the Umayyads* (State University of New York Press, 1994), 37.

replaced the Umayyad by taking over its authority in 750 AD and establishing a capital in Baghdad. It also extended through the Middle East and North Africa but did not control India even at its most expansive point (around 850 AD). This empire is the one which is most commonly associated with the so-called Golden Age of Islam, and traditional accounts attribute to it many developments in science, literature, medicine, and philosophy. It was only brought to an end when invading Mongols captured and sacked Bagdad in 1258. The third empire was the Ottoman Empire (1299 – 1922), which some view as the greatest Muslim empire of all. It endured for 600 years, spanning such great events as the Crusades, the capture of the Byzantine capital of Constantinople in 1453, and the reign of Suleyman the Great in the 16th century. The Ottoman empire began to lose political and military power after the defeat of its army at Vienna in 1683 and ended in 1923 when Mustafa Kemal Attaturk dissolved the empire to establish the modern nation-state of Turkey. The fourth empire to be established (though the Ottoman Empire ultimately outlasted it) was the Safavid Empire (1501-1736). This was perhaps the greatest of all Persian empires, known for its art and architecture as well as its efficient government system.[145] Finally, the Mughal Empire was founded in 1526 and lasted to 1857. It was based in India and enjoyed an extremely rich and prosperous existence with both cultural and economic progress. Although there was no religious controversy, decline ultimately set in as a result of indulgent leaders and a weak army.

## The Golden Age and its Impact on the West (as related by traditional and Muslim accounts)

Muslims and traditional histories emphasize that throughout these five empires, great scholars "genuinely contributed in the development of philosophy and science."[146] They point to Islamic Spain and the Middle East as the real guiding lights for the development of thought in Europe during the Middle Ages, as well as for essential concepts such as the Arabic numeral system. These concepts and innovations created a "great ... debt owed by medieval Europe to the Islamic world," as one source explains.[147] The basic tenets of this view are that the Islamic world, especially during the Golden Age (750-1050 AD), was a period of great learning and innovation for Muslim scholars. The assumption is that the West at this same time

---

[145] Arthur Goldschmidt, *A Concise History of the Middle East*, 11th ed. (Boulder, CO: Westview Press, 2016), 133-34.

[146] The Myth of Islamic Science (http://indiafacts.org/the-myth-of-islamic-science/)

[147] Emmet Scott, *Mohammed & Charlemagne Revisited: The History of a Controversy* (Nashville, TN: New English Review Press, 2012), xi-x

experienced a period of cultural and technological stagnation, and the Renaissance several hundred years later was only possible because Islamic scholars had preserved the classical works that were later "rediscovered" by the West and which stimulated the cultural revival of the Renaissance. Furthermore, the traditional account maintains that scientific discoveries pioneered by Muslim scholars were later of great significance in Europe's own technological boom. These Muslim advances are said to include the following: the astrolabe (for navigation); an early version of the scientific method; the development of algebra, algorithms, and spherical trigonometry; the introduction of "Arabic" numerals (originally from India); advances in anatomy, surgery, and pharmacology; and advances in astronomy, chemistry, and optics.

It has been generally established from historical records that numerous Muslim scholars contributed to diverse fields of study during this time. Al-Farabi (b. 872), Ibn-e-Rushd (b. 1126), and Ibn-Sina (b. 980) were great philosophers who studied and wrote commentaries on Aristotle (as well as on religion and reason), while Ibn-al-Haytham (b. 965) and Abu Musa Jabir-bin-Hayan (b. 721) were famed physicists and astronomers. Al-Haytham is recognized as the "father of modern optics" for his contributions to the understanding of vision, especially in regard to light being reflected into the eye from the outside rather than from the eye itself. In addition, he is recognized as an important contributor to the scientific method because of his use of experiments to verify his theories. Other notable names include Muhammad ibn Zakaria Al-Razi (b. 865), who was the greatest Muslim physician and is credited with the invention of rubbing alcohol; Al-Biruni (b. 973), who specialized in multiple fields that included astronomy, physics, and mathematics; Omar Khayyam (b. 1048), who was a great mathematician, poet, and astronomer; and Al-Khawarizmi (b. 780), who collected and consolidated previous mathematical discoveries, and brought advancements to the fields of astronomy and geography. All of these men are credited with contributing to the cultural splendor and learning that characterized the various Muslim empires, but especially the Abbasid Empire in its zenith as the center of the 300-year Golden Age of Islam.[148]

---

[148] See Ahmed Renima, "The Islamic Golden Age: A Story of the Triumph of the Islamic Civilization," in *The State of Social Progress of Islamic Societies*, ed. Habib Tiliouine (Springer, 2016), 25-52.

# Counterview of the Islamic Expansion and Golden Age

A common explanation of the Golden Age is that Islam itself inspired and nurtured a culture where the arts and sciences could flourish. Revisionist scholars who critique the idea of a Golden Age do so on two bases: first, that many of the innovations originated from conquered peoples and non-Muslim thinkers rather than Arab scholars, and second, that those Muslims who did contribute to their fields did so outside of and sometimes even directly against the religious circles of Islam. Some go so far as to suggest that Islamic culture was a negative influence on the world. As one scholar writes, Islam, unfortunately, contributed to Europe numerous "ideas and attitudes that were far from being enlightened," such as holy warfare.[149] A closer look at the historical records available, as well as recent archeological discoveries, have caused revisionist scholars to seriously question the idea of a Golden Age at all, and certainly to doubt that Islamic culture is the true source of the European Renaissance.[150]

The first of these objections is based on the argument that many or most of the discoveries credited to Islamic culture can actually be traced to the works of conquered peoples, especially Jews and Christians who were educated in the "western" (Byzantine) tradition of learning and contributed to cultural and scientific development during the first generation or two after the Muslim armies had conquered their lands. One scholar, Robert Spencer, enumerates some examples of how the evidence shows major innovations to be the work of non-Muslims; these points are supported by other revisionist scholars as well.

- The architectural design of mosques, especially the domes, was originally from Byzantine models of existing churches.
- The astrolabe was developed by the Greeks long before Muhammad was born (though the Muslims made improvements).[151]
- Christians preserved Aristotle's works during the "Dark Ages," and Christians, such as Huneyn ibn Ishaq (809-873), did most of the translation of the Greek into Arabic.[152]
- The first hospital in Baghdad during the Abbasid period was built by a Nestorian Christian, Abu 'Ali 'Isa ibn Zur'a (943-1008).

---

[149] Emmet Scott, *Mohammed & Charlemagne Revisited*, xx.
[150] Ibid., xvi.
[151] http://www.astrolabes.org/pages/history.htm
[152] John O'Neill, Holy Warriors, 137

- The first Arabic-language medical text was written in Greek by a Christian priest and then translated into Arabic by a Jewish doctor.
- The world's first university may have been the Assyrian Christian School of Nisibis and not Al-Azhar in Cairo.[153]
- The "Arabic" numerals, as well as the concept of the zero, came from India.
- Morera points out "even the Arabic script may have been invented by Christian missionaries from the Christianized Arab city of Hira in ancient Iraq."[154]
- Morera also adds that a tenth-century Muslim Chronicler testified that in Iran the majority of philosophers were still Christian.[155]

Spencer goes on to point out the implications of such evidence: "Islam was not the foundation of much significant cultural or scientific development at all. It is undeniable that there was a great cultural and scientific flowering in the Islamic world in the Middle Ages, but there is no indication that any of this flowering actually came as a result of Islam itself."[156]

In addition to the evidence cited by revisionist scholars, there is also evidence from Muslim scholars themselves that strongly suggests that a number of discoveries credited to Islam did not come from the Arab Muslim conquerors, but rather from the people they had conquered, especially the Persians, the Greek-speaking Christians educated in the Byzantine system, and the Jews. Even Muslim scholar Ibn Khaldun (1332-1406) remarked that most of the Muslim scholars and innovators were non-Arabs of Persian descent[157] (al-Razi, Avicenna, al-Biruni, al-Khawarazmi, Omar Khayyam, al-Farabi, Abu Musa Jabir, al-Kindi, and al-Ghazali) and would most likely have been influenced by Baghdad's pre-Islamic Greek heritage in philosophy and science. According to Serge Trifkovic, a Serbian-American scholar and author of *The Sword of the Prophet*, during this time (900-1200), Jews and Christians translated earlier Greek works on theology, philosophy, medicine, and literature into Arabic.[158] Islam was not opposed to learning from the earlier civilizations and incorporating their science, learning, and culture into its own worldview. The Muslims evaluated this

---

[153] Robert Spencer, *The Politically Incorrect Guide to Islam (and the Crusades)*. (DC: Regnery, 2005), 90-91.

[154] Dario Fernandez-Morera, The Myth of Andalusian Paradise: *Muslims, Christians, and Jews under Islamic Rule in Medieval Spain* (Wilmington, Delaware: ISI Books, 2016), 237.

[155] Ibid., 237.

[156] Robert Spencer, *The Politically Incorrect Guide to Islam*, 89-90.

[157] Morera, *The Myth of the Andalusian Paradise*, 236-7.

[158] Serge Trifkovic, *The Sword of the Prophet Islam – History, Theology, Impact on the World* (Boston: Regina Orthodox Press, 2002), 197.

material according to their religious views and the authority of the Qur'an and made some contributions, but in the end, rejected most of it in favor of revelation alone. Later, Jews and Christians translated the Arabic works into Latin and re-introduced Greek medicine (Hippocrates and Galen) and philosophy (Aristotle and Plato) to the West.

The Muslims did indeed transmit Greek, Hindu and other pre-Islamic knowledge to the West. However, after initially accepting and encouraging its use, the Muslims themselves were not able to make use of this knowledge beyond a superficial understanding due to their rigid view that revelation (the Qur'an) must supersede everything, even reason, and scientific inquiry. This is why Trifkivic asserts:

> The nature of the problem has always been spiritual. Like all totalitarian ideologies, Islam has an inherent tendency to the closing of the mind. The spirit of critical inquiry essential to the growth of knowledge is completely alien to it. All known episodes invoked to counter this simple fact happened in spite of Islam, not thanks to it.[159]

Robert Spencer adds, "Much of the responsibility for this must be laid at the feet of the Sufi Abu Hamid al-Ghazali (1058-1111). Although he was a great thinker, he nevertheless became the chief spokesman for a streak of anti-intellectualism that stifled much Islamic philosophical and scientific thought."[160] Spencer then concludes that for a time the Islamic culture was able to draw on and advance the achievements of the surrounding civilizations, "but when they had taken what they could from Byzantium and Persia, and sufficient numbers of Jews and Christians had been converted to Islam or thoroughly subdued, Islam went into a period of intellectual stagnation from which it has not yet emerged."[161] This suggests that once the talent of recently conquered civilizations had been absorbed, the anti-intellectual emphasis of Islamic leaders choked the innovation so that the discoveries became stagnant until picked up by later Christian and Jewish scholars in the West.[162]

The second main issue that is not raised by Muslim scholars defending the Golden Age is that the Islamic governments did not support a number of these scholars, especially the ones who rejected the core beliefs of Islam. Therefore, what they accomplished was often in spite of Islam rather than

---

[159] Trifkovic, *The Sword of the Prophet*, 200.

[160] Spencer, *Politically Incorrect Guide to Islam*, 91-92.

[161] Ibid., 91-92.

[162] See Robert Reilly, *The Closing of the Muslim Mind*; Emmet Scott, *Mohammed & Charlemagne Revisited*; and Dario Fernandez-Morera, The Myth of the Andalusian Paradise.

because of Islam.¹⁶³ For example, Muhammad ibn Zakariya Al-Razi, one of the greatest of all Muslim physicians, philosophers and alchemists dismissed revelation and considered religion a dangerous thing. Al-Razi was condemned for blasphemy and almost all his books were destroyed later.¹⁶⁴ Avicenna, another great physician, philosopher, and scientist was considered a devout Muslim but held that philosophy was superior to theology. His views were in sharp contrast to central Islamic doctrines, and he rejected the bodily resurrection of the dead. As a consequence of his views, he was severely criticized by the philosopher Al-Ghazali and labeled an apostate.¹⁶⁵ Al-Farabi was also denounced by al-Ghazali for adopting the heretical view that reason was superior to revelation.¹⁶⁶ Averroes (Ibn Rushd) was a Spanish philosopher and scientist who expounded the Qur'an in Aristotelian terms and said that philosophy superseded religion. For this, he was found guilty of heresy, his books were burned, and he was banished from Lucena.¹⁶⁷ Al-Khawarazmi, the great mathematician, had his own problems. Nowhere in his works did he acknowledge Islam or link any of his findings to the holy text, and the historian Al-Tabari even considered him to be a Zoroastrian.¹⁶⁸ Omar Khayyam was highly critical of religion, particularly Islam, and condemned the idea that every event and phenomena were the result of divine intervention. Like many free thinkers of his time, he was denounced as a heretic for spreading ideas that were deemed to counter the teaching of the Qur'an.¹⁶⁹ As Trifkovic notes, one of the less known repercussions of the Islamic Golden Age was that "persecution, exile, and death were frequent punishments suffered by the philosophers of Islam whose writings did not conform to the canon." This

---

¹⁶³ Trifkovic, *Sword of the Prophet*, 196.

¹⁶⁴ S.M. Ghazanfar, *Medieval Islamic Economic Thought: Filling the Great Gap in European Economics* (London: RoutledgeCurzon, 2003), 250. See also Ibn Warraq, *Why I am not a Muslim*, 268. See also, http://www.islam-watch.org/syedkamranmirza/nostalgia-of-islamic-golden-age.htm (accessed 9_27_2016).

¹⁶⁵ Ghazanfar, *Medieval Islamic Economic Thought*, 251. See also http://www.islam-watch.org/syedkamranmirza/nostalgia-of-islamic-golden-age.htm (accessed 9_27_2016).

¹⁶⁶ Richard Walzer, *Greek into Arabic* (Oxford: Oxford University Press, 1962), p. 209. In Ibn Warraq, *Why I Am Not a Muslim*, 263.

¹⁶⁷ http://www.alhewar.com/habib_saloum_averroes.htm (accessed 9_27_2016).

¹⁶⁸ http://www.islam-watch.org/syedkamranmirza/nostalgia-of-islamic-golden-age.htm (accessed 9_27_2016).

¹⁶⁹ https://lifethelove.wordpress.com/2012/09/01/were-there-any-great-muslim-scientists-by-waseem-altaf/ (accessed 9_27_2016). Will Durant, *The Story of Civilization*, vol. 4, "The Age of Faith" (New York: Simon and Schuster, 1950), 322-23.

is also why Trifkovic laments that often "the best Muslims, whether judged by intellectual or political achievement, are usually the least Muslim."[170]

If the driving force behind the "Golden Age" was, in fact, the conquered peoples and a handful of scholars who generally received condemnation rather than respect from the Islamic government, then there is no reason to credit the Qur'an, faith in Allah, or the sayings of Muhammad for this enlightened age. Rather, Muslim scholars were able to contribute to science, philosophy, and the arts due to the rise of rationalism and free-thinking represented by the Mu'tazilites. Revisionist scholars conclude, however, that when the momentum of Islam followed al-Ghazali in his rejection of rationalism, the "closing of the Muslim mind"[171] brought an end to any invention and innovation on the part of Muslim scholars.

## Did Islam Contribute to the European Dark Ages?

Another important question revolves around the claim that Islamic advancements brought Europe out of the Dark Ages and laid the foundation for the later European Renaissance. This is certainly a prevalent view that is promoted by world leaders today. For example, in Obama's speech at Cairo University in Egypt on June 4, 2009, he praised the many virtues of Islam, speaking of "civilization's debt to Islam" and its "innovation" that "carried the light of learning" through the ages and to Europe.[172] This sentiment is clearly an echo of the traditional Muslim view, adopted by many geo-political leaders, that the cultural superiority of Islam during the Golden Age had a profound cultural effect on Europe. One Muslim writer, Ziauddin Sardar, concurs with this view and writes, "the European Renaissance and all the progress in science, technology, medicine, learning and humanism that it produced, was built squarely on the shoulders of Muslim scholars and thinkers. Indeed, the Renaissance is inconceivable without the contribution of Muslim civilization."[173]

However, in addition to the discussion above regarding the evidence pointing to the major contributors to Islamic civilization being often non-Muslims or non-orthodox Muslims, a handful of revisionist scholars in the last century have offered new arguments to support a general claim that

---

[170] Serge Trifkovic, "The Golden Age of Islam is a Myth," FrontPageMagazine.com/Friday, November 15, 2002. http://archive.frontpagemag.com/readArticle.aspx?ARTID=21117

[171] See Robert Reilly, *The Closing of the Muslim Mind*.

[172] President Obama, https://www.whitehouse.gov/the-press-office/remarks-president-cairo-university-6-04-09

[173] Sardar, *Introducing Islam*, 123.

Islamic culture actually had a deleterious effect. This effect can be seen both in the civilizations it interacted with and in the societies that it actually governed. The first argument, which concerns the civilizations around Islamic empires, is promoted by Emmet Scott, a historian specializing in the ancient history of the Near East, who theorizes that Muslim conquests and raids contributed to the so-called "dark ages" of Europe.

Scott offers several main points in support of this claim, which he bases largely on the work of a 20th-century Belgian historian, Henri Pirenne. First, Pirenne and Scott argue that Muslim conquests and continual skirmishes along the vital trade routes of the Mediterranean blocked Western European interactions with the Byzantine Empire, which for hundreds of years was the bastion of Western learning and culture. This would have hindered or perhaps doomed the efforts of European scholars who sought to make intellectual advances in the midst of political and military chaos that followed the loss of Roman structure and authority. Scott notes that the former Graeco-Roman civilization in Europe before the rise of Islam was largely "urban, literate, and learned, and characterized by what could be called a rationalist spirit."[174] After the Muslim conquest, this same part of the world was described as a "society that was overwhelmingly rural, generally illiterate, had a largely barter economy, and tended to be inward-looking rather than open and syncretic."[175] Most academics account for this decline and decadence as a gradual result of the fall of Rome to the barbarians. However, as Pirenne and Scott point out, before the conquest by the Muslims, the former "barbarians" (Germanic tribes) were assimilating well into the Christian society, and even bringing economic growth and development to the European urban centers, which calls into question the common view that European society of this time was in serious decline.[176]

Second, Pirenne and Scott argue that Muslim forces had several key negative influences that Muslim forces exerted on the West. These include cutting off the trade of Egyptian papyrus (which led to a shortage of readily-available writing materials in Europe and forced a dependence on expensive parchment),[177] the influence of Islamic-style theocracy (which they argue helped bring Europe to accept a papal rule and later a medieval theocracy that eventually became corrupt),[178] and even the concept of Holy War – used in the Crusades[179] – and the Inquisition, which they document

---

[174] Emmet Scott, *Mohammed & Charlemagne Revisited*, vii.
[175] Ibid., vii.
[176] Ibid., 160-61.
[177] Ibid., xxi.
[178] Ibid., 236.
[179] Ibid., 235.

as having been used in Muslim territories fifty years prior to the great Spanish Inquisition.[180] These influences would have led to a decrease in literacy and trade as well as provided the idea for several of Europe's less-laudable acts, such as the attacks against Jewish villages during some of the Crusades and forced conversions of Jews and Muslims in Spain during the Reconquista. For these reasons, ranging from the economic woes caused by the naval blockade of trade on the Mediterranean Sea to the Catholic Church's attitude toward apostasy and "Holy War," Scott and Pirenne conclude that the impact of Islam on the West had many detrimental consequences and thus "caused" the Dark Ages in Europe. Regardless of whether the reader finds their arguments persuasive, it is nonetheless intriguing to try to envision what Europe would look like today if Islam had not been able to exert so much global control and influence over the last 1400 years.

## The Myth of Andalusia

One common argument for the existence of an Islamic Golden Age is the example of Muslim rule in the Spanish region of Andalusia. This medieval culture is frequently held up as an example of how the three Abrahamic faiths, Judaism, Christianity, and Islam, were able to function under a benevolent Muslim government that allowed a high level of religious tolerance, societal order, and cultural productivity. In contrast, the argument is made that Christian Europe was plunged into chaos and barbarism after the fall of Rome. Thus, according to this view, the Arabs "brought one of history's greatest revolutions in power, religion, culture, and wealth to Dark Ages Europe" as they were "generally religiously tolerant."[181] This perspective also paints the Muslim culture as "[respectful of] Christians and Jews as 'People of the Book'" and maintains that "[m]odern historians seem to agree that the invasion was not particularly cruel, or destructive," as one historian has summarized. [182] Finally, it maintains that the Qur'an is the source of tolerant behavior and jihad is merely an "inner struggle" rather than a violent and large-scale conquest.

However, in his recent study, *The Myth of the Andalusian Paradise*, Dario Fernandez-Morera collects a body of compelling evidence that suggests that much of the positive view of multi-cultural tolerance practiced in Muslim-controlled Spain during the "Golden Age" has no legitimate basis in reality. He argues that its promotion as such has been more to advance

---

[180] Ibid., 240.

[181] David Levering Lewis, *God's Crucible: Islam and the Making of Europe, 570-1215* (New York: W.W. Norton, 2008), xxii-xxiii.

[182] Colin Smith, *Christians and Moors in Spain* (Warminster: Aris & Phillips, 1988), 1:10.

a vision of medieval Islam as being enlightened and tolerant (even superior to Christianity) than to objectively study the historical evidence. First, the chronicles and eyewitness accounts from this time period record ruthless invasions where churches were pilfered and burned or converted to mosques. Libraries were burned, just as they were in Zoroastrian Persia and Christian Alexandria. Crosses were destroyed wherever they were found. Morera reports that "Religious and political persecutions, inquisitions, beheadings, impalings, and crucifixions" reached a height unequaled before in Spain.[183] Slavery was rampant, and slaves made up one of the main exports. Indeed, many Christian women were taken as sex slaves and Christian men were made eunuchs to guard the harems.

In addition to the brutal invasion tactics, Morera's evidence also points to the creation of a violent and unsophisticated culture after the conquest: killings for power were common and violence was the major method for social control. Even though the European culture of Spain was much more advanced than the culture of the invading Muslims, who were mostly illiterate Bedouins, Christians were looked down upon and Jews were held in contempt.[184] In addition, the Maliki School of Islamic jurisprudence, which is very strict and unfavorable to non-Muslims, was instituted throughout the area in order to maintain Muslim control.

Finally, Morera argues that Andalusian society was hardly multi-cultural. Care was taken by Muslims not to pollute themselves by contact with Christians and Jews, whether that be from verbal greetings or using the same utensils. Morera also demonstrates that the Christian *dhimmis* of Spain did not benefit much from Islamic "toleration." Instead, "they were by definition a subaltern group, a fourth- or fifth- class marginalized people in a hierarchical society" and "they were the victims of an extortion system, the dhimma, that gave them the choice that gangsters give to their victims: pay to be protected, or else."[185] Rather than being the tolerant, multi-cultural paradise presented by many scholars today, Islamic Spain is described by Morera as a "multicultural society wracked by ethnic, religious, social, and political conflicts that eventually contributed to its demise – a multicultural society held together only by the ruthless power of autocrats and clerics."[186] According to Morera's research, for the Jews and Christians in Spain who were subjected to the rule of Islam, Al-Andalus was certainly not the tolerant, peaceful, and progressive paradise that many scholars and politicians promote today.

---

[183] Morera, *The Myth of the Andalusian Paradise*, 120.

[184] Ibid., 64.

[185] Ibid., 239.

[186] Ibid., 4.

## Implications

Muslim scholars, as well as many non-Muslim scholars, promote a view of Islam that emphasizes its status as one of the greatest civilizations of all time, and assume that during the Middle Ages the cultural heritage of Islam was the force that not only preserved Western civilization but spurred it on to the great achievements of the Renaissance and the Enlightenment. However, the evidence that is used to support this view is more controversial than has been generally acknowledged. Seventh-century archeology, chronicles, and eyewitness accounts from the medieval period, and even a more critical examination of the traditional histories of scholars and innovations all cast a certain degree of doubt upon the accepted Golden Age narrative. This in turns raises other significant questions. For example, if later traditions do not match up with seventh-century archaeology, how can Muslims verify the existence of the early caliphs, historicity of early conquests, or basis for religious beliefs? If the Golden Age was greatly exaggerated and overrated, what does this indicate about Islam in general? Does Islam have a good historical claim to being a religion that promotes peace and tolerance of other faiths? Clearly, careful historical research and the freedom to draw conclusions unbiased by mainstream interpretations is essential for discovering and answering some of the most significant questions of history – questions which otherwise never come to light because they do not concur with the standard account. Ultimately, then, it is very important to base conclusions on the best evidence. In the case of Islam's Golden Age, this seems to include giving serious consideration to the evidence which indicates that Islam may have been more of a detrimental force than an incubator of culture and learning.

## Apologetic Conclusions

Muslims often refer to Islam as the foundation of great cultural and scientific flowering throughout the Middle East and beyond during the Middle Ages. How can Christians demonstrate that the evidence does not support these claims in a number of ways? The discipline of Apologetics can actually be a great tool in situations like these, where history and theology are woven together. It can help build skills for Christians to logically evaluate evidence and theories while also providing the tools for them to successfully reach out to Muslims with the gospel. There are basically three reasons for Apologetics – preparation, defense and refutation. *Preparation* is important in Apologetics because it prevents Christians from being converted to other religions by building up their faith. This often takes place when the believer is confronted by other beliefs and forced to learn more about his own religion in contradistinction to the beliefs of others. In order for a believer to "give an answer," he must be informed about his own beliefs as well as the beliefs of his inquisitor. Another very important role of Apologetics is the *defense* of Christianity against attacks by other religions or doctrines. Christians need to be able to use the art of persuasion in order to commend and defend the beliefs of Christianity to those of other faiths. The third role of Apologetics is the *refutation* of heresy, as Christians must be ever vigilant in their assault against doctrines and ideas that seek to destroy orthodoxy by subterfuge or false beliefs.

When applying these aspects of apologetics to Islam, Christians must first understand that the early Muslim conquests may have been so devastating to the European economy that they, in fact, contributed to the rise of the Dark Ages. In addition, the Golden Age was probably overrated, and the purported scientific and mathematical discoveries of the period should often, in reality, be attributed to non-Muslims and Muslim non-conformists rather than devoted Muslim scholars. Furthermore, primary source materials reveal that a peaceful coexistence of Jews, Christians, and Muslims in Al-Andalus was more mythical than factual. Therefore, the modern view of a tolerant multicultural society under Islamic dominance does not seem to be supported by the evidence. Christians also need to understand that the tensions between rival Christian groups in the Middle East, as well as in Spain, brought weakness and disunity, making these areas ripe for conquest. This particular situation should cause Christians today to realize that they need to seek unity in the face of persecution, especially in regard to the Christians in the Middle East.

In addition to understanding both the Muslim and Christian position, Christians need to be able to defend what they believe and realize that right beliefs bring about right actions. The Bible encourages Christians to stand firm in the truth so that they will not give in to false doctrines and misconceptions (Eph. 6:10-18; 2 Tim. 4:3-4). Defending what is true is crucial in a Christian's witness to Muslims. It is also necessary that Christians demonstrate a supernatural love based on the mercy of Christ and the Father's desire to bring Muslims into the true kingdom of God. Otherwise whatever gains attained through reason will be lost due to a lack of relationship.

Finally, Christians must be able to refute error when it is presented, though this should also be done with gentleness and respect (1 Peter 3:15). For example, it is important to refute certain viewpoints that are untrue. One of the "mantras" that is repeated over and over by Muslims as well as non-Muslims is that Islam is a religion of peace. However, Christians need to realize that the evidence of constant warfare with the West, and especially with Christians and Jews, casts serious doubt on this claim. If Islam is not inherently supportive of co-existence and peace, then assuming it to be so is not only erroneous but also as potentially catastrophic as it was for the seventh-century peoples who assumed that the invading Muslims would cause them no harm.

## Building Bridges to Understand

One important topic to build a bridge towards is the discussion of how verses in the Qur'an, as well as in the Hadith, tell Muslims to subdue all non-Muslims. These views need to be compared with the verses in the Bible that demonstrate that Jesus Christ is the only one who can bring peace to this world.

| Islam | Christianity |
|---|---|
| "*Fight those who believe not in Allah nor the Last Day, nor hold that forbidden which hath been forbidden by Allah and His Messenger, nor acknowledge the religion of Truth, (even if they are) of the People of the Book, until they pay the Jizya with willing submission, and feel themselves subdued.*" (Q. 9:29) | "I have said these things to you, that in me you may have peace. In the world you will have tribulation. But take heart; I have overcome the world." (John 16:33) |
| *The Messenger of Allah said: "I have been commanded to fight against people till they testify that there is no god but Allah, that Muhammad is the messenger of Allah, and they establish prayer and pay zakat."* (Sahih Muslim 1:33) | "Peace I leave with you; my peace I give to you. Not as the world gives do I give to you. Let not your hearts be troubled, neither let them be afraid." (John 14:27) |

According to these verses, Islam will always be at war. Allah gave all Muslims a mandate to conquer all nations and people until they have submitted either by converting to Islam or by paying the jizya and agreeing to the terms of a "protected" citizen. Christianity, in contrast, rose out of persecution, and because Jesus had submitted to death in place of sinful man, only he can provide the true peace for which the world yearns.

Another important bridge relates to understanding the history of Islam and science. During the Golden Age of Islam, the Muslim world may have been relatively more advanced than parts of the Christian world; however, it seems that many of the scientific advances were borrowed from other cultures conquered by the Muslims. In addition, a number of the Muslim scholars were considered heretics or rebels and their work was discredited and their books were burned. This provides a good opportunity to explain how Christianity is well suited to advance the cause of science since the God of Christianity is understood as both the creator of all things and the one who created the laws of science to be orderly and consistent so that mankind could benefit from using reason to make new discoveries. In Islam, reason was made subordinate to revelation and science, and this often led to the rejection of innovative thinking through "the closing of the Muslim mind."[187] Since Christianity has a balanced view in regard to reason and revelation, new discoveries and innovative thinking have been highly regarded and supported throughout history.[188]

Finally, many have promoted Muslim rule in al-Andalus as a model of multiculturalism and tolerance that we should follow in our present situation. However, the evidence reveals that only the Arabic culture was given positive approval, and both Christianity and Judaism were scarcely tolerated and were regarded as "inferior" religions. Thus, a good bridge to use would be to demonstrate that Islam will never be tolerant of other religions as long as Muslims follow the Qur'an's injunction to subdue all other religions (Q. 9:33, 8:39, 61:9). However, it should be remembered in conversation that Christians also have difficulty being tolerant of other faiths. Therefore, it would be profitable for both Muslims and Christians to dialogue about ways to respect each other's religion. Hopefully, through this process, Muslims will better understand that true toleration will come only when we embrace the fact that all are created in the image of God and he wants everyone to bow before God the Son. Only if we are in Christ can true tolerance be achieved.

### Study Questions:

1. In the seventh century, the Islamic Empire expanded rapidly throughout the Middle East, North Africa, and even Spain. What were some of the reasons for this rapid expansion?

---

[187] Robert Reilley, theme concept from *The Closing of the Muslim Mind.*

[188] The common story of the Church standing against science by banning Galileo's work leaves out one important detail. The leaders who forcibly suppressed his views of the solar system were acting on a recent decision by the Church to officially adopt the views of Ptolemy and his earth-centric model. This was thus more of a political interference and bore no reflection on the Bible's teaching or on the general Christian approach to scientific learning.

2. There were a number of genuine advances in philosophy and science during the Golden Age of Islam. What were some of the positive discoveries made by Muslim scholars?

3. What are some arguments supporting the view that Islam was not the foundation of much significant cultural and scientific flowering in the Islamic world in the Middle Ages?

4. What are some ways that Islam may have contributed to the European Dark Ages? What are some possible negative consequences brought on by the influences of the Islamic conquests?

5. What are some ways that a Christian could use the controversy over the Islamic Golden Age to help Muslims and skeptics separate fact from fiction and then reach out with the gospel of Christ?

6. Explain how some leaders in the multi-cultural movement are promoting the supposed toleration in Islam in order to criticize Christianity and weaken the foundations of Western civilization. Why is their ultimate goal one that is doomed to failure?

# PART 2: BELIEFS AND PRACTICES

# CHAPTER 7 Islamic Doctrine: Five versus Three Equals One?

## Introduction

In some ways, Islam is a complex, multi-layered religion that mixes politics, economics, and social dynamics within a religious structure. The structure itself is based on the Qur'an's pronouncements from Allah, the words of the prophet Muhammad recorded in the Hadith and a complicated system of jurisprudence. On the other hand, the basic doctrines are quite simple, and initiation into the religion calls for only the recitation of one particular phrase with sincerity. In fact, the religious studies author Reza Aslan states, "Contrary to perception, the Pillars are not oppressive obligations – quite the opposite. These are highly pragmatic rituals, in that the believer is responsible only for those tasks that he or she is able to perform." Aslan also reminds his readers that the "primary purpose of the Five Pillars is to assist the believer in articulating, through actions, his or her membership in the Muslim community."[189]

These practices are what make Islam very much a religion of orthopraxy, a religion of action rather than of doctrine. The Pillars make Islam a relatively easy religion to follow because everything is laid out in advance, and the many routines only solidify the actions. Ergun Caner, a former Muslim, remarks, "The devout Muslim must unite belief (imam) with practice (din). The combination of right principles with dedicated performance will guide the Muslim through the course of his life into the hereafter."[190] These "pillars" are not found specifically in the Qur'an, but Muhammad supposedly specified the practices, and they can be found in the various Hadith collections.

This chapter will provide an introduction to the Five Pillars and the Six Beliefs of Islam so that the reader will gain a general understanding of the core doctrine of Islam. There are a number of similarities in the beliefs of Islam and Christianity, but there are also some very important differences. For example, while Islam shares a strong view of monotheism, the belief in one God, it also adamantly rejects the Christian doctrine of the Trinity, the deity of Christ, the historicity of the crucifixion, and the accuracy of the Bible. These major differences are important enough to devote a later chapter to their in-depth discussion, but this chapter focuses

---

[189] Reza Aslan, *No god but God*, 145.
[190] Ergun Caner and Emir Caner, *Unveiling Islam* (Grand Rapids: Kregel, 2002), 122-23.

on explaining the beliefs and outlining a Christian response to each of the six major beliefs of Islam. Hopefully, this will help the reader better assess the distinctions between Islam and Christianity.

## The Pillars

While these five "pillars" are not specifically laid out in the Qur'an, there is an early Hadith tradition that Muhammad had stipulated five practices to guide his followers in fulfilling their obligations to Allah.[191] They are called "pillars" because they are the five religious duties that form the foundation of every believer's faith.

### Shahadah

This is the recitation of the creed of Islam – "there is no god but Allah, and Muhammad is his prophet (*rasul*)." The recital of the creed is performed multiple times a day as part of the required prayer obligations, and it emphasizes the belief in the absolute oneness of God (the *tawhid*). A person becomes a Muslim by reciting the Shahada in Arabic with a sincere heart: "La ilaha illa Allah wa-Muhammad Rasul Allah." Reza Aslan comments, "This deceptively simple statement is not only the basis for all articles of faith in Islam, it is in some ways the sum and total of Islamic theology. This is because the Shahada signifies recognition of an exceedingly complex theological doctrine known as *tawhid*."[192] All of Islam, in actuality, revolves around this concept of absolute monotheism. Even the second half of the creed, focusing on the prophet, still emphasizes the centrality of Allah. It contains two notable elements: first, that Muhammad is the prophet of Allah but not his associate or any kind of deity to be worshipped; and second, the word "Islam" or "submission" is drawn from this core idea that everything is about the ultimate reality of Allah and humanity's duty to submit to him. The person who recognizes these twin realities and reacts by submission to Allah is thus called a "Muslim," or literally "one who submits."

### Salat

The second Pillar is the practice of prayer, called *Salat*, which is a ritualized and obligatory act performed five times per day while facing Mecca. These times are also fixed as being sunrise, noon, afternoon, sunset, and evening. They typically take place in the context of communal prayer at the mosque, as men line up in rows, with the edges of their feet touching the feet next to them and perform a series of movements in unison while

---

[191] Bukhari, Sahih, I, II, chapter 2, no. 7, 17.
[192] Reza Aslan, No god but God, 150.

chanting specific Qur'anic verses. A *qibla*, or notch in a building, shows the direction of Mecca towards which Muslims should pray. The direction was originally toward Jerusalem, but this was later changed to Mecca (see Sura 2:144-50).

## Zakat

This is the practice of giving a 2.5% tithe to the mosques for distribution to the needy. It is obligatory for faithful Muslims to contribute. The word "zakat" literally means "purification," and it is intended to remind Muslims of their obligations to the sovereign will of Allah (another aspect of submission). In addition to this mandatory tithe, additional money can also be contributed for the poor, an action which will bring merit to the giver from Allah and contribute to the Muslim's store of good deeds.

## Sawm

This is an observance of fasting during the Arabic month of Ramadan (9th month of the Islamic year), intended to commemorate the time of Muhammad's first revelation (according to tradition). During this month, Muslims are not allowed to eat or drink during the day, but once night falls they may eat and drink as they desire. The meal before sunup is known as the *suhoor*, and the *iftar* meal is eaten after sundown. The focus of this ritual is intended to be the purification of one's life for the service of Allah, and to aid in this goal, a practice of reading through the Qur'an during the 30-day period is advocated. The end of the month of fasting is marked by "Eid al-Fitr," or the Festival of the Breaking of the Fast, which is the most widely celebrated holiday in the Muslim world.

## Hajj

The *Hajj* is the pilgrimage to Mecca. It takes place during the last month of the Islamic year, and all Muslims hope to make the journey at least once in their lifetime. Such a pilgrimage is supposed to be a privilege and an honor to the pilgrim, but it is not actually obligatory to those who cannot afford to make the pilgrimage. In reality, most Muslims never fulfill this pillar due to the lack of finances, time, or opportunity. When a Muslim pilgrim does reach Mecca, he performs certain rituals such as walking around the Ka'aba seven times, kissing the black stone, and "stoning Satan" by throwing stones at three masonry pillars that represent Satan and two of his helpers. Other events revolve around certain traditional activities performed by Muhammad while he was on his pilgrimage, such as praying at the Grand Mosque, as well as emulating the panicked search Hagar made for water by running between the hills of Safa and Marwa and then drinking from the well of ZamZam. As with the other four pillars, fulfilling the Hajj is meant to solidify a Muslim's devotion to Allah. This is perhaps why Reza Aslan says, "More than anything, the Five Pillars are meant as a metaphor for Islam; they are a summary not just of what is required to be a member of the *Umma*, but also of what it means to be a Muslim."[193]

## Implications

For Muslims, the focus of the Pillars is to remind them of Allah and his will in the midst of sin and the present world – he is "the one who is greater." However, the spiritual growth from this view of God is dynamically different from the Christian understanding of spiritual growth. Whereas Muslims see external actions and ritual as a way of achieving inward purification, Christians believe that the process of becoming holy must begin inwardly, in the attitude of the heart towards God. This heart attitude transforms the whole man, extending to the external actions and practices of life. Some Muslims may object and say that Christians can live an insincere religious life by sinning freely and then asking for forgiveness without repentance. However, the Christian doctrines reflect this transformational concept by emphasizing that faith and works are both needed to demonstrate that a believer's life has been truly transformed.

To understand the core theological differences between Islam and Christianity requires an understanding not only of the five pillars of Islam but also of the six beliefs. In this next section, a summary of each belief will be given from the Muslim point of view, and then a Christian response will be given. This critique is not meant to denigrate Islamic doctrine, but to help the reader understand that there are core differences between Islam and Christianity that must be taken into account in order for fruitful conversations to take place.

## The Six Beliefs of Islam and How they Compare to Christianity

As discussed in the chapter on the Qur'an, the traditional Muslim view holds that Islam is the final revelation of the Abrahamic scriptures. Thus, Muslims believe that Islam is both similar and superior to Christianity since the Qur'an corrects textual corruptions and discrepancies that have crept in over time and distorted the Bible from its original purity. The original version of the Jewish and Christian scriptures are believed to have matched the accounts of the Qur'an exactly since all scriptures from Allah are said to have derived from the same eternal written source in heaven, but over time Muslims believe that Jews and Christians allowed their scriptures to become

---

[193] Ibid., 145.

corrupted.[194] Thus, a final revelation given to a final prophet was necessary to restore Allah's plan for mankind. The core doctrine of Islamic life can be summarized in the six beliefs taught by Islam.

# Belief in one God

> The Traditional Muslim View:
> Say: He is Allah, the One and Only;
> Allah, the Eternal, Absolute;
> He begetteth not, nor is He begotten;
> And there is none like unto Him. (Q. 112)

For Muslims, Allah is not only the one who is, and was, and always will be, but, as al-Ghazali opined, "God is the First, before whom there is nothing, and the Last after whom there is nothing." (Aslan, 151; Q. 57:3) Belief in one God is the core belief of Islam. Muslim doctrine states that everything derives from the understanding that there can only be one god in the universe, and, in a sense, God is the only reality or "the *only* being with real existence."[195] This is the concept of "tawhid," the unity of God, which Muslims believe to be the foundation of Islam. Reza Aslan even goes so far as to say that this concept goes beyond monotheism. "Tawhid means that God is Oneness. God is unity: wholly indivisible, entirely unique, and utterly indefinable. God resembles nothing in either essence or attributes."[196]

For Muslims, all things exist by the will of Allah, and Allah can have or do anything he desires. However, there is one thing that Islamic doctrine teaches that Allah cannot have: he cannot have any partners or any equals. Surah 3:64 says, "People of the Book, let us arrive at a statement that is common to us all: we worship God alone, we ascribe no partner to Him, and none of us takes others beside God as lords." Thus, for Muslims, Allah is totally "other" from mankind or creation, and so cannot be a father, or have a son, or have any associates. This is the reason that Muslims have such difficulty with the Christian concept of the Trinity. If Allah is an absolute unity, then how could the one God also be three Gods? For Muslims, this belief in the Trinity adds something "other" than God to God, which is blasphemy. In fact, to claim that Jesus Christ is God's son is the greatest of all sins in Islam and is known as "shirk," or the worship of anyone or anything other than the one God. Some Muslims even believe that anyone who commits shirk will not be able to receive forgiveness from

---

[194] Riddell, *Islam in Context*, 48.
[195] Reza Aslan, *No god but God*, 151 (emphasis his).
[196] Ibid., 150.

Allah. This is supported by Sura 4:48, which states, "Lo! Allah forgives not that a partner should be ascribed unto Him. He forgives (all) save that to whom He will. Whoso ascribes partners to Allah, he hath indeed invented a tremendous sin." Thus, according to Islam, Christians are the greatest of all sinners since they worship Jesus Christ as God the Son, the second person of the Trinity.

## A Christian Response

It is very important for Christians to assure their Muslim friends that the fundamental belief of Christianity is that there is only one God. As Moses stated in Deuteronomy 6:4-5, "The Lord our God is one Lord; and you shall love the Lord your God with all your heart, and with all your soul, and with all your might." This is the one God who appeared to Moses at the burning bush and called himself "Yahweh," or "I am that I am" in Hebrew (Exodus 3:15-16). This is also the same God who appeared earlier to Abraham.

However, it is also important to explain to Muslims that Yahweh is a triune God. Muslims frequently have misunderstandings about the Trinity that need to be dealt with. For one thing, many Muslims believe that the Trinity is made up of God, Jesus, and Mary. Often, they also believe that Jesus was born biologically through sexual relations between God and Mary. Muslims do not seem to understand how the one essence of God is different from the three persons of the Trinity. Christians do not say one God and three Gods, or one essence and three essences, but rather one essence and three persons. This may be a mystery, but it is not illogical.

In addition, if Allah is a distant, remote being who reveals his will but not himself (Q. 67:12), then it is impossible to know him in a personal way. In Allah's monadic oneness, his attributes stem from his powerful Will, which, because it provides no basis for relationship, often promotes capriciousness. Also, since his power is more important than his other attributes, there is an unequal emphasis on power over his other attributes. Therefore, a follower cannot know Allah or even be sure of the consistency of his attributes. In his absolute oneness there is unity but not the community of the trinity, and because of this lack of relationship, love is not emphasized.

On the other hand, because Yahweh, the God of the Bible, is by nature a triune unity, his attributes stem from his nature. The eternal relationship between the Father, Son, and Holy Spirit within the Trinity promotes love within the Godhead and extends to his creation. Also, since his attributes are based on his unchanging nature rather than his powerful will, all his attributes are equal and promote trustworthiness rather than capriciousness. This means that believers can know God and be sure of his attributes.

In addition, the only way that Jesus Christ, as the second person of the Trinity, could die on the cross to pay for our sins is because God's nature is triune. If Jesus were not God himself, then his death on the cross would be meaningless. Only a triune God, defined as one essence and three persons, could become incarnate in the world through the person of the Son, and still remain the one God of the universe. Yet, this is the God that Muslims reject. For them, Jesus cannot be God nor can God be a Father, for he cannot have a son. Therefore, if Muslims reject God as the Father of Jesus, then Allah cannot be the same as the God of the Bible.

# Belief in the Prophets

### The Muslim View

In order for Allah to make his will known to the people, he sent prophets (*alnabi*) and messengers (*rasul*). A prophet (*nabi*) is a messenger of God who delivers a new scripture, while a messenger (*rasul*) is commissioned by God to confirm and teach existing scripture. Muhammad and Jesus are considered to have had the roles of both a messenger and a prophet. However, since Muhammad received the Qur'an, and the Qur'an is considered to be the final revelation of Allah, he is considered the final and greatest of all prophets, or the "seal of the prophets." 124,000 prophets are supposed to have existed according to the Hadith, though the Qur'an mentions only 25 specifically. A number of these prophets are known from the Old and New Testaments: Adam, Nuh (Noah), Ibrahim (Abraham), Isma'il (Ishmael), Ishaq (Isaac), Ya'qub (Jacob), Yousef (Joseph), Ayyub (Job), Musa (Moses), Harun (Aaron), Dawud (David), Sulaiman (Solomon), Al-Yasa (Elisha), Yunus (Jonah), Yahya (John), and 'Isa (Jesus). Messengers who are not also prophets can be anyone speaking Allah's word, such as imams today. The prophets were to focus on the same fundamental message: reminding people of Allah's existence, the reward for a good life, and a day of judgment and punishment for unbelievers. This message was not always well received, but Allah promised to protect his prophets from any harm (Q. 17:94). Thus, Muslims have a hard time accepting the crucifixion of Christ, as this would go against the principle of God protecting his prophet from a humiliating death.

### A Christian Response

According to the Bible, God's purpose for the use of prophets was to tell the people the story of his redemptive acts in history through preaching, teaching, and writing. The ultimate story is the one about the Son of God coming into the world and dying in order to redeem his followers. Muslims, however, believe that Muhammad fulfills the position of the prophet to come mentioned in Deuteronomy 18:15, where Moses says to the people,

"The Lord your God will raise up for you a prophet like me from among you, from your brothers—it is to him you shall listen." Muslims also claim that the "unlettered prophet written about in the Torah and the gospel" in Surah 7:157 refers to Muhammad as the fulfillment of Deuteronomy 18:15. However, the prophet written about in this passage was to have come from among the Jews, not the Arabs, nor even from among the descendants of Ishmael. The word "brothers" in this passage refers to Jews, or fellow Israelites. In addition, Genesis 17:21 states that God's covenant was established with Isaac, not Ishmael: "My covenant I will establish with Isaac." Even the Qur'an establishes this point (Q. 29:27): "And We gave to Him Isaac and Jacob and placed in his descendants prophethood and scripture." (This verse does not mention Abraham, so Muslims cannot claim that since they are descendants of Abraham through Ishmael then they should be included). In fact, Muhammad would not fulfill the biblical requirements of a prophet of God.

**Deuteronomy 18:18-20** English Standard Version (ESV)

[18] I will raise up for them a prophet like you from among their brothers. And I will put my words in his mouth, and he shall speak to them all that I command him. [19] And whoever will not listen to my words that he shall speak in my name, I myself will require it of him. [20] But the prophet who presumes to speak a word in my name that I have not commanded him to speak, or who speaks in the name of other gods, that same prophet shall die.'

Muhammad contradicted the Bible in a number of places: he denied the deity of Christ, taught that the doctrine of the Trinity was wrong, and called for the destruction of Jews and Christians. Muhammad also taught "in the name of other gods," namely Allah. Deuteronomy 18:21-22 states that a true prophet of the true God can be known by whether the prophecy is fulfilled or not, and if it is not fulfilled, then the one who spoke that word is not a true prophet. According to the Bible, then, Muhammad fails in all these tests and therefore could not have been a true prophet of God.

And if you say in your heart, "How may we know the word that the Lord has not spoken?" — When a prophet speaks in the name of the Lord, if the word does not come to pass or come true, that is a word that the Lord has not spoken; the prophet has spoken it presumptuously. You need not be afraid of him.

However, Jesus does fit the requirements of Deuteronomy 18:15-18. Jesus came from a Jewish background (Matt. 1:1-16), spoke the words that God commanded him to speak (John 12:49), claimed to be a prophet (Luke 13:33), and verified this claim by having his prophecies fulfilled (John 2:19). Muhammad also claimed to be a prophet who spoke the word of God, but he was not Jewish and did not fulfill any prophecy. Therefore, he could not be the prophet who was to follow Moses and fulfill the words of Deuteronomy 18:15.

# Belief in the Holy Books

## The Muslim View

According to the Muslim view, whenever there was chaos or confusion on earth, Allah sent scripture through his prophets to guide the people. Over time there were probably many books written, but only five holy books are recognized or accepted by Muslims today. These include the *Suhuf* (revealed to Abraham, but now lost), the *Taurat* (the Torah, given to Moses), the *Zabur* (the Psalms of the Old Testament), the *Injil* (the Gospels of Jesus Christ), and the *Qur'an* (Allah's final message to mankind through Muhammad). Each of these scriptures is supposed to have supported and informed the scripture given before it, so that collectively they form a body of work that saves and benefits mankind. For example, Muslims believe that the *Taurat, Zabur*, and the *Injil* were sent down to the Jews specifically to guide the people of Israel through various stages of their history. However, Muslims believe that, over time, Jews and Christians mixed the truth with error, and these scriptures became so corrupted by the ideas of men that it could no longer be trusted. Therefore, it was necessary for Allah to send down the Qur'an to Muhammad and the Arabs in order to provide a correct and ultimate revelation of Allah's word for all mankind (Q. 3:3-4a). If the Qur'an is the final word of Allah, and the Christian scriptures have been corrupted, then Muslims argue that Christians cannot know anything about the actual life of Jesus Christ or even the true nature of God.

## A Christian Response

The central critique of the Muslim view focuses on the question of the authenticity of the scriptures. Muslims explain the differences between the Bible and the Qur'an by claiming that there are transmission errors and textual corruption in the Bible, while the Qur'an has been perfectly preserved and represents the final corrected revelation from Allah. However, if it can be shown that historical and literary evidence supports a fully preserved Christian scripture (and not a fully preserved Qur'an), this argument becomes untenable. In addition, there is no physical evidence to support Muhammad's denunciation of the Christian scriptures as being riddled with error, since the only differences between the copies in Muhammad's time (the 7$^{th}$ century) and the original texts from the 1$^{st}$ century AD have been shown to be minor copying errors.

There are several tests used for confirming the veracity of ancient documents that demonstrate the reliability of the Christian Bible as an unaltered and uncorrupted document: the bibliographic test, the internal witness test, and the external witness test.[197] The bibliographic test determines whether the current version of a text is consistent with the original version, and uses the time between the first extant (existing) copies and the date of the actual writing. The shorter the gap is, the more reliable the accuracy. While the earliest date for a complete Greek copy of the New Testament, called the *Codex Sinaiticus*, is in the mid-4$^{th}$ century, almost 300 years after the original text was written down, papyrus fragments of the New Testament are as close as 25 or 35 years after the original writing.[198] In contrast to the close proximity of dates for the earliest copies of the New Testament, most ancient documents only exist through copies that were written almost 1,000 years after the original document. For example, the second closest text to the Bible in the ancient world in terms of accuracy is Homer's *Iliad*, for which the earliest known copy only dates to about 500 years after the writing of the original. This makes the New Testament a far more verifiable text than any other in the ancient world by far, outstripping contemporaneous texts by hundreds of years (for example, Tacitus —1,000 years — and Caesar — 1,000 years).[199] In addition, the existence of over 5,800 Greek copies and 18,000 early copies of the New Testament in other languages make it much less susceptible to textual suspicion than Muslims would claim. This large number of early manuscripts allows scholars to compare the various copies for accuracy of transmission and makes it easier to reconstruct the original New Testament text.

The internal and external witness tests are tests that examine whether an ancient document is verified by outside contemporary sources or archeological evidence (external test) as well as whether the authors claim to be eyewitnesses of the events they transcribe (internal test). Up to the present time, no archeological discovery has yet contradicted the Old or New Testament references, and textual support for its veracity has been discovered in everything from Egyptian carvings and Assyrian cylinder rolls to the first-century works of Josephus. Of these discoveries, archaeologist Nelson Glueck has confirmed,

---

[197] Ken Boa, *I'm Glad You Asked: In-Depth Answers to Difficult Questions about Christianity* (David C. Cook, 1995), 90-93.

[198] The John Rylands fragment of the gospel of John (*18.31-33; 37-38)* is dated around 125 AD, around 25-30 years after the original document was completed.
https://www.challies.com/articles/the-history-of-christianity-in-25-objects-rylands-library-papyrus-p52/ (accessed January 1, 2019).

[199] Ken Boa, *I'm Glad You Asked*, 93.

It may be stated categorically that no archaeological discovery has ever controverted a Biblical reference. Scores of archaeological findings have been made which confirm in clear outline or exact detail historical statements in the Bible. And, by the same token, proper evaluation of Biblical descriptions has often led to amazing discoveries.[200]

In comparison, the earliest copy of the complete Qur'an has been dated to around 150 years after the death of Muhammad. If the Qur'an had been completed within 20 years of Muhammad's death, then there should be numerous copies of the Qur'an by the end of the 7th century, given the availability of parchment and even paper (which had been invented in China around 105 BC). The absence of manuscripts of a completed Qur'an, except for fragments, strongly suggests that the Qur'an is not a perfect revelation from Allah transmitted without variation from the lips of Muhammad to the written words on parchment within the lifetime of his followers. If this is a correct assessment of the situation, then Christians should be more confident to ask "when" and "where" questions when Muslims claim that the New Testament has been corrupted and is therefore an unreliable source for contradicting Islamic theology. Indeed, if the New Testament in the time of Muhammad was in the same form as it was in the first century AD, then Muslims would have no basis for the argument that the Bible was corrupted, and the world needed a new revelation from Allah. The evidence tells a very different story from that traditionally believed by Muslims.

# Belief in Angels

## The Muslim View

Muslims believe in an entire supernatural realm, with a particular focus on angels. They believe these beings were created by Allah and, like men, will one day die and be resurrected. However, they do not eat or drink, have no determining gender, and are considered sinless except for those who have fallen away and followed Satan. The angels have different ranks, but the four most important angels are called archangels and are the most powerful in heaven. These mighty angels, according to Islam, are Gabriel, Allah's chief messenger, Michael, Allah's chief warrior, Izrail, the angel of death, and Israfil, who will blow the last trumpet on the Day of Judgment. The fall of Satan (another one of Allah's mighty angels) and his followers resulted in the formation of the demons and the evil jinn, who continually torment and tempt humans. The reason for Satan's banishment from

---

[200] Nelson Glueck, *Rivers in the Desert*, (New York: Farrar, Strous and Cudahy, 1959), 136.

heaven was apparently due to his pride, which is similar to the view that Christians hold. However, the details of the account are quite different. According to the Qur'an, Allah had all the angels come and bow out of respect before Adam when he was first created, but Iblis refused to kneel before a mere created being. Iblis declared with pride, "He was made of clay, but I was made of fire, so I am better than he." For this rebellion, Allah doomed Iblis to live outside of paradise. From then on, Iblis, or Satan, became the chief of all who oppose Allah and his creation, mankind (Q. 15:28-46).

In general, angels were created to praise Allah and watch over mankind, as well as to carry out the will of Allah. Muslims believe that sometimes they were even involved in some of the great battles Muslims had with their adversaries. One of the more interesting beliefs that Muslims have about angels is that they believe that each person has two angels, named *Raqib* and *Atib*, one on the left shoulder and one on the right shoulder, to record each human's good and bad deeds (Q. 50:16-18). Some Muslims believe that during the Day of Judgment these angels will then verify whether a believer's good works will outweigh their bad works. There are also those who believe that there are two fierce angels that visit each corpse in the grave and ask them a series of questions concerning their beliefs in Allah, Islam, and Muhammad. Depending on the response, the angels will transport the souls either to the fiery pit (Gehenna) or to paradise. Overall, there are some similarities between the Christian/Jewish view of the angelic realm and the Islamic view, but there are two particularly strong differences: Muslims believe in the alternate explanation of Satan's rebellion against God, and that the role of the angels in a person's eternal destiny is much more pronounced in Islam.

## A Christian Response

As the book of Hebrews explains, holy and elect angels are "all ministering spirits, sent out to render service for the sake of those who will inherit salvation" (Heb. 1:14). Their purpose is to serve God by watching over humans and working for the good of Christian believers. It is doubtful, however, that each person has been assigned an individual "guardian angel." It is more likely that all Christians are surrounded by a host of angels that guard them against the dangers of this world and the temptations of Satan and his followers (Psalm 91:11).

There are a number of beliefs about angels in the Qur'an and the Bible that appear to be very similar, but each of them also features some very important differences. First of all, both scriptures portray angels as messengers of God who bring timely messages upon special occasions, such as the announcement to Mary that she would give birth to Jesus. However, the Bible does not indicate that angels have the primary role of relaying the exact word of God to his followers. Yet, according to the Muslim account, the angel Gabriel recited the Qur'an to Muhammad over a 23-year period. There was never a direct word from Allah to Muhammad. That means that the accuracy of the revelation was dependent on the angel Gabriel. This is similar to the Book of Mormon, which was supposedly revealed by an angel called Moroni. In both cases, there is no way to verify that what was revealed by these angels was actually from God, especially since Muhammad and Joseph Smith were the only ones who were present.

Another similar belief about angels in Islam and Christianity is that there are good angels and evil angels and that Satan, who rebelled against God due to his pride, leads the evil angels. However, the reasons for this rebellion are different. Rather than linking Satan's fall to a failure to bow before Adam, the Bible teaches that Satan had already rebelled against God before the creation of man, and he was in the garden to tempt Adam and Eve to disobey God and follow him instead. This represents the cosmic battle for power between Satan and God over the soul of man. Satan has been granted power by God and seeks to destroy Christians; however, his power over believers is limited, and Jesus Christ has already defeated him through his death and resurrection (Col. 2:14-15). Christians, therefore, have the power, through Christ, to resist and repel Satan and his demons.

There is one other important distinction between the Muslim belief in angels and the way that Christians view angels. In Islam, there was never a direct word from Allah to Muhammad. Allah is considered too far above man to communicate personally. The Bible, however, reveals a very personal God who is willing to incarnate in a human body so that he can personally redeem his followers. This love was clearly demonstrated in the angelic realm when God the Son revealed himself in a pre-incarnate body as the Angel of the Lord and physically interacted with Adam in the garden (Gen. 3:8), with Abraham in a visit (Gen. 18:2), and with Jacob in a struggle (Gen. 32:22-31). The Allah of Islam would never stoop so low to raise man up so high, but the God of the Bible does because he loves his people with an everlasting love (Jeremiah 31:3).

# Belief in the Day of Judgment

### The Muslim View

Muslims believe that after death, there will be a day of judgment when everyone will be resurrected and then judged according to their works (Q. 39:68). Believers who have more righteous deeds than evil ones hope to be rewarded with entrance into Paradise (Q. 23:102-4). Their hope is based on the promises of Allah in the Quran such as can be found in the following verses:

And those who believe and do righteous deeds – We will surely remove from them their misdeeds and will surely reward them according to the best of what they used to do. (Q. 29:7).

And those whose scales are heavy [with good deeds] - it is they who are the successful. But those whose scales are light - those are the ones who have lost their souls, [being] in Hell, abiding eternally. (Q. 23:102-4)

On the final Day of Judgment, then, the scales will be brought out and Allah will weigh these works based largely on how faithfully Muslim believers have followed the Five Pillars of Islam. Good and evil deeds are examined, but even if the scales are judged favorably, Allah in his sovereignty can arbitrarily decide to reject the evidence and send the individual to hell.[201] On the other hand, some Muslims believe that Allah will rescue undeserving Muslims from hell in order to demonstrate his grace and mercy. In addition, some Muslims believe that Muhammad himself will intercede for his followers who fall short on their record of good deeds and rescue them from the horrors of hell. Non-believers, however, will not be shown any mercy, and their only destination will be the fires of hell.

### A Christian Response

Muslims believe in sin, like Jews and Christians, but reject the idea of original sin, or Adam's sin nature being passed down to every living human. Instead, they believe that all sins are forgivable by Allah except the sin of blasphemy or associating Allah with anyone or anything else (*shirk*). Sin is also considered a private matter, and each person must pay for their own sins. Therefore, Muslims consider the substitutionary death of Christ on the cross for a Christian's sins to be unjust. Muslims will say that salvation is achieved by a combination of Allah's grace and their good works, but in the end, Islam can only logically be viewed as a religion of salvation by works: if Allah's grace is dependent on a person's good works outweighing the bad works, then a person's works still determine their destiny. On the other hand, Christians believe that they will never have enough good works to be righteous before God. This is why the Bible teaches that believers are not saved by works, but by grace through faith alone (Ephesians 2:8-9).

## Belief in the Decrees of Allah (or Predestination)

### The Muslim View

Islam holds strongly to the belief of Allah's sovereignty over all things. For Muslims, everything exists by the will of Allah, and since Allah can do

---

[201] Riddell, *Islam in Context*, 48-9.

anything he desires, it logically follows that he has full control over all the actions of mankind. We can see this view described in Surahs 74:31 and 35:8, which state, "Allah leads astray those he wills, and also guides those whom he wills." If this is true, then what role does man have in his own destiny? This question of balance between Allah's predestination and man's free will, or sovereignty and responsibility, as Christians usually put it, was divisive in the early Islamic theological debates. As described in the chapter on theology, the Mu'tazilites believed that everybody had been given power by Allah to make choices regarding how to live, while the traditionalists argued that this doctrine limited Allah because he predestined all things, including the actions of individuals. In the end, the traditionalists won the debate because most people agreed that Allah would not have true control if he allowed people to choose as they desired. If Allah can do anything, they reasoned, he could not be disobeyed or rejected. Even today most Muslims believe that Allah is in control of all history and that their own personal lives are predestined in terms of everyday circumstances as well as ultimate salvation. This is the reason for the common use of "in sh'allah," or "if Allah wills it," which suggests the idea that Allah has total control over all people and events. For many, this belief leads to fatalism and passivity, while others find that it frees them from worries about matters outside their control. For the latter, this belief may give them great courage in times of hardship or when things go wrong. The former, however, may try to escape their fate by seeking the protection of Qur'anic charms or trusting in the intercession of Muhammad in the Last Day. Muslims call this resignation to fate *kismet*. One writer describes Allah's complete control over everything in this way: "Kismet makes the Muslim fanatically self-sacrificing in war, resigned in defeat, in bereavement and disaster, and inactive in the presence of preventable evil, such as epidemics, because these could be called the 'Will of Allah.'"[202]

## A Christian Response

In regard to the way they respond to the belief in predestination, Muslims and Christians differ in significant ways. For a Muslim, Allah only loves those who do his will, and thus he does not love the unbelievers (Q. 3:31-32; 30:43-45). On the other hand, while the God of the Bible loves those who are good, he also loves sinners and gave his life for them (Romans 5:1-10). In addition, the Allah of the Qur'an is a distant God with whom man cannot have a relationship (Q. 112:1–4), while the God of the Bible is one who wants to have a relationship with man (John 1:11-14; 15:9-15). Furthermore, Allah is portrayed in the Qur'an as the best of deceivers (Q. 3:54, 4:142) as well as the author of evil (Q. 113:1-2). Since Muslims believe that by nature Allah's sovereignty is unlimited, he is under no

---

[202] Jay Smith, 1995 Article: http://www.debate.org.uk/debate-topics/theological/6belief/

obligation to be good, or just, or righteous. In the Bible, however, God is infinitely righteous and holy (Psalm 77:13; 99:9). God doesn't seek blind obedience, but rather a relationship. Relationships require trust and free will. Therefore, because of God's own nature, he created man with a nature that has free will so that humans can love God based on their own free choice rather than because of a resignation to his will. The Bible also teaches that man is created in God's own image (Genesis 1:27); this is in contrast to the Muslim view that man is created as Allah's slave (Q. 25:63). True love requires free choice. Finally, the God of the Bible is holy and cannot tolerate evil (Habakkuk 1:13). This is why he cannot allow anyone to be in heaven no matter how many good works they perform. Only perfection is acceptable. However, the Bible teaches that no human being is perfect. This is why Jesus Christ had to take our place and die for the sins of mankind. He was the only one holy enough to satisfy the requirement of perfection.

## Implications

If scholars such as Yehuda Nevo,[203] Karl-Heinz Ohlig, and Volker Popp[204] are correct in their presupposition that Islam is a man-made religion, then a logical deduction from studying its theological tenets may be that Islam could have been created in part due to the rejection of what was taught about Jesus (that he was God himself), and also in part because of many things that were not known concerning Christian teaching (such as the role of grace and the full plan of salvation by grace rather than by works). The Muslim rationale for this rejection is that the Biblical scriptures taught these controversial doctrines only out of a corruption of the original text. If it had been understood during the early days of Islam that the Christian and Jewish scriptures were, in fact, accurate, then the premise that the Qur'an was necessary to correct the error would not have been tenable. This incorrect assumption about the errors of the earlier scriptures means that many claims of the Qur'an, and thus of Muslims, are misleading statements.

There are a number of areas where a more accurate understanding of Christianity on the part of Muslims would help Christians be more persuasive in their defense of their own beliefs. Therefore, it is important for Christians to respond to the core Muslim beliefs with the following responses. First of all, it is important to point out that Christians believe in one God and not three separate gods. The Father, Son, and Holy Spirit are three persons that make up the one God – three persons in one essence. This may be a difficult concept to grasp, but it is not contradictory nor

---

[203] Nevo, *Crossroads to Islam*.
[204] Ohlig, *Early Islam*.

illogical. Moreover, because the Christian God is a unity within the community of the Trinity, this explains why God desires his followers to love him and worship him through a relationship. It explains why God could come to the earth as a man and personally take the place of sinners on the cross. The Trinity also explains why God did not have to create a universe to be love. In contrast, Allah is so transcendent and remote that Muslims cannot know him personally or have a relationship.

In regard to the prophets, according to Deuteronomy 18, which Muslims claim prophesies the coming of Muhammad as the prophet that God will raise up, Muhammad actually must be considered as a false prophet because he is not able to pass the tests of a true prophet of God.

In regard to angels, there are similarities between the two religions such as the understanding that angels are messengers of God who also guard humans from temptation and danger. There is also the shared belief in Satan as a fallen angel who is bent on the destruction of mankind. However, the Bible does not indicate that angels would be the ones to reveal the Word of God to the people, as the Gabriel of the Qur'an was tasked. In fact, at one point in the Bible (Gal. 1:8) God warns his people to be on guard so that they would not be deceived even if an angel came and revealed to them a different gospel than what they find in the New Testament. When the Qur'an is compared with the Bible, this is exactly what we see with the core contradictions in regard to doctrine. Therefore, the Gabriel of the Qur'an, and of Islam, cannot be a true angel of God.

Muslims, like Christians, believe in a Day of Judgment when everyone will be resurrected and then judged by God to determine whether they will enter heaven or hell. However, there are a number of ways that the Muslim beliefs deviate from the Biblical account, and ultimately Muslims believe that they will be saved if their good works outweigh their bad works.

Finally, Muslims believe that since Allah can do anything he desires, he, therefore, predetermines all the actions of individuals. This means that man does not have free will, but rather is a slave to Allah, and Allah controls all man's actions. Ultimately, this may lead to a sense of fatalism and passivity since there is little hope that a person's actions can change his or her destiny. This is ironic in a system where people hope that by their actions they will achieve salvation, since, if an omnipotent force already determines all their actions, they really don't have any control over their future. In this way, Islam presents the ultimate system of fatalism.

## Apologetic Conclusions

It would be helpful in conversation with a Muslim friend to first bring up a number of similar beliefs in order to demonstrate that both Christianity and Islam support beliefs that are generally beneficial to society. However, it would also be important to demonstrate that there are some very important differences which highlight how unlikely it is that Christianity and Islam come from the same religious background. These topics would include the Trinity, the crucifixion (and therefore substitutionary death), original sin, the deity of Christ, and the historicity of the New Testament.

## Building Bridges to Understand

Probably the best bridge that can be built in this area would be to demonstrate that the whole focus of Christianity is that Jesus Christ is God himself and that his substitutionary death provides the only way to heaven. This would clarify the main differences between Christian and Islamic beliefs and provide a basis for further discussion.

Here are some ways that Christians can reach out to Muslims in regard to their beliefs:

- **Listen:** One of the most important things a Christian can do in order to effectively reach out to a Muslim is to listen carefully to their explanations of their beliefs. All Muslims believe in the same six central doctrines, but their interpretations can be very different. It is important to make sure that the individual's particular views are addressed.

- **Understand:** It is also essential that Christians understand the beliefs of Muslims, not only from a scholarly point of view, but also on a cultural level. Beliefs are passed down from one generation to another through actions and expectations more than through doctrinal explanations. When Christians demonstrate an interest in knowing more about Islam, then the Muslim is often more open to listening to what the Christian has to say.

- **Compare:** Muslims have many misconceptions about Christianity, which form barriers that separate them from knowing Jesus Christ as Lord and Savior. It is therefore important to point out and correct these misconceptions with well-reasoned arguments so that Muslims can have the opportunity to more clearly understand the claims of Christianity about sin and salvation.

- **Persuade:** The worldview of Muslims is based on presuppositions that support their beliefs and also filter the way that they understand the evidence for Christianity. By recognizing a Muslim's presuppositions,

Christians can assess Islam's foundational beliefs and provide reasonable arguments to support the Bible's truth. Muslims are more willing to explore the inconsistencies of their own beliefs when counter-arguments are presented in a winsome, rational, and loving way.

- **Pray:** It is crucial that prayer is involved throughout the whole process since this is ultimately a spiritual battle and must be fought with spiritual weapons (Ephesians 6:10-18). It is also important to provide hope for Muslims since their religion cannot provide the assurance that many are seeking. These longings are only satisfied through Jesus Christ, which is why it is so important to make sure that every bridge that is constructed links to Jesus Christ on the other side.

### Study Questions:

1. Explain what *tawhid* means and how this view of Allah undergirds all of Islam.
2. What are some similarities between the Six Beliefs in Islam and the major doctrines of Christianity? What are some key differences?
3. What is the prime reason that the Allah of the Qur'an and the God of the Bible cannot be referring to the same God?
4. What are the main arguments a Christian should use in defending the accuracy of the New Testament with a Muslim who says that it has been corrupted?
5. Focusing on the presuppositions for the Muslim worldview, what are some ways that a Christian can reach out to Muslims in regard to their beliefs?

# CHAPTER 8 Sharia Law: External Laws or Internal Sanctification

## Introduction

When Westerners think of Sharia law, their concept is usually centered on excessive punishments, such as being stoned for adultery or having hands cut off for stealing. However, Islam presents Sharia not just as a legal system but as an integral way to fulfill the will of Allah for each person and situation, since Allah's will is to bring about compassion, generosity, and justice. Muslims, therefore, justify these strong measures by arguing that they are used only rarely and in a way that will help people find their way back to Allah. This chapter examines the various aspects of Sharia law, along with the traditional account of its origins, then considers what revisionist scholars believe to be Sharia's current significance and possible historical inconsistencies in its origin story. Does Sharia law have significance today, both to Muslims and non-Muslims? What does it reveal about Islam, both religiously and politically? These are important considerations, both for Christians who come to the issue from a religious perspective and for non-Muslims in general who want to understand the role of social justice and culture in the Islamic worldview.

## The Traditional Muslim View

Muslims believe that Sharia developed from laws which were revealed in the Qur'an, as well as other laws that grew out of Muhammad's own example or rulings that he gave during his lifetime. These secondary laws came from the *sunnah* of the prophet, (meaning his words as well as his actions), and were collected in the written volumes of the *Hadith*. However, if any situation arose where these sources did not offer enough information to make a judgment, then the judges were free to use their intellect, as well as reason, in order to rule in these cases. Thus, as one author declares, "Sharia is derived from the Quran, exemplified in Muhammad's life, and explained by imams."[205]

The word Sharia comes from the Arabic word meaning "path to water," or "pathway to be followed," or even "the pathway for a Muslim to walk," symbolizing a way of life that is followed to please Allah and

---

[205] Nabeel Qureshi, *No God But One: Allah or Jesus?* (Grand Rapids, MI: Zondervan, 2016), 34.

emphasize the fulfillment of his will on an individual's life.[206] Sharia is considered the infallible law of Allah and therefore it must supersede all other codes of law. The areas of life that Sharia dictates behavior for far exceed a simple code of punishment for crimes. Instead, as Scott Bridger, a professor of Islamic studies points out, "Muslims believe Sharia contains a comprehensive system governing every aspect of their lives, from how to brush one's teeth to how to conduct financial transactions."[207] Dr. Shawki Allam, the Grand Mufti of Egypt, compares Sharia to the US Constitution and explains that "Far from a medieval code of capital punishments, the Shari'ah is a dynamic ethico-legal system designed to safeguard and advance core human values." He later argues that,

> The sensationalism over the Shari'ah we see time and again is simply fear mongering. As much as it may bother those who spread hate, American Muslims put core tenets of the Shari'ah into practice every day when they operate soup kitchens, donate their time to community service, get married or divorced, practice their professions, run their businesses, have children, visit the sick, and much more.
>
> Simply stated, the purpose of the Shari'ah is not to establish theocracies, to subjugate non-believers or to subject people to capital punishments. Rather, the Shari'ah aims to facilitate a believer's attaining God's pleasure, secure human welfare in this life and attain human salvation in the hereafter—ideals common to all Abrahamic faiths.[208]

Thus, as Dr. Allam explains, Sharia encompasses every detail of a person's life and informs them on how they should act in various situations: how to dress; how to enter a room; what to eat; how to eat; how to cook; how to relate to others; how wives should respond to their husbands; how women are supposed to behave in public; how to discipline children; how to guide families spiritually; how to handle money, property, inheritance, banking needs, etc. This full and detailed nature of the law, interestingly, is largely responsible for the popularity of Sharia with the average Muslim. Some Muslims today who desire Sharia law do so because they are minority

---

[206] Mark Durie, *The Third Choice: Islam, Dhimmitude and Freedom* (Deror Books, 2010), 40. Nabeel Qureshi, *No God But One*, 33-34. Bill Warner, *Sharia Law for Non-Muslims* (Center for the Study of Political Islam, 2010), 5.

[207] J. Scott Bridger, "What is Shariah Law?" November 4, 2013: https://www.baptistmessenger.com/the-worldview-of-islam-muslim-beliefs-practices/

[208] Shawki Allam, "Shari'ah Law: What it is and what it is not," https://mfaegypt.org/2015/11/08/shariah-law-what-it-is-and-what-it-is-not/

groups in non-Muslim nations, and they hope to insulate themselves through Sharia from the surrounding culture.

In Muslim societies, as well as for Muslims in minority situations, the process of interpreting and applying Sharia is called *fiqh* in Arabic, and this process is carried out by qualified religious scholars who use reason and tradition in order to apply Islamic law to every aspect of life for a Muslim. These Sharia rulings are first divided into two broad areas of guidance, one dealing with religious worship and the other covering worldly matters. These two areas are further divided into three more specific areas: Religious worship and ritual, which covers prayer, fasting, and pilgrimages; private social interactions, such as marriage, business, and ethics; and then public laws, which cover topics such as government, criminal law, and war (Jihad). These divisions are then governed by five categories for classifying various behaviors and actions: obligatory, recommended, permitted (halal), offensive, and forbidden (haram).[209] For example, prayer would be obligatory, meat prepared according to Sharia standards would be permitted, or "halal," and drinking alcohol would be forbidden, or "haram." It will be beneficial to review four general areas of Sharia law in order to better understand the extent of its influence.

## Family Relationships

This aspect of Sharia law deals with the roles of individuals within the context of home and family. Women are given detailed instruction on how they as wives should respond to their husbands, what their duties and responsibilities are, and how to bring up their children and teach them about Islam. Sharia also provides instruction on such small details as how a woman should dress (supplementing the Qur'an, which says women should dress modestly but gives no further details), what types of food she should cook, and how she should relate to men outside the family. The question of why some Muslim women wear clothing that covers most of their body, even their face, often comes up in discussion. Muslim women frequently suggest that this type of dress protects their modesty and even gives them freedom from being treated as a sex object. The Qur'an actually has very little to say about how women should dress. The most important verse in this regard is Sura 24:31, which admonishes women to cover their upper body with their veil. Later traditions, informed by the hadith, led to additional types of coverings traditionally worn in public or in the presence of adult males outside the immediate family. The *hijab* is a veil which

---

[209] The Public Dhikr (Hadra) by Nuh Ha Mim Keller, 1996. http://www.islamicity.com/forum/printer_friendly_posts.asp?TID=990. (accessed October 1, 2018).

usually covers the head and chest. It is also used as a general term for modest dress. A *niqab* is a veil that covers the face, showing only the eyes, and a *burka* is a full face and body covering that is worn in the most conservative Muslim countries. Sharia law gives men similarly comprehensive instruction on how they are to treat their wives, discipline their children, guide their families spiritually, and relate to other men in the community.

## Crime and Punishment

This area is the best-known (and even infamous) aspect of Sharia law outside of the Muslim community. It gives what are often viewed as harsh punishments for theft, lying, murder, rape, and adultery, among other crimes. These range from stoning a couple for adultery or beheading a blasphemer/apostate, to cutting off the right hand of a thief, to a hundred lashes for rape. These serious offenses are known as *hadud and* merit the harsher forms of sharia. *Tazir* refers to severe crimes that do not measure up to the strict requirements of hadud offences, such as receiving 80 lashes for drinking alcohol, though even drug use is sometimes punished by beheading. Muslims, however, point out that such severe punishments are rare and when they are used, it is in such a way that draws the person back towards a proper attitude of submission toward Allah. Thus, Sharia law should not be judged simply because of its strong stance towards crime.

## Inheritance and Property

Sharia also governs the practices of how wealth and property are passed on after death. Because Islam emphasizes the responsibility of men in taking care of the family, property is largely given to male descendants so that they can ensure the wellbeing of everyone else in the family. While Sharia law stipulates that women typically receive only half the inheritance, this is mostly because they are the protected members of the family, and are not usually obligated to support anyone. If they are widowed, they will either marry again or live with relatives. This dictating of how property is received, handled, and passed on is ultimately intended to help communities run smoothly without property disputes or families being in need.

## External Customs

Other aspects of Sharia law deal with slavery and the status of non-Muslims. The Sharia code allows for slavery – anyone captured in Jihad or children of current slaves is a legitimate slave – but dictates at great length how these slaves are to be treated, especially the female slaves. Muslims say that slavery is extinct in most Islamic countries, so these sections would not apply today. The features of Sharia that deal with non-Muslims consider that they are half the worth of Muslims in legal procedures. Also, their testimony is often considered unreliable and does not count for many decisions in the Sharia courts. In addition, they were considered second-class citizens called "dhimmis," and as a "protected" class had to pay a specific tax called the "jizya," which exempted them from military duty and (at certain times) other aspects of Muslim law. However, it also made them subject to a complex set of regulations that prevented them from having certain freedoms that Muslims had. These ranged from dress specifications to giving their seats up to Muslims when asked, to not having political rights. Property and contract laws, on the other hand, applied equally to Muslims and non-Muslims.

The purpose of Sharia is to provide guidance for Muslims in every aspect of their lives so that they will be able to live in accordance with the will of Allah. In this way, as long as they follow the divine law, they will be able to please Allah, avoid punishment in this world and the next, and hope to live in peace with their neighbors. However, Sharia has not brought peace to Muslims or their nations, nor has it created a very tolerant situation for Christians and Jews living under a Muslim government. In fact, as we will demonstrate, sharia has created one of the most intolerant systems of inequality the world has ever seen.

## Counterview

Revisionist scholars discuss Sharia law in two main ways: first, they question the legitimacy of its origins and cast doubt on it really being derived from Muhammad's words and actions, and second, they argue that implementing Sharia law in modern societies is dangerous both politically and ethically. On the first point, these scholars argue that the origins of Sharia are dubious, as they trace their connection to Islamic code mainly through the Hadith and the Sunnah, which were written down 150 to 200 years after Muhammad's death, and thus lack a convincing mandate.[210] Furthermore, some scholars have concluded that many of the Hadith were fabricated at various times in order to favor a particular ruling over another side, and this dilutes the religious forces of the Sharia law even more. It should also be noted that there are a number of contradictions in the Sharia

---

[210] Donner, *Narratives of Islamic Origins*, 20.

code, so it cannot truly be considered to be a perfect or inerrant rule of law, Islamic or otherwise.[211]

On the second issue, which deals with modern implementation of Sharia law, scholar Mark Durie warns that non-Muslims should not mistake the Sharia for an out-of-date relic of the past centuries. Instead, he describes it as "an authoritative application of Muhammad's example in a comprehensive and consistent way, using rigorous principles and Islamic case-law. This is much more inclusive in concept than any penal code."[212] He goes on to explain that the root problem with implementing Sharia law is that Muhammad was not merely a religious figure, but also a political, military, and legal authority. Thus, as Bill Warner, the founder of the Center for the Study of Political Islam, reminds us, "Sharia law is the political implementation of the Islamic civilization."[213] In addition, any consideration of the laws of Islam is equally a religious, juridical, and political discussion.[214] Therefore, because the rules of Sharia define a total way of life, Durie says that "there can be no Islam without Sharia."[215]

Sharia law may have originated from the Hadith and the Qur'an in terms of its principles, but its actual modern form is a sprawling set of codes and rules very similar in its breadth to a nation's entire legal codex. Sharia law manuals contain the entirety of the rules in the form of a systematic reference book. In actuality, only 14% of the total words of Sharia is derived from the Qur'an, while the balance of 86% is found in the Sira and the Hadith. Interestingly, one writer notes, this means that "Islam is 14% Allah and 86% Muhammad," since the Sira records Muhammad's life and the Hadith record his words and actions.[216]

## Sharia Changes

Another important factor to include in our equation is that Sharia continues to change through time, not only due to the continual interpretation of the religious leaders but also due to its intrinsic political foundation. Because Islam has linked itself to the political as well as the theological realm, in some cases the political aspirations of leaders or factions/parties have changed various aspects of the secondary elements (involving everyday applications) of Islamic practice. When political or

---

[211] Ibid., 14.
[212] Durie, *The Third Choice*, 41.
[213] Warner, *Sharia Law for Non-Muslims*, 8.
[214] Durie, *The Third Choice*, 50.
[215] Ibid., 40.
[216] Warner, *Sharia Law for Non-Muslims*, 6.

power goals are involved, the parties have used religious means to promote political ends. This has fundamentally affected many aspects of Islam today, and Sharia law is perhaps one of the best examples. Even if the Sharia law is valued for its ability to create a society of good Islamic order, and not for its historic or theological purity, it nonetheless reveals a flawed religion that has certain portions of its nature formed through conflicting religious and political views between warring factions. At least it cannot be claimed that Sharia law is strictly derived from the Qur'an and Hadith, and thus it should more accurately be regarded in the light of man-made laws created around a religion, rather than laws received from direct revelation.

In addition, Sharia law dictates not only the actions of Muslims but also of non-Muslims. In countries with a Muslim majority, this could mean that non-Muslims would have to subject themselves to state-legislated inferiority. At the very least, it can be surmised that such a rule would not create a society which supported equal rights for all its citizens. At the worst, the fact that fundamentalist groups, in particular, are the ones currently seeking to revert back to a more violent interpretation of the Sharia in order to promote their views is a warning sign of destabilization of the state.

## The Development of Control through the Practice of Dhimmitude

It would be helpful at this point to understand how the practice of *dhimmitude* (forced subordination of non-Muslims) developed since it is inextricably tied to Sharia and provides a portrait of what non-Muslims have had to endure under Sharia domination. After Muhammad's death, the second caliph, Omar, is said to have instituted a series of "conditions" that guided the Muslims in their treatment of the conquered Christians. Rather than execute all the Christians who would not convert to Islam (since this would decimate the pool of needed workers), a third choice was often preferred – paying the "jizya," or head tax, with willing submission and "feeling themselves subdued" (Q. 9:29). In essence, this meant that the subjugated Christians, or non-Muslims, were to purchase their lives back from their Muslim conquerors and live in such a way that they would feel constantly intimidated. In order to regulate this lifestyle, a set of conditions was drawn up called the "Conditions of Omar." It is probable that these conditions were developed long after the time of the second caliph, Omar, but his name and time period are now firmly associated with the rules that guided the treatment of the subjugated class of second-class citizens who became known as the "Dhimmis," or "protected persons."

According to the "Conditions of Omar," the "dhimmis" were expected to agree to onerous conditions in exchange for their lives. The following list is presented through the voice of the captives giving the impression that these conditions were considered to be a fair exchange for safety.

When you came to our countries, we asked you for safety for ourselves and the people of our community, upon which we imposed the following conditions on ourselves for you:

1. Not to build a church in the city – nor a monastery, convent, or monk's cell in the surrounding areas – and not to repair those that fall in ruins or are in Muslim quarters;

2. Not to prevent Muslims from lodging in our churches, by day or night, and to keep their doors wide open for [Muslim] passersby and travelers;

3. Not to display a cross on them [churches], nor raise our voices during prayer or readings in our churches anywhere near Muslims;

4. Nor to produce a cross or [Christian] book in the markets of the Muslims;

5. Not to display any signs of polytheism, nor make our religion appealing, nor call or proselytize anyone to it;

6. Not to prevent any of our relatives who wish to enter into Islam;

7. Not to possess or bear any arms whatsoever, nor gird ourselves with swords;

8. To honor the Muslims, show them the way, and rise up from our seats if they wish to sit down;

9. To host every traveling Muslim for three days and feed him adequately;

10. We guarantee all this to you upon ourselves, our descendants, our spouses, and our neighbors, and if we change or contradict these conditions imposed upon ourselves in order to receive safety, we forfeit our dhimma [covenant], and we become liable to the same treatment you inflict upon the people who resist and cause sedition"[217]

---

[217] Raymond Ibrahim, *Crucified Again: Exposing Islam's New War on Christians* (D.C.: Regnery, 2013), 25-27. See also, Medieval Sourcebook: Pact of Umar: https://sourcebooks.fordham.edu/source/pact-umar.asp

Other restrictions were added over time. Omar reputedly added another one: "that Christians never raise their hands against a Muslim, including in self-defense."[218] In summary, these conditions resulted in extreme restrictions on the lives of the Christians and Jews, especially in the following three areas:

### There were restrictions on expressions of worship:[219]

Churches could not be repaired; crosses and Bibles could not be displayed; and the sounds of Christian prayers, bells, and singing were not permitted beyond the boundaries of the church.

### There were restrictions on freedom:

Proselytizing Muslims was banned, as was any form of blasphemy toward Muslims, the prophet or Islam in general. Also, any Muslim who converted to Christianity was charged with apostasy and subject to the death penalty.

### Christians were assigned an inferior social status:

Dhimmis were very much considered beneath the level of the Muslims. They had to humble themselves before Muslims; their testimony in court was not valid against a Muslim; they could not raise their hand against a Muslim even in self-defense; they could not hold public office or any other position over a Muslim; and a Christian man was forbidden to marry a Muslim woman, even though a Muslim man could marry a Christian woman. Christians and other non-Muslims were simply not considered equal in any way to Muslims.

These restrictions were established in the early days, and during the period of colonialism, they were overturned as the Muslims experienced the humiliation of losing their hegemony to the Western world. Raymond Ibrahim, a writer, and researcher for Gatestone Institute, says that "for the first time in Islam's 1,200 years of existence (at the time), non-Muslim subjects were to be treated as equal to Muslims, and their right to religious freedom and worship was to be guaranteed."[220]

However, as Ibrahim reminds us, "these debilitations and humiliations, which were inflicted upon the Christians of the Islamic world in the past, are at this moment being inflicted upon the Christians of the Islamic world in the present, as a natural consequence of Muslims returning to the

---

[218] Ibrahim, *Crucified Again*, 27.

[219] Summarized from Ibrahim, *Crucified Again*, 28-29.

[220] Ibrahim, *Crucified Again*, 12.

authentic teachings of Islam."[221] In fact, the *Conditions of Omar* is being dusted off and revived in a number of locations in the Middle East. For example, during a Friday sermon, Saudi Sheikh Marzouk Salem al-Ghamdi advocated a return to the past.

> If the infidels live among the Muslims, in accordance with the conditions set out by the Prophet – there is nothing wrong with it provided they pay Jizya to the Islamic treasury. Other conditions are ... that they do not renovate a church or a monastery, do not rebuild ones that were destroyed, that they feed for three days any Muslim who passes by their homes ... that they rise when a Muslim wishes to sit, that they do not imitate Muslims in dress and speech, nor ride horses, nor own swords, nor arm themselves with any kind of weapon; that they do not sell wine, do not show the cross, do not ring church bells, do not raise their voices during prayer, that they shave their hair in front so as to make them easily identifiable, do not incite anyone against the Muslims, and do not strike a Muslim ... If they violate these conditions, they have no protection.[222]

If these were the words of a Muslim fanatic, that would be one thing. However, Ibrahim demonstrates that the Conditions of Omar are very much on the rise again:

> Churches in Muslim countries are regularly bombed, burned, or simply denied permits to renovate or even to exist. Crosses are burned and Bibles are confiscated. Muslim converts to Christianity are often violently attacked and sometimes executed. Christians accused of committing "blasphemy" – which can mean simply discussing Islam, or even Christianity – are assaulted and killed. Jizya is exacted from Christians once again. Christians are forced to convert to Islam. Christian women and children are abducted and raped.[223]

People in the West have a hard time understanding how these things could be going on in the world today, especially since many of the Muslims they know or are familiar with present a very different picture of what they call "moderate" Islam. Political leaders throughout the Western nations have continually made excuses for the actions of Muslim radicals and have aggressively promoted a hollow platitude that Islam means "peace." This obfuscation has only exacerbated the problem and has given radical

---

[221] Ibid., 29.
[222] Robert Spencer, *Muslim Persecution of Christians* (Sherman Oaks: David Horowitz Freedom Center, 2011), 41-42.
[223] Ibrahim, *Crucified Again*, 30.

Muslims even more courage to expand their operations and recruit new warriors for their cause. Ibrahim explains,

> When the West, or at least popular culture in the West, became spiritually bankrupt and began apologizing for itself, Muslims, disgusted, turned back to Islam and its way, the Sharia – all, of course, to Western approval and encouragement. And now the myopic West cannot comprehend that Muslims have gone back to treating Christians in the exact same ways Muslims treated Christians before Muslims began to emulate the West. That history is all but lost. In fact, the cognitive dissonance between what the multiculturalists in the West believe about the benign and even superior culture of Islam, and what is reported as actually taking place in the Muslim world, is so great that many Westerners simply cannot take in the facts.[224]

One of the implications of this pattern is that Sharia is used to transform a non-Muslim host country into a sharia-compliant country. Then, as the population of Muslims increases, more demands are made, and the oppression of Christians becomes greater. It is a form of coercion.

The French philosopher, Jacques Ellul, illustrates this pattern by tracing the infiltration of Islam into France through three stages: The first stage involved small groups of immigrant workers coming from North Africa, mainly Algeria, Morocco, and Tunisa. The second stage began when the worker's families were allowed to join them. The third stage is the result of the minor inroads made by the initial immigration becoming major obstacles in French society today. Ellul observes that these small steps ended up with the proliferation of mosques, the demands made by Islamic communities for special privileges, the destruction of churches, and the move of millions of Muslims into Islamic communities in the outskirts of our cities and to villages in our provinces![225]

Ellul's overall comment on this predictable progression may be a warning to other countries experiencing mass migration from Muslim countries today: "Rather than integrating Muslims into French society, we witness the integration of France into Islam."[226]

We can also see this trend in a study performed by Peter Hammond, a former director of Intervarsity Christian Fellowship. In the chart below,

---

[224] Ibrahim, *Crucified Again*, 17.

[225] http://www.faithfreedom.org/jacques-ellul-on-the-impossibility-of-integrating-muslims-in-western-societies/ (Accessed on October 2, 2018).

[226] www.faithfreedom.org/jacques-ellul-on-the-impossibility-of-integrating-muslims-in-western-societies/

note how the rise of the Muslim population in a country not only results in greater influence but also there is a greater call for Sharia in all aspects of life, for the Muslim as well as the non-Muslim. There is also a trend of more violence committed by Muslims in their host countries as their numbers increase.

## Influence through Demographics[227]

| Extent of Muslim Influence by the Numbers | Countries in this percent level |
|---|---|
| **Less than 1%** <br><br> Muslims are regarded as peace-loving and not a threat; Muslim groups begin to work the system and push for an equal voice | United States, Australia, Canada, China, Italy, Norway |
| **At 2% and 3%** <br><br> Proselytizing of minorities and major recruiting in jails and gangs takes place (Muslims expect majority governments to be compliant); will use our political systems, our constitutions based on freedom, and our educational systems against us | Denmark, Germany, United Kingdom, Spain, Thailand |
| **From 5% on** <br><br> Disproportional influence; they will begin under-the-table coercion through the demand for halal food and religious "rights"; there is a push for the acceptance of Sharia law | France, Philippines, Sweden, Switzerland, The Netherlands, Trinidad & Tobago |
| **10% or more of population** <br><br> Violence is often used in order to voice complaints and pressure the majority government; any non- | Guyana, India, Israel, Kenya, Russia |

---

[227] Adapted from Peter Hammond, "What Islam Isn't," FrontPageMagazine.com, Monday, April 21, 2008.

| | |
|---|---|
| Muslim action that offends Islam will bring violence and threats | |
| **After reaching 20%**<br><br>Riots become commonplace, Jihad militias form, persecution of Christians takes place, as well as church and synagogue burning | Ethiopia |
| **At 40%** you will find "widespread massacres, chronic terror attacks and ongoing militia warfare" | Nigeria, Bosnia, Chad, Lebanon |
| **From 60%** you may expect "unfettered persecution of non-believers and other religions, sporadic ethnic cleansing (genocide), use of Sharia Law as a weapon and Jizya, the tax placed on infidels" | Albania, Malaysia, Qatar, Sudan |
| **After 80%** expect "State run ethnic cleansing and genocide" | Bangladesh, Egypt, Gaza, Indonesia, Iran, Iraq, Jordan, Morocco, Pakistan, Palestine, Syria, Tajikistan, Turkey, United Arab Emirates |
| **Near 100%** will "usher in the peace of 'Dar-al-Salaam' -- the Islamic House of Peace -- there's supposed to be peace because everybody is a Muslim" | Afghanistan, Saudi Arabia, Somalia, Yemen |
| But there is no peace! | Which Muslim majority country in the world has a thriving economy with freedom, security, and true peace for all of its citizens? |

## Comparison of "Stages"

It is evident from the comparison above that there are a number of similarities between the response of the church to Islam in the 7th century and the 21st century. There are four general stages that are represented at both times -- denial, apathy, "complacent ignorance," and fear. In regard to denial, those living outside the Middle East and North Africa in the centuries following the rise of Islam denied that there was much going on. When they did comprehend the gravity of the situation, they were apathetic about getting involved. In fact, it took almost 400 years for the church to launch a counter-attack (the Crusades). As one writer notes, there was also "complacent ignorance,"[228] because the Christians outside of the strike zone were more concerned with their own peace and security rather than learning more about the enemy and seeking to rescue their brothers in Christ. Finally, there was fear – fear of getting involved, fear of retaliation, and fear of the unknown. We see the same responses today.

## Similar Patterns

In the 7th-century, these same patterns that we observe today developed in the borderland between the Arabs and the Christians. As the Arab horde moved northward behind the retreating Byzantine forces, some non-Chalcedonian Christian groups, who had been persecuted under the Byzantine rule, at first embraced the new religious movement as the "rod of God's anger" intended "to deliver [them] from the Byzantines,"[229] and they felt relief from what they considered an oppressive former regime. On the other hand, the "Byzantine polemicists saw Islam as a 'Satanic plot' to destroy Christian Faith."[230] Some of the sources cited religious devotion by the invaders and some cited brutality and godlessness. Overall, there seemed to be a sense of ambivalence and unpreparedness. At first, the new regime ruled from a distance and made light economic and civil demands. This further pleased the non-Chalcedonian Christians. However, as the Muslims gained more power, the suppression of Christian rights increased. In time, Christians were brutally persecuted, churches and Bibles were burned, crosses were banned and public preaching was denied. As the number of Muslims in the general population grew, many of the remaining Christians were faced with three choices: convert, submit and pay, or die.

---

[228] Robert Wilken, "Christianity Face to Face with Islam," *2009*. https://www.firstthings.com/article/2009/01/christianity-face-to-face-with-islam.

[229] "'Christianity and Islam' from Oxford Islamic Studies Online," November 13, 2014 http://bridgingcultures.neh.gov/muslimjourneys/items/show/198.

[230] Ibid. (Gaudeul, vol. 1, 65).

Bill Warner notes how this pressure by the implementation of Sharia on Christians eventually resulted in the nations of Turkey, Egypt, North Africa, Lebanon, Syria, Iraq, and Ethiopia to become Islamic and the Christians to become dhimmis. He explains,

> Jihad placed Muslims in political control and established Sharia law. Then all of the Christians became dhimmis. Centuries of the jizya tax and third-class status caused them to convert. It was Sharia law and the dhimmi status that destroyed Christianity in Islamic lands. Western civilization cannot survive under Sharia law.[231]

We see many of these same patterns reappearing in the 21st century, especially in the Middle East. For example, as ISIS has been on the move in Iraq, they have been greeted with open arms by their fellow Sunni Muslims who hold disdain for the present U.S. built Iraqi government. As ISIS gains more power, there is greater suppression of the rights of Christians and those they consider to be Muslim "infidels." Christians are faced with horrendous persecution as they experience torture, rape, crucifixion, and beheadings. Their churches are burned, crosses are banned, and public proclamation of their Christian faith brings swift martyrdom. In the end, they are given three choices: convert, submit and pay, or die (or flee before this happens). With meticulous and brutal conviction, parts of the Middle East are being "cleansed" of any Christian presence – a presence that has survived for almost 2,000 years.

## Solutions

Are there any ways to break this pattern and bring true peace to the Middle East? The growth of "power Islam" seems to catapult forward when there is a political vacuum to fill. In the 7th century, the retreat of the Byzantine forces left the Levant (the area that includes Palestine, Israel, and Syria) unguarded. In the 20th century, there was a retreat of colonial forces that had provided modernization and movement toward Westernization. While the colonial forces were in control, the Middle Eastern Christians had been able to experience a type of "Golden Period" where the *dhimmi* status was lifted and they were able to build churches, receive better opportunities for education, and make advances in society. However, the colonial forces turned the power back over to the Muslims, and in a relatively short time, the rejection of western values provided an impetus to revive a socio-economic-religious worldview based on 7th century Islam. Because Islam is a theocracy, the success of "power Islam" has encouraged militant groups

---

[231] Warner, *Sharia Law for Non-Muslims*, 31.

to believe that God is on their side. This, in turn, has fueled their belief that they have a mandate by God to subdue the rest of the world (the *Dar al-Harb*, or "house of war") under the *Dar al-Islam*, or the "house of Islam" (or "house of submission" to God).

Durie says this is the reason most Muslims believe that Sharia should be the foundation for legislation, and it is also the reason that many constitutions in Muslim-majority countries demand Sharia law over any other legal system. After all, a nation cannot be Muslim without Sharia as the basis of the government, and, if sharia is the supreme guide over all that a Muslim does, then it should also be the supreme guide for the nation. However, as evidenced by countries that have the strictest sharia-dominant governments, like Iran, Afghanistan, Saudi Arabia, and Sudan, this preference for sharia has not produced model states.[232]

Some believe that a secularization of Islamic countries needs to take place, involving the "separation of mosque and state." With this type of separation, the state would protect the freedom of the religion and the religion would respect the role of the state. Then, when there is a proper balance between these "two worlds," there can be peace. However, a theocratic nation, which Islam requires, will always be at war with the secular state.

## Is Sharia Compatible with the U.S. Constitution?

As more refugees from Islamic countries make their way into America, some have asked whether Sharia is compatible with the U.S. Constitution. First of all, American democracy is based upon the U.S. Constitution. The Constitution protects the rights of all of its citizens in regard to religious freedom, privacy, and private property. The Constitution also allows people to follow their conscience with respect to behavior, culture, and lifestyle, as long as it does not infringe on the rights of others. Muslims find that many of these things are compatible with sharia and therefore are able to fit in with American lifestyles. However, there are other aspects of sharia that are not compatible at all and should not be practiced in a democracy, such as forced prayer, the requirement of halal food for non-Muslims, and a ban on legal activities for non-Muslims, etc.

Bill Warner believes that "there are no common principles between American law and Sharia,"[233] and lists a number of restrictions to the freedom all Americans presently enjoy. Under Sharia law, he says, there is

---

[232] Durie, *Three Choices*, 50.
[233] Warner, *Sharia*, 3.

no freedom of religion; there is no freedom of speech; there is no freedom of thought; there is no freedom of artistic expression, and there is no freedom of the press. He also points out that there is no equality of peoples, for under Sharia a non-Muslim can never be equal to a Muslim. In addition, under Sharia law, there is no equal protection, but rather "justice is dualistic, with one set of laws for Muslim males and different laws for women and non-Muslims."[234] Therefore, Sharia is incompatible with democracy since non-Muslims are not equal with Muslims.

This tension between democratic principles and Sharia law is amply demonstrated in the new constitutions of Iraq and Afghanistan, which are still largely based on Sharia. Even with all the recent influences of America in these two countries, any success of implementing democratic ideas into these societies is doomed because sharia law will not tolerate the freedoms established in the constitutions of democratic nations. Furthermore, if an Islamized society is required for Sharia to be followed consistently by Muslims, there will always be the push for more and more Sharia compliance in the democratic society where Muslims are in the minority. Even a small percentage of Muslims in a society can cause large ripples by their persistent push for sharia-compliant demands. We can see this process at work in the "creeping Sharia" taking place here in America.

## Ten Steps of Creeping Sharia

Sharia is political as well as religious. We can, and should, resist the political aspects of Sharia since the whole purpose of Sharia is to undermine our political system and install Sharia as the only law of the country. "Creeping Sharia" seeks to replace the legitimate government of the host country. The higher the population of Muslims, the stronger the push for Sharia. Here is an example of how ten possible steps may be implemented by Muslims to transform our society as Sharia uses our own compliance to religious demands against us.

First, there is a demand for prayer times at schools.[235] After all, Muslims are required to pray five times a day, so in a democratic nation the public schools should respect the religious needs of Muslims and accommodate this "request." Second, then comes the demand for a special room for prayer that can only be used for prayer. It would be too difficult to keep changing the room around for the prayer times, so a separate room would have to be set aside to fulfill this "request." Third, there would be a demand

---

[234] Ibid., 3.

[235] The first part of this scenario is based on the actual plans outlined on the web by a Muslim.

for new plumbing for foot washing, etc. After all, proper prayers cannot be performed without the proper ablutions. Taxpayers would be asked to pay for these "requests." Fourth, Muslims will have an opportunity to explain the practice of prayer. In order to give a reason for their demands, Muslim religious leaders would be asked to give their religious reasons for their "requests." This would enable Muslims to teach Qur'anic material in the schools. Fifth, there would be a demand for halal food. After all, non-Muslims should not expect Muslim children to be forced to eat food that has not been prepared according to religious requirements. In time more of the food would become halal in order to make it easier to fulfill the "requests" of the Muslims. Sixth, special concessions for Ramadan would be requested. Since fasting is required of all Muslims during the month of Ramadan, schools will be asked to make special allowances for Muslim students since they would not be at their best during these times. Schedules for non-Muslim students would have to be re-configured. Seventh, there would be a demand for Sharia-compliant clothing. Beyond the requests that scarves and hijabs be allowed for the females, special requests for sportswear would also be made. Eighth, there would be demands for Sharia family law. This leap would be made easier with all the concessions made through the school system. The requests would begin with allowances for domestic issues such as marriage counseling, divorce cases, inheritances, and other family matters, but it would then escalate to the ban of alcohol, a push for Sharia finances, and a different level of treatment for honor killings and rape. Ninth, Muslims would demand to be recognized as a minority with special treatment in jobs, appointments, and civil rights. Even though Islam is not a "race," this distinction would be used in order to gain popularization and acceptance of the "requests" made in this area. Tenth, finally there would be a demand for Sharia law instead of the U.S. Constitution. The "request" would be for Muslims to handle their own matters according to the rule of Sharia rather than the Constitution of the United States. After all, the Constitution does not make a provision against religion, so Islam, as a religion, should be allowed to have accommodations made in order to fulfill its rightful religious needs. Some may think that this scenario is over the top, but as Bill Warner points out, "Even though Sharia violates every principle of our Constitution, it is being implemented today, because Americans are unaware about Sharia or its meaning."[236] All ten of these steps have already been tested in various parts of America, with different results. It is only a matter of time if Europe is our example of the movement toward Sharia compliance.

---

[236] Warner, *Sharia*, 9.

## Sharia is Not Equitable

Another reason to reject Sharia in the West is that it is not equitable for all people. It discriminates against women and all non-Muslims. It is not a system of true justice and should be rejected by all non-Muslim societies. As Mark Durie, author of a book on Sharia, notes, "For Sharia to be followed consistently and comprehensively – and this is most important – it requires an Islamized society."[237] Thus, once Sharia is allowed to operate in a democratic society, the push for more and more compliance to Sharia standards will not cease until the whole society is put under the thumb of Sharia. We already looked at the inequality of Sharia in regard to Christian dhimmitude, as well as the possible outcome from creeping Sharia. Another good example of this inequality can be found in the treatment of women, even in Muslim cultures.

Muslims will say that the status of women under Sharia is one of privilege because it is the man's responsibility to take care of the family's economic, religious, and social needs. The Qur'an (4:34) relates that this is because "Allah has made men superior" to women and given men more strength and wisdom in order to be "managers of the affairs of women." However, this often relegates the women to a status of dependency where they have less rights than men, less freedom, and fewer legal claims. For example, a man can divorce his wife by saying "I divorce you" three times in the presence of witnesses, but the wife has to go through a difficult Sharia court procedure. In addition, since the women are often prevented from working outside the home, they have less means to earn a living. One of the most heartless rulings is that the wife is often not given custody of the children. In regard to marriage, the Qur'an (4:34) states that if the wife is not obedient, the husband should first admonish her, then refuse to share his bed, and last to beat her. In Sura 2:223, wives are said to be the "tilth" (fertile lands) for their husband's sexual desires and are not allowed to refuse their husband's desires. The rights are supposed to be equal, but they are not so. Women are responsible for the household and the family but are restricted in the greater society. The Qur'an even refers to women as inferior to men because men work to take care of women and therefore have a superior position (Q. 2:228, 4:34). In addition, the inheritance of women is half that of men (Q. 4:11), and their testimony in court is half that of a male (Q. 2:282). In the religious domain, women cannot take any leadership roles and have to pray separately from the men in the mosque. Women also have to cover themselves to safeguard their modesty and not distract men.

---

[237] Durie, *The Third Choice*, 49.

One of the most egregious practices involving Muslim women is the prevalence of Female Genital Mutilation (FGM). Even though the practice is not promoted in the Qur'an or the Hadith, it is prevalent in many parts of the Muslim world. The World Health Organization estimates that more than 200 million girls and women alive today have undergone this brutal procedure.[238] This practice has had a long history in Islam, for John of Damascus, in his 8th-century treatise, *The Heresy of the Ishmaelites*, mentions female circumcision as one of the distinctive customs practiced by those who would soon become known as Muslims.[239]

In these and many other ways, women are basically second-class citizens in the world of Islam. This contrasts sharply with the status of women in the New Testament where Paul explains that "There is neither Jew nor Greek, slave nor free, male nor female, for you are all one in Christ Jesus" (Galatians 3:28). If we are all one in Christ, then we have the exact same status in Christ and as Christians. As we have seen, this is not the case in Islam.

Another egregious practice that is still quite prevalent in Islam is human slavery. Most people are only familiar with the European slave trade, but the Islamic slave trade spanned a greater time period and involved a greater number of black Africans. In one study, it is estimated that 17 to 20 million slaves were captured in Africa and transported to the Islamic world between 650 and 1920 AD, while 11.7 million were taken from Africa across the Atlantic and into parts of Europe between 1450 and 1900 AD.[240] It is also estimated that the mortality rate during transit in the Islamic slave trade ranged between 80-90 % among the men (due mainly to castration casualties), while the mortality rate hovered around 10% for the European slave trade (due to trans-Atlantic travel and disease). It is also the case that in the Islamic slave trade two out of three slaves were women because one of the chief purposes of slavery for Muslims was sexual exploitation. For the European slave trade, two-thirds of the slaves were male and were required mainly for agricultural work. Another little-known view held by Muslims is that blacks historically were considered inferior to other races. For example, a famous Muslim scholar, Al-Jahiz (781-869 AD), once wrote, "We know that the Zanj (blacks) are the least intelligent and the least discerning of mankind, and the least capable of understanding the consequences of actions."[241] This was not the view of earlier cultures, which seemed to have a more neutral view of blacks, but it became prevalent in

---

[238] http://www.who.int/reproductivehealth/topics/fgm/prevalence/en/ (accessed 10/1/2018).
[239] Daniel Janosik, *John of Damascus, First Apologist to the Muslims* (Wipf & Stock, 2016), Appendix C, 268.
[240] Ralph Austen, *African Economic History* (Currey and Heinemann, 1987), 275.
[241] Jahiz, Kitab al-Bukhala ("Avarice and the Avaricious")

seventh-century Arabia as Blacks became identified with the slave class after the Islamic conquest of Africa.[242] Davis Goldenberg, for example, notes that in ancient Greece and Rome people were not defined by their color.[243] However, this changed during the expansion of Islam when Goldenberg relates that "We first see this... explicit link between skin color and slavery in Near Eastern sources beginning in the seventh century."[244] It seems, then, that the Muslim view toward women and blacks is not one of equality, but rather of an inferior class of humans. Many Muslims also believe that all non-Muslims are inferior and therefore need to be converted to Islam in order to be recognized as equals (Q. 61:9, 48:28, and 9:33). This attitude does not resonate well with the principles of the Bible or the ideals of a free society such as we have in America.

## The Goal of Sharia

Ultimately, the goal of Sharia is to become the law of the land, so in this way, it is totally incompatible with the U.S. Constitution. Thus, Sharia should not be allowed in America except for practices that do not conflict with American laws and policies. Muslims have a right to practice their religion in America, but they do not have the right to alter the beliefs or practices of other religions or legitimate lifestyle choices.

## Building Bridges to Understand

How should Christians respond to the problem of Sharia? We first need to understand Islam better, especially in the way that Sharia is intricately involved in every aspect of the religion and its political ambitions. Understanding Sharia will help us to better understand Islam. We also need to get to know Muslims so that we can put a face to Sharia and build relationships based on understanding and love rather than ignorance and fear. We need to fight the creeping Sharia that seeks to slowly erode the U.S. Constitution as well as the will of non-Muslim Americans to counter the rise of Islam in the world. We cannot afford to shuffle over to the sidelines. We need to hold fast to our Christian doctrine as well as the core of American values. We need to learn how we can turn this controversy into a transformation. Muslims need Jesus!

Michael Youssef, a Christian pastor, reminds us that, "In contrast to Christianity, Islam is a religion of law, blind submission, fear, and

---

[242] David Goldenberg, *The Curse of Ham, Race and Slavery in Early Judaism, Christianity, and Islam,* (Princeton University Press, 2005), 170.

[243] Goldenberg, David, *The Curse of Ham,* 200.

[244] Ibid., 170.

punishment. Under theocratic Islamic rule, submitting to the ruler is equal with submitting to Allah. Islam doesn't simply require belief in Allah, the Koran, Muhammad as the prophet, and the Day of Judgment. Islam demands surrender and submission."[245] Christians, on the other hand, are to win over their enemies through love and compassion. Christians are also taught to confess their faults and to seek forgiveness. These things are central to Christianity, but they are relatively unknown in Islam. A loving, compassionate approach could be a powerful witness to Muslim friends.

Another way to help Muslims understand some of the stark differences between Islam and Christianity is to compare some of the harsh Sharia commands with the grace of God revealed in Scripture and through the life of Jesus Christ. Hopefully, when Muslims see how many of the principles of Sharia counter the grace and freedom of the gospel, they will be more attentive to what you share with them about Jesus Christ and Christianity. In the chart below, the left-hand column lists some of the inhumane commands of Sharia. In the center column is the source. Then, in the right-hand column, there are verses and ideas that you can share with your Muslim friends to demonstrate that Christianity is very different from Islam in these particular ways.

| Sharia command | Source: Qur'an or Hadith | Gospel of Grace: Christianity |
|---|---|---|
| "We gave Moses the Scripture" (Q. 6:154). "This is my path, leading straight, so follow it, and do not follow other ways" (Q. 6:153) | | "For the law was given through Moses; grace and truth came through Jesus Christ" (John 1:17). |
| 1. Islam commands offensive and unjust jihad | Sura 9:29 | Then Jesus said to him, "Put your sword back into its place. For all who take the sword will perish by the sword. (Mat 26:52). |

---

[245] Michael Youssef, *Blindsided: The Radical Islamic Conquest* (Kobri, 2012), 83.

| | | | |
|---|---|---|---|
| 2. | Islam orders apostates to be killed | Sura 9:11-12 | "You have heard that it was said, 'You shall love your neighbor and hate your enemy.' But I say to you, love your enemies and pray for those who persecute you" (Mat 5:43-44). |
| 3. | Islam orders unmarried fornicators to be whipped and adulterers to be stoned to death | Sura 24:2 for fornicators; stoning was left out of Qur'an by Uthman, but supplied in the hadith | Jesus said to them, "Let him who is without sin among you be the first to throw a stone at her" (John 8:7).<br><br>"Flee from sexual immorality. . . do you not know that your body is a temple of the Holy Spirit within you, whom you have from God?" (1 Cor. 6:18-19) |
| 4. | Islam commands that homosexuals must be executed | Abu Dawud, no. 4447 | "Do not be deceived. . . men who practice homosexuality. . . will [not] inherit the kingdom of God. *And such were some of you*" (1 Cor. 6:9-11). [We can be changed by God's grace] |
| 5. | Islam commands that a male and female thief must have a hand cut off | Sura 5:38; Buhkari, Punishments, no. 6788 | Jesus said to the thief on the cross, "Truly, I say to you, today you will be with me in paradise." (Luke 23:43)<br><br>"Let the thief no longer steal, but rather let him labor, doing honest work with his own hands, so that he may have something to share with anyone in need" (Eph. 4:28). |

| | | | |
|---|---|---|---|
| 6. | Islam allows husbands to hit their wives | Sura 4:34 | "Husbands, love your wives, as Christ loved the church and gave himself up for her." (Eph. 5:25)<br><br>"Likewise, husbands, live with your wives in an understanding way, showing honor to the woman as the weaker vessel, since they are heirs with you of the grace of life, so that your prayers may not be hindered" (1 Peter 3:7). |
| 7. | Islamic law can still demand a literal eye for an eye | Sura 5:45 | "You have heard that it was said, An eye for an eye and a tooth for a tooth.' But I say to you, do not resist the one who is evil. But if anyone slaps you on the right cheek, turn to him the other also." (Mat 5:38-39) |
| 8. | Sharia allows for FGM | The Prophet (peace be upon him) said to her: 'Do not cut severely as that is better for a woman and more desirable for a husband.'– *Sunan Abu Dawûd*, Book 41, #5251. | "Husbands, love your wives, as Christ loved the church and gave himself up for her." (Eph. 5:25) |
| 9. | Slavery is still being practiced in Islam | | "There is neither Jew nor Greek, slave nor free, male nor female, for you are all one in Christ Jesus" (Galatians 3:28). |

## The Best Strategy

I like the approach that Nabeel Qureshi follows best. He first lists a number of similarities between Islam and Christianity to demonstrate that many Muslims are seeking to follow Sharia in order to please Allah and earn his favor. Then he points out that the main difference between Islam and Christianity is that while Muslims follow a legal code, Sharia, as their "path," Christians do not follow a mere code, but they follow a person, the Lord Jesus Christ. As Qureshi says, "The way of life in one religion is through the law, while in the other it is through faith in a person."[246] Jesus Christ is the person that all Muslims need to be introduced to, and we have the honor and privilege of being the ones that God uses to share with them the one who is the "Way, the Truth, and the Life" (John 14:6).

### Study Questions:

1. Sharia is based on the Qur'an and the Hadith. What are some general problems with claiming to base God's eternal law on these particular documents?

2. What does Sharia reveal about Islam, both religiously and politically?

3. Who are the "dhimmis" and what were some of the conditions they were forced to endure under Muslim domination? How would life under Dhimmitude be destructive for a Christian's faith?

4. What are the "Conditions of Omar," and what are some of the ways that these rules control the Christians living under Sharia law?

5. Why would the more fundamentalist groups (like ISIS) be the ones most in favor of forcing Sharia on the rest of the population, whether a person is Muslim or non-Muslim? What do they hope to gain?

6. How does the increase in the percentage of Muslims in a non-Muslim country affect the behavior of the Muslims toward their host country?

7. What are some ways that Christians should respond to efforts to establish Sharia in the United States? How can our understanding of Sharia be used to witness to our Muslim friends?

---

[246] Qureshi, *No God But One*, 31.

# CHAPTER 9 Sin and Salvation in Islam: Works Alone or Grace Alone?

## Introduction

Today the Muslim concept of salvation is drastically different from the Christian view. Perhaps the best statement to frame the Islamic view of salvation is from Ron Rhodes: "A weak view of sin will always lead to a weak view of salvation."[247] In other words, Islam minimizes the reality of human sin to such an extent that for the Muslim there is no need for a savior. Each individual Muslim is said to have the ability to save himself. In his book, *One with God*, Kärkkäinen writes that when it comes to salvation issues, Islam and Christianity are at opposite poles. He says, "In Islam salvation is based on good works, whereas in Christianity salvation comes by faith in the righteousness of God."[248] As we have already seen with our overview of the early Islamic development of theology, this statement may be too simplistic. However, when we analyze the origin of sin in Islam, it will become apparent that there are crucial distinctions between Christianity and Islam. In addition, a number of reasons for the foundational differences between the two views on salvation will be clarified in this chapter.

## The Origin of Sin for a Muslim

It all begins in the garden of Eden. For Muslims, Eden was originally in heaven or Paradise. Adam was created here when Allah formed him from the clay and breathed his own spirit into man's soul (Q. 38:71-72). Eve was formed out of Adam, though the Qur'anic account does not explain how this took place. The Qur'an also does not name Adam's wife, though she is known by Muslims as "Hawa."

While in the garden, Allah taught Adam the names of the animals, which Adam learned with exceptional ability. Allah was pleased with his new creature and ordered all the angels to fall down to him in prostration. All the angels except one, Iblis, obeyed and prostrated themselves before Adam. Iblis refused to bow down to Adam, a mere man. The Qur'an says that Iblis was arrogant and thought he was better than man because he was

---

[247] Ron Rhodes, *Reasoning from the Scriptures with Muslims* (Eugene, Oregon: Harvest House, 2002), 233.

[248] Veli-Matti Karkkainen, *One with God: Salvation as a Deification and Justification* (Minnesota: Liturgical Press, 2004), 135.

created from fire instead of clay. For his arrogance, Allah eventually cast Iblis out of Paradise.

Allah gave Adam and Hawa freedom to eat any of the fruit in Paradise except from a certain tree that was forbidden to them. They were told not even to go near it. However, over time Iblis, while he was still in Paradise, continued to entice them to seek immortality by eating the fruit of the tree. As the days went by, Adam continued to think of the tree and living forever in paradise. At one weak moment, he forgot the warning from Allah, took some of the fruit and ate it together with Hawa. At once they realized that they had disobeyed Allah and they felt deeply ashamed. Adam pleaded with Allah to forgive him, and because Adam was sincere Allah relented and forgave him. However, the consequences of this action terminated their life in Paradise, and they were sent to the earth.

Muslims generally believe that Eden was just a testing ground and Allah always intended to send Adam and his wife to the earth. This relocation was not a punishment, however, since Allah had forgiven Adam of his transgression before sending him to earth. Adams' "sin" was that he had forgotten Allah's warning, and this led Adam to disobedience. However, this action did not have any effect on Adam's nature, nor did it affect the rest of the creation in any adverse way. Thus, because Adam could be restored to his position before Allah by asking for forgiveness and receiving Allah's mercy, there was no lingering curse on the rest of mankind. Adam may have taken a fall, but this did not result in the Fall of man and the rupture of man's relationship with God that Christians refer to as original sin.

Though there are similarities in the Muslim story of Adam with the Old Testament narrative, there are some fundamental differences. In fact, the view of sin portrayed in the Muslim narrative forms the watershed or the crucial dividing point between Christianity and Islam. All other major distinctions between the two religions, in regard to sin and salvation, stem from these foundational differences.

Not only is the view of salvation in Christianity diametrically opposite from Islam, but the definitions of sin and grace are dramatically different as well. The underlying difference is really the fact that Islam minimizes the impact of human sin to the point where a savior figure is no longer needed. Salvation can thus be earned or achieved by a Muslim, and the matter of sin and forgiveness are between the individual and God.

In order to gain a more complete picture of what sin and salvation mean to a Muslim, we will first survey the Muslim beliefs as they are expressed in four areas: the view of sin, the need for atonement, the place for good works and the assurance of salvation. Then, we will contrast these beliefs with the Christian view in order to clarify the similarities as well as the differences. In the end, it will be apparent how these opposite beliefs impact the two religions in fundamental ways.

# The Traditional View of Islam

### 1. View of Sin

According to the traditional Muslim view, which was recounted above, there is no original sin, and Adam instead made a mistake in forgetting the covenant he made with Allah. Likewise, all men after him commit sins due to weakness and forgetfulness, but this does not mean that they are depraved. Humans can live a righteous life by following Allah's law. As Geisler indicates, "whereas in Christian theology man's disobedience is viewed as a fundamental turning point in his relationship to God, according to the Muslim perspective this was only a single slip on Adam and Eve's part that was completely forgiven after their repentance."[249] Thus, unlike in the Christian version of the Fall, there was no effect on the nature of man or the rest of creation. Instead, Adam was expelled from Paradise to Earth, which means that mankind started from Paradise and is now trying to regain Paradise through their actions in the world. For Muslims, however, the transition from Paradise to earth was not a punishment, but rather a promotion to come down to earth to rule as God's viceroy. Although Adam disobeyed God after he repented of his "mistake" he was fully restored. As Kateregga declares, "Man is not born a sinner and the doctrine of the sinfulness of man has no basis in Islam."[250]

### Meaning of Sin for a Muslim

One of the words for sin in Arabic is *dharb*. It refers to any action that goes against the commands or wishes of Allah. Since it deals with a person's deeds, sin for a Muslim is an act and not a state of being. Though the Qur'an says that all people are prone to sin, Allah will be merciful to the ones who turn to him and repent of their sins: "The (human) soul is certainly prone to evil, unless my Lord do bestow His Mercy: but surely my Lord is Oft-forgiving, Most Merciful" (Q. 12:53). Therefore, sin is something that can be circumvented by discontinuing a certain action or avoiding temptation. In addition, since it is not considered a state of being, a person should be able to overcome sin on their own simply by living what the Qur'an and the culture consider an upright life. This means that a savior is not necessary

---

[249] Norman Geisler and Abdul Saleeb, *Answering Islam: The Crescent in Light of the* Cross (Grand Rapids, MI: Baker Books, 2002), 42.

[250] Badru Kateregga and David Shenk, *Islam and Christianity: A Muslim and a Christian in Dialogue* (Herald Press, 2011), 134.

for salvation. However, every Muslim must strive to overcome the sin in their life. These sins are categorized in various ways.

## Categories of Sin

This is a complex subject, and it can sometimes be confusing because Muslims will categorize sin in different ways. Most will follow tradition and divide sins into major and minor ones. However, others believe there are a number of gradations of sin. The least offensive to Allah would be **mistakes**[251] (caused by forgetfulness), then **immorality**,[252] **transgressions**,[253] and then **wickedness and depravity**.[254] The greatest sin, however, is ascribing a partner to God, which is called **Shirk**.[255] Some would say that the greatest sin is against Allah, then against the Brotherhood (other Muslims), and then against mankind as a whole. This would account for the degrees of punishment warranted in the Qur'an for punishment due to transgressors according to these gradations, with sins against Allah, such as Shirk (association of another being with Allah), and apostasy (rejecting Allah as the true God), being worthy of death. Sins against other Muslims would merit punishment ranging from death, to the loss of limbs (for stealing), to the loss of property or the payment of a fine. Sins against those outside the Muslim faith would often bring only minimal punishment.

Another way to categorize sins in Islam is found in the Hadith. For example, in Sahih Bukhari, one of the most important collections of the sayings of Muhammad, there are seven major sins (Al-Kaba'ir) listed:

> "Avoid the seven noxious things"- and after having said this, the prophet (saw) mentioned them: "associating anything with Allah; magic (equivalent to Witchcraft and Sorcery in English); killing one whom Allah has declared inviolate without a just case, consuming the property of an orphan, devouring usury, turning back when the army advances, and slandering chaste women who are believers but indiscreet."[256]

---

[251] ayyia, khatia (Suras 7:168; 17:31; 40:45; 47:19 48:2)

[252] itada, junah, dhanb (Suras 2:190,229; 17:17 33:55)

[253] haram (Suras 5:4; 6:146)

[254] ithm, dhulam, fujur, su, fasad, fisk, kufr: (Suras 2:99, 205; 4:50, 112, 123, 136; 12:79; 38:62; 82:14)

[255] (Sura 4:48)

[256] Al-Bukhari 6857.

However, according to 'Abdullah ibn 'Abbas "Seventy is closer to their number than seven," (and some references even say 700).[257] Here is a typical list of the seven deadly sins from the Qur'an:

1. Shirk – polytheism
2. Sihr – magic
3. Murder
4. Usury (charging interest)
5. Consuming wealth or property of orphans
6. Fleeing from battle
7. Accusing chaste women of adultery

**Some of the 70 would include**

- Not Praying
- Not paying Zakat
- Not fasting on a Day of Ramadan without excuse
- Not performing Hajj
- Fornication and Adultery
- Homosexuality (sodomy)
- Lying about Allah and His Messenger
- Pride and arrogance
- Drinking alcohol
- Gambling
- Frequent lying
- Giving and accepting bribes
- Breaking contracts
- Making statues
- Offending and abusing Muslims
- Offending people and having an arrogant attitude toward them

---

[257] Although this tradition is missing from the canonical Hadith collection, it is found in the Tafsir al-Tabari 9207.

- Persistently missing Friday Prayers without any excuse
- Deceiving and plotting evil
- Cursing or insulting any of the Companions of Allah's Messenger

In addition to this, all other transgressions would be considered "small faults," and as long as the major sins are avoided, and the minor sins do not persist and become major sins, then the minor sins will be forgiven by Allah.[258] This view seems to be supported in the Qur'an (Q. 4:31):

> Allah says, "*If you avoid the great sins [daba'ir or dharb – punishable in the afterlife] which you are forbidden to do, We shall remit from you your (small) sins [sayyi'a], and admit you to a Noble Entrance (i.e. Paradise).*

However, since there is no official list of the minor sins, these are interpreted in a variety of ways, and often there is confusion about how these transgressions should be dealt with.

A helpful guide that explains the complexity of views on sin in Islam was written by Ibn Hazm of Cordoba in the 11th century AD (994-1064). He called his list the "Five Precious Gifts" (Mawahib) that "ensured salvation except for those who are doomed."[259] He wrote that (1) Allah pardons minor sins (sagha'ir) as long as grave sins (kaba'ir) are avoided. (2) If Allah grants sincere repentance of grave sins before death, even if the sins are many, their grave sins will become void. (3) If good actions and evil actions are equibalanced, then they will not be held responsible for anything they have done. "The good deeds will drive away the evil deeds" (Q. 11:114). (4) Allah counts an evil action once and a good action ten times, and gives double measure to whom he pleases. (5) Even for those who die having done more evil than good, they can be released from eternal punishment after a time and be transferred to Paradise based upon the "strength of intercession."[260] Note that according to this view only the *kafir*, or infidels, would remain in hell after a period of punishment and payment for their sins. All the Muslims would eventually be released to Paradise.

## 2. Atonement or Salvation from Sin

Since humans can live a righteous life, Muslims believe there is no need for someone else to provide atonement or "save" them from sin. In Islam,

---

[258] See Shaykh al-Islam Ibn Taymiyah said in Majmoo' al-Fataawa (15/293)

[259] Ibn Hazm, Risalat al-Talkhis, 133-134.
[260] Camilla Adang, Maribel Fierro and Savine Schmidtke, *Ibn Hazm of Cordoba: The Life and Works of a Controversial Thinker* (Brill, 2013), 430.

one only needs to seek (tawbah) repentance, which means "to return." As the Qur'an states,

> O my Servants who have transgressed against their souls! Despair not of the Mercy of Allah: for Allah forgives all sins: for He is Oft-Forgiving, Most Merciful. Turn ye to our Lord (in repentance) and bow to His (will), before the Penalty comes on you: after that ye shall not be helped. (Q. 39:53)

Also, Rhodes adds that Allah "has no need to satisfy his own justice" since he can forgive out of his will.[261] Because of this, atonement cannot fit into the Muslim paradigm of sin and salvation because ultimately Allah's Will is inscrutable. Allah's law keeps a person on the straight path and the reward is Paradise.[262] Thus, it would make more sense to say that salvation in an Islamic context really only refers to the afterlife.[263] In this regard, Moucarry, a Syrian evangelical Christian and expert in Islamic studies, says that when Muslims "speak of salvation in Islam, what is meant is the way Muslims fulfill their religious obligations so that on the Day of Resurrection they escape God's judgment, receive forgiveness and enter paradise."[264] Even if a person fulfills all the good works and lives a good life, Allah may still say in the end that he will not accept the person into paradise. Muslims still hope in the mercy of Allah, however, believing that they can perform adequate works to merit his favor.[265]

### 3. Good works are thus sufficient

The Qur'an teaches that salvation, which is basically a reprieve from hell and acceptance into paradise, comes through pleasing Allah with good works. Good works outweigh bad works, so if sufficient good has been done, the believer will enter paradise:

And those whose scales are heavy [with good deeds] - it is they who are the successful. But those whose scales are light - those are the ones who have lost their souls, [being] in Hell, abiding eternally. (Q. 23:102-3).

Thus, Muslims would say that God's sovereignty and man's natural capacity to please him and do his will are the two elements which together bring about salvation.[266]

---

[261] Ron Rhodes, *Reasoning from the Scriptures with Muslims*, 235.
[262] Ibid., 233.
[263] Geisler and Saleeb, *Answering Islam*, 122.
[264] Chawkat Moucarry, *Faith to Faith: Christianity and Islam in Dialogue* (Inter-Varsity Press, 2001), 101.
[265] Ibid., 104.
[266] Ibid., 104.

J.P. Edwards explains that even in Islam sin will keep a person out of heaven. Sin must be atoned for, but this is required of individuals for their own sins.[267] In addition, "Atonement is not by sacrifice, but rather doing prescribed good deeds." (Q. 7:8-9). The greater weight of good deeds cancels out a person's bad deeds. However, no one will know if they have enough good works until the final judgment.[268]

Based on these components, the concept of Christian "grace" or God's unmerited favor resulting from a substitute (atonement) is unnecessary for salvation. Ironically, the concept of grace is seen as an affront to Allah's sovereignty and man's responsibility. Those who claim grace are said to only seek an easy way out of the duty of living a righteous life, and perhaps even jeopardize their afterlife in paradise (since they failed to live a life pleasing to Allah).

### 4. Assurance of Salvation

Finally, according to Moucarry, salvation in Islam has four components: faith, obedience, repentance and the Prophet's intercession on the last day.[269] In regard to faith, Muslims believe that having faith means that one assents to the truths revealed in the Qur'an. Some, such as Muhammad Abul Quasem, say there are two means of salvation: faith (*iman*) and action/works (*amal*). In addition, faith has three essential ingredients, "belief in the oneness of God, belief in the prophecy of Muhammad, and belief in life after death."[270] Others say there are five main objects for faith: belief in "God and his attributes, the prophets and their virtues, the angels, the sacred books, and the day of resurrection."[271] These beliefs represent most of the six core beliefs in Islam.

Secondly, Muslims believe in salvation through obedience, which is the observance of religious duties. Without obedience, however, there would be no faith. In this sense, faith is a function of obedience and is actualized through works. Works follow the five pillars of the confession of faith, prayer, fasting, almsgiving and hajj. This is why Quasem reminds his readers that, "Belief alone is not enough."[272]

---

[267] J.P. Edwards, "Sin and Its Solutions In Islam And Christianity," www.ciu.edu:Nov. 16, 2010, 3.

[268] Ibid., 3.

[269] Moucarry, *Faith to Faith*, 101. In Islam, similar terms regarding salvation are shared with Christianity, but the meaning is often quite different.

[270] Geisler and Saleeb, *Answering Islam*, 123.

[271] Ibid., 123.

[272] Muhammad Quasem in Geisler and Saleeb, *Answering Islam*, 123.

Thirdly, Muslims believe that repentance is necessary for salvation. Repentance means to turn away from sin and ask for forgiveness from Allah so that he would intercede for them (Q. 40:3). In a sense, without intercession (God's mercy) no one can be saved. This appears at first to be similar to the Christian view but is only superficially alike because in Islam Allah simply pardons sin. No sacrifice for sin is required. Therefore, Christ's death on a cross is not needed.[273] Some Muslims believe that Muhammad will be able to intercede for sinners, but intercession by Muhammad is based on Muhammad being the last prophet of God and is found only in the hadiths, not in the Qur'an.

Thus, salvation for Muslims is achieved by faith in Allah and his messenger, and ultimately by Allah's mercy (and perhaps the intercession of Muhammad or others). However, even faith in Allah and his mercy is measured by a person's good works outweighing their bad deeds to the extent that in a very real sense their salvation, or entrance into Paradise, is dependent on what they do or do not do. If God's mercy enters into the picture, it is mostly arbitrary. This often produces a fatalistic view of the future since Muslims neither know whether their good works will outweigh their bad works (there is no "cosmic scorecard" they can refer to), nor are they assured that God's mercy will save them from hell. Perhaps this is why some choose the path of active jihad, clinging to Muhammad's promise that if they are killed while fighting the infidel, they will gain instant entrance into Paradise (Q. 3:195, 2:244, 4:95).

In summary, in Islam there is no "original sin," but rather Adam merely made a "mistake" by forgetting the covenant he made with God. In this way, he did not commit a sin that transformed his nature. Therefore, men are responsible for their own "sins," which are committed because they are weak and forgetful, but not depraved. Atonement, then, or reconciliation with Allah, is not necessary in Islam because people are able to free themselves from the bondage of sin in their own strength (Q. 23.102-3). And even though it is understood that ultimately salvation is dependent on Allah's grace, which is capricious since he makes arbitrary decisions and he has no need to satisfy his own justice, most Muslims still hope that in the end they will end up in paradise. They may not have the assurance that Christians claim, but their dependence on good works at least gives them the sense that they are doing all they can on their own. The rest they leave up to Allah.

---

[273] Ibid., 4.

# Examination of Islamic View of Sin and Salvation

These four primary beliefs in Islam (the view of sin, the need for atonement, the place for good works and the assurance of salvation), are very different from those of Christianity, and these differences often leads to religious and even cultural clashes. However, there are also many similar aspects woven through the two contrasting religions. How does this fit together? The answer, perhaps, is that Islam may have adopted the outward characteristics of the Judeo-Christian religion, but substituted new foundational premises. The result is that the conclusions drawn from those premises are markedly different. This can be seen in the consideration of the human problem, also discussed as "sin and salvation." In the discussion above, the Islamic understanding of these issues starts with a root cause, offers a solution, and concludes with an optimal outcome: the problem of mankind is ignorance, which is solved by the guidance which Allah offers, and the intended result is success (in this life and the next). Christians, however, have a different set of premises and thus a different conclusion: The root problem of man is a sin nature that causes him to be disobedient, the solution is atonement or forgiveness through the substitutionary death of Christ, and the intended outcome is victory in terms of salvation.

These very different ways of defining "sin" thus lead to contrary understandings of God and salvation. As Mark Drurie says, "Whereas Islam sees the world as divided into winners (the rightly guided) and losers (the ignorant), in Christianity the world is divided into the lost (the unsaved) and the found (the saved)."[274] It is very important, therefore, to realize that when a Muslim and a Christian are discussing their faith, although they both use the words "sin," "grace," and "salvation," those words have completely different meanings depending on who is using them! In addition, while Islam sees ignorance as the human problem, Christianity sees sin as the real problem because it separates us from a holy God. Therefore, Muslims say they need guidance in order to have success, while Christians seek forgiveness in order to attain salvation.[275] Since their understandings of the human predicament are so different, their search for solutions will be very different as well. These dissimilar beliefs can be understood better when we compare the four areas involved: the view of sin, the need for atonement, the place for good works and the assurance of salvation.

---

[274] Durie, *The Third Choice*, 19.
[275] Ibid., 19.

# View of Sin

## Christian View

In Christianity, sin separates us from God and must be dealt with. However, man is incapable of redeeming himself from sins that are committed against God and therefore needs a divine savior who can atone for his sin and satisfy God's divine justice. Since this is beyond our ability, no amount of good works will be adequate to save us from eternal separation. Even the faith we need to accept Christ's atoning death is a gift from God through his grace, or unmerited favor. It is all the work of God. The Islamic view of humanity, however, does not acknowledge fallenness or depravity.[276] In Islam there is no conversion or regeneration, just remembering.[277]

Perhaps this is why Fazhur Rahman says that "For Islam, there is no particular "salvation": there is only "success [falāh]" or "failure [khusrān]" in the task of building the type of world order we are describing."[278] Faruqi even goes so far to say that, strictly speaking, salvation does not exist in Islam because it is not needed. Man has been endowed with all that is necessary to fulfill the divine will.[279]

### 1. In Christianity an atonement is necessary

Wayne Grudem defines Atonement as "the work Christ did in his life and death to earn our salvation."[280] Basically, Christians believe that God in his justice demands that there would be payment of the penalty for sin, which is death, and yet in his love God desires to forgive us for our sins and restore us to fellowship with him. As sinners worthy of death, we need a sinless advocate who by his own death could act as a substitute and pay the penalty for our sins. Jesus Christ is the only one who could do this. In a way, Jesus restored us to a righteous position where we enjoy an at-one-ment relationship with God instead of his wrath for our actions against him. Therefore, without the work of Christ on the cross on our behalf we could not be reconciled with God, nor would we be able to have any assurance of being with him in heaven.

In Islam, people believe they are able to free themselves from the bondage of sin in their own strength. In this belief there is a lack of

---

[276] Geisler and Saleeb, *Answering Islam*, 122.

[277] Ibid., 124. Quoted from Hasan Askar and Weibrecht Stanton.

[278] Fazlur Rahman, *Islam, 2nd Edition* (Chicago: University of Chicago Press, 1979), 63.

[279] Moucarry, *Faith to Faith*, 101.

[280] Wayne Grudem, *Bible Doctrine: Essential Teachings of the Christian Faith* (Zondervan, 1999), 248.

understanding the depth of our sins and total depravity of our souls. In regard to the rejection of total depravity, Geisler says that the Islamic view is not consistent with reality. He points out that even Muslims have to admit that human beings are sinful and the Qur'an attests to this: "if God were to punish men for their wrong-doing, He would not leave, on the earth, a single living creature" (Q. 16:61). Thus, Muslims would have to concur with the Bible which states that no one is righteous and sinless except Jesus, which the Qur'an also affirms (Q. 3:46, 19:19).[281]

Muslims also conclude that atonement is unnecessary because Allah makes arbitrary decisions. He says, "Let it be" and it is done. "He has no need to satisfy his own justice."[282] Thus, forgiveness is by Allah's will, not by justification. Perhaps this is why Moucarry says, "Islam does not acknowledge our moral downfall and consequently the necessity of our redemption."[283]

### 2. Good works are not enough

All other religions, in one way or another, set up a system that provides some kind of hope for eternal reward based on what committed followers do in their words, thoughts, and deeds. However, Christianity teaches that no amount of good works will ever be enough to pay the penalty for our sins because God's justice is higher than any of our deeds.

On the other hand, "salvation" according to the Qur'an is through pleasing Allah by good works (Q. 23:102-3). For a Muslim, this means that what you do is more important than who you are, whereas the focus in Christianity is on the inner being of man. Following this difference, Michael Youssef comments that, "the main emphasis in Islam is on external behavior, not the inward transformation of the heart, mind, and will. Islam is a religion of rituals and external acts – overt behavior that one must engage in with the hope of receiving Allah's favor."[284]

## Why Good Works?

Michael Youssef recognizes that "salvation" as Christians define it is not a concept that Muslims accept. Therefore, it may not be accurate to say that Muslims believe in a "salvation by works." According to the Qur'an, man is born into a natural state of purity (or "fitrah," Q. 30:30), and

---

[281] Norman Geisler, Answering Islam, 285.

[282] Rhodes, *Reasoning from the Scriptures*, 235.

[283] Moucarry, *Faith to Faith*, 110.

[284] Youssef, *Blindsided*, 85.

remains so until he makes himself guilty by doing a guilty deed (disobeying Allah).[285]

Therefore, since Islam does not view man as having a sinful nature, his nature does not need to be transformed.[286] This may be why the Palestinian-American philosopher, Ismail al-Faruqi, writes, "in the Islamic view, human beings are no more 'fallen' than they are 'saved.' Because they are not 'fallen,' they have no need of a savior. But because they are not 'saved' either, they need to do good works – and to do them ethically – which alone will earn them the desired 'salvation.'"[287]

Instead of "salvation" in a Christian sense, Faruqui believes religious justification is the motivating force for doing good works. Therefore, he claims that "only [the] works and deeds constitute justification in God's eyes." Thus, he believes it is not salvation by works, but rather religious justification by works that provides hope for Muslims. In other words, Muslims hope to escape hell by doing enough good works to justify themselves before Allah and gain his mercy.

However, Faruqui's explanation of justification still falls short because it focuses on the outward works of a person rather than the inward nature. This superficial "salvation" does not deal with sin as a part of man's essential nature and therefore excludes the need for forgiveness. Indeed, as Youssef points out, "according to Islam, forgiveness is not an essential part of Allah's nature."[288] However, if our sin nature truly separates us from a holy God, then without forgiveness there is no hope. Thus, this lack of forgiveness may be another reason for good works on the part of Muslims, because if they never experience the forgiveness of God, then all they have to justify themselves before Allah are the works that they do. This may be why Youssef concludes that "Muslims live their lives in fear of offending Allah and suffering an eternity in hell. The Muslim experience is an experience of continual spiritual anxiety because a Muslim can never be assured of having done enough good deeds and religious rituals to have earned acquittal before the eternal Judge." (Youssef, 85).

## The Muslim Dilemma

This lack of assurance leads to a very real existential crisis for many Muslims. They need more than just the hope that good works will gain Allah's favor. Some will conclude that Allah, in his mercy, will grant them

---

[285] Geisler, *Answering Islam*, 43.
[286] Youssef, *Blindsided*, 85.
[287] Isma'il al-Faruqi, *Islam* (Nils: Argus Communications, 1984), 9.
[288] Youssef, *Blindsided*, 85.

entrance into paradise, but their theology provides only a flawed view of grace and mercy. Therefore, they are left without a foundation to understand total forgiveness, creating an existential desire that cannot be fulfilled by their beliefs.

While Christians view Christ's sacrifice as the bridge between sin and grace, Muslims reject the concept of unmerited favor because they do not consider their natures to be corrupted or in need of transformation. In fact, Geisler reminds us that Islamic theology is "violently opposed to salvation by grace through faith, based on the crucified and risen Christ."[289] Thus, if they don't need a savior, then they must save themselves. Therefore, the need for good works comes in. When they realize that they cannot be assured that they will ever have enough good works, then their only resort is the mercy of Allah. However, mercy is a difficult concept since it lies too close to unmerited favor or "grace," a concept which leads naturally to the need for some kind of intercession and thus even a savior figure. But this goes against their entire theology of man's uncorrupted nature. Therefore, in the attempt to be their own savior, they are ultimately prevented from embracing the only savior who can truly save them from their sins. This is why Youssef writes that,

> "Even the most devout and pious Muslim has no assurance of winning Allah's favor and entering paradise. A Muslim could conceivably observe all the tenets of Islam throughout his or her life and still be rejected by Allah in the end. There is no assurance of salvation in Islam."[290]

## No assurance of Salvation

Comparatively speaking, then, the differing diagnoses of humanity's conditions are met with different solutions by each. As one Muslim puts it, "In Islam, humans are not seen as being in such a hopeless situation before God: we are seriously ill, but not spiritually dead."[291] However, as Edwards points out, "Islamic theology presents man with a more hopeful beginning, but a less assured end than Christianity, which robs men of all hope in themselves, but offers a guarantee of righteousness, peace, and paradise unmatched by Islam."[292] Thus, Christianity's solution for sin seems to both satisfy God's justice and bridge the gap between God's sovereignty and man's free will.

---

[289] Geisler, *Answering Islam*, 271.

[290] Youssef, *Blindsided*, 85.

[291] Moucarry, *Faith to Faith*, 101.

[292] J.P. Edwards, "Sin And Its Solutions In Islam And Christianity," www.ciu.edu:Nov. 16, 2010, 1.

## Muslims Reject Divine Justice

The "less hopeful beginning" and "more assured end" that Christianity offers hinges on a key concept that Islam fundamentally rejects: divine justice. This is the essential quality that Christians believe God possesses and which can only be satisfied by the atonement of a sinless savior. According to J.D. Greear, there are four reasons why Muslims reject the Christian's view of "divine justice." First of all, if Jesus' death on the cross is necessary to enable God to forgive, then God's power is limited. This implies that something must happen first before God can act, which limits God's actions and therefore, according to Islam, must be inaccurate. Second, it makes us more merciful than God since we can forgive without demanding a sacrifice, but God cannot. Third, Muslims do not believe that guilt can be transferred to someone else, even if Jesus were deity. Each person is responsible for his own destiny (Q. 6:164 and Q. 2:233). Fourth, Muslims do not believe that someone else can pay for sins. A person's sin must be weighed against one's good works. The individual must bear the weight of his own sins.[293] Clearly, Muslims and Christians define not only justice differently but also have different understandings of what it means to forgive, what mercy actually is, and the concept of payment or propitiation (a Latin term meaning to conciliate or appease a person or deity).

## Implications and Apologetic Conclusions

In conclusion, salvation for Muslims is achieved by faith in Allah and his messenger, and ultimately by Allah's mercy (and perhaps the intercession of Muhammad or others). However, even faith in Allah and his mercy is measured by a person's good works outweighing his or her bad deeds to the extent that in a very real sense their salvation, or entrance into paradise, is very dependent on what that person does or does not do. If God's mercy enters into the picture, it is mostly arbitrary. Therefore, there is no room for grace or the idea of atonement in this religious worldview. This often produces a fatalistic view of the future since Muslims neither know whether their good works will outweigh their bad works, (there is no "cosmic scorecard" they can refer to), nor are they assured that God's mercy will save them from hell. Perhaps this is why some choose the path of active jihad, clinging to Muhammad's promise that if they are killed while fighting the infidel, they will gain instant entrance into paradise (Q. 3:195, 2:244, 4:95).

This is why it is so important for Muslims to understand the biblical view of sin and salvation. Muslims need to understand the gravity of sin so

---

[293] J.D. Greear, *Breaking the Islam Code* (Harvest House, 2010), 61.

they will realize their need for a savior and their utter helplessness to save themselves. Without this realization, then it is very difficult to convince a Muslim of his need for Christ. Muslims need the grace of God and the Holy Spirit working in their lives. Otherwise, their dependency on their own works will lead to legalism, which is the natural outcome of the Islamic definitions of sin, grace, and salvation. Due to this focus, Muslims have no way of understanding the concept of grace as anything but a form of "cheating" on a divine test. Thus, Muslims view legalism positively because it is an outward sign of piety and hard work, while Christians view it negatively due to their theological definition of "grace," leading to further difficulties in dialogue between the two religions. How can we overcome these difficulties?

## Building Bridges to Understand

Works versus faith as the basis of salvation is understood very differently by Muslims and Christians. Every known religion in the world has one of two methods for finding favor in the eyes of the deity: good works that earn merit, or a free gift of grace (unmerited favor) from the deity to the human. Islam holds more of the former belief while Christianity holds only the latter. Surah 5:9 explains, "To those who believe and do deeds of righteousness hath Allah promised forgiveness and a great reward." This highlights well the combination of Allah's grace and the believer's works, which together save the Muslim from punishment in hell and reward him or her with divine favor.[294] However, this makes salvation ultimately more of a reward than the free gift the Bible teaches that it is. Ephesians 2:8-9 is a good verse to help explain this concept: "For by grace through faith you have been saved, not by works, so that no one can boast." Christians, therefore, believe that works flow out of a true believer in gratitude and obedience to God, but that those works cannot lend even the slightest benefit to their actual salvation since that is the free gift of God alone and is 100% reliant on him. Such a contrasting view of salvation can give a Christian the opportunity to point out God's gracious love and mercy. A good verse to share at this time is Romans 5:8, "but God shows his love for us in that while we were still sinners, Christ died for us." First, ask your Muslim friend how many good deeds would be sufficient enough to merit God's favor. Then, ask them what they think is God's greatest demonstration of love. Share with them Romans 5:8 and emphasize that God's greatest demonstration of love came through providing his Son, Jesus, as the payment for our sin. This provision is an act of God's grace

---

[294] In fact, technically a Muslim's good works must outweigh his evil deeds to earn him entrance to heaven, but Allah can will the Muslim's entrance despite a negative balance if he, Allah, so wills it.

that rules out any possibility that we could work for our salvation. It also assures Christians that they can never lose what they did not gain through their own works (John 10:28). This is the assurance that your Muslim friend would very much like to have. Therefore, it is very important to be sensitive to this need and share with them the hope that you have.

Finally, it may be helpful to bring in the verse from the Qur'an on crucifixion (Q. 4:157) and use it to compare the Muslim denial of the crucifixion with the Christian belief that without a crucifixion there cannot be a death that paid our debt. We would then still be in our sins with no escape from hell. If God is the only one who can pay the price for our sins, and no amount of good works will be enough, then we begin to see how much Christian salvation rests on the good work of Christ on the cross. Because Jesus did the work and paid the penalty, we can "merit" our salvation through his substitution on the cross. Muslims cannot understand how God would die in our place for the sins that we committed. Yet, this radical love is exactly what Muslims need to know in order to experience assurance in their own lives.

### Study Questions:

1. What was the origin of sin according to the Muslim sources? How is the concept of sin different from the Christian view of sin?

2. If the foundations are faulty, then the beliefs are faulty as well. What are some of the faulty foundations Muslims have about sin and how does this affect their resulting beliefs and actions?

3. Why do Muslims put so much emphasis on doing good works? In the end, do the good works bring assurance of their salvation? Why or why not?

4. Islam teaches that the root cause of our problems is ignorance, which can be solved by Allah's guidance. A Christian believes that the root cause of our problems is a sin nature that causes us to be disobedient. The solution is atonement or forgiveness through the substitutionary death of Christ, and the intended outcome is victory in terms of salvation. Muslims, however, do not really seek salvation. What is it that Muslims seek and how is this an insufficient goal?

5. Given that Muslims do not have assurance that they will be accepted by Allah into Paradise, how can this dilemma be used to help them understand why the Christian view of the sin problem and its solution is the only reasonable belief?

# CHAPTER 10 Eschatology: Waiting for the Mahdi or the Messiah?

## Introduction

Dr. Michael Youssef, who studied Islamic movements at Emory University, claims that for almost fourteen hundred years the main goal of Islam has been to conquer the world and bring all people under the subjugation of Islam.[295] This may seem like a bold statement, but a number of scholars point out that this view can be clearly evidenced in the Qur'an, the Hadith, the commentaries, and the writings of Muslim scholars from the very beginning up to the present.[296] It is also evidenced in the type of expansion that has taken place and can be seen even in the recent migrations from Islamic countries into the non-Muslim West. Another author, Joel Richardson, in his book *The Islamic Antichrist*, contends that,

> In order to understand Islam properly, one must understand the way that Islam understands itself. Islam views itself as the only true religion - indeed the only religion worthy to be practiced. As such Islam has as one of its goals, total world domination. Islam's driving goal is to literally eradicate what it sees as the false and misplaced worship of all other religions. Until the day that everyone says, "none has the right to be worshipped other than Allah," Islam will continue its fight against unbelievers and unbelieving nations.[297]

This goal of Islam to build a world empire may not be something that is laid out in a single document, but it can be demonstrated through various writings of Muslims over the centuries. For example, in one of the hadiths, Bukhari wrote that Allah's Apostle (Muhammad) said, "I have been ordered to fight the people till they say: 'None has the right to be worshipped but Allah.'"[298] The Qur'an states, "Fight those from among the people of the Book, who believe not in Allah, nor in the Last Day, nor hold as unlawful what Allah and His Messenger have declared to be unlawful, nor follow the true religion, until they pay the tax considering it a favor and

---

[295] Youssef, *Blindsided*, 101.

[296] William Wagner, *How Islam Plans to Change the World* (Grand Rapids, MI: Kregel, 2004).

[297] Joel Richardson, *The Islamic Antichrist: The Shocking Truth about the Real Nature of the Beast* (Los Angeles: WND Books, 2009), 138.

[298] Sahih Bukhari Volume 9, Book 84, Number 59, Narrated Abu Huraira.

acknowledge their subjection" (Q. 9:29). This is followed by Surah 9:33 which states, "He it is Who sent His Messenger with guidance and the religion of truth, that He may make it prevail over every other religion." Ibn Khaldun, a 14th-century Muslim historian wrote, "In the Muslim community, the holy war is a religious duty, because of the universalism of the (Muslim) mission and (the obligation to) convert everybody to Islam either by persuasion or by force."[299] The 20th-century Islamic scholar, Al Mawdudi, said this about global domination: "Islam is not a normal religion like the other religions in the world, and Muslim nations are not like normal nations. Muslim nations are very special because they have a command from Allah to rule the entire world and to be over every nation in the world."[300] Finally, Omar Ahmed, a former Chairman of the Board of CAIR (Council on Arab-Islamic Relations), a Muslim civil rights and advocacy group, boasted that "Islam isn't in America to be equal to any other faith, but to become dominant. The Quran should be the highest authority in America, and Islam the only accepted religion on earth."[301] In his book titled *How Islam Plans to Change the World*, William Wagner says the premise of his book is simple: "Islam is a world religion with a well-defined culture and a developed strategy for taking control of the world."[302]

Christianity is a religion that calls sinners to surrender willingly to a God who loves them, while Muhammad and his followers encourage the spread of Islam by force. At this point, someone may raise the objection that Christians say, "we will win the world to Christ," so what is the difference? A key difference is that Jesus Christ came and died in our place so that all who believed in him would have eternal life. In Matthew 11:28-30 Jesus said, "Come to me, all you who are weary and burdened, and I will give you rest. Take my yoke upon you and learn from me, for I am gentle and humble in heart, and you will find rest for your souls. For my yoke is easy and my burden is light." In other words, Jesus comes as the "Prince of Peace," while Islam advocates constant war until all people submit to Allah.[303]

The bigger question may be, "who will win?" Samuel P. Huntington, in his 1993 article, "Clash of Civilizations," predicted the present conflict

---

[299] Ibn Khaldun, *The Muqaddimah*, trans. by Franz Rosenthal (New York: Pantheon Books Inc., 1958) Vol. 1:473

[300] Mark A. Gabriel, *Islam and Terrorism* (Lake Mary Florida, Charisma House 2001), 81.

[301] Report in the San Ramon Valley Herald of a speech to California Muslims in July 1998; quoted in Pipes, *CAIR: Moderate Friends of Terror*, New York Post, April 22, 2002.

[302] Wagner, *How Islam Plans to Change the World*, 11-12.

[303] However, in the Second Coming, the Bible teaches that Jesus will overcome all of his foes.

we now have between the Christian West and Islam and put forth the view that Islamic extremism would become the biggest threat to world peace.[304] Huntington received harsh criticism for his thesis shortly after his book came out in 1996, but after the turmoil of these last 20 years, the conflict between Christianity and Islam seems to be growing in intensity.[305] Michael Youssef, in his book *Blindsided*, argues that "Militant Islamists view Christianity as the foremost foe of Islam" and then outlines four primary reasons why the clash of these two religions is taking place at this time.[306] First, Islamic militants assume that Christian values pervade Western society the way Muslim ideology pervades Islamic society. Therefore, they assume that the perverse values and practices that pervade Hollywood and the corrupt business world must be the result of Christian influences on the society. Second, Islamic militants see Christianity as the dominant force in the Western world, and therefore, if Christianity can be subdued or eradicated, then Islam will be able to easily subdue the West for Allah. Third, Muslims view our Western tolerance, our lenient immigration rules, and our "politically correct" suicidal decisions that seek to destroy the very fabric of America as weaknesses that will allow them to exploit the West, infiltrate our government, and undermine our society. In regard to this point, Joel Richardson tells of a Muslim who stood up in the midst of a dialogue with Christians and said, "Thanks to your democratic laws, we will invade you. Thanks to our religious laws, we will dominate you."[307] Fourth, Islamic extremists blame the Christian West for many of the problems that plague the Middle East today, such as poverty, civil unrest, and oppression, as well as the introduction of anti-Islamic features of American culture. The greatest blame, however, is reserved for America's continued support for Israel.[308]

Coming from a similar perspective, William Wagner, a missionary strategist, and religious scholar, believes that Islam has a three-pronged strategy that guides many of the movements: "Jihad (holy war), Da'wah (missions), and mosques (presence)."[309] Jihad is used in order to engage the West on the battlefield, Da'wah in the public arena, and mosques in the religious circles. The key to bringing these three initiatives together seems to be found in Islamic Eschatology, or the views of the end times. In a sense, Islam has always been a religion that looked to the end in order to shape

---

[304] Samuel P. Huntington, "The Clash of Civilizations?" Foreign Affairs, Vol. 72, No.3 Summer, 1993), 22-49.

[305] http://www.e-ir.info/wp-content/uploads/Clash-of-Civilizations-E-IR.pdf

[306] Youssef, *Blindsided*, 102-3.

[307] Richardson, *Islamic Antichrist*, 145; Abdullah Al-Araby, *The Islamization of America: The Islamic Strategy and the Christian Response* (Booklocker.com, 2003), 8.

[308] Youssef, *Blindsided*, 102-103.

[309] Wagner, *How Islam Plans to Change the World*, 12.

the present, for the Qur'an promised that it is in the next life that followers would be rewarded, and fantasies fulfilled. This is also one of the reasons that Muslim suicide bombers willingly volunteer to sacrifice their lives to kill the infidel, for Islamic traditions promise that the one sure way to enter Paradise is through "martyrdom."[310] Radical Muslims will say, "We love death while you love life," with the point being that this is the reason that they will win in the end. What is it about their view of the end times that could persuade them to destroy their own lives, as well as the lives of others, in order to gain what they consider the greatest good? What does their Eschatology teach and how does it impact their goal for domination?

Islamic prophecy points to a small town in Syria, called "Dabiq," as the site of Armageddon, or the last battle, for the Muslims. They believe that the "armies of Rome," represented by the US forces together with the coalition of Western nations, will be vanquished once and for all leaving the world open to Muslim dominance.[311] This is why ISIS wanted to draw the United States into the battle for Iraq and Syria. The Muslim leaders were confident that they would succeed in fulfilling the prophecy found in the Hadith.[312] What is more, the followers of ISIS believe that they will be able to make this happen and therefore set the stage for the final act in history. They hope to bring about the resurrection and the day of judgment that will separate Muslims from non-Muslims, those who go to their reward in Paradise, and those who will be punished forever in the fires of Hell (Jahannam). The danger of ISIS, then, is not that the end times are imminent, but that the leaders of ISIS believe they have an active role in bringing these things about.

It is important to note that most Muslims that we meet in America are similar to us in their values and they may deny that Islam seeks to be the only religion in the world They may also refute the belief that the goal of Islam, especially evidenced by their eschatology, seeks to rid the world of all Christians before the end comes. Thus, they would probably claim that ISIS has a wrong view of the end times. However, the beliefs of ISIS support many features that most Muslims believe and follow. More importantly, the views of ISIS are supported by the Qur'an and the Hadith. This chapter will examine the predominant beliefs of Muslims in regard to the end times and then compare them with the beliefs of Christianity.

---

[310] See Qur'an 4:74; 9:111; Sahih Bukhari 52:54; 52:46; 20:4678; 20:4655.
[311] Sahih Muslim 2897, Book 54, Hadith 44.
[312] Glenn Beck, *It IS About Islam* (Simon and Schuster, 2015), 19.

## The Traditional View

Eschatology has to do with those things that cover both what will happen after death as well as the events that will lead up to the end of time. Doctrinally, Muslims do not view this life as the end, but rather the beginning of the next life. Thus, what is done in this life is very important because it will determine, to some extent, the destination of the afterlife. Christians and Muslims do share some of the views concerning the end times. For example, in both religions Jesus plays a central role when he returns at the end. Muslims also hold similar views as Christians regarding judgment in that they believe in a resurrection of the good and the evil (Muslims and non-Muslims), that we all will face the final judgment, and that eternal life in Heaven (Paradise) will be reserved for the saved, and Hell for the lost. There are also some major differences, as will be detailed later in the chapter. In addition, there are some differences between the Sunni and the Shiah views, especially in regard to their messiah figure who is known as the Mahdi. Shias believe that he will be the 12th Imam following Ali's line and Sunnis believe that he will make himself known by his great leadership skills and devotion to Allah. In the end, though, both look to the Qur'an and the Hadith to support their views on the events that will take place.

One of the primary questions involves what happens after death. What happens when a Muslim dies? What are the steps involved? First of all, the Qur'an (56:83) says that the soul of the dying person comes to their throat and two angels, named Munkar and Nakir, come to remove the soul from the body. They will ask three questions: "Who is your God?" (answer: Allah); "Who is your prophet?" (answer: Muhammad); and "What is your faith?" (answer: Islam). Answering correctly is all-important because the answers will determine what will happen to the body as it awaits the resurrection. Believers who answer correctly will be comforted in the grave, but non-believers will be tormented. However, knowing the answers to the questions will still not assure a person's final destiny, for that cannot be known in Islam. Even Muhammad prayed often that he would be kept from punishment in the afterlife.[313]

While the order of the major end time events are not always clear in the Qur'an and the Hadith, they are generally marked by a series of signs, both major and minor.[314] One of the most important signs is that a great leader of the family of Muhammad, known as the Mahdi, will return (from

---

[313] Bukhari, volume 2, book 23, # 454 and 456.

[314] Dr. Samuel Shahid wrote a book called *The Last Trumpet*. He attempts to show that the major concepts of Islamic eschatology were borrowed from the Hebrew Scriptures, the Christian New Testament, and the concepts of Zoroastrianism.

hiding or just emerge from among the people) and come into power. He will bring "justice and true belief" just at the end of time.[315] He will be the final caliph and usher in the beginning of the end times, and Jesus (Isa) will then come back from heaven and aid the Mahdi in a series of great battles. Their primary enemy will be the false Messiah, known as the Dajjal. In time, the Jesus (Isa) defeats the Dajjal, and the remaining Christians will be persuaded to become Muslims because the Jesus (Isa) will abolish the Jizyah, the head tax on non-Muslims, and thus reduce the choices to either conversion or death. The Mahdi continues the process of spreading Islam, bringing an age of defeat for all other religions and military success for Muslims. The Madhi and Jesus (Isa) build the new kingdom of Islam together, ushering in a time of Islamic dominance. Afterward, it is said that Jesus (Isa) will get married, have children, and reign gloriously for 40 years before dying a natural death. His death will be the last event before the Judgment Day. These ideas originated from the Hadith, but the account developed its current form during the time of the Abassid Empire (200-300 years after Muhammad's death).[316]

Many minor signs of the end times are also mentioned in the Hadith, including: women outnumbering men 50 to 1, the Arabs conquering Constantinople (Istanbul), Mecca being reduced to ruins; an increase in ignorance about the faith, the arising of false prophets; an increase in wars, and calamities arising that cause people to long for death.[317] The last four signs are clearly similar to Christianity and are more typical examples of end times in other traditional religions. Others, such as the first three, are unique to Islam and are more unusual in their claims.

All of this leads up to Judgment Day, also known as the Day of Reckoning. There are many different versions of exactly what will happen, but the main idea is that all people are resurrected and separated into those who are Muslims and non-Muslims – the latter will be cast into Hell and the Muslims will then be judged according to their works. Part of this process involves crossing a razor-sharp bridge called the Bridge of Sirat. Those who safely reach the other side will find themselves in Paradise, but those whose sins are too great will fall off and find themselves in Hell unless the mercy of Allah intervenes. Those who cross successfully will then gather at the Pool of the Prophet where Muhammad will begin to intercede with Allah for the faithful so that they can enter Paradise. When they enter Paradise or *Jannah* in Arabic, they will find everything they long for in this

---

[315] see "Mahdi" entry in Oxford Dictionary of Islam. John L. Esposito, ed., *The Oxford Dictionary of Islam* (Oxford University Press, 2003).

[316] http://christinprophecy.org/articles/islamic-eschatology/ (accessed 1/1/19). See also Joel Richardson, *The Islamic Antichrist*, 31-32, 58-59, 71-75.

[317] http://christinprophecy.org/articles/islamic-eschatology/ (accessed 1/1/19).

life. According to the Muslim view, Paradise will have seven levels with the most faithful Muslims dwelling at the highest level.[318]

Paradise is described as a beautiful garden with every delight imaginable, and where everyone will be happy and fulfilled (Q. 13:23-24). Believers will be surrounded by family and friends and will also be served by beautiful eyed maidens that will meet their every need (Q. 55:56-7; 56:35-8). There will be food of every kind, rivers of water, milk, honey, and wine that will not intoxicate (Q. 56:11-24), and delicious fruits of all kinds. Muslims also point to a verse in the Qur'an that indicates that on the Day of Resurrection some will see God, which they believe will be a joy that surpasses all others (Q. 75:22-23). The unbelievers, on the other hand, will not see God but will be cast into the fires of Hell for eternity.

The hope of Muslims is that they are found obedient to Allah, so that they may reap the rewards of a life of service to him and to one another. Fear is seen as a motivating factor, even a healthy one, pushing the believer to work hard and trust in Allah's mercy for the end of days. Some Muslims are even saying that the rise of the caliphate and the disintegration of the West already mark the beginning of the end.[319] Others believe that this is the time when Islam will bring the New Order (new era) to the whole world ushered in by the Muslim Mahdi (messiah), and the Muslim Jesus (Isa al-Masih), who will both work together to battle against the Muslim antichrist, who is known as the Dajjal. Together, these three major signs are thought to indicate the beginning of the end. This is why it is important to examine these three figures in more detail.

## The Mahdi

The first of the major signs refers to the Mahdi, or the "Guided One." He is the central figure in the Islamic end-time scenario and is universal among both Sunni and Shia Muslims.[320] The Mahdi is Islam's messiah, or savior, and his appearance is comparable to the return of Jesus Christ for Christians. Interestingly, in a Pew article published in 2012, the number of Muslims in the world who believed the Mahdi would return in their lifetime was over 50%.[321] According to the Hadith and other traditions, the Mahdi will descend from the family of Muhammad (through Fatima) and will

---

[318] http://christinprophecy.org/articles/islamic-eschatology/ (accessed 1/1/19); http://aboutislam.net/counseling/ask-about-islam/islam-armageddon-end-times/.

[319] Beck, *It IS About Islam*, 21.

[320] Richardson, *The Islamic Antichrist*, 22-23.

[321] http://www.pewforum.org/2012/08/09/the-worlds-muslims-unity-and-diversity-3-articles-of-faith/ (accessed 7/25/18)

fulfill a number of prophecies. He will be a devout Muslim, and will be viewed as an "unparalleled spiritual, political, and military world leader."³²² As the final caliph of Islam, the Mahdi will lead a revolution to establish a new world order. At this time, the traditions state that the Mahdi will lead his army from the east and they will conquer Israel carrying the black flag.³²³ After killing many Jews, Jerusalem will serve as the center of Islamic rule in the world.³²⁴ During this time of the Mahdi's reign, a peace agreement will be made between the Muslims and the West, mediated through a Jew from the priestly class, for a period of seven years. At the end of the seven-year period, after the Mahdi has caused Islam to be the only religion practiced on the earth, he will then die.

## The Muslim Jesus

The coming of the Muslim Jesus is the second most important event among major signs. According to Islam, Jesus is not God in the flesh/the Son of God. Rather, they do not believe that Jesus ever died on a cross for the sins of mankind.³²⁵ Instead, Muslims believe that he ascended to heaven and remains alive with Allah. He will return again to finish his ministry and complete his life. He is not considered a savior, merely a prophet in the long line of prophets. For example, the Qur'an states in 43:59 that Jesus "was no more than a servant: We granted Our favor to him, and We made him an example to the Children of Israel." (43:59) Muslims also believe that his return will not be to restore the nation of Israel to the Jewish people. Rather, he will come back and declare himself to be a Muslim, perform the pilgrimage to Mecca (hajj), oversee the enforcement of Islamic sharia law throughout the world, and lead many Christians to convert to Islam. He will also testify against those who called him Son of God and abolish Christianity through three specific acts: he will break crosses (meaning that he will abolish the worship of the cross and eliminate all other religions except Islam); he will kill all swine (meaning that he will mandate sharia accepted food); and he will abolish the Jizyah tax, which was the price that non-Muslims had to pay in order to be classified as protected citizens. This also means that the only choices remaining for Christians will be to accept Islam or die.

---

[322] Richardson, *The Islamic Antichrist*, 31.

[323] Richardson, *The Islamic Antichrist*, 25-6. Tirmidhi, as quoted by Zubair, *Signs of Qiyyamah*, 42.

[324] Muhammad ibn Izzat and Muhammad Arif, *Al Mahdi and the End of Times* (Dar Al Taqwa Ltd., 1997), 40.

[325] The Qur'an denies that he was ever crucified (Q. 4: 157).

Some of the hadith state that Jesus' return will take place at "the white minaret in the eastern side of Damascus"[326] during the time of prayer. The Mahdi will ask Jesus to lead the prayers, but Jesus will defer to the Mahdi, indicating that his role is to support the Mahdi.[327] They will then work together to make Islam the only religion practiced throughout the world. During this time Jesus will kill the Dajjal, the Muslim antichrist (or anti-Mahdi), and bring peace to the world. The traditions also state that Jesus will get married, have children and, after forty years, die a natural death. He will then be buried next to the prophet Muhammad.[328]

## The Dajjal, Islam's Antichrist

The third primary character in Islamic eschatology is known as Al-masih Ad-Dajjal (the messiah, the deceiver). The traditions relate that he will be given great powers to do miracles in order to deceive people. Traditions also describe him as blind in one eye[329] and having the word "kafir"[330] (infidel, unbeliever) written between his eyes (on his forehead), which only true Muslims will see.[331] He will also claim to be divine, even claiming to be God himself.[332] Therefore, Muslims believe that he will impersonate Jesus Christ in order to deceive people and turn them away from Islam. They also believe that he will recruit an army made up mostly from the Jews and fight against the Mahdi and the Muslim Jesus. However, the Muslim Jesus will kill the Dajjal and establish peace on the earth.[333]

Once the Dajjal has been dealt with and the entire population of the world has submitted to Allah, then the Day of Reckoning will come. Everyone who has ever lived will be resurrected in a physical body, joined with their soul, and gathered together at the place where they will be judged by Allah. Those who have faithfully followed Allah, or gained his favor, will be set aside to prove their faith by making it over the razor-thin bridge of Sirat and to gain entrance into Paradise. Those who have opposed the will of Allah will be cast into the fires of Hell for eternal torment. When it comes to the end, every Muslim wants to be on the side of Allah, and

---

[326] Sahih Muslim, book 041, #7015.
[327] Muslim, book 001, #0293.
[328] Dawud, Book 37, #4310.
[329] Sahih Muslim, 041, #7005.
[330] K, F, R – assumed but not written out.
[331] Muslim, 041, #7009.
[332] Philips, *Ad-Dajjal*, found in Richardson, *The Antichrist*, 73.
[333] Sahih Muslim, 041, #6924

when the end determines the beginning of eternal life in Paradise or in Hell, then it becomes everything.

## 12th Imam

There is one other area of prophecy concerning the end times that needs to be discussed. Although there are many similarities between the beliefs of the Sunni and Shia Muslims, there are also some distinctions that need to be understood. For example, one of the main differences between Sunni and Shia Muslims in regard to the end times is that Sunnis believe the Mahdi has not yet been born, and therefore his identity is not yet known. At the right time, they believe Allah will have the Mahdi appear in order to initiate peace and justice throughout the world. The Muslim Jesus (Isa) will appear at that time as well to join the Mahdi in preparing the world for the Day of Judgment.[334]

However, for 85% of the Shia who call themselves "Twelver Shia," the Mahdi is known as Muhammad ibn Hassan al-Mahdi and is the 12th Imam in the line of the 4th Caliph, Ali ibn Talib. Therefore, according to the traditions, he would be a direct descendant of Muhammad through his daughter Fatima. He is said to have been born in 869 AD, and *Twelvers* believe he is still alive in a period of hiding, or occultation until the time is right for his appearance. At a time of great chaos, tyranny, and suppression, the 12th Imam will emerge as the messiah, along with the Muslim Jesus, to fulfill the mission of bringing peace by establishing Islam as the dominant faith throughout the world. There are a number of Middle Eastern leaders, such as the former Iranian President Mahmoud Ahmadinejad, and the present Grand Ayatollah Khamenei, who are strong followers of the 12th Imam. They believe they can hasten the return of the Mahdi through an apocalyptic event, such as the destruction of Israel. They also believe it is the responsibility of the government to prepare the way for the Mahdi.[335]

## Conclusion of The Traditional View

For the most part, the average Muslim has a minimal understanding of what is supposed to happen in the end according to the traditional beliefs. They are often more concerned with their individual eschatology rather than the universal eschatology of the theologians and scholars. In regard to their individual eschatology, Muslims are very much aware that

---

[334] Beck, *It Is About Islam*, 24-25.

[335] Beck, *It Is About Islam*, 24-25; see also http://www1.cbn.com/onlinediscipleship/12th-imam-key-facet-of-islamic-prophecy-fuels-middle-east-turmoil

they are responsible for doing everything they can in order to avoid Allah's displeasure so that they will have a better chance of making it to Paradise. Paradise itself is usually described as a beautiful extension of all the good things on the earth, and they know that they need to do all that they can in order to merit entrance to this realm after death. The bigger picture that makes up universal eschatology is often pushed to the periphery of their beliefs, except where it overlaps with their obligations to follow the Qur'an and the will of Allah, for they believe their individual destiny is often determined by how well they succeed in carrying out the universal goals of Islam. The universal eschatology revolves around the three major signs: the Mahdi, the Muslim Jesus, and the Dajjal. These figures dominate the events of the end times and mark the progression of the events themselves. The focal point of all these events is to demonstrate that Islam will eventually gain control of the whole world and bring everything under the rule of Allah. Once this has been secured, the judgment will come with those who believe in Allah hoping to gain a place in Paradise, while those who have rejected him will find their eternal abode in Hell.

This next section will deal with a critical examination of the claims of Muslims in regard to events they believe will occur in the future and a comparison of the three main figures from both the Muslim and the Christian perspective. This comparison will reveal that even though there are some similarities in their understanding the events of the end times, the actual evidence reveals that the main figures involved are diametrically opposite in their character, intent, and ultimate role.

## Counterviews

Before dealing with comparisons of eschatology between Islam and Christianity, it will be helpful to discuss several areas of concern regarding the formation of Muslim views regarding end time events. The first area of concern involves the reliability of the Islamic sources. While the Qur'an discusses judgment, Paradise, and Hell, it does not mention the coming of the Mahdi or false messiah or similar details about the end times. Rather, many of these elements are from the Hadith and offer less-than-substantial proof of their literary veracity. A number of the views contradict each other; many can also be traced from other extant religious traditions and from folklore. All of this makes it difficult to know how much it is reasonable to trust these sources, casting doubt on the cohesion of the entire eschatology of Islam. Shrouding the end point of life and the world in superstition and a less-than-substantiated revelation make it difficult to reconcile these doctrines of judgment, Paradise, and Hell with the larger claims of Islam.

## Copy Cat Religion

A different concern involving the sources of Islam may suggest that many of the traditions describing the events of the end times have been copied from, or influenced by, earlier religions such as Judaism, Christianity, Zoroastrianism, and even paganism.[336] While this could be argued to be the Islamic "correction" of corrupted sources, it is an equally plausible explanation that the Hadith borrowed heavily from these sources and intermixed them to make a new account. It could have borrowed from Judaism a lot of stories of the prophets in the Old Testament, and from Christianity the stories of Jesus and Mary, though these stories are often distorted and retold in an Arabized fashion. Some of this material focuses on end-time events, such as the return of the Muslim Jesus, but it is from Zoroastrianism that many of the traditions that relate to the Islamic end times are found.

Zoroastrianism is from Persia (modern day Iran) and has roots that go back to the time of Moses and even Abraham. Zoroastrianism contains well-developed traditions that deal with end time events, such as the appearance of a savior, the resurrection of the dead, victory over evil with reward in Paradise and rejection in a fiery Hell when the world is judged by the one supreme God.[337]

For example, in regard to individual eschatology, Zoroastrians believe that at death there are two spiritual creatures waiting by the dead body with the evil one trying to drag the soul off to Hell and the good one protecting the person's soul. The soul is taken to a bridge that it must cross in order to get into Paradise. The bridge, called "Chinvat," will be broad and comfortable for the righteous and narrow and perilous for the wicked one. It is at this point that the souls are assigned to Paradise or Hell, or a possible middle state, according to their works in this life. In regard to universal eschatology, Zoroastrians believe that during resurrection the physical body is united to the soul. These events are very similar to the events now described in Muslim traditions. In addition, the concept of the maidens of Paradise, al-hurs, or the houris, may have come from Zoroastrianism.[338] The fires of Hell are a common theme in Zoroastrian eschatology and they also play a dominant role in motivating Muslims to stay on the "straight path." Some other practices that may have been adopted from Zoroastrianism are the five daily prayers (Jews had three per

---

[336] See Samuel Shahid, *The Last Trumpet* (Xulon Press, 2005).

[337] http://www.cais-soas.com/CAIS/Religions/iranian/Zarathushtrian/z_influence_abrahamic.htm; Encyclopedia Iranica, www.iranicaonline.org/articles/eschatology.

[338] Encyclopedia Iranica, www.iranicaonline.org/articles/eschatology.

day), the call to prayer, the ablution before prayer, a covering for the head during prayer, and a direction to face during prayer. There is also a story of a night journey to heaven described in Zoroastrian literature, one which existed well before the time of Muhammad and his particular night journey from Mecca to Jerusalem where it is believed he ascended up into heaven for a visit.[339]

The implication of all of this is that if many of the eschatological views in Islam come from other religions, then how can it be viewed as the only correct view? If many of these ideas were patterned after the traditions of other religions, then this would indicate that either Muslims borrowed many of their ideas from other religions, meaning that Islam is a man-made religion, or, as Muslims would argue, Islam communicates the corrected view and therefore should be the only view represented.

## 72 Virgins in Paradise

One of the main criticisms of the Islamic view of individual eschatology is that Paradise is often portrayed as a man's sexual playground with a bevy of virgins created by Allah to satisfy every man's desires. Other than the celestially created "maidens" with large, beautiful eyes, wives and daughters are scarcely mentioned in the narratives of Paradise. Indeed, there are some hadith that relate one of Muhammad's visions of Hell where he states that most of the inhabitants were women.[340] So, the question often arises, "What do women have to look forward to in a Paradise made to satisfy men's desires?" In contrast, one of the chief replies from Christians when they are asked about their views on heaven is that they "want to see Jesus." One of the focal points for Christians seems to be the physical presence of God among his people, whereas the Muslim Paradise seems to be a place where many of the forbidden things of this world will be paramount in Paradise. For example, if marital fidelity is expected on earth, then how can promiscuity be something that is promoted in the afterlife? Yet, this seems to be one of the foundational characteristics of the Muslim Paradise.

One question that comes up often in regard to jihad concerns the promise of 72 beautiful, black-eyed perpetual virgins as wives in Paradise to Muslim men who die in battle against the infidel. This promise even applies to the "shahid" (martyr) who commits suicide in order to kill non-

---

[339] https://www.mythicistmilwaukee.com/mythicistmilwaukeeblog/2014/12/11/islam-zoroastrianism-parallels (accessed 1/1/2019).
[340] al-Bukhari vol. 4:464, vol. 2:161; Muslim, vol. 1:143, 147.

Muslims or other Muslims who are deemed to be heretics.[341] They are told that they will go straight to heaven and their reward will be pleasures beyond belief, including the service of 72 virgins (known as the houri, pl. hur). The Qur'an, hadith and Islamic scholars all mention that virgins will be awarded to Muslim men in Paradise. For example, the word "hur" is used only four times in the Qur'an, in the passages 44:54, 52:20, 55:72, and 56:22, and each time the translation reads, "And we shall join them to Companions, with beautiful Big and lustrous eyes." This promise is actually made to any man who merits Paradise, not just the "shahid." It is also true that the number 72 does not appear anywhere in the Qur'an. From where, then, did this idea of martyrs being rewarded with 72 virgins in Paradise come? According to al-Tirmidhi (824-892), one of the first to write on this topic, a martyr has seven special favors from Allah. One of those is that he will be saved from the punishment of the grave. Another is that he is protected from the terror of Judgment Day. A third is that he will marry 72 wives from the beautiful virgins of Paradise.[342] Many other hadith and traditional sayings seem to verify this number of women given to each man. Various Muslim scholars say that while the exact number of virgins cannot be determined, their opinion is that the hadith that mention the narrations of these beautiful maidens is sound (good). For example, Shaykh Gibril F. Haddad says that each man will have two wives in Paradise, along with up to a hundred concubines, while the Shuhada (martyrs) will have 72 wives.[343] These traditions are often brought up by those who recruit terrorists for suicide bombings. However, other Muslims, like the reform-minded Irshad Manji, believe that the use of the word "virgin" or "maiden" is a mistranslation, and the Arabic word *houri* should be translated as "raisin"! "In other words, martyrs would get raisins in heaven, not virgins."[344]

Christophe Luxemberg, a scholar of ancient Semitic languages, claims that much of the Qur'an came from an earlier Syriac source, and when the Arabic in the Qur'an is transliterated and translated back into Syriac the word "houri" referred to white, crystalline grapes that were part of the lush

---

[341] Although suicide is forbidden in the Qur'an (Q. 4:29), those who commit suicide in order to carry out their obligation to jihad are praised as faithful martyrs rather than mere "suicide bombers."

[342] Al-Tirmidhi, Vol. 4, Ch. 21, No. 2687

[343] http://www.webcitation.org/64zXNO08I

[344] http://www.theblaze.com/news/2016/06/01/islam-scholar-says-theres-a-major-problem-with-the-claim-that-muslim-martyrs-get-72-virgins-after-death-and-its-all-about-the-translation-of-virgins/

fruit found in the gardens of heaven, rather than celestial virgins.[345] This would greatly disrupt the propaganda of those trying to recruit suicide bombers. Who would want to give their life away for a box of raisins!

In conclusion, the Qur'an and Hadith give the impression that if a Muslim dies in battle (holy jihad), then Allah will reward him with an automatic pass to Paradise. This is still only a conjecture, not a verified certainty. The reward of 72 virgins seems to have come much later, with Tirmidhi's special favors for those martyrs killed in battle. Today, this view seems to be a common belief, especially held by radical Islamists. Interestingly, there are some Muslims who try to counter the Islamists by claiming that the word "hur," which is often interpreted as "beautiful maiden," or "virgin," may instead simply mean "beautiful crystalline grapes," and have nothing to do with eternal virgins in heaven given to Muslim men as a reward for their sacrificial actions. This interpretation is not accepted by many, but it fits the context much better.

In the end, though, it seems that the promise of 72 virgins as a reward for faithful service unto death for Muslim men was built upon false foundations, misinterpreted words, and a dose of wishful thinking.

## The Grand Delusion

Perhaps the greatest concern in regard to Islamic eschatology is the way that the three main figures in their apocalypse (end time events) seem to be diametrically opposite to the three main figures in Christian eschatology. Following are some charts based on the research of Joel Richardson[346] that will compare the various descriptions of these major figures and provide persuasive evidence revealing that in many ways the roles are polar opposites. For example, Muslims believe that the Muslim Jesus, along with the Mahdi, will attack the Dajjal (Muslim anti-Mahdi) who will be opposing the work of the Mahdi and helping the Jews. However, if the Dajjal is really the Christian Jesus, then the Mahdi and the Muslim Jesus will be trying to kill the real Jesus, while the Muslims will be following the "false" Jesus and trying to kill all the Christians in the name of Allah. This may sound confusing at this point. Hopefully these charts will clarify what may end up being the grand delusion of all time.

---

[345] Christophe Luxemberg, *The Syro-Aramaic Reading of the Koran: A Contribution to the Decoding of the Language of the Koran* (Berlin: Verlag Hans Schiler, 2007), 352. In Syriac, the word hur is a feminine plural adjective meaning white, with the word "raisin" understood implicitly.]

[346] Joel Richardson, *The Islamic Antichrist*, 33-50, 61-69, 77-80.

## Comparison 1: Is the Muslim Mahdi the Christian Antichrist?

A comparison between the Christian Antichrist and the Muslim Mahdi reveals a number of similarities that may point to the same false religious leader. The following chart compares the Christian antichrist with the Muslim Mahdi and reveals some stark similarities between the two figures who may end up being the same individual.

### Table 1: Muslim Mahdi and the Christian Antichrist

| Christian Antichrist | Muslim Mahdi |
|---|---|
| The term antichrist is mentioned only once in the Bible. 1 John 2:18: "Children, it is the last hour, and as you have heard that antichrist is coming, so now many antichrists have come." <br><br> • Also known as the "beast" in Revelation (Rev. 13:4) <br> • "the man of sin" or the "man of lawlessness" (2 Thess. 2) <br> • "the oppressor" (Isaiah 14) <br><br> He will be a powerful political and military world leader. He will be the "beast" who will rule of the ten nations detailed in Daniel 7 and Revelation 13. He will be given authority over every tribe, people, language, and nation" (Rev. 13:7). | Muslims view the Mahdi as one who will be victorious over all religions and will rule the whole world from Jerusalem with great political and military power. <br><br> (Tabari, Dala'il al-imama , Najaf edition, 1369), p. 249) <br><br> As the final caliph of Islam, the Mahdi will lead a revolution to establish a new world order. |
| **Comparison 1: Universal false religious leader** ||
| The Christian Antichrist will be the universal false religious leader who will lead the whole world astray: "all inhabitants of the earth will worship the beast" (Rev. 13:8). The False Prophet will assist him. | The Mahdi will also be known as a spiritual world leader, and known as the leader of a worldwide religious movement promoting only Islam and forcing non-Muslims to convert and worship Allah alone. |

|  | Islam will be the only religion allowed. Through this he will institute a "new world order." The Muslim Jesus will assist him. |
|---|---|
| **Comparison 2: Targeted campaign against Jews and Christians** ||
| The Antichrist will target those who resist his plan to establish his religion as the only one in the world. He will be given power to "make war on the saints and to conquer them (Rev. 13:7) | The Mahdi has a special calling to convert Christians and Jews to Islam. If they do not accept Islam, they will be killed (Richardson, 42). One famous hadith makes the point that even if the Jews hide behind rocks to try and escape even the rocks will cry out and reveal their presence (Muslim, 041, #6985) |
| **Comparison 3: Military attack against Israel and the Temple mount** ||
| The antichrist will attack Jerusalem in order to conquer it (Ezekiel 38:9-12). He will set up his throne in the Temple (2 Thess. 2:4) | The Mahdi will also attack Jerusalem and conquer it for Islam (Tirmidhi, as quoted by Zubair, Sins of Quhanna, 42 – in Richardson, 45). He will make Jerusalem the center of Islamic rule. (Izzat and 'Arif, *Al Mahdi and the End of Time*, 40). |
| **Comparison 4: Seven-year treaty with Israel** ||
| The Antichrist will initiate a treaty with Israel for seven years prior to attacking the city (Daniel 9:27). This will give the Israelis a false sense of security. Isaiah refers to this covenant as a "covenant of death." (Isaiah 28:14-15) | The Mahdi will make a peace treaty for seven years with a Jew from the priestly class (Richardson 47); (Tabarani, as related by Hadrat Abu Umamah, as quoted by Zubair Ali, *Signs of Qiyammah*, p 43 and Abduallah, p. 55) |

| Comparison 5: Changing the laws and times ||
|---|---|
| The book of Daniel points out that the antichrist "will speak against the Most High and oppress his saints and try to change the set times and the laws" (Daniel 7:25) | As a Muslim, the Mahdi will seek to change the time and implement the Muslim calendar, which begins with the Hijrah, or Muhammad's escape (migration) to Medina in 622 AD. The Mahdi will also implement shariah throughout the world, the Islamic law based on the Qur'an and the Hadith, or the sayings of Muhammad.<br><br>"Only Islam fits the bill of a system that has its own unique calendar, a week based on its own religious history, and a clear system of law that it wishes to impose onto the entire earth." (Richardson, 48) |
| Comparison 6: Riding on a White Horse ||
| Revelation 6:1-2 portrays the rider on a white horse as a counterfeit Christ who triumphs over the people. However, this is only a false imitation of Christ's true triumphal appearance on a white horse found later in Revelation 19:11. | The Mahdi is said to be the fulfillment of this passage in Revelation (Rev 6:1-2), and he will ride the white horse in victory over the world as he brings Islam to all people and all countries. (Richardson, 50) also (Izzat and 'Arif, *Al Mahdi and the End of Time*, 15, 19). |

**Comparison 2:** Will the Muslim Jesus turn out to be the False Prophet of the Bible? Note the similarities between these two end time figures. Both will seek to lead Christians away from the true Jesus Christ of the Bible. Could it be that the Christian false prophet and the Muslim Jesus are one and the same?

## Table 2: The Muslim Jesus and the False Prophet

| Christian False Prophet | Muslim Jesus (Isa) |
|---|---|
| Description of the Christian False Prophet<br><br>The Christian False Prophet is mentioned in the book of Revelation (16). He will deceive many and try to lead people away from Jesus Christ. | Description of the Muslim Jesus<br><br>According to Muslims, the Muslim Jesus was not crucified, but taken up to heaven alive and awaits his return to earth. He will return from heaven and help the Mahdi conquer the world for Allah. He will kill the Dajjal and persuade many Christians and Jews to convert to Islam. |
| **Comparison 1: The unholy partnership** ||
| The False Prophet in the Bible is the assistant to the Antichrist. He is able to perform miracles. His purpose is to deceive people in order to get them to follow the Antichrist. | The Mahdi and the Muslim Jesus form an unholy alliance. The Muslim Jesus is subordinate to the Mahdi and seeks to force Christians to follow the Mahdi. |
| **Comparison 2: Chief Enforcer** ||
| The False Prophet will give people two options: to worship the Antichrist or die (Rev. 13:15) | The Muslim Jesus comes to convert the Christian world to Islam. He will institute Islamic law all over the earth. He will abolish the Jizyah tax (protection money), and without this alternative the only two choices left for the non-Muslim will be to convert to Islam or to be executed by the Mahdi and the Muslim Jesus. |
| **Comparison 3: Executioner** ||
| Revelation 13:15 indicates that the False Prophet will kill all who refuse to worship the image | The Muslim Jesus will establish a system of law that will enforce the mass extinction of |

| | |
|---|---|
| of the first beast (another name for the Antichrist). According to Revelation 20:4 they will be beheaded. This is one of the preferred ways for Muslims to execute non-believers. It has been this way for 1400 years. | everyone who refuses to convert to Islam. One of the favorite ways of execution for Muslims is beheading. |

### Comparison 3: The Biblical Jesus and the Dajjal

Could it be that the person that Muslims fear most, the Dajjal, could really be the biblical Jesus Christ? This would be ironic in a tragic sense for the one that they need most to follow, the true Lord and Savior, Jesus Christ, would be twisted into the most hated and fearful creature imaginable for Muslims. This is certainly something that only Satan could devise.

### Table 3: The Muslim Dajjal and the Christian Jesus

| Christian Jesus | Muslim Dajjal |
|---|---|
| Jesus Christ is the Son of God, Second person of the Trinity, and truly God himself | The Muslim Dajjal is the false Messiah, or the Antichrist figure for Muslims. |
| The Christian Jesus will claim to be one with the Father and the true Christ (Messiah) | The Dajjal will claim to be Jesus Christ. |
| The Christian Jesus will make salvation possible for many Jews during the tribulation. Satan will seek to destroy Jesus and his followers. | He will defend Israel against the Mahdi and the Muslim Jesus, who will seek to destroy the Dajjal. |
| The Christian Jesus is appearing to many Muslims in dreams and visions leading them out of Islam and into a relationship with him. | It is also believed by Muslims that the Dajjal will "deceive" many Muslims into leaving Islam. |
| The False Prophet will try to kill Jesus Christ | According to Islamic eschatology, the Muslim Jesus will kill the Dajjal |

## Polar Opposites

This would be especially ironic if the Muslim False Prophet were already here on earth claiming to be Jesus Christ when the real Jesus Christ appears and the Muslims will claim that he is the Dajjal. Everything would be topsy-turvy. On the one hand, the real Jesus Christ would be mistaken for the Dajjal, Islam's antichrist, and on the other hand the Christian False Prophet would be accepted as the Muslim Jesus, and the real Christian Antichrist would masquerade as the Muslim Mahdi. Again, we can see how Islam is diametrically opposite to Christianity in core areas. We need to be aware of these differences and able to help others make these very important distinctions.

Table 4: Polar Opposites

| Christian View | Muslim View |
|---|---|
| Muslim Mahdi = Christian Antichrist | Muslim Mahdi = Messiah |
| Muslim Jesus = Christian False Prophet | Muslim Jesus = true Prophet of Islam |
| The Dajjal = Muslim Antichrist = Christian Jesus Christ (??) | The Dajjal = Muslim Antichrist |

## Implications

It seems that today scholars look at the similarities between Christianity and Islam and try to say that Christian doctrine is often mirrored by Islamic beliefs. However, in this case, the image that portrays Islam seems to be clearly a distorted reversal of Christian beliefs. This may be why Joel Richardson calls Islamic eschatology an "anti-parallel" of Christian theology, especially in reference to the three major figures of Islam. What Christians see as the savior (Jesus Christ), Muslims see as the deceiver and destroyer (Dajjal), and what Christians see as the Antichrist and the False Prophet, Muslims see as their messiah (the Mahdi) and his helper (the Muslim Jesus) who will destroy the one they interpret as the great deceiver and destroyer (Jesus Christ of the Bible). In this way, could it be that Islam is the "anti-parallel" counterfeit of Christianity? The implications of this would be far-reaching, for it would mean that if Christianity is the true religion then Islam is the strongest adversary and the ultimate enemy of Christ. Could Islam represent the "spirit of the antichrist" that the apostle John writes about in his letter:

1 John 4:1-3 English Standard Version (ESV)

4 Beloved, do not believe every spirit, but test the spirits to see whether they are from God, for many false prophets have gone out into the world. ² By this you know the Spirit of God: every spirit that confesses that Jesus Christ has come in the flesh is from God, ³ and every spirit that does not confess Jesus is not from God. This is the spirit of the antichrist, which you heard was coming and now is in the world already.

We know that Islam vehemently rejects the belief that Jesus Christ is God, and therefore even though they will agree that the Jesus of the Qur'an was a prophet and messenger from God, they will not accept any evidence that Jesus Christ is God himself. As John clearly states, this is the spirit of the antichrist, and we need to passionately reject this deceptive and destructive view.

A further implication may be found in the Islamic practice of *taqiyya*, which allows Muslims to mislead non-believers in regard to the nature of a Muslim's own belief in order to avoid persecution. This practice allows Muslims, both Shia and Sunni, to lie to non-Muslims in a time of war, persecution, or even minority status if the lie will protect Muslims and further the goals of Islam. In his article on taqiyya, Raymond Ibrahim quotes a Muslim authority, Sami Mukaram, who says,

> Taqiyya is of fundamental importance in Islam. Practically every Islamic sect agrees to it and practices it ... We can go so far as to say that the practice of taqiyya is mainstream in Islam, and that those few sects not practicing it diverge from the mainstream ... Taqiyya is very prevalent in Islamic politics, especially in the modern era.[347]

For Christians, it is difficult to accept that any religion that claims to be a revelation from the true God would freely resort to deception. However, taqiyya may play a major role in shielding the true nature of Islam behind a screen of duplicity and obfuscation. For example, how many times have Muslims defended their religion as a "religion of peace" while the majority of the terrorist activity in the world is carried on by Muslims?[348]

---

[347] Sami Mukaram, *At-Taqiyya fi 'l-Islam* (London: Mu'assisat at-Turath ad-Druzi, 2004), 7, quoted in Raymond Ibrahim, Beware Islam's Doctrine of Deception, PJ Media, September 24, 2015: http://www.meforum.org/5522/ben-carson-taqiyya.

[348] https://www.statista.com/topics/2267/terrorism/

## Apologetic Conclusions

The important message for Christians to realize is that the Bible states clearly that the last days will be filled with deception. It would make sense that Islam may be the greatest deception used by Satan to destroy Christianity throughout the world. In his book, *The Islamic Antichrist*, Richardson writes that, "The biblical picture of the last days is one where deception is the absolute rule of the day. In virtually every passage where the New Testament discusses the end times, the author stresses that believers must guard against deception."[349] One example of this can be found in Matthew 24:3-4 where Jesus told his disciple, "Watch out that no one deceives you." A little further he says, "At that time many will turn away from the faith and will betray and hate each other, and many false prophets will appear and deceive many people…. For false christs and false prophets will appear and perform great signs and miracles to deceive even the elect – if that were possible. See, I have told you ahead of time." (Matthew 24:10-11, 24-25). The apostle Paul also warns Christians to be aware of the dangers that will take place during the end times:

**2 Thessalonians 2:9-12** English Standard Version (ESV)

⁹ The coming of the lawless one is by the activity of Satan with all power and false signs and wonders, ¹⁰ and with all wicked deception for those who are perishing, because they refused to love the truth and so be saved. ¹¹ Therefore God sends them a strong delusion, so that they may believe what is false, ¹² in order that all may be condemned who did not believe the truth but had pleasure in unrighteousness.

Is it possible that one of the powerful delusions that God sends will be the lie embodied in Islam, especially in the way that beliefs concerning the end times point to a very different Christ and a very different gospel?

## Building Bridges to Understand

In creating a bridge, it would be good to start with some of the similarities in regard to the end times, such as Jesus playing a central role in both Christian and Muslim views, and both religions believing in a resurrection of the dead, a final judgment, a literal heaven and hell, eternal life in heaven (Paradise) for the saved, and eternal life in hell for the lost. Then, it would be helpful to point out the specific areas where Christ will be the triumphant one in Christianity. It will be important to demonstrate that Christians view Jesus as God himself, and this is important not only for the outcome of the last battle but also for each believer as they will need

---

[349] Richardson, The Islamic Antichrist, 160.

to face Christ in the judgment. However, for Christians who have put their trust in Jesus Christ, they will not have to fear the judgment. This is not true for Muslims. This may be an opportunity to help Muslims see that Christianity offers a much better option: Christ has done it all. We cannot work our way into heaven (Eph. 2:8-9). This is especially important because Islam offers no sure salvation and therefore no real hope.

There is also the issue of deception (*taqiyyah*). If even Allah cannot be trusted, then how can Muslims trust anything in the Qur'an, the Hadith, or even promises from their leaders in regard to their own eternal destination? What does history tell us about the broken treaties? What does the fact that most Islamic majority countries are struggling to get into the 21$^{st}$ century and are still under constant strife? Where is the peace? It certainly is not apparent in Islam. Lambert Dolphin, a physicist, and theologian, comments, "The end of the age we live in is marked by deception on a world-wide scale because truth has been so widely and universally rejected by mankind. This is the clear statement of Paul when he speaks about the appearing of the man of sin" (2 Thessalonians 2: 3-12).[350] The whole idea of the prevalence of deception (taqiyyah) in Islam can be used to challenge the idea that Islamic leaders can be trusted. It is also good to compare it with the uprightness of Jesus Christ and the selfless loyalty of his disciples.

Since Joel Richardson's ideas have been heavily used in this chapter, it would be fitting to close with a summary of some of the ideas that he advocates for building bridges with Muslims:[351]

- Never underestimate the power of the gospel: "It is the power of God for the salvation of everyone who believes." (Romans 1:16)

- How can they hear without a preacher? (Romans 10:14) We must be willing to go to them.

- We need to reach out in love rather than fear (or despite our fears). Our struggle is not against flesh and blood, but rather against the rulers, authorities, powers, and spiritual forces (Ephesians 6: 10-12)

- Our critique is against Islam, not Muslims. We are commanded to love Muslims, for even though they are far from the true God, they are made in the image of God and need to "come home." (Muslims are not our enemy so much as Islam is).

- The majority of Muslims that we meet will be just like us: they desire to live a good life pleasing to God.

---

[350] Lambert Dolphin, http://www.ldolphin.org/islam.shtml (accessed 7/25/2018).
[351] adapted from Richardson, *Islamic Antichrist*, 203-209.

- We should see them as sincere God seekers.

- We should not see Muslims as "others," but rather as "another" one of God's creatures.

- We need to be confident that God wants us to be overcomers: We need to overcome our fear with love; we need to overcome hatred with reconciliation.

These are all helpful pointers for us to follow as we reach out to Muslims around us and seek to lead them to the one who has already conquered death. Jesus Christ has a wonderful eternal plan for every person who calls on his name and walks in his footsteps. The true path to heaven can only be found in the one who says "I am the way... follow me." (John 14:6, Matthew 16:24).

### Questions for Study:

1. What are some of the positions on eschatology that are similar in both Christianity and Islam?

2. What are the main differences in the positions on eschatology between Christians and Muslims?

3. How is the Muslim Jesus different from the Jesus of the Bible?

4. How are the three main figures in Islamic eschatology – the Mahdi, the Muslim Jesus, and the Dajjal – an "anti-parallel" to the three main figures in Christian eschatology – Jesus Christ, the antichrist, and the false prophet?

5. What are some ways that you can use this information on Islamic eschatology to build a bridge to your Muslim friend or neighbor?

6. What would be some of the implications concerning the end times if Christianity is true and Islam is false?

# CHAPTER 11 Sects and Schools: What is the Real Agenda?

## Introduction

Non-Muslims tend to view Islam as a monolithic religion in which Muslim followers all believe the same thing and follow the same traditions. The emphasis on the use of Arabic in the mosque prayers and for the proper interpretation of the Qur'an only emphasizes a certain uniform system of belief and practice. However, there is great diversity among the people who make up Islam, and this can be seen in the various sects that have developed over the years. The Qur'an and the Hadith both teach that there should be unity in Islam, but they also point out the inevitable diversity of any human institution.

In Surah 42:13, the Qur'an teaches that there should be no divisions within Islam:

> He has ordained for you of religion what He enjoined upon Noah and that which We have revealed to you, [O Muhammad], and what We enjoined upon Abraham and Moses and Jesus - to establish the religion and not be divided therein.

This may have been the intent for the religion of Islam, but, as we shall see, there were forces working from the very beginning to separate followers and bring divisions. For example, a Hadith attributed to Tirmidhi (no. 171) states that the prophet himself said there will be 73 sects and only one will lead to paradise:

> The Prophet (PBUH) is reported to have said, "if the people of Israel were fragmented into seventy-two sects, my Umma will be fragmented into seventy-three sects, and all of them will be in Hell fire except one group." The companions asked Allah's messenger which group that would be. Whereupon he replied, "It is the one to which I and my companions belong."

It seems, then, that from the beginning there was the realization that many diverse sects would form, yet only one would be identified as the true path to Allah. In this case, Tirmidhi is assuming that a Muslim will find the right path by following the sunnah of Muhammad and living their life according to the words of the Qur'an. This is still very much the ideal for Muslims around the world. However, since the number of sects in Islam now number far more than 73, it is sometimes difficult to determine which group has the correct interpretation and the right practices that will give them a chance to get into paradise. In this chapter, a number of the major divisions will be examined, and the similarities and differences will be highlighted in order to better understand how belief and practice in Islam is often determined by might rather than by mind.

## Traditional Muslim View

It may be true that there are many diverse groups in Islam, but it must also be understood that most of these groups fall into one of two main divisions, the Sunni and the Shia. Most Muslims will identify themselves within these two systems since most of the sub-groups were originally derived from one or the other. In this section, each of the major groups will be described and certain aspects will be highlighted in order to provide more insight into some of the events taking place in the Muslim world today that impacts the rest of the world. Then, in the counter-view section that follows, various reasons for the formation of the divisions and the consequent practices will be assessed and evaluated in order to provide a clearer picture of a possible way forward in regard to relations with Islam and the Western world.

### Sunni Muslims

The largest "denomination" of Islam is made up of Sunni Muslims. The various Sunni groups and sub-groups make up 85-90 % of all Muslims. The word *Sunni* comes from "sunnah," which refers to the teachings, actions, and example of the prophet, Muhammad. Those who follow or maintain the sunnah of Muhammad are therefore called Sunni Muslims. According to Muslim tradition, Muhammad did not appoint a successor to lead the community after his death. Therefore, his followers elected one of Muhammad's close companions to be the first caliph or religious successor to the prophet. Abu Bakr, Muhammad's father-in-law, was chosen by consensus to be the first one to fill this position.

Following Abu Bakr were other companions of the prophet, Umar ibn al-Khattab, and Uthman ibn Affan. The fourth caliph elected by consensus was Ali ibn Abu Talib, Muhammad's cousin, and son-in-law. These first four leaders were called the "Rashidun" or "the rightly guided caliphs," and they tried to provide an example to other Muslims by strictly obeying the commands of the Qur'an and the traditions of the prophet. Islam remained centered around the words and actions of Muhammad, and in time, according to Muslims, the sayings of Muhammad were passed down and recorded as the Hadith, and the religious practices established by Muhammad became the sunnah. Together these two sources provided the basis for Islamic law called *Sharia*.

During the first century of the Abbasid Empire (750-850 AD), Sharia was established through four schools of religious thought, or jurisprudence, known as *Madhabs*. These four schools of jurisprudence (or interpretation) are the Hanifite, Malikite, Shafi'ite, and Hanbalite Madhabs. The largest number of Muslims follow the Hanifite school, which was founded by Abu Hanifa al-Nu'man ibn Thabit (d. 150 AH/767 AD). It favors the use of rational judgment in determining what is best for the common good, and it is most influential in Iraq, Pakistan, India, and Central Asia. The Malikite school was founded by Malik ibn Anas (d. 179 AH/795 AD) and it uses consensus and analogy in order to determine the right path. It is most influential in North Africa, Egypt and eastern Arabia. The third school, the Shafi'ite, was begun by Muhammad ibn Idris al-Shafi'i (d. 204 AH/820 AD). It accepts the authority of the Hadith, in addition to the Qur'an, and de-emphasizes the role of reason. It is most influential in Indonesia. Finally, Ahmad ibn Hanbal (d. 241 AH/855 AD) founded the last madhab called the Hanbalite school. The Hanbalites maintain that the Qur'an is the supreme authority, though they also accept the Hadith as authoritative. This is the smallest of the four major schools of jurisprudence, but it is the forerunner of the Wahhabi-Salafist movement and has played a major role in the rise of power in Saudi Arabia.

All of these schools seek to apply and instill the will of Allah in their legal works through strict adherence to the Qur'an and the sunnah of Muhammad, though some have a greater reliance on reason. They are also considered orthodox in their teaching and usually display mutual tolerance for the others, though there were often periods of great rivalry as different schools postured for power in the development of the various Islamic empires. However, most Sunnis today consider their view of Islam to be the only correct interpretation, so there is often intolerance and persecution directed at other forms of Islam, especially Shi'ism.

## Shia Islam

The second largest division of Muslims, the Shi'ah, make up around 10-13 % of all Muslims, and comprise the majority of the population in Azerbaijan, Bahrain, Iran, and Iraq. The name is derived from the "shia Ali," or the party or partisans of Ali, the fourth elected caliph and the son-in-law of Muahmmad. Shi'ah believe that the caliph should be a direct descendent of Muhammad rather than a leader selected by consensus from the general followers. Thus, they reject the legitimacy of the first three Rashidun caliphs and claim that Ali was the first true leader of the faithful after Muhammad.

This split between the Sunni and the Shia developed through three phases. The first point of division took place in 632 AD when Abu Bakr was selected to succeed Muhammad rather than Ali, who was a blood relative. The Shia believe that before his death Muhammad conveyed to Ali that he would be the one to succeed him after his death. However, the previous pledge by Muhammad was overlooked and Ali was denied leadership at that time. Later, after the assassination of the third caliph, Uthman, Ali was selected by consensus to take on the role of caliph. However, this choice was disputed by Muawiyah, a relative of Uthman, who desired the position for himself.[352]

This quarrel culminated in the battle of Siffin (657 AD) during the First Fitna, or Civil War, between the forces of Muawiyah and Ali. Muawiyah wanted Ali to punish the murderers of Uthman and therefore would not pledge his allegiance to Ali until that was accomplished, while Ali said he would not pursue the murderers until Muawiyah pledged his allegiance and accepted his authority. Since Ali was not able to follow through, Muawiyah brought his forces up against Ali's army near the Euphrates river. After three days of a battle, which neither side wanted to start, Ali called for arbitration in order to stop the bloodshed. This brought an end to the battle, but it also was seen as weakness on the part of Ali and led to the decline of his rule. After four years, Ali was assassinated by a Kharajite ("one who leaves"), a former follower who had separated from Ali's camp and decided that piety rather than blood should determine the choice for the leader of the faithful. Ali's son Hasan was put forth for the next caliph, but Muawiyah persuaded him to withdraw, and after a treaty was signed the people selected Muawiyah to lead them.

Years later (680 AD), when Ali's son Husayn, who was considered the third caliph in the Shia line, went up against Muawiyah's son, Yazid, his army was intercepted at Karbala, Iraq, and Husayn was captured and beheaded. This further infuriated the Shi'ites because the treaty between Hasan and Muawiyah had stipulated that after Muawiyah's death the people would select the next caliph. However, Muawiyah had chosen his own son to follow in his footsteps. This triple betrayal at the hands of the opponents of Ali's family set in motion a rift that still exists between the Sunnis and the Shias.

Though both Shia and Sunni Muslims follow the same Five Pillars and hold the Qur'an and the sunnah of Muhammad as their supreme authority, there are a number of differences between the two systems. Minor differences on the Shia side range from condensing the five daily prayers into three, more leniency during the month of fasting, and religious observances to honor their past leaders such as pilgrimages to the shrines of various leaders and passionate displays of loyalty.

---

[352] The irony of this dispute is that both Muawiyah and Ali were descendants of Abd Manaf; Muawiyah through the Umayyad branch of the family and Ali through the Hashim branch to which Muhammad also belonged.

There are also some crucial differences as well. First of all, Shia Muslims consider the transmitters of the Sunni collections to be unreliable because they do not give preference to Ali and are sometimes narrated by enemies of the Shia, so different Hadith collections by Shia scholars are preferred. Secondly, while Sunni Muslims consult the four Madhabs, which use consensus for making decisions concerning the Muslim faith, Shia Muslims believe that the Imams, or the descendants of Ali's family line, are the true caliphs, or rightful successors of Muhammad. These first twelve Imams were considered infallible, so their decisions had spiritual and political authority over the community. They were also the ones consulted in regard to questions of jurisprudence and Qur'anic interpretation.

Shiah Islam is even divided into three branches according to the number of Imams accepted. The majority group follows the teachings of the twelve traditional Shia Imams, and therefore the followers are called Twelvers. They believe that the twelfth Imam, a descendent of Ali, who disappeared in the tenth century, is still alive and in occultation, or hiding. He is known as the Mahdi, a messiah figure, and they believe he will restore the purity of the faith as well as appear again before the Last Judgment (end times). The other two groups, which developed due to disputes over the successions of the Imams, are the Seveners *(Isma'ilis)*, who believe that the seventh Imam should have been Isma'il instead of his younger brother Musa al-Kazim, and the Fivers *(Zaydis)*, who followed Zayd instead of his brother Muhammad al-Baqir. Thus, the Fivers end their list with Zayd, and the Seveners end their list with Isma'il. However, the Twelvers are by far in the majority, and therefore most Shi'ites follow the teachings of their twelve Imams, especially Jafar al-Sadiq, who was the sixth Imam.

## Sufism

Another important group in Islam is Sufism. It is not really a sect, but a mystical and ascetic branch of Islamic teaching that deals with purification of the inner self. The word *Sufi* means "woolen" and refers to the woolen garments worn by followers and signifies the rejection of worldly pleasures. Most Sufis are Sunni, but Sufi are represented in both major branches. In many ways, it is a reactive movement that arose to counter the rigid ritualism of orthodox Islam. Sufis want a relationship with God, which orthodox Islam will not really allow since Allah is considered too far removed from mankind. Sufis strive to obtain a direct experience of God. Some practitioners even speak of not just experiencing God, but becoming God themselves by annihilation and being absorbed in the divine. Martin Lings, an English convert to Islam, and a highly respected Sufi states, "Sufism is nothing other than Islamic mysticism."[353] He also relates that Sufism is to

---

[353] Martin Lings, *What is Sufism?* (Cambridge: The Islamic Texts Society, 1993), 15.

Islam "what the heart is to the body."³⁵⁴ In this way it is very much a religion of the heart for an Islam that is often overly concerned with the external behavior of Muslims. In a way, Sufism provided a counterpoint between legalism and inner experience and taught that original Islam was much more concerned with spiritual matters rather than the materialistic concerns that seem to be emphasized in the Qur'an. There are also a number of elements that may have been influenced by Christian mysticism as well as Buddhist and Hindu beliefs. This may be why one scholar says that Sufism "originated in pious asceticism and cut across all social and religious divisions."³⁵⁵ Two of the most important Sufi leaders in Islam were al-Ghazali, who sought to synthesize the legalistic and mystical schools of Islam, and the poet Rumi, whose words still reach out across the ages to Muslims and non-Muslims alike.

## Ahmadiyyah Muslim Community

A group that does not fit neatly into the Sunni or the Shia camp is the Ahmadiyyah Muslim Community, founded in India by Mirza Ghulam Ahmad in 1889. It started out as an eschatological movement in which Ahmad claimed to be the promised Messiah (second coming of Christ) as well as the Mahdi who would bring in the end times. For most Muslims these claims are blasphemous, and so from the beginning, the Ahmadis were considered heretics (*kafirs*) or non-Muslims. However, Ahmadis consider themselves to be true Muslims, and they claim to practice a pure form of Islam re-established by the teachings of their prophet. They also seek to end religious wars and seek to bring back the justice and peace advocated by Muhammad. In fact, Ahmad encouraged his followers to see themselves as leading a revival that would reject the radical tendencies found in many Islamic groups and "restore the relationship of love and sincerity" between God and his creatures.³⁵⁶ Ahmadis believe that their founder fulfilled the Qur'anic prophecy of the Second Coming of the Holy Prophet. They also believe that he was "the Messiah for the Christians and Muslims, Krishna for the Hindus, and Buddha for the Buddhists."³⁵⁷ In fact, they believe that his mission was to "bring about the renaissance of Islam, to bring all the followers of the various religions into the fold of Islam and to establish its supremacy over all other religions, ideologies, and creeds."³⁵⁸ However, most Muslims believe that the prophet Muhammad was the last prophet of

---

³⁵⁴ Ibid., 106.

³⁵⁵ Douglass Pratt, *The Challenge of Islam: Encounters in Interfaith Dialogue* (Burlington, VT: Ashgate, 2005), 68.

³⁵⁶ A.R. Dard. *Life of Ahmad (PDF)*. Islam International Publications, 2008, XV. Retrieved 30 June, 2016.

³⁵⁷ Dard, XIV.

³⁵⁸ Dard, XIV-XV.

Allah, and therefore they reject the words and intentions of Ahmadi and his followers. Today the Ahmadis have expanded to over 200 countries and number between 10-20 million worldwide.

## Baha'i

Most people in the West who are familiar with the Baha'i Faith are not aware that this new religion first developed as an offshoot of Shia Islam in the nineteenth century. It all began in 1844 when a young Shia Muslim in the city of Shiraz, Iran, named Muhammad Ali, became convinced that he was the Bab or the forerunner of the Mahdi to come. The Bab's teachings came under severe persecution from the Muslims, especially since he taught that Muhammad was not the final prophet, and he was arrested and then executed in 1850. Thirteen years later, one of his followers, Husayn Ali Nuri, claimed an angel appeared to him while he was in prison to inform him that he was the chosen one, or the Mahdi. He began to refer to himself as the Baha'u'llah, or "the Glory and Splendor of God," the Promised One that the world was waiting for. In time Husayn Ali was exiled to Haifa, Israel and spent the rest of his life writing scriptures for the Baha'i Faith. Today the movement has over five million followers in 200 countries.

Followers of Baha'i believe that religion is evolving and so their prophet, the Baha'u'llah, and his teachings supersede Muhammad, the Qur'an, and all other religious systems. Just as the Baha'u'llah is the fulfillment of all the Messianic roles in the major world religions, Baha'i claims to be the ultimate fulfillment of all religions. As the pinnacle religion of the world, it can afford to accept the good things found in other religions because they are lesser revelations leading to the most complete revelation found in Baha'i. Thus, it not only accepts these things, but it also absorbs them. In the teachings of Lao-tze, for example, they say that the primary teaching was reverence. The identifying characteristic for Brahmanism was sacrifice. For Buddhism it was renunciation. Under Moses, the people learned righteousness. Through Jesus came a deeper understanding of love. Through Muhammad came the teaching of submission to God. Finally, Baha'u'llah, the greatest of all these teachers, founded the greatest of all these religions based on the principle of unity: unity of God, unity of religion, and unity of humanity. Supposedly this is the last and greatest principle in the progression of revelation.

The major goal of Baha'i, then, is to unite all of mankind into one religious kingdom. In order to do this, all the religions of the world would have to bow to a great unifying one. Baha'i claims to be the religion that would bring all others together. The reason the Baha'is can say this is that they believe that underneath the different patterns of ritual and worship, all religions are in complete agreement in regard to all the important things. They also believe that Baha'u'llah were the highest and most complete manifestation of God. Therefore, his writings should be the most complete revelations known to man. However, because Baha'is deny that Muhammad is the final prophet, both Sunni and Shia Muslims reject Baha'i as a heresy and continue to persecute believers who still live in Islamic countries.

## Alawites

The Alawites are another offshoot from Shia Islam that Christians should know about, since the present leader of Syria, Bashar al-Assad, ascribes to this form of Islam. The name *Alawi* means "followers of Ali," and today the Alawites represent around 20 percent of the population in Syria, as well as minorities in Turkey and Lebanon, with a total of around 4 million people. Alawites follow a branch of the Twelver school of Shia Islam, and are thought to be descendants of the eleventh Imam, Hasan al-Askari (d. 873). However, they tend to add some syncretistic elements to their beliefs, such as a divine triad comprised of Ali, Muhammad, and Salman the Persian. According to their theology, these three Muslims are the three current emanations of the one God. Ali represents the incarnation of the deity in the triad and is called the "Essence" or the "Meaning" of God, while Muhammad, whom Ali created of his own light, represents the Name, and Salman the Persian is the Gate.[359] In addition, through their contact with the Byzantines and the Crusaders, Alawis added other Christian elements to their creeds and practices such as celebrating Christmas, Easter, and the Epiphany. In other ways, their doctrines incorporate Gnostic, neo-Platonic, and heretical Islamic beliefs and practices. Even with all the syncretistic additions, Alawites still claim to be Muslims. However, Sunni scholars generally disavow this claim and consider them to be pagans or non-Muslims. Even the great scholar Ibn Taymiyya was virulently anti-Alawite and accused them of aiding the enemies of Muslims. Al-Ghazali, the great Muslim philosopher, also considered Alawites to be non-Muslims. Today there is a movement to downplay the former syncretism and connect the Alawites more firmly within the Twelver belief system. This has been encouraged by the Iranian regime, which is also a strong advocate of Twelver Shia beliefs.

## Druze

Another Shia sub-group that contains syncretistic elements is the Druze faith, with around 2 million adherents in the Levant region (Syria, Lebanon, Israel and Jordan). It is believed that they developed in the eleventh century as an offshoot of the Ismaili sect of Shia Islam (Seveners). They are considered heretical and non-Muslims by other Muslims because of their

---

[359] "Alawi Islam." Globalsecurity.org

syncretistic beliefs that incorporate elements of Ismailism, Judaism, Christianity, Gnosticism, Neo-Platonism, and even Hinduism. For example, they believe in a form of reincarnation in which the soul continues to reincarnate as a human until it unites with the Cosmic Mind and achieves ultimate happiness.[360] They are also considered heretical because of their belief that the third Fatimid caliph of Egypt, al-Hakim bi-Amr Allah, was a manifestation of Allah and will return as the Mahdi on judgment day. Like the Alawites, the Druze tend to keep their beliefs secret in order to ward off persecution and gain acceptance in the greater world of orthodox Sunni Islam.

## Wahabbism

Sunni Muslims seem to be less drawn to heresy, but they have their own excesses that tend toward hyper-fundamentalism rather than syncretism. Wahhabism is an example of this trend. Wahhabism is a fundamental revival of seventh-century Islam by the eighteenth-century teacher Sheikh Muhammad ibn Abd-al-Wahhab in Saudi Arabia. It is derived from the Sunni Hanbali school of interpretation via the writings of Ibn Taymiyya (d.1328). In some ways the Kharijites of first century Islam could have been an early model for Wahhabis today since they, too, only wanted to follow the pure, original teaching of Muhammad. Wahhabism rejects all innovation in Islam after the prophet Muhammad's time in the seventh century. They are rigid in their interpretation of Sharia and intolerant of Sufism and innovation. Wahhabism was instrumental in bringing the house of Saud into power, which is why it is the official creed of Saudi Arabia. Since it is also linked to Salafism ("following the forefathers of Islam"), Wahhabism teaches that they have the right interpretation of the Qur'an, they consider moderate Muslims to be infidels, and they seek to convert all Muslims to their form of belief. They also seek to dominate the world for Islam, according to the Qur'an (Q. 8:39, 9:33, 61:9) and the Hadith (Sahih Muslim #1731). Even though Wahhbism is a minority position overall in the Muslim world, it is thought to be foundational to Muslim terrorist groups operating today, especially those who believe in the destruction of non-Muslim societies like America.

## The Nation of Islam

There are some sub-groups in Islam that began far from the foundational moorings and then tried to reform their beliefs in order to come in line with orthodox Sunni Islam. The Nation of Islam, one of the only sub-groups to develop in America, has this record. The Nation of Islam was founded in Detroit in 1930 by Wallace Fard Muhammad. He wanted

---

[360] http://www.druze.org.au/religion/

to resurrect the spiritual, social and economic condition of black men and women and looked to Islam for a solution. However, the original beliefs did not look very much like Sunni Islam in the Middle East. It was more of a mixture of Islam and Black Nationalism. First of all, his followers came to believe that Fard Muhammad was the Messiah for the Jews and the Mahdi of the Muslims. They also believe that the Arabian Muhammad was not the final prophet, but rather they hold that Elijah Muhammad, the successor to Fard Muhammad, was the final "messenger of Truth." They also believe black people were the original race on the earth and only allow blacks to be a member of the movement. Due to these heretical differences, traditional Islam rejected the Nation of Islam and did not consider them to be true Muslims. However, the son of Elijah Muhammad, Warith Deen Muhammad, abandoned the beliefs of the Nation of Islam in 1976 and turned to orthodox Islam, naming his new organization the American Society of Muslims. Not everyone agreed with this move, and the present leader of the Nation of Islam, Louis Farrakhan, revived the former group in 1979 with the earlier heretical teachings. Under Farrakhan, the NOI once again grew, but it was still viewed as a heresy by most orthodox Muslim groups. More recently, after a bout with cancer, Louis Farrakhan has reached out to orthodox Islam, and in time may follow Malcolm X and Warith Deen Muhammad on the road toward orthodoxy.

## Political Groups

It would be helpful to be familiar with some of the political groups that have influenced the West and challenged Christians on the nation's campuses, in the courts of law, and in the halls of Congress.

### Muslim Brotherhood (Al-Ikhwan Al-Muslimun)

The Muslim Brotherhood was founded by an Egyptian scholar, Hassan al-Banna in 1928. It is now the largest Sunni movement in the Arab world and accepts Muslims from all four Sunni schools of thought. The Brotherhood seeks to re-establish the caliphate and pushes for stricter Islamization of society. This is why the formation of Islamic courts of law, or Sharia, in the West is seen as essential to the development of the end goals of the Brotherhood. Underlying all that it does, the Muslim Brotherhood looks to the Qur'an and sunnah as sole guides for faith. One of their mottos describes this well: "Allah is our objective; the Qur'an is the Constitution; the Prophet is our leader; jihad is our way; death for the sake of Allah is our wish."[361]

---

[361] Helbawy, K., (2009) *The Muslim Brotherhood in Egypt: Historical Evolution and Future Prospects*, p.65

## CAIR

The CAIR website states, "The Council on American-Islamic Relations (CAIR) was established in 1994 to challenge stereotypes of Islam and Muslims."[362] In many ways it has grown to be the leading organization in the United States dedicated to promoting an Islamic perspective on a number of different fronts. According to the website, "the vast majority of CAIR's work deals with civil rights and anti-defamation." However, they also detail acts of destruction and desecration of Islamic places of worship, support educational efforts to promote Islam in the US, advocate for freedom of religion and freedom of conscience on behalf of Islam, denounce terrorism and religious intolerance, and oppose racial and religious profiling. However, in 2007 CAIR was included in a list of organizations that were labeled as unindicted co-conspirators of a Hamas funding project involving the Holy Land Foundation, which was indicted. In 2008 the FBI labeled CAIR as a front group for Hamas.[363] A book published in 2009, titled *Muslim Mafia: Inside the Secret Underworld That's Conspiring to Islamize America,* by Paul David Gaubatz and Paul Sperry, portrays CAIR "as a subversive organization allied with international terrorists."[364] CAIR has denied these allegations, and under the Obama administration, the organization has regained some of its former influence. CAIR continues to present itself as a staunch supporter regarding "America's founding principles and religious pluralism," but at the same time, they have organized political action to protest aspects of US counterterrorism policy as well as downplay the concern of Christian groups concerned with the rise of Islamic terrorism in the US.

## Jamaat-e-Islami

Another important political group to be familiar with is the Jamaat-e-Islami founded by Abul Ala Maududi in 1941. This is the oldest religious party in Pakistan, and it was formed in order to aid the new state of Pakistan to develop a government that was totally ruled by Sharia. Maududi was very much opposed to the Western social and economic structures, such as secularization, capitalism, and socialism. He favored the founding of a caliphate with Islamic economic laws and believed that politics was integral to the Islamic faith. Western ideas and methods were antithetical to the ways of Islam and therefore would not work in a truly Islamic society. Maududi further believed that only a complete Islamic state

---

[362] http://www.cair.com/about-us/cair-who-we-are.html#Introduction

[363] http://www.breitbart.com/national-security/2015/12/15/fbi-chart-documents-portray-cair-hamas-related-organization/

[364] Doyle, Michael, "Judge: Controversial 'Muslim Mafia' used stolen papers," Charlotte Observer, November 10, 2009

would be able to bring about the type of revolution necessary to subdue the whole world under the domain of Islam.

### Gülen Movement

The last of the political groups to review is the very influential Gülen movement established in the 1970s by Turkish Islamic scholar Fethullah Gülen. This movement is very active in education with over 1,000 private schools and universities in over 180 countries in the world (including even American charter schools). It promotes interfaith dialogue as a way to seek inroads into the communities and foreign governments and advocates cooperation between different religions. The movement has garnered praise for its advocacy of science, education, and interfaith dialogue, but critics have also pointed out that it often uses these means as a way to infiltrate non-Muslim societies.

## The Counter View

One of the central struggles within Islam is the ongoing conflict between the Sunni and the Shia Muslims. Historically, both sides claim the greater legitimacy, the former through succession of the chosen political leaders, and the latter through direct bloodlines going back to Muhammad himself. The Shia also claim to carry the superior leadership through their spiritual leaders, who will culminate in the Imam Mahdi, the one who will appear at the end times and lead the Muslims in the final battle against the infidel.

One Muslim scholar, Murtaza Hussain, however, believes that the Sunni-Shia conflict narrative is "misguided at best and disingenuous at worst." He reasons that, "The conflict which some claim exists today between Sunni and Shia Muslims is a product of very recent global events, blowback from the 1979 Iranian Revolution and the petro-dollar fuelled [sic] global rise of Wahhabi reactionaries," and driven by modern politics rather than the continuation of a 1400-year grudge war between Sunnis and Shias. A Shi'ite Saudi economist, Ihsan Bu-Huleiga, agrees with the political assessment, but not the timeline: "The differences between groups in Islam have always existed, but it is only when you mix them with politics that it becomes really dangerous—dangerous like an atomic bomb."[365] Indeed, throughout the Middle East, most of the wars and political conflicts pit Sunnis against Shiites. However, is the root of this schism found in the decision over the right of succession, or have these battles been fought for political and economic sway?

---

[365] Yaroslav Trofimov. May 14, 2015 Wall Street Journal. "Sunni-Shiite Conflict Reflects Modern Power Struggle, Not Theological Schism."

In a recent dissertation, Michael Bufano concludes that the split between Sunnism and Twelver Shi'ism was the product of several centuries of various theological factions (such as the Kharajites, the Qadarites, Mu'tazilites, and the Ash'arites) wrestling with the early theological issues and sorting out which beliefs would become standard, or orthodox. He suggests that "many do not realize how long it took for the important differences between what became known as Sunni and Shi'i Islam to become solid and fixed as they now seem to be. In other words, in the first few centuries of Islamic history, the term Shi'ism can only be applied retrospectively to a diversity of political sects and religious movements, many of which had little in common."[366] Thus, it is possible that the Sunni-Shi'a divide did not begin to develop until the tenth century during the Abbasid era and reach fruition until the sixteenth century under the Safavid era. This means that the process to consolidate these two main branches of Islam took almost 1,000 years.[367] This reminds us that much in Islam may be retrofitted to accommodate later views, which would explain many of the contradictions and historical gaps that mark the development of early Islam. Just as there is a 9th-century view of how the Qur'an was canonized rather than 7th-century narratives from eyewitness accounts, in the case of the Sunni-Shia divide we may have a 16th-century invention rather than the real story.

Another question may also be significant, "Why does it matter?" In the chapter on the development of Islamic theology, it was demonstrated that theology because it is so often linked with politics in Islam, was subverted by power. In turn, this quest for power tends to use religion as its stepping stool for conquest and control. Thus, it is possible that the early movement toward a new religion in the seventh century may have been inspired by the religious goal of unifying Judaism and Christianity, with its various branches (Monophysites, Nestorians, and Melkites), under one religion. This first appealed to a number of those who were conquered, but after a while, the leaders of the new religion realized that they could only manage the population through political manipulation and "theological" control. Thus, it is possible that as Islam moved through various stages of development, Muslim leaders needed to exert more authority over the non-Muslims in order to maintain their religious dominance. Today this ever-escalating need for power and control seems to be reflected in the many battlefronts between the Sunni and the Shia for control over Islam.

---

[366] Michael Bufano, *A Reconsideration of the Sunni-Shi'a Divide in Early Islam* (Clemson University, 2008).

[367] Bufano, *Reconsideration*, 146.

The main problem with this is that the rest of the world seems to be caught in the middle.

## Implications

If the Sunni-Shia split did not occur in the 7th century over the dispute concerning the rightful successor to the leadership of Islam, but rather was a gradual development over centuries, then what does this indicate about the early history of the religion and its development? First of all, if the terms "Sunni" and "Shia" were not in use until the 10th century, this may support the view that the traditional narrative of the selection process for the new leader after Muhammad is incorrect. Indeed, since the historical existence of the first four caliphs, including Ali, is absent, then it is possible that this narrative of a dispute between the group that advocated selection by consensus and the group that advocated selection by heredity may merely be a scenario that was retrofitted from the tenth century after a long litany of theological and political disputes had coalesced into two main camps.

Historically it is certain that there were factional disputes within the early developers of the religion of Islam. However, the evidence better supports the view that these theological and political disputations were not along traditional Sunni-Shia lines, but rather indicate the eventual outcome of a religious revolution that first sought to bring the various Jewish and Christian factions together but ended up as a religion driven by political power to the point that in the end it rejected the very impetus of its original design. In other words, if the crafters of the religion of Islam, such as Muawiyah, Abd al-Malik and al-Hajjaj, were trying to create a religion that would unify the other major religious influences in the Middle East, what they ended up with is a religion that distorts the Mosaic legal system of the Jews, rejects the gospel of salvation of the Christians, and dooms its followers to the whimsy of a God they cannot relate to and a future that offers no assurances of a paradise beyond the grave.

Another implication of the Sunni-Shia divide is that it indicates that Islam is very much controlled by political ambitions: theological Islam has been trumped by political Islam. The practices (orthopraxy) in Islam cannot be separated from its beliefs (orthodoxy). Therefore, religion and politics, belief and power, become intertwined. Furthermore, the tendency is to mandate religious devotion through force rather than freedom of choice. We see this especially in the various political groups that have sprung up from both Sunni and Shia Islam, such as Wahhabism, the Muslim Brotherhood, CAIR, Jamaat-e-Islami, the Gülen Movement, and even more so with the Taliban, Al Qaeda, Hezbollah, Hamas, and ISIS. All these groups have made political Islam the force behind their ideology and the pathway to reaching their goals.

On the other hand, Christianity is not dependent on political institutions. In fact, the main point of Jesus' answer to the Pharisees concerning the Roman coin was to demonstrate that the core of Christianity is separate from the power of the state (Matthew 22:18-22). The real power in Christianity comes from the gospel of Jesus Christ. However, the real power in Islam comes from the followers submitting to the demands of the religious leaders which are based upon the commands in the Qur'an (Q. 3:18-20).

## Apologetic Conclusions

Christians need to understand the different groups that make up Islam in order to better explain Christian beliefs to Muslim friends. Some of the reasons for the development of the different sects in Islam are similar to the reasons that there are different denominations in Christianity. Christian leaders through the centuries have interpreted the Bible differently and these different interpretations have brought about different emphases in styles of worship, views of doctrine, and ways to interpret Scripture. These differences have led to the three major branches of Christianity (Catholic, Orthodox, and Protestant), and numerous denominations, especially among the Protestants. There have also been a number of heresies that have developed along the way.

Muslim leaders have also been responsible for leading groups of Muslims in various directions according to their interpretations, practices, and cultural background. However, since Christianity is based on core beliefs that all Christians (except for heretics) accept, such as a triune God, the deity of Christ, and salvation through faith, rather than on what they do, having different denominations can be a healthy way to meet the diverse personalities of cultures and peoples.

On the other hand, the emphasis in Islam is unity in the Umma and this usually is interpreted as all Muslims conforming to the same beliefs, as interpreted by the leaders of their sect, and following the same practices, as modeled by Muhammad. Innovation is discouraged and violation of Sharia is met with harsh consequences. One of the main reasons for these core differences between Christianity and Islam is that theological Islam was overshadowed by political Islam. The supreme goal in Christianity is to love the Lord with all your heart, soul, strength and mind, and then to love your neighbor as yourself (Mark 12:29-31). The supreme goal in Islam is to bring the whole world under the dominance of Allah (Q. 8:39, 9:33, 61:9). Love will free the soul, and dominance will enslave. These two systems are inherently incompatible and, unfortunately, will continue to build an insurmountable divide.

The prevalence of Sufi Islam may be a result of political Islam as well. If Allah is considered unknowable in orthodox Islam, and therefore inaccessible to humans, then it is impossible to have a personal relationship with Allah. However, there is a deep longing in the soul of man to have intimate knowledge of God. In Christianity there are ways for believers to fulfill this longing, and some denominations even go to extremes in order to promote ways to experience the fullness of God. On the other hand, the strict Sunni belief system does not allow Muslims to have a relationship with Allah, and since Islam is considered an all-encompassing system, including social, religious, cultural, and political aspects, these attempts to cultivate a deeper relationship with Allah are often squelched. However, this desire is so strong that Sufi groups have often found ways around the strict views of Sunni or Shia Islam and developed strong pockets of followers, especially from the more artistic and philosophically-minded Muslims. One thing for Christians to recognize is that Sufis are often the ones who are more open to the gospel since their hearts are already softened toward having a relationship with God.

## Building Bridges to Understand

The Sufi need for relationship can help Christians reach out to Muslims by stressing the love that God has for us and the reason that Christ came in the flesh. He wanted to break through that divine and human barrier. He also needed to become a man in order to die in our place.

It is also important to stress to our Muslim friends that Christians are also divided over many issues, often because of personal desires rather than biblical ones. Many of the differences among Christians are not about the fundamentals of the faith, but rather secondary issues. Christians therefore need to model forgiveness and tolerance with each other. We should not be afraid to admit to our frailties, especially if our weakness can reveal God's strength and holiness.

The problems between Sunni and Sufi branches can also be used to challenge Muslims to seek true forgiveness in Jesus Christ. Grudges carried over generations prevent people from true forgiveness. Only Christ can give the peace that passes understanding that will bring healing to such deep divides.

This is why it is so important for Christians to reach out to Muslims in truth and love. Muslims need to see what true Christianity is like, and they need to know that Christians truly love them. Building relationships with the Muslims we meet is the first step to bridging the gap that only Christ can fill. As we share the gospel with our Muslim friends, we can become part of the solution.

**Study Questions:**

1. Name three or four ways in which Sunni Islam and Shia Islam are similar.

2. What are the main differences between Sunni and Shia Islam? How important are these differences?

3. What is political Islam and how has it influenced the religion of Islam?

4. Explain some of the reasons that Sunni Muslims view other breakaway groups, such as the Ahmadiyyah Muslim Community and the Baha'i, as heretical groups.

5. How does the historical view of a tenth-century starting point for a retrofitted explanation of a seventh century Sunni-Shia split cast doubt on the veracity of some of the other origin stories for Islam (such as the religion, the Qur'an, and Muhammad)?

6. What would be a good approach to use with a Sufi Muslim in order to help them understand the core beliefs of Christianity?

# PART 3: JIHAD, CRUSADES, AND ISIS

# CHAPTER 12 History and Meaning of Jihad: A Struggle Against Violence or a Violent Struggle?

## Introduction

One of the most controversial issues brought up today in discussions about Islam is the topic of Jihad. Non-Muslims often associate the word with "holy war," conjuring up images of turbaned warriors with curved scimitars and black flags.[368] It may come as a surprise to these westerners, then, that the concept of jihad is a complex one, with the word itself having several possible interpretations. Even all Muslims do not agree on jihad's true meaning or its role in the practice of Islam. Some Muslims today claim that jihad defines a personal struggle each believer has within themselves in order to fully submit to Allah. These Muslims vehemently oppose the other interpretation, which is that jihad provides the rationale for their political and military conquests in order to advance the cause of Islam and bring the world under the domain of Allah. In this muddle, many political leaders and Western scholars emphasize the peaceful, internal struggle interpretation of jihad. Others, however, point out that Islamic history itself undermines this view, as it has been a history of conflict and conquest from its inception, and directed primarily against Christian territories, as Bernard Lewis points out:

> For almost a thousand years ... Europe was under constant threat. In the early centuries it was a double threat—not only of invasion and conquest, but also of conversion and assimilation. All but the easternmost provinces of the Islamic realm had been taken from Christian rulers, and the vast majority of the first Muslims west of Iran and Arabia were converts from Christianity. North Africa, Egypt, Syria, even Persian-ruled Iraq, had been Christian countries, in which Christianity was older and more deeply rooted than in most of Europe. Their loss was sorely felt and heightened the fear that a similar fate was in store for Europe.[369]

Naturally, such clashing views lead to some important questions. If Islam is a religion of peace, why are there so many Muslims who claim they

---

[368] See Mark Hartwig, "Spread by the Sword?" http://www.answering-islam.org/Terrorism/by_the_sword.html

[369] Bernard Lewis, *Islam and the West* (New York: Oxford University Press, 1993), 13.

are true followers of Muhammad and the Qur'an constantly at war with each other and all other nations and people? Can "jihad" lead to both peace and war? A survey of the various views of jihad throughout the history of Islam will help resolve these questions. This chapter will also explore the concept of jihad politically, theologically, and culturally in order to determine how it is used in different contexts and what it means for Christians in the West today.

## The Traditional Muslim View

Examining the traditional Muslim view of Jihad is a somewhat complex task, as it involves two conflicting viewpoints today and various interpretations over the past centuries. The Moderate View, which is often emphasized by Muslims and non-Muslim leaders alike in the West, is the most complex. It also is argued by various sources to be a far more recent interpretation than the Fundamentalist View. Before discussing these two views, a general definition of the word "jihad" should be noted. Its basic sense is to "struggle" or "persevere" toward some goal. The word is derived from the Arabic root, "jahada," and for Muslims this struggle is often understood in the context of religious duty. It is therefore often linked with the phrase *al-jihad fi sabil Allah,* meaning "struggle, or striving, in the path of God." This term occurs often in the Qur'an and Hadith, commanding faithful Muslims to carry out jihad for Allah.[370] How and where exactly this struggle is carried out, however, is the true center of controversy.

### Moderate Muslim View

The Moderate View of jihad hinges around the concept of "greater and lesser jihad." Moderate Muslim scholars explain that the struggle of jihad is best understood not as a holy war but as having two meanings: an inner spiritual struggle, called the "greater jihad," and an outer physical struggle against the enemies of Islam, called the "lesser jihad." This dual understanding is said to have come from Muhammad who once told his followers returning from a military campaign, "this day we have returned from the minor jihad to the major jihad."[371] Thus, this view holds that the most important struggle humans can have is the struggle to gain mastery

---

[370] Ahmed Al-Dawoody, *The Islamic Law of War: Justifications and Regulations*, (Palgrave: Macmillan, 2011), 56. "Seventeen derivatives of jihād occur altogether forty-one times in eleven Meccan texts and thirty Medinan ones, with the following five meanings: striving because of religious belief (21), war (12), non-Muslim parents exerting pressure, that is, jihād, to make their children abandon Islam (2), solemn oaths (5), and physical strength (1)." There are many references in the Hadith to Jihad, and there is also a chapter in the Hadith collection of Al-Bukhari that focuses entirely on Jihad.

[371] Hadith (Fayd al-Qadir) vol. 4, p. 511.

over personal desires in order to submit fully to the will of Allah. If military action is taken, it must be only when necessary to protect the faith, and therefore only carried out defensively and along carefully defined terms of engagement, such as not harming women and children or those who are disabled. Significantly, this "lesser" or defensive jihad must be previously authorized by proper authorities, such as key religious scholars or prominent governing officials, to ensure that the threat is imminent, and the cause is truly one of defense.[372]

In order to support this view of jihad as a defensive mechanism, moderate Muslim scholars interpret the history of Islam as being primarily one of co-existence, where military action as a means of Jihad is used only rarely. One example of this need for military jihad, according to Muslim scholars, was during the defensive battles against the Christian Crusaders when they invaded Palestine. Another time was during the early period of Islamic conquests when the Muslims were being attacked by Byzantine and Persian forces. Instances where unprovoked and violent warfare was undertaken in the name of Islam are categorized as instances of misuse of the concept of jihad, where political or religious groups hijacked the idea of jihad to gain power and control over infidels, or even when splinter groups attacked orthodox Muslims with the claim that they, the splinter group, represented Muhammad's true followers. Thus, the Moderate view maintains that true military jihad is rare and carefully controlled. Therefore, if there were incidents that misused extreme violence, the Moderates would not tend to interpret these travesties as legitimate instances of jihad. Instead, these unauthorized acts of violence would be deemed unIslamic and the perpetrators would be treated as infidels of the faith. Most importantly, they argue, jihad should not be viewed as a declaration of war against other religious groups, especially Jews and Christians, who should be protected and respected because they worship the same God that Muslims do.

Indeed, moderate Muslims point to Qur'anic verses which emphasize the co-existence of religions and the doctrine of "just wars." Sura 2:256, for example, is one of the most significant verses as it states that "there can be no compulsion in religion." Thus, as medieval scholar Ibn Taymiyya (1263-1328 AD) theorized, Muhammad himself would have never sanctioned the killing of non-believers who refused to convert, as this would contradict the non-compulsion principle.[373] Without a justification for offensive action, defensive or "just" war is the only acceptable type of violence; Sura 22:39-40 and Sura 2:190 state that any attacks against non-believers must be a defensive response to oppression and injustice. This is why moderate

---

[372] Sardar, *Introducing Islam*, 60-61.
[373] Reza Aslan, *No god but God*, 85.

Muslim scholars would argue that Islamic terrorist groups are not following true Muslim guidelines and therefore are distorting the true meaning of jihad.[374]

Beyond these basic tenets of Greater and Lesser Jihad, moderate Muslims in the West generally also believe that non-Muslims do not understand the true meaning of jihad. Reza Aslan expresses these views well, arguing that there are a number of misunderstandings that have promoted various false stereotypes of jihad. For one thing, Aslan claims that Islam has often been portrayed as a "warrior religion" that inspired the Muslim horde to charge across the Middle East with a holy passion. However, he believes this "deep-rooted stereotype of Islam as a warrior religion has its origins in the papal propaganda of the Crusades when Muslims were depicted as the soldiers of the Antichrist in blasphemous occupation of the Holy Lands."[375] In addition, Aslan says that during the Middle Ages the Holy Roman Empire was trying to distinguish itself as important in the face of all the Islamic advances in philosophy and science by labeling Islam as the "religion of the sword," thus projecting a Western superiority over Muslim actions.

Furthermore, Aslan advances the Moderate perspective by arguing that non-Muslims were not forced to convert to Islam by military force. He maintains that neither Muhammad nor the Qur'an sanctions this behavior, and that early Muslims did not encourage it. Instead, he reasons that "the financial and social advantages of being an Arab Muslim in the eighth and ninth centuries were such that Islam quickly became an elite clique," and therefore the benefits of joining the new religion attracted nonbelievers to embrace Islam for themselves.[376]

However, the main area of confusion, moderate Muslims argue, is the true meaning of the word "jihad." They refute the popular view that the concept of jihad means "holy war" and seek to reclaim its true meaning, which they argue is that of an inner struggle for purity before Allah. This argument has been voiced in Western academic circles as well, as was expressed in the Spring 2002 Harvard graduation speech by a senior named Zayed Yasin who stressed that jihad in its truest and purest form, the form to which all Muslims aspire, is the determination to do right to do justice even against your own interests. It is an individual struggle for personal

---

[374] Ibid., 87.
[375] Ibid., 79.
[376] Ibid., 80.

moral behavior. Especially today, it is a struggle that exists on many levels: self-purification and awareness, public service and social justice.[377]

Several professors at Harvard University spoke in support of this non-violent interpretation. Among them, David Mitten, a convert to Islam, stated that true jihad is "the constant struggle of Muslims to conquer their inner base instincts, to follow the path to God, and to do good in society."[378] Roy Mottahedeh, the chairman of the committee on Islamic studies at Harvard, added that a majority of learned Muslim thinkers "insist that jihad must be understood as a struggle without arms"[379] in all cases except defense and justice. John Esposito, a professor at Georgetown University, explained these views further by concluding that "in the struggle to be a good Muslim, there may be times where one will be called on to defend one's faith and community. Then [jihad] can take on the meaning of an armed struggle."[380]

Thus, the Moderate View is generally supported by western academics (and political leaders) in their views that jihad is first an inner struggle (Greater Jihad) and only second a defensive military option (Lesser Jihad). The legitimacy of this interpretation is supported from the Qur'an and various sayings of Muhammad, and therefore the Moderates believe Muslims who view jihad as a mandate for aggressive violence have tragically ceased to follow true Islam.

## The Fundamentalist Muslim View

Leading Muslims who support the Fundamentalist View of jihad insist that only Muslims should speak for Islam, claiming that Islam is not a religion of peace. For example, Al-Baghdadi, the self-proclaimed leader of the Islamic State Caliphate, has said, "Islam was never a religion of peace. Islam is the religion of fighting. No one should believe that the war that we are waging is the war of the Islamic State."[381] It is important to note that fundamentalists trace this understanding of jihad all the way back to the

---

[377] Daniel Pipes, "Jihad and the Professors,"Commentary, November 2002: http://www.danielpipes.org/498/jihad-and-the-professors (accessed 7/26/2018).

[378] David Mitten, Harvard Islamic Society: http://www.discoverthenetworks.org/printgroupProfile.asp?grpid=7406 (accessed 7/26/2018).

[379] Roy Mottahedeh, "Islam and the Opposition to Terrorism": https://www.nytimes.com/2001/09/30/opinion/islam-and-the-opposition-to-terrorism.html (accessed 7/26/2018).

[380] Daniel Pipes, "Jihad and the Professors,"Commentary, November 2002: http://www.danielpipes.org/498/jihad-and-the-professors (accessed 7/26/2018).

[381] http://www.dailymail.co.uk/news/article-3082114/ISIS-execute-26-civilians-fighters-reach-gates-ancient-Palmyra-Syria.html

first days of Islam. Some of the hadiths relate what Muhammad himself had to say about jihad:

> I have been commanded to fight people until they testify that there is no god, but Allah and that Muhammad is the Messenger of Allah, and perform the prayer, and pay zakat. If they say it, they have saved their blood and possessions from me, except for the rights of Islam over them. And their final reckoning is with Allah.[382]

Even the popular 14th-century compilation of Islamic law called *The Reliance of the Traveler* says that "Jihad means to war against non-Muslims, and is etymologically derived from the word *mujahada*, signifying warfare to establish the religion."[383] In addition, one of Islam's most prominent scholars, Ibn Khaldun, compared the mission of Islam with the mission of other religious groups. His understanding was that in regard to the other major religions in the world, "the holy war was not a religious duty for them, save only for purposes of defense." However, the mission given to Islam was different. He relates, "In the Muslim community, the holy war is a religious duty, because of the universalism of the Muslim mission and the obligation to convert everybody to Islam either by persuasion or by force."[384] Hassan al-Banna, the founder of the Muslim Brotherhood, wrote about the centrality of jihad as well. He said that "Jihad is an obligation from Allah on every Muslim and cannot be ignored nor evaded... The verses of the Qur'an and the Sunnah of Muhammad (PBUH) are overflowing with all these noble ideals and they summon people in general to jihad, to warfare, to the armed forces, and all means of land and sea fighting."[385] In contrast to the many leaders who try to reduce jihad to a struggle that individual Muslims have with themselves in order to become better Muslims, there are many voices throughout the history of Islam who have boldly defined jihad as active warfare against the infidel until all people submit to Islam. These fundamentalist Muslim protest the interpretation of Islamic doctrine by non-Muslims, use the Qur'an and Hadith to support their views and emphasize that history supports their interpretation of a militaristic struggle in jihad.

---

[382] Bukhari, Book 1:Volume 8: Hadith 387; Sahih Muslim 1:31-34

[383] *Reliance of the Traveller*, Revised Edition (Beltsville: Amana, 1988), 599.

[384] Ibn Khaldun, *The Muqaddimah*, 183.

[385] Hasan al-Banna, *Kitabul Jihad*, in Milestones, ed. A.B. al-Mehri (Birmingham, England: Maktabah, 2006), 220.

## Counterview

How non-Muslims and Westerners understand and respond to the concept of jihad is, as has been indicted, a complex subject. The current trend among influential Muslims is to adopt the position of reformers, seeking to define jihad as a personal struggle or, at most, self-defense against a specified enemy. For example, the Council on American-Islamic Relations (CAIR) insists that Christians exaggerate the role of jihad and make it out to be "holy war" when it is simply a "broad Islamic concept that includes struggle against evil inclinations within oneself, struggle to improve the quality of life in society, struggle in the battlefield for self-defense (e.g., having a standing army for national defense), or fighting against tyranny or oppression."[386] On the other hand, revisionist scholars argue that jihad, both in Qur'anic teaching and in Islamic history, has always included the concept of a "holy war" with offensive tactics against non-believers. For example, in his book, *The History of Jihad*, Robert Spencer "shows that jihad warfare has been a constant of Islam from its very beginnings, and present-day jihad terrorism proceeds along exactly the same ideological and theological foundations as did the great Islamic warrior states and jihad commanders of the past."[387]

Being thus in a kind of agreement with the Fundamentalist View, such scholars warn of the deadly peril faced by Western societies whose leaders generally dismiss violent jihad as the product of a few unbalanced terrorists, and who give little credence to the argument that aggressive jihad is supported in any way by the Qur'an or orthodox Muslim teachings. If violent jihad is in fact supported or even mandated by Islamic doctrine, revisionists point out, there is no reason to expect violence and terrorism to diminish or die a natural death.

Revisionist scholars bring up historical and textual evidence to argue that, as Paul Fregosi puts it, "the purpose of jihad became, and basically still is, to expand and extend Islam until the whole world is under Islamic rule."[388] Another author, Jacques Ellul, emphasizes jihad's essentially religious nature and pointed out jihad's inescapable connection to every Muslim: "Jihad... forms part of the duties a believer must fulfill; it is Islam's

---

[386] Daniel Pipes, Jihad: How Academics Have Camouflaged Its Real Meaning, http://historynewsnetwork.org/article/1136.

[387] Robert Spencer, *The History of Jihad: From Muhammad to ISIS* (Bombardier, 2018). Book promotion, Amazon.com.

[388] Paul Fregosi, *Jihad: Muslim Conquests from the 7th to the 21st Centuries* (New York: Prometheus, 1998), 20.

*normal* path to expansion."[389] This section examines these and other claims by revisionist authors, focusing on the historical evidence, texts from the Qur'an and Hadith, and critiques of the Moderate View which form the core of these counterview arguments.

In terms of historical evidence, the past 1300 years offer a wealth of information about Islam's growth and expansion. As has been noted in a previous chapter, the 700's – 1500's AD saw a concerted and persistent effort to spread Islamic control over large swathes of land in the Middle East, North Africa, and even parts of Europe. Bernard Lewis writes of this period, "For more than a thousand years, Europe, that is to say Christendom, was under constant threat of Islamic attack and conquest. If the Muslims were repelled in one region, they appeared in greater strength in another."[390]

Logically, these constant battles cannot be attributed to a strategy of defensive jihad, as no historical accounts record instances of Islamic terrorists or believers being brought under attack when the land was initially acquired by Muslims. (The Crusades could well be argued to be an instance of defense, but it should be recalled that the land was initially acquired by Muslims from non-Muslims years before.) Thus, if the conventional definition of 'defense,' which is seeking to retain land that one already possesses or owns, then aggressively assuming control of lands already occupied by others cannot be termed a defense. One other possible scenario of 'defense' might be a situation where the peoples of other lands were persecuting Muslims, and defeating the persecutors brought about the secondary consequence of Muslim forces acquiring new lands after the battles were over. Historical records can answer whether the latter situation actually occurred; and from earlier chapters tracing the expansion of Islam, the evidence is very clear that Islam was the aggressor most of time. Thus, the conquest of these lands is much more readily explained by the conclusion that early Muslims viewed their work as an offensive jihad, with the goal of conquering land in the name of Allah (Q. 8:39), or simply conquering out of non-religious motivations.

Going back even further in history, revisionist scholars argue that Muhammad himself waged mostly offensive battles against Mecca. This pattern of warfare seems to have been established soon after Muhammad and his followers arrived at Medina, where the earliest biographies record

---

[389] Ibid., 20. Quoted in the foreword to Bat Yeor's *The Decline of Eastern Christianity Under Islam: From Jihad to Dhimmitude: Seventh-Twentieth Century* (Farleigh Dickinson, 1996), 19.

[390] Bernard Lewis, *From Babel to Dragomans: Interpreting the Middle East* (Oxford: Oxford University Press, 2004), 126.

that they engaged in over seventy battles.[391] Only one, the Battle of the Trench (627 AD), was defensive in terms of protecting the Muslims' lives and property. However, it can be argued that Muhammad's early life and sayings in Mecca, recorded in the Qur'an and Hadith, do indicate an emphasis on peace. One revisionist scholar, David Wood, has argued in response to this point that there were actually different "stages" of how the concept of jihad was viewed, corresponding to the status of Muslims in society at the time. These three stages can be titled 'respect,' 'defense,' and 'offense.'

Wood found, first, that the first stage of *respect* applied during the time that Muhammad and the Muslims were in the minority in Mecca and needed to maintain peaceful relationships with the non-believers and patiently bear with those who denied the truth of Islam. Thus, the revelations Muhammad received during this stage called for religious tolerance, such as is recorded in Sura 109:6, which supposedly was revealed in the earliest Meccan period,[392] and maintains that each person is free to choose their own religion ("You shall have your religion and I shall have my religion").[393] Wood calls this first stage "Stealth Jihad" because while Muhammad and his followers were being persecuted by the non-believers, there may have been a call for tolerance in public, but, as later verses indicate, Muhammad may have actually been preaching a subversive messages against the Meccans in private.

However, after the move to Medina when there were enough Muslims to fight defensively against the Meccan opponents, then permission was given to fight against others in order to defend themselves. This brought in the second stage, called "Defensive Jihad." It was during this time that Sura 22:39-40 was revealed and gave permission to fight against those who sought harm to the community.

> Permission (to fight) is given to those upon whom war is made because they are oppressed, and most surely Allah is well able to assist them; Those who have been expelled from their homes without a just cause except that they say: our Lord is Allah...

The third stage, called "Offensive Jihad," began when Muslims established a majority in the area. During this stage, aggressive jihad against

---

[391] Ibn Ishaq/Ibn Hisham, The Life of the Prophet

[392] See Bell's Introduction to the Qur'an, chapter 7, which follows the chronology developed by Theodore Noeldeke. http://www.truthnet.org/islam/Watt/Chapter7.html

[393] See also Q. 73:10-11.

all unbelievers is commanded, including Jews and Christians, until they are subdued. Sura 9:29 represents this stage when it says,

> Fight those who do not believe in Allah or in the Last Day and who do not consider unlawful what Allah and His Messenger have made unlawful and who do not adopt the religion of truth from those who were given the Scripture - [fight] until they give the jizyah willingly while they are humbled.

It is important to note that in this passage, the Muslims were commanded to fight anyone who did not accept the religion of Islam and believe in Allah or follow the laws found in the Qur'an. Over the years, then, David Wood argues that the Muslims began with tolerance toward all those around them when they were in the minority, but once they had achieved the majority status and had power and authority due to their military strength, a call was sent down through revelations from Allah so that fighting unbelievers was a continual command until all non-believers were converted or became subdued under the rule of Islam. Revisionist scholars point to this pattern of jihad development being demonstrated during not only during the early years of Islam but extending through history wherever Islamic forces captured and conquered non-Muslim lands, throughout the Middle East, North Africa, and even along the borders of Europe.

Literary evidence is also offered by revisionist scholars to support these historical arguments and to counter the claims of the Moderate View of jihad. Using verses from the Qur'an and Hadith in this way naturally is very closely tied to the early history of Muhammad and the birth of Islam. Do these sources support a 'greater and lesser Jihad' concept, or do they command offensive jihads of conquest, as the fundamentalist Muslims claim? The difficulty in answering or even discussing this question is that the Qur'an actually contains passages that support both interpretations. For example, Sura 109:6 says, "You shall have your religion and I shall have my religion," and Sura 2:256 clearly states "There is no compulsion in religion." On the opposite end of the spectrum, Sura 9:5 says to "slay the idolaters wherever you find them," and Sura 9:29 encourages Muslims to "fight those who believe not in Allah." Some moderate Muslims explain these contradictory instructions by saying that the more violent verses were only for the time when Muhammad was leading the early Muslims, and once Islam was established, the peaceful verses took precedence over the outdated ones. However, this explanation actually goes against the Qur'an's own instruction on its interpretation: "We do not abrogate a verse or cause it to be forgotten except that We bring forth [one] better than it or similar to it. Do you not know that Allah is over all things competent?"[394] This method of interpretation is called the Doctrine of Abrogation, and it essentially calls for this practice of substituting verses that were revealed to Muhammad later in his ministry for earlier verses on the same subject, letting the later verses supersede the earlier.

For example, a verse such as Sura 9:5, known as one of the "sword verses," is considered according to the Doctrine of Abrogation to supersede as many as 114 other verses calling for tolerance and peace.[395] This is because it is said to be part of the last series of revelations given to Muhammad before his death in Medina. David Wood uses the Doctrine of Abrogation to support his argument of the three stages of Muslims' view of jihad, and writes that "when Muslims rose to power, peaceful verses of the Qur'an were abrogated by verses commanding Muslims to fight people based on their beliefs."[396]

These teachings were also carried on through various Hadith narratives, and there are many examples of Hadiths promoting a violent form of jihad (struggle against non-Muslims through force). For example, in Al-Bukhari (8: 387) Muhammad is recorded as saying, "I have been ordered to fight the people till they say: 'None has the right to be worshipped but Allah.' And if they say so, pray like our prayers, face our Qibla and slaughter as we slaughter, then their blood and property will be sacred to us and we will not interfere with them except legally and their reckoning will be with Allah." In Sahih Muslim (1:33), the Messenger of Allah is recorded as saying, "I have been commanded to fight against people till they testify that there is no god but Allah, that Muhammad is the messenger of Allah, and they establish prayer and pay zakat." It is noteworthy that in both of these hadiths violence is sanctioned until the person says the Shahada, prays and pays the zakat, which means that conversion to Islam has taken place. Daniel Pipes also points out that in the Hadith collection of al-Bukhari he finds that "there are 199 references to jihad, and every one of them refers to it in the sense of armed warfare against non-Muslims."[397]

Most Muslims accept the Doctrine of Abrogation today and have done so historically. One of the great commentators of the Qur'an, Ibn Kathir (1300-1373), concluded in his writings that the verse that advocates "there is no compulsion in religion" (Q. 2:256) has been abrogated. He

---

[394] See also Q. 16:101.

[395] https://www.politicalislam.com/abrogation-and-the-koran/

[396] David Wood, http://www.answeringmuslims.com/p/jihad.html

[397] Daniel Pipes, "Jihad: How Academics Have Camouflaged Its Real Meaning," http://www.daniepipes.org.

concluded, "Therefore all people of the world should be called to Islam. If anyone of them refuses to do so, or refuses to pay the Jizyah, they should be fought till they are killed."[398] Thus, the historical and literary elements come together with the Doctrine of Abrogation to create what revisionist scholars claim is a clear picture of Islamic doctrine gradually promoting a version of jihad that is based on physical violence and has decreasing tolerance towards unbelievers throughout the chronologically-placed Suras and Hadiths.

The final noteworthy argument that revisionist scholars make is that the Moderate View of jihad as a whole cannot be sustained in the light of the evidence detailed above. As additional support for this claim, scholars point out a flaw in one of the key arguments made by Muslims advocating the Moderate View: the famous Hadith that explains the concept of Greater and Lesser Jihad is actually only found in a 12th century book written by Yahya ibn al 'Ala, called *The History of Baghdad*. In this book, In this book the author relates, "The prophet returned from one of his battles, and thereupon told us, "you have arrived with an excellent arrival, you have come from the Lesser Jihad to the Greater Jihad – the striving of a servant against his desires." However, this story is totally absent from the traditional hadith collections. It also directly contradicts the Qur'an (4:95-96), which states, "Allah prefers the mujahidin over those who remain [behind] with a great reward." This passage and its late creation would seem to indicate that some Muslims want to promote the idea of the "greater" jihad so that they can get away from the violence of the "lesser" jihad. Peter Townsend concludes, "It should be clear from the above that the idea that 'jihad against the self' is the most important form of jihad has no basis whatsoever in orthodox Islamic teaching."[399]

Besides abrogation and this unsupported hadith, revisionist scholars also argue that some of the more popular Qur'anic verses quoted to support the Moderate View are taken out of context. These verses would be used to argue a general theological point, such as regarding internal jihad, but actually, they cannot be supported from the full text they are drawn from. A significant example of this is Sura 5:32, which says that "if any one slew a person – unless it be for murder or for spreading mischief in the land – it would be as if he slew the whole people: and if any one saved a life, it would be as if he saved the life of the whole people." Muslims often quote this verse to give the idea that Islam holds all life to be valuable and killing anyone, except those committing murder or mischief, is strongly opposed to Islamic justice. However, the verse is

---

[398] Tafsir of Ibn Kathir, Al-Firdous, Ltd., 1st edition, Part 3, 37-38.

[399] Peter Townsend, *Questioning Islam: Tough Questions & Honest Answers About the Muslim Religion* (Peter Townsend, 2014), 231.

actually addressed specifically to the "Children of Israel" and does not refer to all people. In addition, other verses state that Jews and Christians "spread mischief in the land," where "mischief" is equated with unbelief, which is a great sin and worthy of death. Therefore, the Jews (and Christians) would not be innocent, but instead would merit the punishment mentioned in the very next verse:

> The punishment of those who wage war against Allah and His Messenger, and strive with might and main for mischief through the land is: execution, or crucifixion, or the cutting off of hands and feet from opposite sides, or exile from the land: that is their disgrace in this world, and a heavy punishment is theirs in the hereafter." (Q. 5:33)

Thus, a verse that is supposed to demonstrate the peacefulness of Islam actually condemns unbelievers to the most horrific punishment.

Understanding the context of verses as well as their chronological order is thus the final argument which revisionist scholars make to demonstrate that the original and accurate interpretation of jihad is one of violent conquest for Allah. While peaceful verses, like "Let there be no compulsion in religion" (Q. 2:256) may have been abrogated by later jihad verses, the violent jihad verses have not been abrogated. They are still in effect, according to the Doctrine of Abrogation, and revisionist scholars thus conclude that Muslims are encouraged to "fight until all religion is for Allah" (Q. 8:39).

## Implications

It is clear, then, that these two views of jihad, along with their interpretation of history and the Qur'an, also have very different views on religious violence as it exists today. If the Moderate View is correct, and violence is not a true part of Islam, then terrorists and extremists who insist that it is are really motivated for other reasons – either their own desire for power, or a false understanding of Islam, or both. At any rate, according to the Moderates, it can never become a dominant view because there are no grounds for such beliefs in the Qur'an, nor any good precedent in history. Troublemakers and isolated splinter groups may pop up over the years, but the majority of Muslims will always adhere to the true interpretation and seek jihad only in their hearts as a means of submitting their personal lives to Allah.

But if revisionist scholars are correct, then several very different implications must be noted. First, their argument that violence is integral to Islamic faith necessarily means that violence and oppressive measures will always be encouraged by a careful study of Islam, not suppressed. Second, if their points are valid, then Westerners are being currently deceived by what is effectively Muslim propaganda – a situation which is as dangerous on an individual level as it is on a national and global level. It is also a falsification of history, as the Moderate View seeks to explain or dismiss the large numbers of offensive battles, campaigns, conquests, and raids, some of which have threated the heart of Europe's territory, as in 732 (Battle of Tours) and in 1683 (Battle of Vienna). Such a misrepresentation means that Westerners do not accurately understand the way that Islamic cultures and Christian nations have interacted in the past, which makes it far more difficult to interact wisely in the present. Finally, if the Moderate view is not supported by the Qur'an or by history, then this bears important implications theologically. As William Kilpatrick puts it, "Jihad for the sake of Allah is not some unfortunate deviation from the true faith, it's an integral part of that faith."[400] Christians must especially be aware of this controversy regarding jihad as they seek to engage Muslim friends. Otherwise, they will most likely assume that peace has the same definition and connotations in Islam as in Christianity, when in fact not all Muslims believe that – and when, if revisionist scholars are correct, no Muslim should believe it if they study the Qur'an carefully.

These implications are especially significant if one considers Islam by global numbers. After all, if a bare handful of Muslims oppose the Moderate View and support warfare and terrorism in the name of Allah instead, what does it really matter? Every religion has its extremists, as is often argued by prominent leaders.[401] However, when one actually considers in terms of statistics who support radical Islam, it has been demonstrated by several groups and polls that the "99.9% of Muslims are completely against radical Islam"[402] is not grounded in substantial fact. In December 2015, the Clarion Project released a video called "By the Numbers – The Untold Story of Muslim Opinions and Demographics." A Muslim woman, Raheel Raza, president of Muslims Facing Tomorrow, narrated the film which demonstrated that radical Islam is a bigger problem than most Western governments want to admit. If we divide up the 1.6 billion Muslims into

---

[400] William Kilpatrick, "Needed: A New Church Policy toward Islam," Crisis Magazine, Feb. 4, 2015.

[401] For instance, Pope Francis has said that "it is not right to identify Islam with violence," since all religions have "fundamentalist" groups that do not represent the true goals of the religion. See http://www.haaretz.com/world-news/europe/1.734559; https://www.jihadwatch.org/2016/07/hugh-fitzgerald-pope-francis-and-jihad-credo-quia-absurdum-and-how

[402] https://winteryknight.com/2015/02/03/obama-says-that-99-9-of-muslims-worldwide-reject-radical-islam-is-he-right/ and http://cnnpressroom.blogs.cnn.com/2015/02/01/pres-obama-on-fareed-zakaria-gps-cnn-exclusive/ (accessed 9/29/2016).

five categories – Jihadists (radicals), Islamists, Fundamentalists, Moderates, and Liberals – the Jihadists would only number around 250,000 to 500,000 people, or less than .03% of all Muslims (ISIS: 40,000 to 200,000; Hamas: 30,000; Hezbollah: 15,000; al Qaeda and affiliates: 100,000; Iranian Revolutionary Guard: 15,000 to 100,000).[403] However, the next two groups contain much larger spheres that support the radical ideology of the Jihadists, especially their beliefs on jihad and sharia, but use different tactics and often work within the cultural and political systems. The first of these two groups are the Islamists, represented by the Muslim Brotherhood, Hamas supporters, and CAIR. The third sphere, the Fundamentalists, make up the greater proportion of Muslims who favor radical views.

It is difficult to arrive at a specific number of Muslims that are represented by these three groups, but a recent Pew Report[404] indicates that these "spheres of radicalization" demonstrate that consistently over 20-25% of all Muslims, especially those in Muslim majority countries, accept and support active jihad and strict sharia law in order to fulfill their obligations to Allah. For example, the Pew Report found that of the 39 Muslim countries polled, 27% of all Muslims believe apostates from Islam should be killed. This represents 237 million people. In addition, 53% of Muslims, or 469 million, support sharia as the law of the land, and over 50% of these are in favor of whippings and amputations, as well as stoning for adulterers. Altogether, then, these three spheres represent 20-25% of all Muslims or roughly 320-400 million people. Most of these Muslims are not involved in the terrorism directly, but they are certainly part of the community that supports and encourages the views and actions of the jihadists and Islamists involved in carrying out the atrocities, all in the name of the religion of Islam.

The impact of these numbers should not be overlooked when considering the implications of Moderate vs. Fundamentalist views of Islam. If 20% of Muslims around the world encourage fundamentalist views and 53% support the implementation of Sharia law, then this paints a very different picture of global Muslim views on jihad than Moderate View proponents have popularly suggested. Westerners should be aware of how peace and violence have historically been defined in Islamic cultures, and

---

[403] Source Clarion Project data: CIA, Amnesty International, CNN, BBC, International Institute for Strategic Studies, Bipartisan Policy Center's Homeland Security Project, Guardian.

[404] "The World's Muslims: Religion, Politics and Society", *Pew Research Center*, April 2013 pp. 16-20

http://www.pewforum.org/files/2013/04/worlds-muslims-religion-politics-society-full-report.pdf .

they should also be wary of assurances of 'mainstream' Islam's peace when such claims are not supported by specific facts.

## Apologetic Conclusions

The theological foundations of jihad are ultimately found in understanding the nature of Allah, as well as clearly distinguishing the difference between peace in Islam – which is literally 'submission' in the text – and Western or Christian definitions of peace. Jihad is integral to Islam because jihad flows from the nature of Allah and his relationship with Muslims and with non-Muslims. First, the prime expression of Allah is his will. This is part of the fundamental belief in Islam that "there is only one God" who is absolute over all things, as well as absolutely other in nature (Q. 112:1-4). Allah is affirmed as being able to do anything, including making what is right, wrong, and making that which is wrong, right. Thus, his righteousness is subordinate to his power, and his power is rooted in his absolute will.

Sura 9:51 explains the logical result of this divine nature, which is the acceptance of Allah's pre-determined plan. After all, nothing can possibly happen to a person without it being the specific will of Allah. The verse declares, "Nothing shall ever happen to us except what Allah has ordained for us. He is our Mawla (protector). And in Allah let the believers put their trust." The prime expression from Allah, then, is his will, and pure will demands submission rather than love. Thus, the relationship between Allah and man is based on man submitting to Allah. It is for this reason that Islam means "submission," and a Muslim is "one who submits." Allah will then give power to his followers as they submit themselves to his will.

This is the point at which "submission" is usually supposed to equal "peace" (which is usually defined as the absence of hostilities and thus harmony and serenity between people). However, this is not logically an exact equivalence, since submission to one person does not necessarily entail submission to others. If Allah's expressed will is to conduct violence against others, such as non-Muslims or those who have broken his law, then following that will is still 'submission' even as the follower commits bloodshed to achieve it. In such cases, submission and peace – obeying Allah and living in harmony with others – could not co-exist. It is along this line of reason that Anjem Choudary, an Islamic spiritual leader in the UK, has stated, "You can't say that Islam is a religion of peace, because Islam does not mean peace. Islam means 'submission.' So a Muslim is one who submits. There is a place for violence in Islam. There is a place for Jihad in Islam."[405]

---

[405] CNN news, April 5, 2010

In addition to understanding the theological implications of jihad, it is important apologetically to see that jihad as a holy war actually carries out a return to the roots of Islam. What is the relationship between peace and power? Some moderate Muslims seek to focus on power as the means to peace. For instance, Muslim author Imran Hostein states that there are five functions of power in Islam: as a deterrent for attack, for responding to aggression, to fight for the oppressed and weak, to persuade others of the truth, and finally to establish justice and societal order.[406] In this way, a good use of power brings peace. The problem with this argument is that the idea of using power for a primary goal of peace, rather than a primary goal of submission to Allah's will, actually contradicts not only the theological implications of Allah's nature but also the example of Muhammad and his instructions in the Qur'an. The conflict of physical jihad toward non-Muslims began with Muhammad and his followers, and it is only reasonable to expect that it will continue. As Bernard Lewis explains, "The presumption is that the duty of jihad will continue, interrupted only by truces, until all the world either adopts the Muslim faith or submits to Muslim rule."[407] Thus, it is only when all are under Muslim rule that there can finally be peace in the sense of an absence of hostilities. While SaLaaM (peace) may be the ultimate goal, iSLaM (submission) is the current goal of every faithful Muslim. Though the two words, peace, or SaLaaM, and submission, iSLaM, share the same consonantal root, S-L-M, they have very different meanings. Otherwise the word MuSLiM, or "one who submits" would also have to mean "one who brings peace." However, no one makes this suggestion. In fact, if the nature of Allah is power through his absolute will, submission brings division rather than peace. In Muslim tradition, the world is divided between those who submit to Allah (the House of Islam, known as "Dar al-Islam,"), and those who do not submit (the House of War, known as "Dar al-Harb"). Christians who engage their Muslim friends in apologetic discussions about jihad must remember these semantic differences as well as learn to view them from the theological perspective of Allah's ultimate will and its demand for submission.

In order for Islam to actually be a religion of peace rather than of submission, therefore, the very essence of the faith would have to change. As Nabeel Qureshi argues, a "return to roots" reformation that focuses on Muhammad's life and the 7th-century society would ultimately create a more radical form of Islam, not a more peaceful or "progressive" one:

---

[406] Imran Hosein, *The Function of Power in Islam*, http://www.themodernreligion.com/pol/power.htm

[407] Bernard Lewis, *The Crisis of Islam: Holy War and Unholy Terror* (New York: Random House, 2004), 31-2.

The notion that reformation should lead to peaceful expressions of a religion is predicated on the assumption that the origins of that religion are peaceful… Since violence is built into the very origins of Islam, the religion would need to be re-envisioned in order to produce a peaceful religion that is internally consistent. Emphasis would have to be drawn away from the Qur'an and Muhammad's life, or the records of their contexts would need to be disavowed. This would not be a reformation but a progression of Islam.[408]

Understanding jihad in an apologetic context thus requires a basic understanding of the theological relationship between divine will and human submission, the difference between submission to Allah and peace towards mankind, and the historical and literary difficulties in re-defining Islam as a religion that advocates the use of power to create 'peace' in a non-violent sense of the word.

## Building Bridges to Understand

Christians discussing jihad with their Muslim friends will almost inevitably stumble upon the issue of peace and what its true definition is, as well as what it should look like in everyday life. Some key contrasts between Muhammad and Jesus' descriptions of peace may be helpful in discussion, with the goal of clearly illustrating what kind of spiritual peace Jesus offers those who follow him.

First, the contrast between depictions of violence and peace in the Qur'an and in the Bible (particularly the New Testament) can be explored. The verses from the Qur'an and Hadiths that have been discussed in this chapter demonstrate that taking the Doctrine of Abrogation into account, the core of Islam is built upon a foundation of violent jihad that must be waged until Judgement Day. As one writer puts it, "Islam allows no permanent peaceful coexistence and co-equality with infidels. Superiority is such a central aspect of Islamic thought that domination is the only worthy expression of Islam's greatness."[409] In stark contrast to this destructive and ultimately very earthly viewpoint, the New Testament shows that Jesus' explanation of his ministry was to bring peace by restoring a spiritual relationship between God and his people. Physical violence and earthly conflicts are continually de-emphasized in comparison. For example, John 14:27 records Christ as saying, "Peace I leave with you; my peace I give to

---

[408] Nabeel Qureshi, *Answering Jihad: A Better Way Forward* (Grand Rapids, MI: Zondervan, 2016), 77.

[409] Youssef, Blindsided, 92.

you. Not as the world gives do I give to you. Let not your hearts be troubled; neither let them be afraid." Even the famous 'sword passage' – often quoted to link Jesus's teaching with militaristic views – is best understood as a metaphorical sword. Matthew 10:34 records the words, "Do not think that I have come to bring peace to the earth. I have not come to bring peace, but a sword." However, the sword refers to the relational separation that occurs between those who believe in Christ and those who do not, even within a family. Jesus was asking for unqualified allegiance and explaining that any relationship that hindered a Christian from being willing to forsake worldly goals and commitments for the sake of Christ must be severed. This call, then, is again a spiritual one rather than a physical call for worldly power or conquest.

Other New Testament verses further illustrate this contrast between the Qur'an and the Bible's teaching on warfare. In Hebrews 4:12, the biblical author uses a sword as a metaphor for the word of God, which spreads the gospel to the whole world. The apostle Paul, in Ephesians 6:12, further emphasizes the spiritual nature of a Christian believer's struggle: "For we do not wrestle against flesh and blood, but against the rulers, against the authorities, against the cosmic powers over this present darkness, against the spiritual forces of evil in the heavenly places." Christians can point out that this emphasis on spiritual struggle is perhaps most powerfully exemplified in the gospel accounts of Jesus' response in the Garden of Gethsemane to his disciple Peter's cutting off the ear of one of the arresting men in the crowd. Christ rebuked Peter[410] and healed the man, thus ending the only time in the gospels that a sword actually comes into play.

The conclusion that Christians can point out from such a discussion is, ultimately, the difference between the "kingdoms" which Jesus and Muhammad sought to build. Muhammad called not only for spiritual submission to Allah and his will but also physical submission of those around him. Jesus, on the other hand, called for disciples whose hearts would be radically changed, promising them that they would suffer in the world for their faith, not prosper, and urging them to store up spiritual treasure in heaven. Thus, Jesus' peace is given immediately to his followers and is not dependent on their circumstances, while Muhammad's promise of peace can only be fulfilled when the world submits (which the Qur'an says will be Judgement Day). Because of this difference, Christians can offer their Muslim friends an immediate peace through Christ that will change their lives, giving them a right relationship with God which will then flow into a right relationship with others. This is the way that Christ called for

---

[410] The words of Christ in Matthew 26:52 are ironic in regard to this discussion, for Jesus said, "all who take up the sword will perish by the sword."

his kingdom to be spread on earth – through suffering and love reaching out to every person, no matter how violent or unlovely that person might be. When seen in this light, the "kingdoms" of Islam and of Christianity cannot have a greater contrast.

**Study Questions:**

1. What is meant by the "greater jihad," and what are the main arguments for this view?

2. How would a radical Muslim defend political or violent jihad? What Qur'anic verses would they use?

3. What are some indications that Muhammad was involved in radical jihad? What are some verses in the Qur'an, Hadith or biographies that would support your argument?

4. What are the three stages of Jihad according to David Wood? What are characteristics of these stages today and how are they influenced by the increase in the number of Muslims in the population of a non-Muslim country?

5. What would be the most effective way to counter the view of jihad and help Muslims realize that true peace can only come through Jesus Christ?

# CHAPTER 13 Crusades: Christian Holy War or Delayed Response?

## Introduction

Whenever the subject of the Crusades comes up in conversation, it seems to touch a raw nerve and causes Christians in the West to feel defensive as well as apologetic. Many view the Crusades as a medieval forerunner of European imperialism characterized by aggression, a desire for expansion, and wanton destruction. This volatile issue has also become an obstacle in discussions between Christians and Muslims. The core issue is often over who started the fight as well as which side caused the most death and destruction. It is crucial that both Christians and Muslims understand the historical record of this controversy since tensions are still high and situations are still volatile. The main apologetic question deals with whether the Crusades were really a delayed response to centuries of Muslim aggression or acts of unprovoked hostility by European Christians against the Islamic world. There are a number of responses that have been proposed in regard to this subject including the suggestion that the Crusades were both a delayed response as well as an unprovoked hostile action.

Critics of Christianity say the Crusades represented a low point for Christianity because Christians did not follow Christ when they took it upon themselves to initiate the fight against the Muslims, but rather weaponized their faith in order to justify their own Holy War against the Muslim world. For example, the 1995 BBC television series on the Crusades, presented by Terry Jones, portrayed the Crusades as "a long, misguided war of intolerance, ignorance, and barbarism against a peaceful and sophisticated Muslim world."[411]

Ironically, this western view of the Crusades may have grown out of the criticism of some of the Protestant reformers in the 16th century, as well as Enlightenment thinkers like historian-philosophers David Hume and Voltaire, who strongly denounced the Crusades. Hume quipped that the Crusades were "the most durable folly that has yet appeared in any age or nation."[412] Voltaire described the Crusades as an "epidemic of fury which lasted for 200 years and which was always marked by every cruelty, every

---

[411] Donald E. Queller and Thomas F. Madden. *The Fourth Crusade: The Conquest of Constantinople*, 2nd ed. (University of Pennsylvania Press, 1999), 1.

[412] Christopher Tyerman, *The Debate on the Crusades*, (New York: Manchester University Press, 2011), 81.

perfidy, every debauchery, and every folly of which human nature is capable."[413] The historian Edward Gibbon (1737-1794) wrote that, "The principle of the crusades was a savage fanaticism," and "the lives and labours of millions, which were buried in the East, would have been more profitably employed in the improvement of their native country."[414]

However, the beginning of the negative view of the Crusades may have actually started when Protestant reformers in the 16th century blamed the Catholic Church for the crusading movement. One Catholic writer, Stephen Weidenkopf, comments that "most Protestant critics viewed the Crusades as the creation of the anti-Christ to increase Church wealth" and believed that the Crusaders themselves were nothing more than instruments of "Catholic bigotry and cruelty."[415] Even the influential 20th century British writer, Steven Runciman, in his book on the Crusades, concluded that the Holy War in itself was "nothing more than a long act of intolerance in the name of God."[416] The consensus of these scholars and philosophers is that the spirit of the Crusades certainly did not represent the spirit of Christ or the true purpose of the gospel. In other words, if the crusaders were true to Christ in their endeavors, they would not have taken up the cross of the Crusades, or the sword of war, and they would certainly not have associated themselves with the horrific events that took place in the long war against Islam.

These same critics of the Crusades also point to the long-standing animosity of the Muslim world as evidence of the negative influence the Crusades have had on Christian-Muslim relations over the centuries. For example, shortly after the attacks of September 11, 2001, former president Bill Clinton suggested to the students at Georgetown University that the sack of Jerusalem in 1099 by Christian Crusaders was ultimately to blame for the horrific attacks on America a thousand years later. After describing the brutal details of the massacre of Jews and Muslims at the hand of Christians on the Temple Mount, Clinton then concluded, "I can tell you that that story is still being told today in the Middle East, and we are still paying for it."[417]

---

[413] Rodney Stark, *God's Battalions – The Case for the Crusades* (New York: HarperCollins, 2009), 6.

[414] Edward Gibbon, *The History of the Decline and Fall of the Roman Empire*, (1776), ch. 61 p. 1086. Or, Edward Gibbon, *The History of the Decline and fall of the Roman Empire*, 6 vols. (New York: The Nottingham Society, n.d.), 6:228-30, passim.

[415] Steve Weidenkopf, *The Glory of the Crusades* (El Cajon, California: Catholic Answers, 2014), 16.

[416] Steven Runciman, *A History of the Crusades*, vol. 3 (Cambridge: Cambridge University Press, 1951-54), 480.

[417] Thomas Madden, Jonathan Riley-Smith article. See also Robert Spencer, PC, 141.

On the other hand, a number of Christian scholars view the Crusades as a delayed response against the Muslims for subduing half of the Christian territory and devastating the church. One writer remarks, "It is a fundamental error and popular historic revisionism to say that Christians suddenly decided to lead a Crusade against the Muslims. It is a gross distortion of the historic record. In reality, the Muslims attacked and captured Jerusalem and many of the early 'Christian Holy Lands' to the degree that finally the Christians fought back to regain their lands taken by Islam."[418] According to this view, "the Crusades were the reaction and response to more than four centuries of Islamic military expansion and religious imperialism which had captured more than two-thirds of the Christian world."[419]

Were the Crusades a delayed response to centuries of Muslim aggression, or were they acts of unprovoked aggression by European Christians against the Islamic world? As usual, there are two sides to this controversy. One side argues that the Crusades were "a totally 'offensive war' of aggression and hostility against Islam – inspired by a corrupt Papacy and motivated by greed and plunder."[420] The other side interprets history differently and claims that "the Crusades were, in reality, a 'defensive war' against centuries of Muslim aggression and imperialism toward Christianity."[421] This chapter will seek to navigate both the negative and positive historical interpretations in order to determine the view that is best supported by the evidence.

## The Traditional Muslim View

It is difficult to find references to the Crusades by Muslims during the time the Crusades were taking place. One reason may be that the word "Crusaders" (*Salibiyyun*) was not used in the literature at that time. The Western invaders were consistently called the *Faranj* (Franks), and the attacks from European Christians were considered secondary matters in comparison to the numerous struggles for power within the Muslim world.[422] Bernard Lewis, an eminent historian of Islam, notes that in the Arabic historiography of the period "the terms *Crusade* and *Crusader* do not appear at all," and that "with few exceptions, the Muslim historians show little interest in whence or why they had come and report their arrival

---

[418] J.L. Williams, *A Christian Perspective on Islam* (Wake Forest, NC: Integrity Publishers, 2008), 68.
[419] Ibid., 68.
[420] Ibid., 68.
[421] Ibid., 68.
[422] Lewis, *Islam and the West*, 12-13.

and their departure with equal lack of curiosity."[423] Carole Hillenbrand, in her book detailing the Islamic perceptions of these battles with Christian forces, refers to the "Crusades" as a Western concept. She explains, "It has no particular resonance for Islamic ears and the Muslim historians are not concerned with it. For them, these are simply wars with an enemy – in this case, the Franks, as distinct, say, from the Fatimids."[424] Muslim scholars did not treat the topic of the Crusades as an isolated topic in any surviving work, though "snippets of information" can be found in "Arabic annals, biographical dictionaries and other literary works of the twelfth to fifteenth centuries."[425] However, Hillenbrand points out that since the "Muslim sources show little interest in the activities and motivations of the other side," it is difficult to reconstruct the flow of events between the Christian and Muslim forces from a Muslim perspective.[426]

However, this lack of historical background has not prevented modern Muslim scholars from promoting a perspective that the Christian Crusades have not ended, and therefore "the Christian powers of the West remain determined to destroy Islam."[427] For example, Dr. Abdullah Mohammad Sindi, A Muslim professor who has taught in several American universities, claimed,

> Of all the religious wars in human history waged by any religion, at any place, and at any time, <u>none</u> have been bloodier, more genocidal, more barbaric, and more protracted than the 200-year "holy wars" by the Western Crusades against the Arabs and Islam… The objective of the Crusades was simple, to destroy the Arabs (whether Muslim or Jew) in the Holy Land of Palestine and its environs.[428]

Dr. Sindi also likens the recent wars on Afghanistan and Iraq to the past "Western terrorist Crusades," and therefore concludes that the Crusades are still continuing. According to this perspective, the Crusades represented an unprovoked aggression by European Christians against the Islamic world, led by a hypocritical pope and a corrupt Catholic Church. One modern Muslim writer summarizes the Crusades this way:

---

[423] Ibid., 12-13.

[424] Carole Hillenbrand, *The Crusades: Islamic Perspectives* (Edinburgh University Press, 1999), 9.

[425] Ibid., 9.

[426] Ibid., 10.

[427] Ibid., 602.

[428] https://www.radioislam.org/sindi/croisades.htm (accessed 10/8/2016).

In the 11th century, almost a thousand years ago, hordes of Christian warriors bearing a red cross stormed into Syria. They journeyed from all parts of Europe, pillaging and slaughtering innocent Muslims along their way. They captured Jerusalem in 1099 leaving no mosque to pray in, nor any Muslim alive. After a hundred years, with the help of Allah, the Muslims struck back.[429]

Throughout the Middle East, and in many other parts of the world, it seems that today's Arab Muslims are still bitter about the Crusades. They say that references to the Crusades cause them to relive the barbaric aggressions of the Crusaders, and they blame Christians for creating tensions that still impact relations between Christianity and Islam in the present.[430] One example of linking present Christian leaders to the past atrocities of the Crusades occurred in 1981 when Mehmet Ali Agha, who attempted to assassinate the pope, wrote in a letter beforehand, "I have decided to kill John Paul II, the supreme commander of the Crusades."[431] The office of the pope was enough to link a later pope with the 11th and 12th-century ones who called for the Crusades.

Presently, Muslims who believe that the Christian Crusades have not ended emphasize the imperialistic aggression of the past Christian warriors and hold up Muslim leaders who squelched the Crusades, like Saladin, as heroes of the faith and great examples to the faithful. Even men like Seyyid Qutb, one of the earliest leaders of the Muslim Brotherhood, are lifted up as those who follow in the footsteps of the Muslim protectors of Islam during the time of the Crusades. Qutb referred to the Crusades as a "form of imperialism"[432] that sought to confront and annihilate Islam.[433]

The subject of the Crusades often appears currently in propaganda pieces against the Christian West. For example, Abu Musab al-Zarqawi, the

---

[429] The Crusade Through Muslim Eyes, http://www.kalamullah.com/the-crusades.html

[430] It is interesting to note that Thomas Madden, an accomplished medieval historian and specialist on the Crusades, claims there is no connection between the Crusades and the terrorist attacks today. He responds in his review of Riley-Smith's book that, "In the hundreds of interviews I have given since that terrible day [9/11], the most common question has been, "How did the Crusades lead to the terrorist attacks against the West today?" I always answered: "They did not. The Crusades were a medieval phenomenon with no connection to modern Islamist terrorism." Madden, Riley-Smith article

[431] Hillenbrand, *The Crusades*, 602.

[432] Seyyid Qutb, Milestones, 95.

[433] Paul Berman, The Philosopher of Islamic Terror, New York Times Magazine, March 23, 2003.
http://www.nytimes.com/2003/03/23/magazine/the-philosopher-of-islamic-terror.html (accessed 10/6/2016).

founder of the Islamic State of Iraq, would refer to his military exploits as attacks against the Crusaders, who were considered enemies of Islam.[434] Critics cry out that the memory of the Crusades has incited the radical Muslims to seek justice through their own defensive war. The most famous of the anti-Crusader rhetoric is Osama bin Laden's fatwa of 1998 in which he called for the killing of Americans, both civilians and soldiers. Osama bin Laden and other Islamists regularly referred to Americans as "Crusaders." Indeed, bin Laden directed his *fatwa* authorizing the September 11 attacks against the "Crusaders and Jews." He later preached that "for the first time the Crusaders have managed to achieve their historic ambitions and dreams against our Islamic *umma*, gaining control over Islamic holy places and Holy Sanctuaries.... Their defeat in Iraq will mean defeat in all their wars and a beginning of the receding of their Zionist–Crusader tide against us."[435] Thus, for Muslims, it was imperative that they unify in order to defeat the current thrust of the Crusader invasion before more damage to the Muslim nations could take place.

This popular view of Christians as the aggressors has even been promoted in the Western secular media. For example, one scholar writes that the Ridley Scott movie, *Kingdom of Heaven*, proclaimed that "the Crusades were unprovoked campaigns of intolerance preached by deranged churchmen and fought by religious zealots against a sophisticated and peaceful Muslim world. According to the Hollywood version, the blind violence of the Crusades gave birth to jihad, as the Muslims fought to defend themselves and their world."[436] This version of Christianity as the perpetrator and Islam as the innocent victim plays well with Muslim critics, like Abd al-Sabour Shahin, an Islamist writer, who says, "The Muslim nation has never attacked a neighboring nation," and therefore all the battles by Muslim forces have been defensive in nature.[437]

This is also perhaps why Muslims say that the sack of Jerusalem was the "starting point of a millennial hostility between Islam and the West."[438] To support this, they note that the Muslims were caught off guard and were not prepared for the invasion by the waves of Christian attackers from Europe. It took nearly fifty years for the Arabs to mobilize against the invaders. Even John Esposito, director of the Prince Alwaleed Center for Muslim-Christian Understanding at Georgetown University, blames the

---

[434] Jonathan Finer and Craig Whitlock, Washington Post, 11 November, 2005, A21.
[435] Madden, Riley-Smith article
[436] Madden, Riley-Smith article
[437] Abd al-Sabour Shahin, MEMRI Special Dispatch, no. 296 (Nov. 2001).
[438] Amin Maalouf, *The Crusades through Arab Eyes*, trans. John Rothschild (New York: Schocken Books, 1984), xvi.

aggression of the Christian West for strained relations today when he implies that "Five centuries of peaceful coexistence elapsed before political events and an imperial-papal power play led to a centuries-long series of so-called holy wars that pitted Christendom against Islam and left an enduring legacy of misunderstanding and distrust."[439]

In conclusion, the general consensus among Muslims today seems to be that the Crusades were an Unholy War initiated by Christians who were defeated by the true army of Allah. Many Western non-Muslims would also agree with Runciman when he writes,

> In the long sequence of interaction and fusion between Orient and Occident out of which our civilization has grown, the Crusades were a tragic and destructive episode.... There was so much courage and so little honour, so much devotion and so little understanding. High ideals were besmirched by cruelty and greed, enterprise and endurance by a blind and narrow self-righteousness; and the Holy War itself was nothing more than a long act of intolerance in the name of God, which is the sin against the Holy Ghost.[440]

## Christian Counter Offensives

It would seem then, according to Muslims, as well as a number of Western critics of Christianity, that the Crusades represented an unforgivable error by all who name the name of Christ. However, when a careful study of the battles between the Christians and the Muslims is carried out and the motivations of the Crusaders are put into perspective, then a very different explanation supports the view that the Crusades were a delayed response to centuries of Muslim aggression beginning four hundred years before Pope Urban's first Crusade. A historical overview of these events will be useful in developing this paradigm.

The earliest use of the word "Crusader" was in 1577, hundreds of years after the end of the last major crusade. Usually, the Christians who participated in the Crusades were called "pilgrims," "soldiers of God," or ones who "took up the cross."[441] A better term for this "crusading movement" then, would perhaps be "European counter attacks," or

---

[439] John Esposito, *Islam: The Straight Path*, 3rd. ed. (Oxford: Oxford University Press, 1998), 58.
[440] Runciman, *A History of the Crusades*, 480.
[441] Alfred Andrea and Andrew Holt, *The Seven Myths of the Crusades* (Indianapolis, Indiana: Hackett Publishing Co., 2015), xiii.

"Christian counter offensives" against the many Muslim attacks which had begun over four hundred years earlier.

When the horizon is enlarged, it is easier to recall that the initial attacks on the Christians began in the middle of the 7th century when Arab forces took control of Jerusalem, Syria, Persia, and, within the next 100 years, a large swath of territory ranging from the mountains of Afghanistan in the East to the Atlantic shores of North Africa in the West. All but the most easternmost provinces had been taken from Christian rulers, and the House of Islam now ruled over two-thirds of the Christian world. Over the next three centuries, Europe was under constant threat from Islam and hundreds of battles were fought by Christians to defend their lands.

Finally, in 1095, at the call of the highest Christian authority, Europeans were finally ready to unify their forces and mount a counter-offensive in an effort to recover their lost territories and finally free the city of Jerusalem from Muslim control. Thus, the Crusades were not the beginning of the counterattacks against the Muslims, and the view that the Crusades represented the first major clash between Christianity and Islam is simply false. By the time Pope Urban II called Christians to "take up the cross" and sacrifice their lives in an effort to recover the lands that once belonged to Christians, the Crusades were merely the most recent counter attacks in a conflict that had existed between Christianity and Islam from the time Muhammad's followers first turned northward. In order to better understand this perspective, it would be helpful to have a brief overview of the major Crusades as well as a consideration of the various motivations of the men who took up weapons of faith and of war.

## Brief Overview of the Crusades

Most historians place the six major Crusades between the years of 1095-1291 AD. The first Crusade was called by Pope Urban II when he urged Christians in Europe to fight the Muslims in order to recover the Holy Land, especially the city of Jerusalem and the church of the Holy Sepulcher, from the "infidel" Muslims. Two other main reasons often cited for participating in the Crusades would be to provide safe passage for the pilgrims making their way to the holy places of Palestine, and for the crusaders to gain remission of suffering in Purgatory, which was promised by some of the Popes. Some scholars say that the Crusades were four hundred years too late, some say that too many atrocities were committed in the name of Christ, and others point out that "this venture began with an inconclusive Christian victory and ended with a conclusive Christian defeat."[442]

---

[442] Lewis, *Islam and the West*, 12-13

However, perhaps the real significance of the Crusades at this time is that the European Christians realized that something had to be done before Islam made more inroads into Europe.

The First Crusade (1098-1099) was called by Pope Urban II in 1095. This was more than 400 years after the Muslims conquered Jerusalem in 638. In addition to the influence of the pope and a number of powerful noblemen, the first crusade was also inspired by the great preacher, Peter the Hermit. In fact, Peter led a first wave of crusaders in what is known as the "popular crusade." These were mostly poverty-stricken people who were ill-prepared. Most of them perished due to starvation, disease, or through the superiority of the Muslim soldiers. This wave was followed by a number of military forces that were mostly successful. In the end, the crusaders captured Jerusalem in 1099 and set up a Latin Kingdom of Jerusalem that lasted until 1187. This allowed the Christian pilgrims to resume their journeys to the Holy Land and it provided a deterrent to some of the Muslim incursions into European lands.

The Second Crusade (1146-1148) was proclaimed when the Turks conquered one of the Crusader cities, Edessa, in 1144. The main preacher urging people on was Bernard of Clairvaux. However, like the followers of Peter the Hermit in the previous Crusade, most of the crusaders were crushed in Asia Minor in December 1147 before they had a chance to reach the Holy Land. The military achievements were negligible and most consider this crusade to be unsuccessful.

The Third Crusade (1188-1192) was launched by Pope Gregory VII in response to the news of the fall of Jerusalem by the Muslim forces led by Saladin. This crusade was dominated by three strong leaders who, unfortunately, did not always see eye to eye: Emperor Frederick I Barbarossa, King Philip II Augustus of France, and King Richard the Lionheart of England. The only military accomplishment was the conquest of the city of Acre and the reinforcement of the Crusader state called "Outremer" which stretched along the coast. However, Richard was able to reach an agreement with Saladin to allow Christians to make pilgrimages to Jerusalem in safety. In some ways this set up the beginning of the end because Saladin was able to then use his "truce" to retake a number of the cities under control of some of the Christian leaders and send the Christians packing. In some instances, Saladin allowed his soldiers, and sometimes even the religious scholars, to execute the captives instead of exiling them from his newly gained territory.[443]

---

[443] Spencer, *Politically Incorrect Guide to Islam*, 142.

The Fourth Crusade (1201-1204) is generally considered to have been a disaster, and highlighted the reasons that these crusades, launched under the slogan of "Christ commands it," often were anything but Christian. The crusaders were diverted to Constantinople to aid a claimant to the Byzantine throne. Instead of attacking Muslims, the crusaders ended up sacking the city of Constantinople and setting up a Latin Empire of Constantinople (1204-1261) under a Latin Patriarch. This further weakened the Byzantine Empire and earned the everlasting enmity of the Byzantines toward the west, bringing further division rather than reconciliation.

The Fifth Crusade (1218-1221) focused on Egypt in the hope that by breaking Egyptian power the crusaders could then recapture Jerusalem. The only real accomplishment was the siege and conquest of the port city of Damietta, which was later recovered by the Muslims. However, due to infighting and disunity, the crusaders had to settle for an eight-year truce and the recovery of the "True Cross of Christ," which was a relic believed to be the cross used to crucify Christ.

The Sixth Crusade (1228-1229) was essentially a continuation of the Fifth Crusade. This crusade was led by the Holy Roman Emperor Frederick II, even after he was excommunicated by the Pope for failing to commit himself to leading a crusade earlier. Frederick II was able to convince the sultan, al-Kamil, who was involved with another campaign in Syria, to offer a 10-year truce to the crusaders. Essentially, this truce accomplished what the previous four crusades were not able to do, regain Jerusalem, as well as Bethlehem and Nazareth. Frederick entered Jerusalem on 17 March 1229, and the city remained under crusader control until the Turks attacked in 1244.

In the end, some may conclude that the Crusades were "late, limited and unsuccessful,"[444] but others argue that "during the Crusading movement these military events were mostly seen in a positive light throughout Christendom, with popes and saints exhorting Catholic warriors to engage in them."[445] Warriors who participated in these battles did so for a number of reasons, and the next section will examine the most significant ones in order to provide a better understanding of the motivations involved and the sacrifices made.

---

[444] Bernard Lewis, 2007 Irving Kristol Lecture, https://web.archive.org/web/20080213032850/http://www.aei.org/publications/pubID.258 15,filter.all/pub_detail.asp (accessed 10/7/2016).

[445] Steve Weidenkopf, *The Glory of the Crusades*, 9.

## The Motivations of the Crusaders

Critics of the Crusades have generally argued that the basic motivations of the Crusaders were for glory, gore, and gain, or, in other words, power of position, revenge on the infidel, and personal economic gain. However, the historical evidence from the accounts written at that time often tells a very different story.

The Church historian Justo Gonzalez gives eight causes of the Crusades: "lure of romantic adventure, social factors, economic factors, unity of the masses, the unity to the cause, corporate expiation, the code of chivalry, and the vow of the doomed." Gonzalez also concludes that the concept of the Crusades "meant that the violence, pillage, and outright murder... were often seen as acts of virtue in the context of the Crusades."[446]

This view of the religious influence on the Crusaders can be seen in other motivations put forth by other scholars. Jonathan Riley-Smith, for example, lists idealism, adventure, and a sense of fulfilling a vendetta as some of the motivations guiding those going on a crusade, especially for the knights. He says in reference to idealism that "the majority of commentators then and a minority of historians now have maintained that the chief motivation was a genuine idealism."[447] In this case, the idealism was focused on conquering Palestine and releasing the hold on Jerusalem. Riley-Smith also lists the quest for adventure as a motivation, perhaps because there was less opportunity for adventure at home, and the crusades offered an appeal for something that would bring honor as well as a chance to do something for their country and their Lord. A third motivation Riley-Smith mentions is that some of the knights had a deep desire to fulfill a vendetta in regard to the "brothers" in Palestine who had been subjected to the harshness of Islam. This was expressed in a letter to Pope Urban II in 1098 which said, "The Turks, who inflicted much dishonor on Our Lord Jesus Christ, have been taken and killed and we Jerusalemites have avenged the injury to the supreme God Jesus Christ."[448] This was a call to avenge God, who was seen to have been "reproached, banished from his estates, crucified; whom you hear calling, desolate and begging for aid."[449]

One motivation that critics mention, but Riley-Smith discounts, is the view that the crusaders were motivated by crude materialism. He argues

---

[446] Ergun Caner, *Christian Jihad* (Grand Rapids: Kregel, 2004), 119, n.11.
[447] Jonathan Riley-Smith, *The Crusades: A Short History*, 11.
[448] Ibid., 16.
[449] Ibid., 16.

that "this was an age of ostentatious and extravagant generosity,"[450] and the land, possessions, and titles forfeited by the crusaders provides good testimony that the Crusade was not viewed as a way to gain a fortune.

In regard to the call for vengeance, Riley-Smith does admit that this may have spilled over and fueled the fervor for vengeance against the Jews, whom the crusaders saw as another group of people who brought shame upon Christ ("to avenge the injury to Christ's honour" due to the crucifixion). However, when he recounts that some of the men who supported the Crusades were men of great piety, he concludes, "A result, I think, is that we find it easier to accept the crusaders for what they were and, without endorsing what they did, can begin to understand why some of the greatest saints in Christian history – Bernard, Louis, Thomas Aquinas, Bridget, Catherine of Siena – were fervently on their side and why so many men and women were prepared to sacrifice wealth, health, life itself, in a cause which they believed to be just, even salvational."[451]

On the other hand, Ergun Caner, who was formerly a Muslim, does not consider some of the motivations in such a generous light. In a chapter that he titles "Sanctified Slaughter: When the Body of Christ Became the Army of God," Caner expresses his deep reservations regarding some of the motivations of the Crusaders. He considers that the "most deeply disturbing motivation for the majority of the soldiers was the explicit promise of salvation for martyrdom."[452] This refers to the offer given by Pope Urban when he granted remission of sins, and therefore the promise of salvation, to all those who would die in the Crusade, whether through battle or through the dangers of the journey.

It is interesting to compare Pope Urban's offer of salvation with Osama bin Laden's promises to his followers in a fatwa he delivered to the world. In the 11th century, Pope Urban said, "All who die by the way, whether by land or by sea or in battle against the pagans, shall have immediate remission of sins. This I grant them through the power of God with which I am invested."[453] In bin Laden's call to jihad on February 23, 1998, he reminded Muslims that Allah said: "O ye who believe, give your response to Allah and his Apostle when He calleth you to that which will give you life. And know that Allah cometh between a man and his heart, and that it is He to whom ye shall all be gathered" (Q. 8:24). In other words, bin Laden was calling all Muslims to join in the cause of Allah and fight against the enemy without concern for their life, for Allah assures that

---

[450] Ibid., 14.
[451] Ibid., 256-7.
[452] Ergun Caner, *Christian Jihad*, 105.
[453] Ibid., 107.

their destiny will be with Him if they die in the battle. These promises for eternal life would certainly motivate many people on both sides of the fight. However, Caner is offended that "the institutional representation of Christianity stooped to such a level of evil enterprise"[454] rather than appeal to a higher calling of following Christ in his example of sacrifice and love.

This last motivation, based on sacrifice and love, is one that Thomas Madden highlights in his review of Riley-Smith's book. Madden maintains that one of the misconceptions of the Crusades is that the actions of the crusaders contradicted the teachings of Christ, who taught his followers to love their enemies and to turn the other cheek when they were persecuted. However, the Bible also teaches that God has placed leaders in positions of authority. In Romans 13:4, the Bible states that the leaders are "God's servant for your good. But if you do wrong, be afraid, for he does not bear the sword in vain. For he is the servant of God, an avenger who carries out God's wrath on the wrongdoer." Later, Augustine developed his just war theory, based on verses like this, which taught that in a defensive war legitimate authorities could use violence to stop or prevent a greater evil.[455] Scholars critical of the Crusades argue that any warfare is an act of evil. However, as Riley-Smith notes, "the concept that violence is intrinsically evil belongs solely to the modern world. It is not Christian."[456] Weidenkopf adds that "The modern world sees violence as inherently evil, but Augustine believed violence could be used for legitimate reasons including the restoration of order and property. In special circumstances, war could be a holy undertaking."[457] Thus, "Using Augustine's writings, the Church identified four criteria that must be satisfied: a just cause, which can involve past or present aggression; proclamation by legitimate authority; defense or recovery of rightful possessions; and right intention or pure motives of the participants. Additionally, war should be undertaken only as a last recourse and the violence unleashed must be proportionate to the threat."[458]

Thomas Madden believes that the Crusades met Augustine's criteria of just war since they were carried out in response to earlier attacks against Christians and their Church. According to Madden,

> The First Crusade was called in 1095 in response to the recent Turkish conquest of Christian Asia Minor, as well as the much earlier Arab conquest of the Christian-held Holy Land. The

---

[454] Ibid., 107.
[455] Ibid., 220-221.
[456] Thomas Madden, Riley-Smith article.
[457] Steven Weidenkopf, *The Glory of the Crusades*, 48.
[458] Steven Weidenkopf, *The Glory of the Crusades*, 48.

second was called in response to the Muslim conquest of Edessa in 1144. The third was called in response to the Muslim conquest of Jerusalem and most other Christian lands in the Levant in 1187. In each case, the faithful went to war to defend Christians, to punish the attackers, and to right terrible wrongs.[459]

Madden maintains that the supreme motivation for the one who "took up the cross" was the motivation that comes as an act of love. He explains that "the faithful went to war to defend Christians, to punish the attackers, and to right terrible wrongs."[460] These were noble motivations and were carried out as a sacrifice on the part of the Crusader, who was really fulfilling an act of penance. This is why, Madden says, the indulgence that Pope Urban II offered was a just motivation. According to Madden, "Crusaders who undertook that burden with right intention and after confessing their sins would receive a plenary indulgence. The indulgence was a recognition that they undertook these sacrifices for Christ, who was crucified again in the tribulations of his people."[461]

In this sense, the Crusades were not just ordinary wars, but rather holy wars made holy by the sacrifices made by the pilgrim warriors. The "Crusade provided a way for them to serve God and to do penance for their sins."[462] Without this understanding of the penitential character, Madden says that the real motivation of the Crusaders cannot be fully understood: "Take away penitence and the Crusades cannot be explained."[463] This sacred act, supported by the indulgences granted by the Pope, explains why many believed that their salvation lay in fighting the Holy War that God had called them to. Though some may have had mixed motives, for most it was not the desire for wealth, or power, or other worldly desires, but for the love of God and the love of his people.

## Differences in the Islamic view of Holy War

For Muslims, their jihad, or Holy War, was also in obedience to Allah. However, their commands came from the Qur'an and the call was to fight against all non-believers until all submitted to Islam, as we read in Q. 8:39: "And fight with them until there is no more persecution and religion should be only for Allah; but if they desist, then surely Allah sees what they do."

---

[459] Thomas Madden, Riley-Smith article.
[460] Ibid.
[461] Ibid.
[462] Ibid.
[463] Ibid.

According to the biographies of Muhammad, and a number of Hadith traditions, he did not teach "peace and tolerance," but rather led armies and ordered the assassinations of his enemies. This foundational perspective led to Islam's own version of the "Crusades" when they invaded Syria and surrounding Christian territory in the mid-600's and up through the middle of the 8th century until almost two-thirds of the former Christian lands were under the domination of Islam. In addition, what is known as the Islamic world today is the result of centuries of brutal warfare against the lands of the Christians and the Jews. This is perhaps why historian Steven Weidenkopf says, "The seventh-century rise of the militaristic and imperialistic movement known as Islam, and its subsequent conquest of ancient Christian territory, was the prime cause for the creation of the Crusading movement and the reason for its longevity."[464] Weidenkopf also explains the important distinction between the Christian and Muslim views on Holy War.

This understanding of holy war differs greatly from the Muslim teaching on jihad. Jihad is incumbent upon all Muslims and is a foundational teaching of Islam. Christian holy war is not incumbent on every believer; indeed, participation in the Crusades was always voluntary, and violence is seen as a necessary evil that can only be entered into for serious and just reasons. Christian teaching even places restrictions on the nature of warfare and on the intentions of those who participate; jihad harbors no such limitations. The main purpose of jihad is offensive through the conquering of territory in order to spread Islam throughout the world; Christian holy war is defensive and primarily involves the recovery of territory lost to an aggressor.[465]

## Why the Crusades Failed

As Weidenkopf indicates, Jihad, or Holy War, has been a part of Islam since its inception. In a sense, Islam cannot exist without this form of Jihad because the overarching command from Allah is for Muslims to subdue the whole world under Allah (Q. 8:39). Islam cannot fulfill this command without force. On the other hand, Christianity is to be spread by love and persuasion. This is why the Crusades, in the end, were not successful. The heart and mind have to be wooed by Christ. In the end, the Crusades failed because they represented actions that were not representative of Christ and the gospel.[466] As one author says,

---

[464] Weidenkopf, *The Glory of the Crusades*, 36.
[465] Ibid., 48-49.
[466] See J.L. Williams, *A Christian Perspective on Islam*, 69.

While warfare is inevitable in a fallen, rebellious and sinful world, it is always a blatant blemish on the face of Christianity when it is initiated in the name of Jesus Christ! Warfare always falls woefully short of the agape love of Jesus Christ that clearly instructs us to "love our enemies" (Matt. 5:44). At best, the Crusades were largely a denial of that foundational truth of the Christian faith.[467]

The Crusades may have failed in achieving the main objective of recovering and retaining Jerusalem and surrounding lands that once belonged to Christians. However, they did initiate a new awareness of the Muslim world and its achievements in science and technology, and the translations of classical Greek works by Christians into Arabic helped jumpstart a new interest in the ideas of Aristotle and other Greek philosophers, which contributed to the rise of the Renaissance. On the other hand, since the initial call by Pope Urban was for a Christian "Holy War," carried out under the leadership of the Church rather than through civil authorities, it was doomed to failure from the start.[468] There were ample reasons for European Christians to defend themselves against the constant threat of the Islamic invasion of their lands, but this should have been the duty of the State rather than the Church. Otherwise, the tendency toward a theocracy, or a government in which God and his laws is recognized as the supreme authority over all secular institutions, would lead to a political state much like that which is present today in Islam.

## A Delayed Response

There is good evidence to suggest that the Crusades were not acts of unprovoked aggression by Europe against the Islamic world, but rather a delayed response to centuries of Muslim hostility against the Christian world. First, there were the Arab conquests of the Middle East, North Africa, and Persia in the first one hundred years. Then there were several hundred years of almost continual battles along the border areas between Europe and the new Islamic empire until Pope Urban called for a unified response to the dangers present on many borders.

Some may still want to assert that the pope should not have interfered with civil matters. However, something needed to be done, and calling the response of thousands of Christians to defend their lands as well as seek to recover the former lands of Christians should not be deemed an

---

[467] Ibid., 69.

[468] Ironically, part of the reason for this failure may have been that the Catholic Church and the State were practically intertwined at that time.

unprovoked act of aggression. In regard to this particular criticism of the Crusades, Bernard Lewis has a word for these critics:

> I would not wish to defend the behavior of the Crusaders, which was in many respects atrocious. But let us have a little sense of proportion. We are now expected to believe that the Crusades were an unwarranted act of aggression against a peaceful Muslim world. Hardly. The first papal call for a crusade occurred in 846 C.E., when an Arab expedition from Sicily sailed up the Tiber and sacked St. Peter's in Rome. A synod in France issued an appeal to Christian sovereigns to rally against "the enemies of Christ," and the Pope, Leo IV, offered a heavenly reward to those who died fighting the Muslims. A century and a half and many battles later, in 1096, the Crusaders actually arrived in the Middle East.[469]

Again, the Crusades may have been a "late, limited, and unsuccessful imitation of the jihad" that ultimately failed, but it was certainly not merely a "long act of intolerance in the name of God." A response was long overdue, and many responded to the call with their honor, their lives, and their fortunes. The least that can be done is to set the record straight and let the evidence speak for itself.

## Apologetic Conclusions

There are a number of apologetic issues that could be dealt with on this subject, but perhaps the most helpful path would be to deal with some of the myths that surround today's views of the crusades so that Christians would have guidance on how to best respond to Muslims in regard to the questions that are brought up. Robert Spencer, the director of Jihad Watch and author of a number of books opposing Islam, mentions nine myths in his book on the Crusades. Following are some of the myths that may come up in conversations.

The first myth promoted by critics is that the Crusades were an unprovoked attack by Europe against the Islamic world. This is false, as was mentioned above because the Muslims were the ones who first invaded the lands of the Christians. Damascus was taken in 635, and Jerusalem was conquered in 638. In one hundred years Muslims had conquered two-thirds of the lands occupied by Christians, and had taken control of the Middle East, North Africa, part of Spain and even parts of India. Muslims were the aggressors and Christians faced increasing persecution. During this time, Christians were often given three choices: convert to Islam, die, or submit to Islamic control and pay the Jizya, a humiliating poll tax (actually a head

---

[469] Lewis, 2007 Irving Kristol Lecture.

tax). This was not a defensive war on the part of Islam; it was a continual series of unprovoked attacks at the hands of the Muslims to seize and control the lands once owned by Christians, as well as other non-Muslims.[470]

The second myth is that the Crusades were an early example of the West's predatory imperialism. This is also false. Pope Urban II called the First Crusade at the Council of Clermont in 1095 in order to initiate a long overdue defensive act. For over 400 years the Muslims had control of Jerusalem and at this time a group of more radical Muslims were attacking the Christians making pilgrimages to the Holy Land. Pope Urban said that without any defensive action, "the faithful of God will be much more widely attacked" by the Turks. In his speech in 1095, Pope Urban II stated,

> They have killed and captured many, and have destroyed the churches and devastated the empire. If you permit them to continue thus for a while with impunity, the faithful of God will be much more widely attacked by them. On this account I, or rather the Lord, beseech you as Christ's heralds to publish this everywhere and to persuade all people of whatever rank, foot-soldiers and knights, poor and rich, to carry aid promptly to those Christians and to destroy that vile race from the lands of our friends…. Moreover, Christ commands it.[471]

Pope Urban II may have been too presumptive in assuming that his call for action was the will of God, but his concern was more than justified by the evidence of prolonged Muslim aggression.

The third myth is that the Crusades were fought by Westerners greedy for gain. Though some Christians went on the crusade with hopes of becoming rich, most noblemen who gathered together armies from among their families, friends and servants lost immense sums of money, as well as their loved ones, through these very costly endeavors. Many of the men took on holy orders, such as the Knights Templar and Hospitallers, and became monks during this time and therefore turned away from worldly gain. In addition, the commitment to take up the cross often involved selling off land and other possessions in order to pay for the long journey to the holy land. There were few men who gained monetarily from the Crusades, and many gave up everything. It is estimated, for example, that

---

[470] Andrea, *The Seven Myths of the Crusades*, 28.

[471] http://sourcebooks.fordham.edu/halsall/source/urban2-fulcher.html (Accessed 10/07/2016).

many of the knights did not return home,[472] and over half of the commoners ended up sacrificing their lives to the cause.

Another myth is that the Crusaders established European colonies in the Middle East. However, this was not an imperialistic venture to colonize the Middle East. A colony is a land that is ruled by a far-off power. Examples would be past colonies in Virginia (Britain), Australia (Britain), and the Dutch East Indies. There were Crusader states, but they were not ruled by Western powers. Rather, they were self-ruling. They did not have any economic arrangement with any European countries, and they did not ship off any wealth from the lands that they ruled. Indeed, the states were established primarily to provide protection for Christians making pilgrimages to the Holy Land. Even the major state called "Outremer," which means "overseas," indicated that the new settlements were to be self-governing and with limited contact. In the end, this lack of support from Europe probably was the major cause that the Crusader states were later taken over by the Muslims.

The fifth myth brought up by critics is that the capture of Jerusalem was unique in medieval history and led to the Muslim mistrust of the West. This is also misleading. It was common practice at that time that if a city rejected terms of peace from an invading army then if the city walls were breached and the people overwhelmed by the invading army, the people of the city were at the mercy of their conquerors. The massacre by the crusaders of the Jews and Muslims in Jerusalem was brutal, but it was not unique for that time.

Another myth about of the Crusades is that they were called against Jews in addition to Muslims. Though a number of Jews were killed by crusaders on their way to free Jerusalem, the attacks were opposed by the local bishops and widely condemned at the time as a violation of the Crusades aim, which was not directed against the Jews. The main reason for the hostility against the Jews was for their complicity in the death of Jesus Christ. They were called "Christ killers" even though they were not the ones to crucify Jesus.

The final myth that needs to be dealt with is that the Crusades were bloodier than the Islamic jihads. Atrocities were committed by the Christian crusaders against the Muslims, and by the Muslims against the Christian crusaders. However, the crusades lasted less than 300 years. The Muslim jihad has continued for almost 1400 years. Both sides can recount horrific deeds done in the name of God by their opponents. However, both accounts violate the actions of those who claim to follow God. War is

---

[472] Riley-Smith, *The Crusades: A Short History*, 11: about 10% of the over 100,000 in the first Crusade were knights.

always brutal and this is the prime reason it should be the last resort in any confrontation.

There are several conclusions that should be considered. The teachings of Christ do not mesh with the slaughter of the Crusades. Not everything done in the name of Christ should be attributed to Christianity.

Also, Muslims will often bring up the Crusades when defending today's terrorism. What should be the appropriate Christian response? First of all, the question should not be dodged. Christians should admit that many actions committed by the Crusaders were wrong and contrary to the teachings of Jesus. Secondly, this would be an opportune time to remind them that Jesus willingly died on a cross to set men free, while Muhammad taught his followers to kill those who would not submit to their religion.

## Building Bridges to Understand

As in most apologetic controversies, understanding the truth about the Crusades helps Christians to assess both sides so that they can better appreciate the criticism of the one side and the positive points of the Christian side. For example, Muslims will often bring up the horrors of the massacres carried out by the Christian warriors. However, since there were also atrocities committed by Muslims, factual presentations of the evidence can help Christians today balance their response by upholding the valor of the Christian warriors on the one hand and admitting the consequences of sin on the other. It would not be helpful, or accurate, to blame all the atrocities on one side. Perhaps a more balanced perspective can be ascertained from the evidence when one concludes that the Crusades were not launched as "an assault on a peaceful, sophisticated, cosmopolitan, and tolerant Eastern world by fanatical barbarians from the West," nor were they "noble and righteous ventures fought by heroic and selfless Latin Christians," but rather that they were the result of centuries of tension between two religions that are fundamentally incompatible.

Some Christians have wondered if they should apologize to Muslims in order to get past the Crusades and not let the topic shut down their witness. However, Bernard Lewis thinks this would be "political correctness run amok." When he heard about Pope John Paul II apologizing to Muslims for the Crusades, Lewis "made the point that the Crusades, as atrocious as they were, were nonetheless an understamble response to the Islamic onslaught of the preceding centuries, and that it was ridiculous [for Pope John Paul II] to apologize for them."[473]

Perhaps it would be better to admit that the Crusades were a belated and ineffectual response to the Muslim jihad, and that the Crusaders were imperfect men and women who were trying to fight a spiritual war with temporal weapons. This is why apologetics is so important. Christians need to realize that the real battle is "not against flesh and blood, but against the spiritual forces of darkness" (Ephesians 6:10). Therefore, in order to "have divine power to destroy strongholds... arguments and every lofty opinion raised against the knowledge of God," we need to "take every thought captive to obey Christ" (2 Corinthians 10:4-5). The first step in this process is to understand both sides of the issue so that we can then defend what is true and refute what is in error. Thus, in regard to the topic of the Crusades, Christians need to be open with their Muslim friends about the failures on the part of the Christians, but they also need to be able to respond to the false representations brought up by others.

### Study Questions:

1. If a Christian friend came up to you and said that they find the Crusades to be a deeply embarrassing episode in the history of Christianity, what would you say to them in order to help them think through the issues?

2. What are some of the main arguments Muslims and critics of Christianity give in regard to the Crusades?

3. How would you defend the position that the Crusades were basically launched as a delayed response to centuries of Muslim aggression?

4. What are the similarities and differences between Muslim Jihad and a Christian view of a "just war"?

5. What is the best way to respond to your Muslim friends when they ask you how you can support the actions of Christians during the Crusades?

---

[473] Martin Kramer, Apologize to Bernard Lewis, Sandbox, March 17, 2007. http://martinkramer.org/sandbox/2007/03/apologize-to-bernard-lewis/. (Accessed 10/07/2016).

# CHAPTER 14 Radical Islam: What is ISIS and What do they Want?

## Introduction

At the time of this publication, ISIS has been on the decline. However, this group represents many radical groups that have gone before it and other groups that will rise up in its place. Therefore, we can use this recent manifestation of the face of radical Islam to help us understand the core motivations of similar groups — past, present, and future.

According to numerous polls, including a recent Pew poll, most views of ISIS in Muslim majority countries were overwhelmingly negative.[474] It is understandable that most Muslims would not want to be associated with a group that is known for harsh, barbaric treatment of others, such as beheading victims on video, burning captives alive, and making sex slaves of thousands of women. Victims of these atrocities have included moderate Muslims, Christians, Jews, or other non-Muslims.

Most moderate Muslims would never think of acting this way against their non-Muslim neighbors. Thus, they want to distance their beliefs from those of the Islamic State. Numerous leaders in the West have supported the Muslim majority by claiming that ISIS is not a true representative of Islam. In a speech on September 10, 2014, President Obama stated that ISIL is not "Islamic" and that "no religion condones the killing of innocents."[475] In November of 2015, Hillary Clinton said: "Let's be clear, though. Islam is not our adversary. Muslims are peaceful and tolerant people and have nothing whatsoever to do with terrorism."[476] Shortly after the Bataclan massacre in Paris, French President Francois Hollande went so far as to say, "Those fanatics have nothing in common with the rest of the Muslim faith."[477] Indeed, as Mark Durie, a scholar in linguistics and theology has pointed out, since 9/11 "the slogan 'Religion of Peace' has been steadily promoted by western leaders in response to terrorism."[478] Non-Muslim

---

[474] http://www.pewresearch.org/fact-tank/2015/11/17/in-nations-with-significant-muslim-populations-much-disdain-for-isis/

[475] http://foxct.com/2014/09/10/full-transcript-of-pres-obamas-isis-speech/

[476] http://www.nationalreview.com/aNovemberrticle/427444/why-does-left-continue-insist-islamic-terrorism-has-nothing-do-islam-jonah-goldberg

[477] http://www.mediaite.com/online/french-president-hollande-attackers-have-nothing-in-common-with-muslim-faith/

[478] http://ijr.com/opinion/2015/12/251190-islam-religion-peace-came-politicians-need-stop-saying/

leaders have also gone to extraordinary efforts to convince citizens in Western countries that groups like ISIS have nothing in common with Islam, and which, contrary to the actions of the terrorist groups, these leaders say should be regarded as a religion that promotes peace and not conflict.

In regard to this almost universal aversion to linking Islam and terrorism together, Robert Spencer, the director of Jihad Watch, notes, "[F]or virtually every authority in the Western world and many Muslim leaders as well, the Islamic State is a vicious perversion of the Qur'an, the Sunnah, and the Sharia of Allah – they insist that whatever the group is to be called, it must not be called "Islamic" or identified in any way with the religion of Islam."[479]

In contrast to the many who argue that ISIS is not truly Islamic, Nabeel Qureshi, a former Muslim and author of *Answering Jihad*, aptly represents non-Muslims who accept ISIS, as well as its sister groups al-Qaeda and Boko Haram, as the self-avowed champions of true Islam that they themselves claim to be. Their form of Islam is deeply embedded in the Qur'an and the life of Muhammad and this emphasis on foundational texts is often far greater than moderate Muslims. Qureshi adds,

> There can be no doubt by any useful definition of Muslims that Islamic terrorists are Muslim. They worship Allah, they strive to follow Muhammad, they perform their Islamic duties, and they have great concern for the international Muslim community. Relatively speaking, they tend to place more emphasis on the foundations of Islam than do average Muslims in the West who proclaim that Islam is a religion of peace.[480]

If this is true, why are the world's Western leaders so adamant about denying the Islamic connection with these terrorist groups? Qureshi indicates that,

> When the leaders and media members insist that these groups are not Islamic, they are either speaking out of ignorance or intentionally engaging in propaganda. These three groups are dynamic expressions of the modern Islamic reformation, and their interpretations of the Qur'an and hadith, in terms of being devoid of accreted tradition, are among the most pure in the Islamic world.[481]

---

[479] Robert Spencer, *The Complete Infidel's Guide to ISIS* (D.C.: Regnery, 2015), 222.

[480] Quereshi, *Answering Jihad*, 91.

[481] Ibid., 88.

It would seem, then, that polar views prevail when it comes to interpreting whether ISIS is Islamic or not.

This chapter will summarize the background of ISIS and deal with the ideology and beliefs of this new movement. These views will also be compared to the more moderate Muslim views in order to determine which side better represents the historical beliefs of Islam. Then, in light of the core motivations of ISIS and similar jihadi groups, a critique of the present situation will be made in order to resolve the cognitive dissonance between the two views which, on the one hand, say that the Islamic State is not Islamic, and on the other hand claim that "ISIS is Islamic, very Islamic."[482]

## Background and History of ISIS

Although the distant roots are found in Muhammad and the first Caliphate, the Islamic State began in Iraq as the Jama'at al-Tawhid, or the Party of Monotheism and Jihad. It was founded by Abu Musab al-Zarqawi in 1999 after he was released from a Jordanian prison after serving five years for waging Jihad against the government. In time, Zarqawi joined with Bin Laden's al-Qaeda and changed the name of his group to al-Qaeda in Iraq (AQI). Under Zarqawi's leadership AQI was known for courageous and daring exploits against the infidel in the name of Islam. Zarqawi was known as a brilliant tactician as well as the chief promoter of the shocking violence that ISIS is notorious for now. He also contributed to a twenty-year plan that seems to be on schedule as it has successfully entered the sixth out of seven phases. It would be helpful to summarize these phases.[483]

- **Phase 1: The Muslim Awakening** (2000-2003). This was designed to provoke the West into responding to the new threat. This phase was very successful considering the devastation brought about by the 9/11 attack.
- **Phase 2: Opening Eyes** (2003-2006). This phase used propaganda and recruitment in order to educate Muslims of their ideological goals and reawaken Muslims to the core beliefs of the Qur'an and Muhammad. Again, judging by the number of Muslims involved in jihad around the world and the number of terrorist attacks that

---

[482] Graeme Wood, "What ISIS Really Wants," The Atlantic Monthly, March, 2015. http://www.theatlantic.com/magazine/archive/2015/03/what-isis-really-wants/384980/ (Accessed 9/5/2016).

[483] Adapted from Beck, *It Is About Islam*, 69-71.

have taken place since 9/11 (over 29,000),[484] this phase would also have to be judged successful.

- **Phase 3: Arising and Standing Up** (2007-2010). This phase would involve the expansion process throughout Iraq, Syria and the surrounding areas. This growth was greatly expedited by the pullout of the U.S. troops from Iraq.

- **Phase 4: Collapse** (2010-2013). This period was marked by the collapse of a number of Muslim governments as revolution spread across the Middle East during the "Arab Spring." Even though many of these protests ended up bringing chaos to the host countries, this all played nicely into the hands of the terrorists.

- **Phase 5: Caliphate** (2013-2016). In this phase the Islamic State would be formally announced, and due to the weakness of the Western nations and their lack of desire to keep up the fight, the Caliphate would grow over time in strength and territory. This goal has been accomplished and al-Baghdadi has guided the Caliphate through the initial steps toward its goal of a world order under the Muslim community of believers.

- **Phase 6: Total Confrontation** (2016-2019). The hope of this phase is for the Caliphate to draw into battle the Western forces, as well as Israel, in order to decimate the enemy.

- **Phase 7: Definitive Victory** (2020). After vanquishing the Western forces and ridding the world of the nation of Israel, the Caliphate hopes to be embraced by the 1.6 billion Muslims in the world. At this time, it would be the only superpower in the world and all remaining non-Muslims would be under the control of the Caliphate.

If the Caliphate continues to have success, then the West is in for a more widespread confrontation with a greater emphasis on infiltrating Western countries and carrying out its goals for domination of the world in the name of Allah.

In June of 2006, the forward momentum of the movement took a detour when Zarqawi was killed in a U.S. airstrike. However, by October the organization recovered and renamed itself the Islamic State of Iraq (ISI). When Obama withdrew the troops from Iraq in 2011 the ISI took advantage of the absence of U.S. troops and the weakness of the Shia government in Baghdad to gain control over territory in Iraq and Syria. ISI

---

[484] https://www.thereligionofpeace.com/attacks/american-attacks.aspx

extended this advantage by fomenting unrest in Syria in order to expand their control. They were successful in helping to ignite a Syrian civil war, and in April of 2013 renamed the organization as the Islamic State of Iraq and the Levant (ISIL or ISIS).[485] In 2014, Ayman al-Zawahiri, who assumed control of al-Qaeda after the death of bin Laden, ended the relationship with ISIS because it was considered too extreme.[486] In June of 2014, however, ISIS declared the formation of a new Caliphate with Zarqawi's former lieutenant, Abu Bakr al-Baghdadi, as the caliph – the successor of Muhammad and the spiritual leader of Islam. The acronym was again changed to IS for the Islamic State, which is the preferred name for their organization.

Abu Bakr al-Baghdadi, whose given name is Ibrahim Awad Ibrahim al-Badri, was born in Samarra, Iraq, to a Sunni family in 1971. He distinguished himself when he was young by his serious study of the Qur'an and his strict standards. He pursued his religious studies at the university and received his Master's (1999) and Ph.D. (2007) in Qur'anic studies from the Saddam University for Islamic Studies.[487] Through his strong devotion to religious matters, as well as relationships with Islamists, al-Baghdadi gravitated towards violent ultra-conservatives in the Islamist movement in the late 1990s and embraced Salafist jihadism.[488] In 2004, after the U.S. invasion of Iraq, al-Baghdadi was arrested by the Americans and placed in prison for his connections with terrorist groups. However, he was not considered dangerous and was released in December of 2004.

Through his prison connections, he found out about al-Zarqawi's AQI and soon joined up with the organization. He was respected for his scholarship and steadily rose through the ranks. After the death of Zarqawi's successor, Abu Omar al-Baghdadi in 2010, Abu Bakr al-Baghdadi was chosen to lead the movement. In June of 2014, after waiting for the U.S. to withdraw its troops, al-Baghdadi declared the formation of a Caliphate and shortened the name of his organization to the Islamic State (IS). As a Caliphate, the Islamic State claims religious, political and military authority over all Muslims worldwide. In regard to core ideology and beliefs, IS follows the Salafi school (Wahhabism), which follows a traditional, literal interpretation of the Qur'an and Hadith. Governed by strict Salafist doctrine, the Islamic State seeks to revive what it refers to as "Pure Islam," and it considers all other Islamic groups to be inferior or illegitimate.

---

[485] The Levant includes Syria, Lebanon, Jordan, and Israel.
[486] Spencer, *The Complete Infidel's Guide to ISIS*, 8.
[487] http://www.bbc.com/news/world-middle-east-35694311
[488] http://www.bbc.com/news/world-middle-east-35694311

The end goal for IS is apocalyptic, and they believe they can usher in the End Times. This is why they seek to lure the U.S. and its allies to the Middle East. Ultimately, they believe they are fighting to prepare the way for the Mahdi, or the "divinely guided one." According to their interpretation, in the End Times the Mahdi will come, along with the Muslim Jesus, in order to establish a worldwide Muslim caliphate where people are either converted to Islam or killed. The Islamic State believes that they will help initiate the coming of the Mahdi by marshaling Muslim forces against the infidels. They also believe the Muslim Jesus will return to the earth, break the cross, kill swine, and abolish the Jizya – in effect abolishing all religions except Islam. Without the protection money as an option (the jizya), then the only two choices left for non-Muslims will be to convert to Islam or die.

## The View from ISIS

Instead of listening to non-Muslim leaders tell us about what Muslims believe, Muslims should be asked what they believe about their own religion. A good place to go for a view concerning ISIS would be their slick new magazine called Dabiq[489] (named after the city where the apocalyptic battle of Armageddon is prophesied to take place).

In the most recent issue (no. 15) there is an article written by a former "Christian" who accepted Islam and joined the Islamic State. His article, called "Words of Sincere Advice," begins with a passionate call to Islam filled with verses from the Qur'an. For example, he calls his readers to the straight path of Islam (Q. 6:153), and he calls all Muslims to form one nation under Allah (Q. 21:92), which is a call to join the Islamic State. He then gives advice about what the readers should do after rejecting the corrupted world of the West, which he likens to the pre-Islamic condition of Jahiliyyah. The first step he advocates is for the readers to pledge their life to the Islamic State, and follow the prophet, who said, "Whoever dies unbound by a *bay'ah* (pledge of allegiance) has died a *Jahili* death." In conjunction with this obligation, they should then "rush to perform Hijrah" and travel to the "land of Islam" (the new Caliphate) in order to join up with the Islamic State. If this is not an option at the time, then the writer encourages Muslims to use the opportunity of living among the infidels to wage jihad where they are.[490] Indeed, the argument is put forth that the "real jihad" is not giving da'wah, or simply telling non-Muslims about Islam, but rather "the real da'wah is waging Jihad!" Action is called for, he

---

[489] Dabiq, issue 15, 26-29. http://www.clarionproject.org/factsheets-files/islamic-state-magazine-dabiq-fifteen-breaking-the-cross.pdf. (Accessed 8/18/2016).

[490] Dabiq, issue 15, 26-29.

continues, in order to fulfill the obligation of spilling the blood of the disbelievers, for the command is clear: "Kill the disbelievers, as Allah said, 'Then kill the polytheists wherever you find them'" (Q. 9:5).

The goal of this jihad against the non-believers, since "disbelievers are a clear enemy" (Q. 4:101), is to scare them and terrorize them "until every neighbor fears his neighbor." Furthermore, the author states that the "Crusader nations and their citizens" are not innocent because the Western democracies fight against the Muslim nations. Therefore, he says to his reader, "it becomes even more obligatory for you to attack the Crusader nations and their citizens in their homelands as done by the likes of the Caliphate's soldiers." His final plea to the former Christian is for him to prove his love for Allah by following Muhammad, who said that he "would have loved to fight for Allah's cause and be killed, then be revived and killed again." The promise was also given that if they followed Muhammad's example against the infidel, then Allah would love them and forgive them of their sins. (Q. 3:31). The final "word of advice" for his reader was to make "simple and effective" plans to "cause the most damage and panic" in order to bring "death and injury to the enemy of Allah, the disbelievers."

The next article in the magazine, titled "Why We Hate You and Why We Fight You," is even more direct in its assertion that fighting against the infidel is commanded by Allah. Contrary to the politically correct narrative that the violent attacks carried out by ISIS are senseless and un-Islamic, the author calls this view "foolish" and proclaims that ISIS is "in fact completely Islamic." Of his six reasons the Islamic State hates the West, the first one sums it all up.

> We hate you, first and foremost, because you are disbelievers; you reject the oneness of Allah – whether you realize it or not – by making partners for Him in worship, you blaspheme against Him, claiming that He has a son [Christ], you fabricate lies against His prophets and messengers, and you indulge in all manner of devilish practices. It is for this reason that we were commanded to openly declare our hatred for you and our enmity towards you... We have rejected you, and there has arisen, between us and you, enmity and hatred forever until you believe in Allah alone'" (Al-Mumtahanah 4 [i.e., Quran 60:4]). Furthermore, just as your disbelief is the primary reason we hate you, your disbelief is the primary reason we fight you, as we have been commanded to fight the disbelievers until they submit to the authority of Islam, either by becoming Muslims, or by paying jizyah – for those afforded this option ["People of the Book"] –

and living in humiliation under the rule of the Muslims [per Quran 9:29].[491]

Clearly, when ISIS is allowed to speak for itself, the reason they give for their actions is that everything they do and say is based squarely on the commands of the Qur'an and the words and actions of the prophet. Thus, if anything, ISIS seems to represent a return to the first century model of conquest and expansion carried out under Muhammad and his loyal followers. It would be exceedingly useful, then, to compare the successful military actions of the conquering Arabs in the 7th century with the present practices of ISIS in order to understand how ISIS operates today. From this comparison and assessment, it will be easier to determine whether ISIS follows the Qur'an and Muhammad more religiously than moderate Muslims or whether it is just a renegade heretical group that blasphemes the name of Allah.

## Implications

As noted in previous chapters, in the 7th century, as the Arab horde moved northward behind the retreating Byzantine forces, some non-Chalcedonian Christian groups, who viewed Islam as the "rod of God's anger" intended "to deliver [them] from the Byzantines,"[492] felt relief from what they considered an oppressive former regime. On the other hand, the "Byzantine polemicists saw Islam as a 'Satanic plot' to destroy Christian Faith."[493] Some of the sources cited religious devotion by the invaders and some cited brutality and godlessness. Overall, there seemed to be a sense of ambivalence and unpreparedness. At first the new regime ruled from a distance and made light economic and civil demands. This further pleased the non-Chalcedonian Christians. However, as the Muslims gained more power, the suppression of Christian rights increased. In time, Christians were brutally persecuted, churches and Bibles were burned, crosses were banned and public preaching was denied. As the number of Muslims in the general population grew, many of the remaining Christians were faced with three choices: convert, submit and pay, or die.

We see many of these same patterns reappearing in the 21st century, especially in the Middle East. As ISIS began their campaign in Iraq they were greeted with open arms by their fellow Sunni Muslims who hold disdain for the present U.S. built Iraqi government. As ISIS gained more power,

---

[491] Dabiq, Issue 15, 31.
[492] 'Christianity and Islam' from Oxford Islamic Studies Online", November 13, 2014 http://bridgingcultures.neh.gov/muslimjourneys/items/show/198. (Sahas, 23)
[493] Ibid. (Gaudeul, vol. 1, 65).

there was greater suppression of the rights of Christians and those they consider to be Muslim "infidels." Christians experienced horrendous persecution as they faced torture, rape, crucifixion, and beheadings. Their churches were burned, crosses were banned, and public proclamation of their Christian faith brought swift martyrdom. In the end they were given three choices: convert, submit and pay, or die (or flee before this happens). With meticulous and brutal conviction, parts of the Middle East are being "cleansed" of any Christian presence; a presence that has survived for almost 2,000 years.

It is evident from the comparison above that there are a number of similarities between the response of the church to Islam in the 7th century and the 21st century. There are four general stages that are represented at both times -- denial, apathy, "complacent ignorance," and fear.

In regard to denial, those living outside the Middle East and North Africa in the centuries following the rise of Islam denied that there was much going on. When they did comprehend the gravity of the situation they were apathetic about getting involved. In fact, it took almost 400 years for the church to launch a counter-attack (the Crusades). As one writer notes, there was also "complacent ignorance,"[494] because the Christians outside of the strike zone were more concerned with their own peace and security rather than learning more about the enemy and seeking to rescue their brothers in Christ. Finally, there was fear – fear of getting involved, fear of retaliation, and fear of the unknown. We see the same responses today. [Apathetic/distant problem/complacent ignorance/fear: pull together response today and end in fear, which leads to denial and this will lead into the next section.]

First, there is widespread denial. The most common form of denial is to say that the atrocities committed by the Islamists are not "true Islam." [Is there an underlying reason for this widespread denial?]

Many are apathetic because the Middle East is far away and the persecution of millions of Christians is still considered a "distant problem." One of the main reasons for this indifference on the part of Western Christians is due to "complacent ignorance"; the focus for many Christians is on self-interest, and as long as there is relative peace and prosperity at home, then persecution of Christians elsewhere is excused or dismissed. Finally, there is fear. This fear can actually drive the apathy, fuel the "complacent ignorance," and even sanction denial because it strikes at the deepest level of our being. Michael Dougherty, a senior correspondent at

---

[494] Robert Wilken, "Christianity Face to Face with Islam" *(First Things,* January 2009*).*

*TheWeek.com* says, "Fear of Islamic radicalism cows the West into silence on Christian persecution."[495]

## Push to a Logical Conclusion

In order to understand what is really going on today in regard to ISIS, we need to reveal the core motivation of their actions. Many in the western world, most likely influenced by fear, deny that ISIS has anything to do with the religion of Islam. However, the leaders of the Islamic State assert boldly that all that they do is strictly motivated by their submission to Allah and their slavish adherence to the Qur'an and the sunnah of the Prophet. Indeed, their war cry, "Allahu Akbar" (God is greater), has become the universal call to submit to the violent Jihad verses in the Qur'an (of which there are over 150). Hassan al-Banna, the founder of the Muslim Brotherhood (1928) made it very clear as to what Jihad was all about: "It is the nature of Islam to dominate, not to be dominated, to impose its laws on all nations and to extend its power to the entire world."[496] Sayed Qutb, the famed spiritual leader of the Muslim Brotherhood, declared that all non-Muslims should be considered "infidels," therefore justifying the Qur'an's mandate to fight against them "wherever they are found."[497] (In other words, there are no "innocent" non-Muslims). More recently, Al-Baghdadi, the self-proclaimed caliph of the new Islamic State, urged his followers to "Support the religion of Allah through jihad in the path of Allah. Go forth, O mujahideen, in the path of Allah. Terrify the enemies of Allah and seek death in the places where you expect to find it, for the *dunya* [worldly life] will come to an end, and the hereafter will last forever."[498] Hasan al-Banna, Sayed Qutb, and al-Baghdadi claim to be the true voices of Islam today. Why, then, do we allow non-Muslim pundits, reporters, and politicians to tell us what Muslims believe about Islam?

Furthermore, it is undeniable that the actions of these Muslim leaders are derived from their beliefs. They justify their violent attacks by resorting to the Qur'an. For example, Surah 9:5 states, "But when the

---

[495] Michael Dougherty, "Why is the West so afraid of Islam?" http://theweek.com/article/index/265535/why-is-the-west-so-afraid-of-islam (accessed 9/26/2018)

[496] *Middle East Forum*: https://www.meforum.org/articles/2014/confusion-over-jihad (accessed 9/26/2018).

[497] http://www.meforum.org/4818/confusion-over-jihad (accessed 9/16/2014).

[498] Speech on July 1, 2014: http://www.memrijttm.org/in-new-message-following-being-declared-a-caliph-islamic-state-leader-abu-bakr-al-baghdadi-calls-for-jihad-promises-support-to-oppressed-muslims-everywhere-calls-for-people-with-expertise-to-emigrate-to-the-islamic-state.html (accessed 9/16/2014).

sacred months are passed away, kill the idolaters (non-Muslims) wherever ye may find them; and take them, and besiege them, and lie in wait for them in every place of observation." This verse is said to abrogate (nullify) more than 114 other verses that prescribe less severe treatment for non-Muslims. Moderate Muslims may try to claim that these violent verses are not for today, but that does little to change the minds of radical Muslims who are following the accepted interpretation of the last 1400 years. [499]

The Qur'an is also clear in the use of beheading as a punishment for those who oppose Islam. Surah 47:4, "And when you meet those who misbelieve, non-Muslims, while fighting in Jihad, cut off their heads until you have massacred them, and take them captive [referring to the women and children]."

In regard to the many Muslims who are killed by ISIS, the terrorists resort to the practice of *takfir*,[500] where the captured Muslims are first declared to be "*kafir*," or unbelievers, so that they can then be subdued, killed or enslaved. This is a practice that is not currently recognized by the west, which leads to a false supposition that religion is not behind the terrorist attacks. However, the Qur'an makes only too clear that world domination is the ultimate goal for the faithful. Thus, once the unwanted Muslims are either killed or cowered into submission, ISIS will turn to the western world to fulfill the mandate from Surah 8:39, in which Muslims are told to keep fighting until Islam is the only religion: "and keep fighting them until there is no division among you, and Islam is the only religion." Supposedly, then, the peace that is part of the Islamic promise will be manifested when all other religions are wiped out and all the remaining people have submitted to Islam. Clearly this is not the "peace" which western readers have in mind. For example, Anjem Choudary, an Islamic spiritual leader in the UK, supports the view of fighting until Islam dominates the world when he states, "You can't say that Islam is a religion of peace, because Islam does not mean peace. Islam means 'submission.' So the Muslim is one who submits. There is a place for violence in Islam. There is a place for Jihad in Islam."[501]

## The "Islamoscale" [502]

The question that comes up at this point is how can a person determine whether ISIS is correct or the moderate Muslims are correct. In

---

[499] see Trifkovic, *The Sword of the Prophet*.

[500] A Muslim who is said to have committed apostasy, or at least is considered one who has turned away from true Islam.

[501] CBN News, April 5, 2010. http://www1.cbn.com/content/uk-muslim-leader-islam-not-religion-peace.

[502] The "Islamoscale" illustrations and content has been developed by the author.

other words, how can we know which view best represents true Islam? Perhaps one way to understand the difference in views is through something called the "Islamoscale." On this scale, the further to the right you go there is a more literal interpretation of the Qur'an. At the very left liberal Muslims are represented, moderates in the middle, and radical Muslims toward the right side.

## The "Islamoscale"

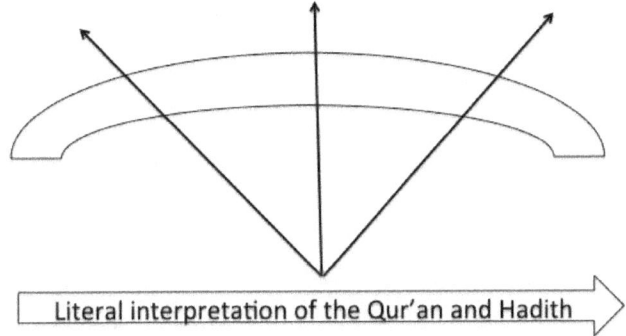

### Interpreting a Verse

How would the different groups interpret one of the verses often cited by the radical Muslims? In Sura 9:29 Allah commands the Muslim believers to "Fight those among the People of the Book who do not believe in Allah nor the Last Day, nor forbid what Allah and His Messenger have forbidden, nor embrace the religion of truth, until they pay the jizya with willing submission and feel themselves subdued."

Liberal Muslims would most likely reply that "This was only for the time of Muhammad." In other words, this verse, and the ones like it, only applied to the time when Muhammad was alive and leading the Muslims. Thus, they are only historical references now and not to be interpreted as applicable for today.

Moderate Muslims would most likely say, "This is only for defensive war and when a proper Jihad has been called by the Muslim state." The assumption here is that the "sword" verses in the Qur'an are still viable for today, but they must be for defensive purposes only, called by a legitimate government, and only against enemy combatants.

Radical Muslims, on the other hand, claim all the fighting verses are for today and against anyone who does not believe that Allah is the true God and that the Qur'an is the true revelation given to Muhammad. In other words, they believe that Muslims need to fight until the whole world is under the domination of Islam. After all, this is what the Qur'an clearly states in Sura 8:39, that Muslims should "keep fighting them until there is no division among you, and Islam is the only religion."

## The "Christoscale"

For comparison's sake, it would be helpful to demonstrate this process from a Christian perspective. This can be done through a "Christoscale," which also depicts the most literal interpretation of the Bible toward the right side of the scale.

## The "Christoscale"

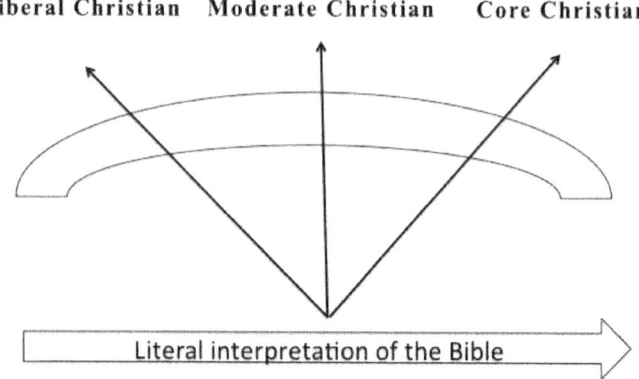

The verse in Matthew 16:24 where Jesus says to his disciples, "Take up your cross and follow me," should be a good verse to use for the comparison. Liberal Christians would likely interpret this injunction by Jesus as an encouragement to be nice to everyone and seek a pathway to peace. Moderate Christians would likely say something like, "We should try to be good examples to others so that our witness may lead them to Christ." However, the words of Jesus are far more challenging than this. Core Christians would properly interpret the words of Jesus as a challenge to "live sacrificially and seek to actively reach out in word and deed in order to win the world for Christ." Thus, when the Bible is followed more literally, the interpretation demands a lot more from the follower. In the same way, if a Muslim followed the Qur'an literally, then there would be a much greater chance that the understanding would shift toward the right side of the Islamoscale. This is certainly the case when the actions of ISIS are compared to the commands of the Qur'an. In fact, it can be said that if ISIS is not Islamic, neither is the Qur'an, for ISIS does nothing that the Qur'an does not command. The chart below (ISIS and Qur'an chart) demonstrates that all the brutal actions for which the world condemns the followers of ISIS are supported in the Qur'an.

## ISIS and Qur'an Chart

| ISIS | Qur'an |
|---|---|
| Terrorism | "Strike terror into the hearts of the enemies of Allah" (Q. 8:60) |
| Blasphemy against Allah: Death | Qur'an 5:33-34 |
| Blasphemy against the Prophet Muhammad: Death – even if the accuser repents | Qur'an 33:57 |
| Blasphemy against islam: Death | Qur'an 9:12 |
| Apostasy: Death | Qur'an 4:89 |
| Fighting and killing non-Muslims | Qur'an 2:216 |
| Sodomy (homosexuality): Death for the person committing the act, as well as for the one receiving it | Qur'an 4:15-16 |

| | |
|---|---|
| Theft: Cutting off the hand | Qur'an 5:38 |

It is also important to note in the chart below (ISIS and Muhammad chart) that if ISIS is not Islamic, neither is Muhammad, for ISIS does nothing that Muhammad did not first do fourteen centuries ago.

## ISIS and Muhammad chart

| ISIS | Qur'an |
|---|---|
| Terrorism | "I have been sent with the shortest expressions bearing the widest meanings, and I have been made victorious with terror..." (Sahih Bukhari 4.52.220). |
| Collateral damage (killing of innocents) | "when asked about the women and children of the polytheists being killed during the night raid, said: they are from them." (Muslim 4321) |
| Mutilation | "If Allah gives me victory over the Quraysh at any time, I shall mutilate thirty of their men!" (Ibn Ishaq 387; Al-Tabari, vol. 7, p133 |
| Torture | "Torture him until you extract what he has" (Ibn Ishaq, 515) |
| Killing the men and taking the women and children as slaves | Massacre of the Banu Qurayza: Muhammad was responsible for the death of over 600 men (Ibn Ishaq) |

Thus, it is clear that while the world demonizes the brutal acts by the followers of ISIS, they are simply carrying out the commands of the Qur'an.

In recognition of this record, Graeme Wood, a journalist for Atlantic Monthly, writes,

> Virtually every major decision and law promulgated by the Islamic State adheres to what it calls, in its press and pronouncements, and on its billboards, license plates, stationery, and coins, "the Prophetic methodology," which means following the prophecy and example of Muhammad, in punctilious detail. Muslims can reject the Islamic State; nearly all do. But pretending that it isn't actually a religious, millenarian group, with theology that must be understood to be combatted, has already led the United States to underestimate it and back foolish schemes to counter it.[503]

The bottom line, then, is that ISIS follows the Qur'an and Muhammad more than most Muslims. Therefore, we need to accept their word, as well as the evidence of what they are doing, and admit that ISIS is Islamic. To do otherwise would be denying reality.

## Apologetic Conclusions

If the evidence supports the view that ISIS is Islamic, then why are so many Western leaders refusing to admit this obvious declaration? For example, President Obama made a point of saying the Islamic State is "not Islamic," despite pressure from critics. At a Summit on Terrorism, even though all the examples of terrorism pointed to Islamic perpetrators, Obama refused to allow Islam to be joined to the word "terrorism." Instead, he refutes the notion that ISIS is Islamic.

Recently, John Kerry reminded reporters that jihadis "define a great religion Islam in a way that doesn't reflect that religion. They steal it, hijack it."[504] Even Pope Francis avoids using the word "Islam" when he speaks of terrorists, and he rejects the notion that Islam is inherently violent. Instead, he sidesteps the main issue by claiming that all religions have fundamentalists who resort to violence in order to further their goals. By equating Islamic terrorists with fundamentalists of other religions, like Christianity, however, the Pope overlooks a key difference between Islam and Christianity: the terrorism in Islam is supported by the example of Muhammad and the teachings of the Qur'an (Q. 8:39, 60), but it is rejected in the New Testament and by the words of Jesus. It is interesting to note that the official magazine of the Islamic State, *Dabiq*, responded to Pope

---

[503] Wood *The Atlantic Monthly*, March 2015.

[504] https://timesofindia.indiatimes.com/john-kerry-interacts-with-iit-delhi-students/liveblog/53940540.cms (accesed 9/26/2018).

Francis and insisted that Islam should be identified as violent and that the Pope needed to face this reality.[505] According to the Muslim authors, "waging jihad — spreading the rule of Allah by the sword — is an obligation found in the Quran."[506] In addition, they wrote "The blood of the disbelievers is obligatory to spill by default. The command is clear. Kill the disbelievers, as Allah said, 'Then polytheists kill the wherever you find them.'"[507] The 6th Chinese military strategist century, Sun Tzu, once said "know your enemy."[508] This advice is still very relevant. In order to defeat extremist Islamic ideology, these leaders need not only to admit its existence, but they also need to realize that denying the truth does not change reality.

In his excellent article on Islam in the Atlantic Magazine, Graeme Wood concluded that, "The reality is that the Islamic State is Islamic. *Very* Islamic. Yes, it has attracted psychopaths and adventure seekers, drawn largely from the disaffected populations of the Middle East and Europe. But the religion preached by its most ardent followers derives from coherent and even learned interpretations of Islam."[509] Denying the truth of this statement does not change reality.

The rationale for the obfuscation that is taking place seems to be that if these leaders give in and admit the connection, then ISIS will have the recognition and legitimacy that they want. Then ISIS will be able to woo even more Muslims to their battlegrounds in support because they will have won the ideological debate and the pressure will be on the moderate Muslims to either join the cause or be relegated as hypocrites (Q. 3:167).

These Western leaders seem to be promoting a multi-cultural hope that the radical Muslims will lose the battle when the moderate Muslims recognize that the pluralism of the West is more attractive than the radical agenda. In other words, these Western leaders believe that if they demonstrate how inclusive the West is, even promoting Islam above other religions and Muslims above other people, that the average Muslim would desire the Western lifestyle and ideology more than the fundamental Muslim one. However, what they don't realize is that the fundamental draw of Islam is to the core of Islamic beliefs, and these are counter to Western values, especially the multi-culturalism that is pushing the whole

---

[505] *Dabiq*, vol. 15, 75.
[506] *Ibid.*, 78.
[507] *Ibid.*, 28.
[508] Sun Tzu, *Art of War*, Chapter 3. http://classics.mit.edu/Tzu/artwar.html (accessed 9/26/2018).
[509] Graeme Wood, "What ISIS Really Wants," *The Atlantic Monthly*, March 2015

agenda. What will happen instead is that the message of the jihadists will be recognized as the true message of Islam and more Muslim young men will flock to ISIS and similar groups in order to defend true Islam. The multicultural effort will backfire and end up putting more gasoline on the fire.

Another reason these leaders may be avoiding linking Islam and terrorism together is that they realize that if they publicly admit that the primary motivation of the terrorists is found in faithfully following the Qur'an and the example of Muhammad, then there could be widespread panic on the part of non-Muslims and violent retaliation on innocent Muslims and their mosques. By continuing to deny the relationship between Islam and the actions of the terrorists, a buffer zone of doubt seems to prevent most non-Muslims from making a firm connection. Therefore, anger and frustration is defused and a backlash against Muslims is prevented. However, if this is the reason for the obfuscation, then it is very likely that a time is coming when that buffer zone mentality crumbles and the fires of retaliation will be ignited. It would be better to face the danger truthfully and help non-Muslims opt for more positive ways to deal with the menace lurking in the shadows.

## The Core of Islam

The West today faces a real dilemma. ISIS claims to be radically Islamic, yet critics claim that ISIS is not Islamic at all. How can we resolve the cognitive dissonance that is taking place? The underlying reason for this dilemma is that the West does not understand the core of Islam. We need to realize that the core of Islam and the core of Christianity (and thus of western values) are polar opposites: one for Power, the other for Love. Islam perceives Allah as a singularity whose essence is pure Will, revealed to man as Power. This is why the proper response for man is total submission to Allah, which defines the word "Islam." However, the mandate from Allah to those who have submitted is that they should then subdue the whole world until all are in submission to the Power of Allah. In order to carry out this mandate, the followers of Islam need to exert power over non-believers, as well as other Muslims who have been deemed, through *takfir*, to be *kafir* (non-believers).

This mandate demands the exact type of behavior that ISIS is displaying right now. Fear is the best tool to demonstrate power over the infidel (Qur'an 59:2) Thus, if we push the core beliefs of Islam to their logical conclusion, it is clear that in this way ISIS supporters are more faithful to the goal of the Qur'an than the many Muslims who would oppose such actions. In regard to this, we may say that "Radical" Islam is closer to the "root" (Latin, *radix*) of Qur'anic teaching than so-called

"Civilized/Moderate" Islam. Perhaps a better comparison would be "Literal" Islam versus "Nominal" Islam, since the latter group often wants to deny many verses in the Qur'an, especially the ones calling for a violent jihad.

In stark contrast to this we have Christianity, the core motivation of which is Love for God and for one's neighbor (Deuteronomy 6:5; Matthew 22:37-40), because the essential nature of God Himself is Love. When Christians seek to live in this love, then their actions bring freedom and true peace, rather than the submission and fear that comes from a pursuit of Power. Thus, "radical" Christians should only become more loving, even as radical Muslims would seek more and more power in a quest for domination and subjugation. The fruit will always show the true nature of the tree. Thus, since ISIS clearly strives to follow the core beliefs of Islam, as their history and own declarations reveal, then we need to recognize it as a valid representation of the religion of Islam.

One lesson that history has taught us is that beliefs have consequences. The history of Islam, combined with an accurate understanding of the Qur'an, has demonstrated that Islam has not been a religion of peace. Furthermore, since the modern terrorists specifically refer to this past and this scripture, it is neither good logic nor good policy to ignore such crucial roots of the current Middle Eastern crisis. A clearer understanding would produce solutions that better understand the motivations and character of the ISIS movement. Subsequently, this would be more effective in meeting the need of the hour while also preparing for future conflicts and implications of radical Islam. A Russian proverb says, "Dwell on the past and you will lose an eye; forget the past and you will lose both eyes." In our present struggle with "literal" Islam, however, if we ignore the past we may literally lose our heads!

## Building Bridges to Understand

Are there any ways to break this pattern and bring true peace to the Middle East? The growth of "power Islam" seems to catapult forward when there is a political vacuum to fill. In the 7th-century, the retreat of the Byzantine forces left the Levant unguarded. In the 20th-century, there was a retreat of colonial forces that had provided modernization and movement toward Westernization. While the colonial forces were in control, the Middle Eastern Christians had been able to experience a type of "Golden Period" where the *dhimmi* status was lifted and they were able to build churches, receive better opportunities for education, and make advances in society. However, the colonial forces turned the power back over to the Muslims, and in a relatively short time, the rejection of western values provided an impetus to revive a socio-economic-religious worldview based on 7th-century Islam. Because Islam is a theocracy, the success of "power Islam" has encouraged militant groups to believe that God is on their side. This, in turn, has fueled their belief that they have a mandate by God to subdue the rest of the world (the *Dar al-Harb*, or "house of war") under the *Dar al-Islam*, or the "house of Islam" (or "house of submission" to God).

Some believe that a secularization of Islamic countries needs to take place, involving the "separation of mosque and state." With this type of separation, the state would protect the freedom of the religion and the religion would respect the role of the state. Then, when there is proper balance between these "two worlds," there can be peace. However, a theocratic nation will always be at war with the secular state, or a Muslim nation that does not follow sharia law.

What should be our Christian response? First of all, Christians should love Muslims because they have also been made in the image of God and need his salvation. We also need to realize that Islam, itself, is the problem, not Muslims. In order to confront heresy, we need to shine the full light of truth on error. If we deny that there is a problem, then we will never resolve it. Thus, our best defense is to construct a proper apologetic approach. First of all, we need to seek to understand Islam. Christians need to be informed of the basic teachings of Islam. Secondly, we need to learn how to defend key Christian doctrines, such as the Trinity, the deity of Christ, the crucifixion, and biblical authenticity. Thirdly, we need to learn how to refute error with gentleness and respect.

This conflict with "power Islam" may last a long time, especially since the foundation of their actions is firmly sanctioned in the Qur'an, the Hadith and the Sunnah of Muhammad. However, we also know that God has a plan for his nations, and we need to realize that in the last two decades more Muslims have come to Christ than in the preceding 1400 years. This is why we need to hold fast to the Word of God, preach boldly, and always be prepared to give an answer for what we believe.

There have been two main responses to jihad recently. Some leaders have repeatedly asserted that radical Islam has nothing to do with Islam, while others seem to view radical Islam as the only form of Islam. However, it is dangerous to measure a religion by extreme positions. Robertson McQuilkin, former president of Columbia International University, often said it is easier to go to one extreme or the other rather than to remain in the center of biblical tension. In this same way, Islam has been cast as either a religion of peace or a conduit of terror. The truth lies in between. As Nabeel Qureshi suggests, Christians may not know how to end the struggle, but they should at least begin "with the truth about Islam and with compassion for Muslims."[510]

## Truth and love

The historical evidence has revealed Islam as a faith where devout believers who follow the Qur'an and Muhammad have consistently come to the conclusion that they are to "struggle" against the non-Muslim world until all people submit to Allah. This is a position that does not promote peace. Facing the truth, then, reveals that there has been a tremendous amount of violence in Islam from its very foundations. This reality has to be acknowledged in order to reach beyond violence to real peace. As Qureshi notes, "As long as Muslims place their primary emphasis on the person of Muhammad and following the teachings of the Qur'an, without successfully supplanting the canonical texts and traditions, the end result will be the same. Islam will direct its adherents to its violent foundations with violent results."[511] Leaders, then, must recognize this truth about Islam in order to carry out the necessary conversations that will allow Muslims and non-Muslims to bring about real change. Otherwise, continued obfuscation and cognitive dissonance will only cloud the real issues and prolong the charade.

However, truth without love will only lead to further rejection rather than persuasion. How can Christians show love to Muslims? First of all, Quereshi suggests that Christians need to be proactive rather than reactive. This means that Christians need to initiate positive relationships with Muslims so that a mutual understanding will develop. This will also reduce the fear Christians often have when they think of the Islamic issues. Instead of fear, which tends to alienate, Christians need to be able to reach out in love.

It also must be understood that fighting will only bring limited solutions and will only prolong the devastation. This is why Qureshi concludes "Fear and fighting both fuel the radical fires. We need something that breaks the cycle, and I think that can only be love." This love puts others above ourselves, even at the cost of one's own life. In a sense, we need radical love in order to fight radical Islam. We need a frame of heart and mind that will shape the way we respond. Qureshi's reflection on the interaction of these two features is very poignant: "That frame of mind is truth and love, and both elements are essential. Without truth we will not

---

[510] Qureshi, *Answering Jihad*, 143.
[511] Ibid., 144.

be able to identify the real problem and without love we will not be able to formulate an enduring answer."[512]

What does this look like in the real world? We need to reach out to Muslims with love and friendship so that we can engage them in conversations that are based on truth rather than lies, the Christian gospel rather than politics, and true peace rather than rhetoric. The gospel is always the way forward, and the love of Christ is always the final solution.

### Study Questions:

1. What are some of the statements that world leaders give when they comment on the terrorist actions of ISIS?
2. What are some of the reasons followers of ISIS give for hating the West and fighting against non-Muslims?
3. What are the best reasons that support the view that ISIS is NOT Islamic?
4. What are the best reasons that support the view that ISIS is Islamic?
5. If ISIS is Islamic as Graeme Wood indicates, what are the main reasons that so many world leaders not only deny this connection, but push hard to promote Islam as a religion of peace?

---

[512] Ibid., 147.

# PART 4: APPROACHES TO REACHING MUSLIMS WITH THE GOSPEL

# CHAPTER 15 Do Muslims and Christians Worship the Same God?

## Introduction

There has been a great deal of confusion brought on by this question, especially in the aftermath of a Wheaton professor's comment affirming that Muslims and Christians do indeed worship the same God. After all, can there logically be more than one God in the universe? If there is only one God, and Muslims and Christians both worship this one God, then they must, by logic, worship the same God.

On the other hand, Muslims do not accept Jesus Christ as the Son of God, and by extension the belief in a triune God. For Muslims, this is the greatest sin a person can commit, for God cannot have an associate. Thus, if Christians worship a triune God, and believe that Jesus Christ is the second person of this triune God, then Muslims would have to say that Christians do not worship the same God. Is there a way past this theological impasse? I believe there is. As a way to bring clarity and resolution to this question, this chapter will explore what we will call the ontological and theological divide, or a comparison of God's existence with his essence as they refer to Islam and Christianity.

On December 15, 2015, Wheaton College placed one of its professors, Larycia Hawkins, on administrative leave for "theological statements that seemed inconsistent" with the Wheaton doctrinal convictions. Prior to this decision, Larycia Hawkins donned a hijab in protest to how she felt Muslims were being treated and stated on Facebook, "I stand in religious solidarity with Muslims because they, like me, a Christian, are people of the book. And as Pope Francis stated last week, we worship the same God." [513] After a tense time of discussion between Hawkins and the Wheaton leadership team, she agreed to resign and part ways with the school.[514]

Shortly after this, a writer for the National Catholic Reporter, Maureen Fiedler, commented in support of Hawkins.

This week, I interviewed a Jewish rabbi, a Muslim imam and scholar, and a Methodist minister about this question: "Do Jews,

---

[513] Nabeel Qureshi, "Do Muslims and Christians Worship the Same God?" RZIM, December 27, 2015. https://rzim.org/global-blog/do-muslims-and-christians-worship-the-same-god/ (accessed 7/25/2018).

[514] Ibid.

Christians and Muslims worship the same God?" All three said, "yes ... basically they do." Now, they recognized some complications, like the Christian belief in the Trinity and that Jesus is called the "Son of God," but they still came away affirming that God is basically one and the same for all three traditions. If we started to recognize and acknowledge the similarities, we might have much less Islamophobia in our world.[515]

Note that the focus is on the similarities between the religious views and not the differences. She does not seem to realize the logical inconsistency in the gulf of meaning between "some complications" in Christian beliefs, such as the Trinity and the deity of Jesus Christ, versus "one and the same."

In his book *Allah*, Lutheran theologian Miroslav Volf also focuses on the similarities and makes the case that Christians and Muslims agree on six claims about God, and therefore worship the same God. These claims are the following:

1. There is only one God, the one and only divine being.
2. God created everything that is not God.
3. God is radically different from everything that is not God.
4. God is good.
5. God commands that we love God with our whole being.
6. God commands that we love our neighbors as ourselves.[516]

Volf explains, "To the extent the Christians and Muslims strive to love God and neighbor, they worship that same true God."[517] Earlier, Volf appeals to the First Letter of John and reminds his readers that, "Whoever does not love, does not know God, for God is love (4.8)."[518]

At one time, Pope John Paul II spoke on this same issue and said, "We Christians joyfully recognize the religious values we have in common with Islam. Today I would like to repeat what I said to young Muslims some years ago in Casablanca: 'We believe in the same God, the one God, the

---

[515] Maureen Fiedler, "Do Christians, Muslims and Jews Worship the Same God?" National Catholic Reporter (January 22, 2016). https://www.ncronline.org/blogs/ncr-today/do-christians-muslims-and-jews-worship-same-god (accessed 7/25/2018).

[516] Miroslav Volf, *Allah: A Christian Response* (Harper One, 2011), 110.

[517] Volf, *Allah*, 123.

[518] Volf, *Allah*, 120.

living God, the God who created the world and brings his creatures to their perfection.'"[519]

This is not a recent view of the Catholic church. In 1076, Pope Gregory VII wrote this to a Muslim leader: "We believe in and confess one God, admittedly, in a different way..."[520] But like many other religious leaders on all sides of the argument, Gregory insisted that *his* version of the Almighty is the one whom the others are unknowingly and incompletely worshiping.

During his presidency, President Bush told Al Arabiya television, "I believe there is a universal God. I believe the God that the Muslim prays to is the same God that I pray to. After all, we all came from Abraham. I believe in that universality."[521] As a Christian, President Bush believed that since there is one universal God, and since Muslims pray to one God, then they must pray to the same God as Christians. His words seem to be supported by the Qur'an, which states, "We believe in that which has been revealed to us and revealed to you. And our God and your God is one; and we are Muslims [in submission] to Him" (Sura 29:46).

In a policy handbook published by the Saudi government, called "Islam: A Global Civilization," the authors promote the connection back to Abraham to make the point that Muslims worship of the same God as the Jews and the Christians:

> One should in fact properly speak of the Judeo-Christian-Islamic tradition, for Islam shares with the other Abrahamic religions their sacred history, the basic ethical teachings contained in the Ten Commandments and above all, belief in the One God.
>
> And it renews and repeats the true beliefs of Jews and Christians whose scriptures are mentioned as divinely revealed books in Islam's own sacred book, the Qur'an.[522]

It seems then, when the similarities are emphasized, that Muslims and Christians must worship the same God. However, the matter is more

---

[519] John Paul II, General Audience, Wednesday 5 May 1999. http://w2.vatican.va/content/john-paul-ii/en/audiences/1999/documents/hf_jp-ii_aud_05051999.html (accessed 7/25/2018).

[520] Douglas Pratt, *The Church and Other Faiths: The World Council of Churches, the Vatican, and Interreligious Dialogue* (Peter Lang, 2010), 281.

[521] http://religion.blogs.cnn.com/2013/09/01/do-christians-muslims-and-jews-worship-the-same-god/ (accessed 7/25/2018).

[522] Published by the Islamic Affairs Department of the Embassy of Saudi Arabia, Washington, D.C. From The Truth About Islam, The Noble Qur'an's Teachings in Light of the Holy Bible, Anees Zaka, Diane Coleman, 2004.

complicated than this. There are some very important differences between the two religions.

When the Law of Non-Contradiction is considered, it helps clarify some of the important differences between the two religions in the understanding of the one God.[523] The Law of Non-Contradiction states that you cannot have two different religions saying the same thing in the same sense at the same time. A corollary of the Law of Non-Contradiction states that if A is true, then B (its opposite) must be false, or if B is true, then A (B's opposite) must be false. Both cannot be true, though both can be false. Thus, if Christianity is true, Islam must be false, or if Islam is true, then Christianity must be false (because they contradict one another in essential areas). Both cannot be true, though both can be false.

What do I say? Do Christians and Muslims worship the same God? Yes, and... no! Let me clarify. First of all, can there logically be more than one omnipotent, omniscient, omnipresent God in the universe? No. Thus, if there is only one God, and Muslims and Christians both worship this one God, then they must, by logic, worship the same God. On the other hand, Muslims do not accept Jesus Christ as the Son of God, and by extension the belief in a triune God. For Muslims, this is the greatest sin a person can commit, for God cannot have an associate. Thus, if Christians worship a triune God, and believe that Jesus Christ is the second person of this triune God, then Muslims themselves would have to say that Christians do not worship the same God (and are guilty of idolatry). Is there a way past this theological impasse? I believe there is: the "Yes" and "No" answer, or the way through the ontological and theological divide.

## The Ontological and Theological Divide[524]

It is understandable that some scholars want to emphasize the similarities between Yahweh and Allah. They point to a common belief in a monotheistic God who is Creator of all things, omnipotent and merciful. They argue that ontologically there can be only one God in the universe.[525] Therefore, since Jews, Christians, and Muslims seek the one God, they are

---

[523] See Norman Geisler, *An Introduction to Philosophy: A Christian* Perspective (Baker Academic, 1987).

[524] Although ontology refers to the "study of being," which may include both existence and essence, I am, for the sake of clarity and consistency, restricting my use of "ontology" to the act of existence, and focusing the term "theology" on the essential nature of God, or, simply put, his essence. Thus, connotatively, "ontology" here refers to God's existence, and "theology" refers to God's essence (or nature).

[525] See Gerald McDermott and Harold Netland, *A Trinitarian Theology of Religions: An Evangelical Proposal* (Oxford University Press, 2014), 69.

seeking the same entity. In a philosophical sense, this may be accurate, especially when we consider the similarities (common traits) which deal with "what he does," or his "doingness," in contrast with his "beingness," or "who he is." Both Christians and Muslims believe there is One God, and that God created the universe. They also believe that God is sovereign and omnipotent and that he will judge the wicked. In addition, they both believe that God has spoken to man through messengers (prophets), angels, and the written word. This is perhaps why Miroslav Volf sums up his views by saying that, "To the extent the Christians and Muslims strive to love God and neighbor, they worship that same true God."[526] However, is this assessment accurate?

In a debate with the celebrated author and former Muslim Nabeel Qureshi, Volf insisted that "Christians and Muslims worship one and the same God, the only God. They understand God's character partly differently, but the object of their worship is the same. I reject the idea that Muslims worship a different God than do Jews and Christians."[527] Volf emphasizes that both Muslims and Christians describe God as loving and just, and therefore, despite their differences, both religions worship the same God. However, knowing "about" is different from "knowing personally."

When the similarities are emphasized, the ontological nature of God is isolated from the theological nature and therefore the focus is on the ontological existence of God (general revelation). However, theologically Muslims and Christians define "God" very differently.[528] Sam Solomon, a Christian scholar, highlights the differences in his book, *Not the Same God*, where he argues,

> ... notwithstanding many apparent similarities, the Allah of Islam as expressed in the Doctrine of Islamic Monotheism (i.e. Tawheed) is the diametric opposite of the Triune Lord God of the Bible – opposite in nature, character, knowability, description, and attributes.... The Qur'an, although seemingly innocent, has as its main objective to undo the message and mission of Christ.[529]

Although both religions claim that God has sent prophets to reveal His will and produce scriptures to guide our lives, Allah and Yahweh cannot be

---

[526] Volf, *Allah*, 123.

[527] Ibid., 14.

[528] It may help if one thinks of ontology, as used here, as "general revelation" (there is a god) and theology as "special revelation" (this is what God is like).

[529] Sam Solomon and Atif Debs, *Not the Same God: Is the Qur'anic Allah the Lord God of the Bible? (Wilberforce Publications, 2016)*, 20, 21.

the same for the following reasons: First of all, their natures are fundamentally different. Allah's nature is based on absolute oneness (Tawhid), which means that there can be no personal relationship with anything or anyone else. The way in which he displays his attributes then, such as his will and his power, are impersonal and often seem capricious to his followers. Also, since his power is more important than his other attributes, there is an unequal emphasis on power over the other characteristics. In the end, a follower of Allah cannot know him or even be sure of consistency in his attributes.

On the other hand, Yahweh is by nature a triune unity, which means that the three persons of the one Godhead have always been in relationship with one another. Therefore, because of this eternal relationship within the Trinity, love is promoted within the Godhead and is extended to his creation. Also, since his attributes are based on his unchanging nature rather than his powerful will, all of his attributes are equal and promote trustworthiness rather than uncertainty. This means that believers can know God and be sure of consistency in his attributes.

Second, Christians understand the nature of God to be triune (Father, Son, and Holy Spirit), which is the only way that Jesus Christ, as the second person of the Trinity, could die on the cross to pay for our sins. If Jesus were not God himself, then his death on the cross would be meaningless. However, Muslims deny that Jesus died on the cross and they reject the belief in his resurrection from the dead. Only a triune God, defined as one essence and three persons, could become incarnate and still remain God of the universe, and yet this is the God that Muslims reject. For them, Jesus cannot be God nor can God be a Father, for he cannot have a son. Therefore, if Muslims reject God as the Father of Jesus, then Allah cannot be the same as the God of the Bible.

Is it possible, however, that Muslims worship the same God as Christians, but they simply misunderstand the God of the Bible? Some would say that the difference is only a matter of degree. For example, David Greenlee, in the *EMS Occasional Paper*, related the response of a Central Asian Muslim who converted to Christianity: "Of course I didn't switch gods when I trusted in Jesus Christ. Why would you even think something like that?" Greenlee then adds, "Among Muslims I know who have turned to faith in Jesus Christ, most—but not all—would say more or less the same thing.[530]

---

[530] David Greenlee, "Do Muslims and Christians Worship the Same God? Missiological Implications of Answering a Divisive Question," (*EMS Occasional Bulletin*, Special Edition, 2016), 13.

The idea here is that most Muslims who come to Christ would not say that when they became a Christian the God, they now worship is different than the God they were seeking before. Most would say that God became real to them, or personal in a way that He was not when they were Muslims. I would answer this by saying that when they were Muslims, they only knew the ontological God and not the theological one. They only knew God from a distance, and not personally. In addition, the god that they "knew" was quite different than the true God who has revealed himself.

This is similar to the contrast between General Revelation and Special Revelation. Through General Revelation (Rom. 1:18-20) we can know that God exists, and we can determine some of his general attributes. However, we can only know God relationally when He reveals Himself to us, and that is the purpose of His Special Revelation. We know of His love for us not only because He revealed this love in the Bible, but even more so because the Word of God "became flesh and dwelt among us" (John 1:14). Ontologically, then, God reveals his existence through General Revelation; it is through his Special Revelation that He reveals His nature as Theos (and this is the study matter of theology).

In the same journal, Fred Farrokh, who is a Christian missionary from a Muslim background, said the following:

> The "Same God Question" appears to me to be a theological optical illusion: "Christians worship one God; Muslims worship one God; physical creation itself points to One Creator. Therefore, Christians and Muslims must indeed worship the same God."
>
> The question I pose to those who argue that Christians and Muslims worship the same God is: Since the Bible teaches that Jesus is God and since Islam teaches that Jesus is not God, then how is it possible that Christians and Muslims worship the same God?
>
> I have never been able to reconcile this "Underlying Question." So, while I can concede that Christians and Muslims both seek to worship God, I believe it is impossible that they are worshipping the same God.[531]

---

[531] Fred Farrokh, "The Question Underlying the 'Same God Question,' with Missiological Implications Thereof." (*EMS Occasional Bulletin*, Special Edition, 2016), 11. [emphasis in the original]

Farrokh states that he has not been able to reconcile the "underlying question" as to how Muslims and Christians can seek to worship the one God. I agree with him that since Islam rejects the deity of Jesus Christ it is impossible that Muslims are worshipping the same God. However, I believe that this conclusion can be reconciled when it is understood that when someone says that both Christians and Muslims must be worshipping the same God since there is only one God, this is only on an ontological basis and not a theological one. What I mean by this is that ontologically, since there is only one God, any religion that seeks to worship the one God would be doing so in the sphere of General Revelation. If there is a rejection of the revealed nature (essence) of God, which is in the realm of Special Revelation, then I would say that particular religion is following after a false god, or at least a distortion of the True God. Thus, when Islam rejects the doctrine of the Trinity, the fatherhood of God, the deity of Jesus Christ, and the resurrection, this clearly demonstrates that the theological understanding of God is not at all the same as it is for Christianity. The divide between the two religions, I believe, becomes insurmountable.

But wait a minute, some will say. What about the Arabic Christians who call the God of the Bible "Allah"? Doesn't this illustrate the fact that Allah and Yahweh are referring to the same God? Actually, when the Arabic Christians refer to "Allah" in their translation of the Bible, they believe that "Allah" is the Father of Jesus and they believe that "Allah" is triune. Therefore, the Allah of the Arabic Christians cannot be the same Allah of the Muslims! This semantic enigma can be cleared up if we remember that words have both a denotative and a connotative meaning. Denotation refers to a dictionary definition, so it would be correct to say that Yahweh and Allah both refer to the concept of God (ontologically), especially for their respective language groups. However, the connotation is determined by what a person conceives about the object of that word (theologically). For example, an Arab Christian may still use the word "Allah" to denote God, but his understanding of that term would be starkly different from a Muslim, for the Christian would recognize that Jesus Christ is God (Allah) whereas the Muslim would never consider that connotation. Thus, denotatively the word "allah" merely refers to "god, deity, etc." (ontology). However, we understand the denotative use by our connotative presuppositions (theology). Therefore, "Allah" for the Muslim cannot be reconciled with the "Jesus is Allah" of the Arabic Christians. There is still a world of difference between the content of the word (connotation), even if the denotation is the same. Without this very important distinction made when we refer to "Allah" and "God" (Yahweh), a lot of Christians will be confused.

Some Muslims may still question this reasoning and emphasize the verses in the Qur'an that relate that Muslims and Christians worship the same God. For example, in Surah 29:46 the Qur'an tells Muslims to say to the Jews and Christians, "Our God and your God is One, and unto Him we surrender." According to Muslims, this should settle the matter. However, as we have noted, since Muslims believe that God is a singularity instead of a Trinity, that Jesus is just a human messenger instead of the Word of God and God himself, and that Jesus was not even crucified on the cross, let alone resurrected from the dead, then there is no place for concluding that superficial assent to General Revelation is enough to claim Theological equality. Ontological similarities do not necessitate theological compatibility.

### Nabeel Qureshi:

When Nabeel Qureshi first became a Christian, he believed that Muslims worshiped the same God as Christians, but simply misunderstood the God of the Bible. However, as he studied the Bible more deeply, he came to realize that Muslims could not believe in the same God because they rejected the very nature of the God of the Bible.[532] The crucial difference, then, is determined by the essence rather than mere existence. Both Islam and Christianity believe that God is one and that He exists. However, when Muslims reject the doctrine of the Trinity, the deity of Christ, the fatherhood of God, and the resurrection, then they have rejected the God of the Bible, and therefore cannot worship the same God as Christians. In the end, Qureshi concluded, "I am confident of my position: *Muslims and Christians do not worship the same God."*[533]

If only Dr. Hawkins had understood that Muslims and Christians worship the same God on an ontological level, and not a theological one, then perhaps the outcome would have been much different. Thus, she might have said something like this: "Since Muslims and Christians both believe in One God, who alone created the universe, they at least share an ontological similarity. However, unless Muslims also accept the doctrine of the Trinity, the fatherhood of God, the deity of Christ, and the actual resurrection of Jesus, then these theological differences will preclude us from acknowledging that they believe in the same God."

After comparing the Allah of the Qur'an and the Yahweh of the Bible, it should be apparent that they could not be referring to the same God. As Nabeel Qureshi states,

---

[532] http://rzim.org/global-blog/do-muslims-and-christians-worship-the-same-god. See also Nabeel Qureshi, Answering Jihad: A Better Way Forward, (Zondervan, 2016), 109-116.

[533] http://rzim.org/global-blog/do-muslims-and-christians-worship-the-same-god

Christians worship a Triune God: a Father who loves unconditionally, an incarnate Son who is willing to die for us so that we may be forgiven, and an immanent Holy Spirit who lives in us. This is not what the Muslim God is; it is not who the Muslim God is; and it is not what the Muslim God does. Truly, the Trinity is antithetical to Tawhid, fundamentally incompatible and only similar superficially and semantically. Muslims and Christians do not worship the same God.[534]

Either the Muslim Allah is the true God, or the Christian Yahweh is the true God, or neither is true. As the Law of Non-Contradiction teaches, they both cannot be true. Therefore, how can we continue saying that "the Allah of Muhammad is also the Father of Jesus"?

Study Questions:

1. What are some of the reasons that people give who say that Allah and Yahweh are the same God? How would you rate these reasons?

2. Is it possible that Muslims worship the same God as Christians, but they simply misunderstand the God of the Bible? Are the differences just a matter of degree? Be sure to back up your answers.

3. In the explanation between ontology and theology, how can we say "yes" and "no" in regard to the question of whether Christians and Muslims worship the same God?

4. How does theology, especially in respect to God's essence, demonstrate that Allah cannot be the same as Yahweh?

5. What is the Muslim concept of "Tawhid" and how is different from the Christian understanding of the Triune nature of God? (How is knowing "about" different from "knowing" personally)?

6. How would you answer a Muslim who claims that Christians and Muslims worship the same God? (Can the Allah of Muhammad also be the Father of Jesus)?

---

[534] http://rzim.org/global-blog/do-muslims-and-christians-worship-the-same-god. See also Nabeel Qureshi, *Answering Jihad: A Better Way Forward*, (Zondervan, 2016), 116.

# CHAPTER 16 How Do You Answer Muslim Objections?

## Definition of Apologetics

Apologetics comes from the Greek word απολογία (apologia), and the verse in 1 Peter 3:15 translates *apologia* as giving an "answer" to any who ask about the beliefs of Christians.

**1 Peter 3:15** English Standard Version (ESV)

[15] but in your hearts honor Christ the Lord as holy, always being prepared to make a defense to anyone who asks you for a reason for the hope that is in you; yet do it with gentleness and respect,

There are basically three reasons for Apologetics – preparation, defense, and refutation. In regard to preparation, one of the primary roles of Apologetics is to prevent Christians from being converted to other religions by building up their faith. We need to **understand** both sides: Christian doctrine and the beliefs of our opponents. Another very important role of Apologetics is the **defense** of Christianity against attacks by other religions or doctrines. If Christianity is true, then Christians should be able to defend what they believe and be prepared to give an answer to anyone who asks for a reason for these beliefs. The third role of Apologetics is the **refutation** of heresy. Christians must be ever vigilant in their assault against doctrines and ideas that seek to destroy orthodoxy by subterfuge or false beliefs. The ultimate goal of Apologetics is to understand what we believe, defend the Christian faith, and refute error so that Christ can be proclaimed, and unbelievers may come to Him as the source of all Truth and the savior of the whole world.

Most Muslims have never spoken with a Christian about the gospel, and most Christians do not know what to say when they do have an encounter with a Muslim. However, there are four major objections that Muslims usually bring up when these encounters do take place. These objections are: how can God have a son; has the Bible been changed; do Christians worship three gods; and did Jesus die on the cross? In order to effectively develop our apologetic approach toward Islam, we will be using four essential questions to frame our discussion:

1. What is the Christian's understanding of this doctrine?

    (Statement of the Christian understanding of the doctrine)

2. What do Muslims believe about this doctrine?

(Explanation of how Islam expresses this particular doctrine)

3. How does the Bible critique Islam's approach to this doctrine?

(Evaluation of the Islamic expression through a biblical critique)

4. How can the biblical critique be used in order to build a bridge with Islam?

(Description of how the biblical critique can be used in order to build a bridge with Islam in this particular area)

## How can God have a Son?

### Christian Doctrine

According to the Bible, Jesus Christ is God the Son, Second person of the Trinity. The Son is eternally existent and God of very God. Through the Incarnation, the Son "took on flesh" in order that He might become man and join Himself to a human nature (John 1:14). The Son did this so that He could die for our sins, redeem us, and provide eternal life in God's kingdom. When we consider scriptural support for these claims we note that the Bible states the Son was sent from the Father (John 3:16-18); the Son was with the Father in the beginning (John 1:1; Phil 2:5-11); Jesus identified himself as God revealed in the flesh (John 8:58); and anyone who has seen the Son has seen the Father (John 14:8). The essential questions that Christians need to be able to answer are: How could Jesus be the Son of God and God at the same time? What does the term, "Son of God" mean? If Jesus is God's Son, then did God have physical relations with Mary and get her pregnant?

### Muslim Beliefs

Muslims will usually focus on what the Qur'an and the Hadith say in regard to the questions they bring up. Then they will turn to reason in order to make Christian beliefs seem illogical. In regard to the question of whether God can have a son, the Qur'an declares that there is one God and therefore there cannot also be a son of God (or an associate of God) as well. A son would indicate that there is an addition to the one God. In the Qur'an, one of the earliest revelations given to Muhammad denies that Allah can beget any other God:

*Say: He is Allah, the One and Only.*
*Allah, the Eternal, Absolute.*
*He begets not, nor is He begotten.*
*And there is none comparable unto Him.*
Surah 112:1-4 (Sura Al-Ikhlas)

Therefore, Jesus is only considered a prophet of God and just a man (Surah 5:75): "Christ the son of Mary was no more than a messenger; many were the messengers that passed away before him." To associate another being with God is the greatest of all sins in Islam, called "Shirk." Apparently, Muhammad misunderstood the term "Son of God" in respect to Christianity and only thought of it in terms of God fathering a child through sexual relations with Mary. This is an abomination to Muslims, as it is to Christians as well. Christians understand Christ being God's Son as an analogical term rather than a physical determination. Muhammad was unable to distinguish between the Christian belief in Jesus as the Son of God and the Arab Pagan belief in idols as offspring of God, such as the so-called daughters of Allah, Al-Lat, Al-Uzza, and Manat. Thus, Muslims cannot reconcile Jesus the man with Jesus the Son of God. Here are some questions that Muslims bring up in order to point out the limitations of the man Jesus in comparison to an all-powerful, all present, and all-knowing God.

If Jesus is God, then why does he not know the date and hour of judgment?

**Matthew 24:36** English Standard Version (ESV)

No One Knows That Day and Hour

36 "But concerning that day and hour no one knows, not even the angels of heaven, nor the Son, but the Father only.

If Jesus were God in the flesh, why did he say the following:

| John 5:19 (ESV) | John 14:28 (ESV) | John 5:30 (ESV) |
|---|---|---|
| 19 So Jesus said to them, "Truly, truly, I say to you, the **Son can do nothing of his own accord, but only what he sees the Father doing.** For whatever the Father does, that the Son does likewise. | 28 You heard me say to you, 'I am going away, and I will come to you.' If you loved me, you would have rejoiced, because I am going to the Father, for **the Father is greater than I.** | 30 "I can do nothing on my own. As I hear, I judge, and my judgment is just, because I seek not my own will but the will of him who sent me. |

In other words, how can Jesus be God if he does not know the time of the Judgment and also says that the Father is greater?

These are just some of the ways that Muslims try to demonstrate that it is illogical to believe that Jesus Christ can be God, for if Jesus cannot do the same things as God then, logically, he must not be God.

### Biblical Evaluation

First of all, Muhammad's misconception of the sonship of Christ is another indication that God did not reveal the Qur'an to him. Otherwise, it would be expected that he would understand the text and the context of the previous revelation from God, the Bible. In the Bible, the term "Son of God" is an analogical term that indicates the relationship that the Second Person of the Trinity has with the Father and the Holy Spirit. Jesus is not inferior to the Father; for he claims that he and the Father are one (John 10:30), as well as if they have seen the Son then they have also seen the Father (John 14:9). Jesus also performed unique miracles that confirmed that he was the Son of God. Thus, the Son is not "another" god but rather the second Person of the One God.

## Building Bridges to Understand

First of all, Christians should explain what the term "Son of God" means in its historic and biblical context. Never does it mean that God has a wife and produces offspring. In addition, Christians should realize that the reference to Jesus as the "Christ" is a title given to the heavenly, eternal Son who is equal to God the Father (John 5:18-24). Christians should also explain the limitations that the Son took on himself in order to become a man. If he did not become fully man, then he could not truly die in our place and bring us redemption from our sins. (Phil. 2:5-8).

John of Damascus demonstrated that even the Qur'an claimed that Jesus was the Word and Spirit of God (*Kalimatullah*, Surah 4:171). Thus, John argued, if Jesus was the Word and Spirit of God, then he must have existed eternally since there could not be a time when God existed without his Word and Spirit. Thus, since there is only one God, then Jesus must also be that same God. In conclusion, Christ must be the image of God to mankind, fully God and fully man, but no less than God himself.

One way to help Muslims understand how the Bible relates the son of God with the one, eternal God can be demonstrated from the book of Revelation. In the beginning of the book, the one God is said to be the Alpha and the Omega, the beginning and the end.

**Revelation 1:8** English Standard Version (ESV)

[8] "I am the Alpha and the Omega," says the Lord God, "who is and who was and who is to come, the Almighty."

However, at the end of the book, Jesus is also said to be the Alpha and the Omega, the beginning and the end. Since there can only be one beginning and one end, then this passage is conflating Jesus as the Son of God with God himself.

| Revelation 22 (ESV) | Revelation 22:16 (ESV) |
|---|---|
| ¹³ I am the Alpha and the Omega, the first and the last, the beginning and the end." | ¹⁶ "I, Jesus, have sent my angel to testify to you about these things for the churches. I am the root and the descendant of David, the bright morning star." |

Muslims may deny this interpretation, but it is a logical assessment of the use of the Greek terms, Alpha and Omega, and the literary principle of conflating two different persons into one.

# Has the Bible Been Changed?

## Christian Doctrine

According to Christian doctrine, the Bible is the word of God revealed to men through the inspiration of the Holy Spirit. Since all the words of the Bible are God's words, they neither contradict each other nor are there any errors in the original documents. Therefore, the Bible is considered to be the supreme authority for Christian beliefs. However, since there are a number of beliefs that Christians have that differ or contradict the Qur'an, Muslims have traditionally held that the Bible must have been corrupted. On whether the Bible has been changed, Edward D. Andrews, author of *THE TEXT OF THE TESTAMENT* writes,[535]

> It should be stated that some Bible copyists were careless, even deceitful. Paleographers have set out four basic levels of handwriting. First, there was the *common hand* of a person who was untrained in making copies. Second, there was the documentary hand of an individual who was trained in preparing documents. The third level was the *reformed documentary* hand of a copyist who was experienced in the preparation of documents and copying literature; and fourth was the *professional hand*, the scribe experienced in producing literature.

---

[535] Edward D. Andrews; Don Wilkins, *THE TEXT OF THE NEW TESTAMENT: The Science and Art of Textual Criticism* (Cambridge, OH: Christian Publishing House, 2017).

We have the 27 books of the New Testament that were penned individually in the second half of the first century. Each of these would have been copied and recopied throughout the first century. Copies of these copies would, of course, be made as well. Some of the earliest manuscripts that we now have indicate that a professional scribe copied them. Many of the other papyri provide evidence that a semi-professional hand copied them, while most of these early papyri give evidence of being made by a copyist who was literate and experienced at making documents. Therefore, either literate or semi-professional copyists produced the vast majority of our early papyri, with some being made by professionals.

The Masoretes (scholar/scribes of the Hebrew OT) were very much concerned with the accurate transmission of each word, even each letter, of the text they were copying. Accuracy was of supreme importance; therefore, the Masoretes used the side margins of each page to inform others of deliberate or inadvertent changes in the text by past copyists. The Masoretes also use these marginal notes for other reasons as well, such as unusual word forms and combinations. They even marked how frequent they occurred within a book or even the whole Hebrew Old Testament. Of course, marginal spaces were very limited, so they used abbreviated code. They formed a cross-checking tool as well, where they would mark the middle word and letter of certain books. Their push for accuracy moved them to go so far as to count every letter of the Hebrew Old Testament.

The meticulous care of the Masoretes in their copying of the Hebrew text was made evident in 1947 when the Dead Sea Scrolls were discovered in the Qumran caves. In the spring of 1947, a Bedouin shepherd threw a stone into a cave, marking an event that would be heard around the world, making the name "Dead Sea Scrolls" more known than any other associated with archaeology. As he released one of his rocks into the cave, the sound of a breaking earthenware jar came back at him. Upon further examination, he discovered the first of the Dead Sea Scrolls. Now, scholars could compare the Dead Sea scrolls that dated to the second and first centuries B.C.E. to The Leningrad Codex, which is the oldest complete manuscript of the Hebrew Bible, using the Masoretic Text, which is dated 1008 C.E. according to its colophon, more than a thousand years difference. A member of the international team of editors of the Dead Sea Scrolls, Professor Julio Trebolle Barrera, states: "The Isaiah Scroll [from Qumran] provides irrefutable proof that the transmission of the biblical text through a period of more than one thousand years by the hands of Jewish copyists has been extremely faithful and careful." (F. Garcia Martinez, Martinez and Barrera 1995, p. 99)

We accept the fact of 1,400 years of 400,000 copyist errors. Bible copyists made mistakes. However, none of those mistakes end up corrupting the Bible. Because we also accept the lifetime work of hundreds of New Testament textual scholars, who have restored the Greek New Testament to a mirror image of the original. We also accept the meticulous care of the Masoretes in their copying of the Hebrew text, which has given us the inspired Word of God, as they preserved textual integrity. Rather than having corrupted translations today, the tens of thousands of Old Testament and New Testament manuscripts have given us the Word of God in our language within the literal translations that are accurate in their rendering of the original language words. Muslims generally are only aware of the first half of the history of the Greek New Testament, where the Greek New Testament was corrupted with copyist errors. They have not been told the second half of the history. There is a Preservation of Scripture, but it is by Restoration.[536]

## Muslim Beliefs

Muslims acknowledge Jews and Christians as "People of the Book" and accept certain parts of the Old and New Testaments: the *Tauret* (the Pentateuch of Moses); the *Zabur* (the Psalms of David); and the *Injil* (the gospels of Jesus).

> *"Dispute not with the People of the Book, save in the fairer manner, except for those of them that do wrong; and say: 'We believe in what has been sent down to us, and what has been sent down to you; Our God and your God is One and to Him we have surrendered.'"* (Sura 29:45)

They believe that these books, in their original form, were sent down as previous revelations from Allah, and therefore should confirm and support the revelation given in the Qur'an: "This Qur'an could not have been forged apart from God; but it is a *confirmation of what is before it*

---

[536] HOW THE BIBLE SURVIVED Careless and Even Deceitful Bible Copyists? https://christianpublishinghouse.co/2019/01/23/how-the-bible-survived-careless-and-even-deceitful-bible-copyists/
How to Count Textual Variants
https://christianpublishinghouse.co/2017/03/31/how-to-count-textual-variants/

..." (Sura 10:37). Thus, the Bible and the Qur'an should agree in regard to their teachings.

The Qur'an is considered to be a direct oral revelation given to Muhammad through the angel Gabriel and later recorded by his followers. It is the most important scripture for Islam and holds the final authority for doctrinal issues as well as all aspects of a Muslim's life, such as social, religious, economic, legal, and governmental. In areas that the Qur'an does not address, it is supplemented by the *Hadith*, or "tradition" (additional sayings of Muhammad and his early disciples). In addition, since the Qur'an is often held to be as eternal as Allah, its pronouncements are believed to supersede any other religious book. Muslims believe that God has revealed his words to many prophets throughout time, but since the Qur'an is the last revelation it must also be the most accurate. Thus, all previous scriptures that contradict the Qur'an must have been corrupted or willfully changed. Here are some surahs that address this position.

*There is among them a section who distort the Book with their tongues: (As they read) you would think it is a part of the Book, but it is no part of the Book; and they say, 'That is from Allah," but it is not from Allah* (Surah 3:78).

*Among them are unlettered folk who know the Scripture not except from hearsay. They but guess. Therefore, woe be unto them who write the Scripture with their hands and then say, "This is from Allah," that they may purchase a small gain therewith* (Surah 2:78-79).

Muslims also believe that God preserves his revelation throughout time. Thus, since the Bible contradicts the Qur'an in multiple areas, the Bible must have been corrupted or changed.

## Biblical Evaluation

The earliest Muslims accepted the reliability of the Bible since the Qur'an seemed to accept what was sent down to the People of the Book as earlier revelation from Allah (Sura 29:45). What changed? As Muslims realized that the teachings of the Qur'an contradicted the teachings of the Bible, they needed to either change the Qur'an to correspond to the Bible or claim that the Bible had been changed and corrupted. Some of the contradictions between the Qur'an and the Bible concern the doctrines of the Trinity, deity of Christ, nature of God, nature of sin, salvation, and end times. There are also a number of differences regarding the prophets named in both the Qur'an and the Bible. There are also a number of problematic claims in the Qur'an that are not supported by the historical, epigraphical, or archaeological evidence. For example, the Qur'an claims to have been written in perfect Arabic because Allah wrote it in heaven (Sura 12:2, 13:37, 41:41,44). However, the Qur'an is not in perfect Arabic. It contains many grammatical errors. Some scholars even say that 20% of the Qur'an is not understandable in Arabic. In addition, there are parts of the Qur'an that are not even in the Arabic language! Over 100 foreign words in the Qur'an are used, including Egyptian, Hebrew, Greek, Syrian, Akkadian, Ethiopian, and Persian. Another claim is that there are no variant readings, lost verses or conflicting readings on various texts (i.e., the Qur'an is perfect). However, many variant readings have been researched and documented. Arthur Jeffery, a noted scholar in this area, gives 90 pages of variant readings. The Yemeni Qur'ans, some of the oldest manuscripts of the Qur'an discovered (early 8th century) also reveal that the Muslim claim of a uniform text can no longer be made. Many Muslims also believe the "original manuscript" which Muhammad himself gathered and constructed is still in existence. However, there are no originals in existence. Some of the manuscripts that are often touted as the original manuscripts copied and sent out by Uthman 20 years after Muhammad's death, The Topkapi and the Samarquand, are actually dated to the end of the 8th century at the earliest. In addition, the traditional account admits that most of the Qur'an was not written down when Muhammad died. It was purportedly committed to memory, written on scraps of leather, bones, sticks, palm leaves, etc., and later compiled by Uthman. These so-called "originals," however, are in a Kufic script that dates it to the 9th century AD (almost 200 years after Muhammad). Due to the lack of early manuscripts, despite the claims of Muslims and the 600 years of additional time, the Qur'an cannot compare to the faithful transmission and reliability of the Bible.

## Building Bridges to Understand

In comparison to the Qur'an, the Bible is reliable. We may not have the original manuscripts, but we have thousands of copies that we can compare. The earliest is dated within 25-35 years of the original (John Ryland manuscript). Due to the great number of early copies and the consistency of the text, Norman Geisler says that the New Testament is 99.5% textually pure. Of the 20,000 lines of text, only 400 are in dispute (about 400 words) and none of them affect significant doctrine. In fact, the Bible that we have now is the same one the early Church Fathers had and the same one that would have been used in the time of Muhammad. Therefore, Muslim claims that the Bible cannot be trusted because it was corrupted over time and changed in significant ways cannot be upheld. In fact, the Qur'an itself testifies that the early Muslims assumed that the Bible was reliable: Say: "O People of the Book! You have no ground to stand upon unless you stand fast by the Law, the Gospel, and all the revelation that has come to you from your Lord" (Surah 5:71). How can the Jew or Christian, *stand fast by the Law and the Gospel*, if the Law and the Gospel have been corrupted or abrogated? Thus, the Qur'an maintains that the

Bible is the word of God and no distinction is to be made between any of the holy books. Therefore, The Torah and the Gospels should be considered to be genuine Scriptures from God and not unreliable or corrupted. The earlier revelations in the Qur'an (from the so-called Meccan surahs) admit that the Jews and Christians received Scripture that should be accepted and believed by the Muslims: But say, "We (Muslims) believe in the Revelation which has come down to us and in that which came down to you (Jews & Christians); our Allah and your Allah is One" (Surah 29:46). In fact, it was not until around 200 years later that the charges of corruption were placed against the Bible (though John of Damascus alluded to this problem in the early 8th century). Therefore, if the Qur'an maintains that the Bible is the word of God, and no distinction is to be made between any of the holy books, then the charge of corruption on the part of the Bible should be dropped. In addition, when compared to all the evidence for the reliability of the Bible, it is the Qur'an that lacks the stamp of divine authority.

# Do Christians Worship Three Gods?

## Christian Doctrine

Christians are monotheists who believe in only one God. However, Christians believe that this one God is also at the same time three persons. Thus, God is Triune. In other words, God is one essence and three persons (The Father is God, the Son is God and the Holy Spirit is God). God is a "plurality of persons within the unity of one essence."[537] Each person has their own role: the Father begets the Son, the Son becomes incarnate and dies on the cross for our sins, and the Holy Spirit is sent to dwell within believers.

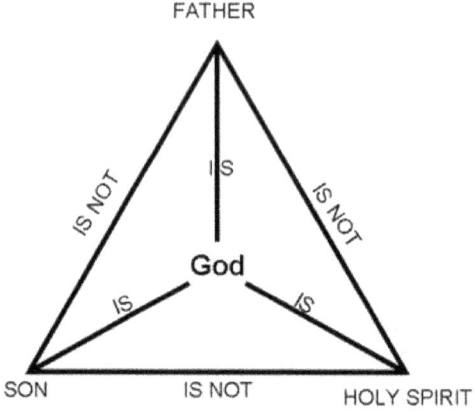

---

[537] Geisler, *Answering Islam*, 263.

## Muslim Beliefs

For Muslims, the concept of the Trinity does not make sense. They will often ask Christians, "how can 1+1+1=1?" Many Muslims also complain that the concept of the Trinity is too complex. As C.S. Lewis put it, sometimes reality is not so simple. "If Christianity was something we were making up, of course, we could make it easier. But it is not. We cannot compete, in simplicity, with people who are inventing religions. How could we? We are dealing with Fact. Of course, anyone can be simple if he has no facts to bother about."[538]

For Muslims, God is an absolute unity (monad). This means that Allah cannot have any associate or anything that would be outside of this absolute unity. Therefore, there can be no plurality in the unity. One result of this belief is that man cannot know Allah since He is totally other and totally transcendent. Therefore, Muslims cannot have a relationship with God.

In the verses in the Qur'an that deny the Trinity, there is a deliberate focus on the belief that Christians must worship three gods. There is also a strong denial that God cannot have a son:

> O People of the Book! Do not exceed the limits in your religion, and do not speak (lies) against Allah, but (speak) the truth; the Messiah, Isa son of Mary is only an apostle of Allah and His Word which He communicated to Mary and a spirit from Him; believe therefore in Allah and His apostles, **and say not,** *Three (thalathatun)*. Desist, it is better for you; **Allah is only one God**; far be It from His glory that He should have a son, whatever is in the heavens and whatever is in the earth is His, and Allah is sufficient for a Protector. (Surah 4:171).

> Those who say, "God is the Messiah, son of Mary," have defied God. The Messiah himself said; "Children of Israel, worship God, my Lord and your Lord." If anyone associates others with God, God will forbid him from the Garden, and Hell will be his home. No one will help such evildoers. Those people who say that God is **the third of three** are defying [the truth]: there is only One God. Surah 5:72-73.

In this last passage, it seems that the Quran erroneously assumes and condemns Christians for believing in three gods consisting of the Father, Mary his wife, and Jesus their offspring. However, Christians have never believed that the Trinity is comprised of three separate gods, nor have they believed that Mary is part of the Triune nature of God.

---

[538] C.S. Lewis, *Mere Christianity* (Harper One, 2015), 145.

## Biblical Evaluation

It seems that a major problem for Muslims is that they cannot grasp the concept of a triune God. They want to ridicule the idea of a Trinity by claiming that mathematically it does not add up. However, the proper math is not 1+1+1=1, but rather 1x1x1=1 or $1^3$ (or one essence and multiple persons). A better construct, perhaps, is to say that $\infty \times \infty \times \infty = \infty$. Whatever the math, the actual nature of God is far beyond any construct that man can conceive. In fact, if God exists on a number of dimensions beyond our three-dimensional universe, then it is understandable that we can only grasp a hint of his true nature. We simply are too limited to comprehend the breadth and length and height and depth of the nature of our God. However, this does not excuse Muslims for trying to put God in a box and limiting the very nature of the one who transcends all of nature.

There also seems to be a fixation and misunderstanding concerning the makeup of the three persons of the Trinity as well as the role of Mary as the mother of Jesus. For example, Surah 5:116 seems to imply that the Qur'an indicates that Christians believe that the Trinity is made up of the Father, Son (Jesus), and Mary.

> And when Allah will say, "O Jesus, Son of Mary, did you say to the people, 'Take me and my mother as two gods besides Allah?' (Surah 5:116) [Jesus denies this]

This has never been the belief of Christians. Early Christians may not have understood the relationships between the Father, Son, and Holy Spirit, but they never would have included Mary in any aspect of the Trinity.

Apparently, there was a heretical sect of fanatical women in 4th century Arabia, called the Collyridians who worshiped Mary as a Goddess. However, this group had been condemned by the orthodox church and was not in existence at the time of Muhammad.

There is also the persistent criticism on the part of Muslims that Christians believe that Jesus was conceived through physical relations between God and Mary. However, this has never been a belief of Christians either. Even Lactantius, a Christian scholar writing in 306, said this in response to this erroneous view:

> He who hears the words 'Son of God' spoken must not conceive in his mind such great wickedness as to fancy that God procreated through marriage and union with any female, - a thing which is not done except by an animal possessed of a body and subject to death.

In conclusion, the Islamic rejection of the Trinity is based on a misrepresentation of the biblical view of what it means for Christ to be God's Son. This is a further indication that the Qur'an could not be the revealed word of the one God.

## Building Bridges to Understand

True Christianity has always portrayed Jesus as God. Therefore, Christians should demonstrate that the Bible states that the One God is also at the same time three persons. First of all, the Bible is clear in stating that there is only one God: "Hear O Israel, the Lord our God is One Lord" (Deuteronomy 6:4). Then, in the New Testament God is known as "Father": "Our Father in heaven" (Matthew 6:9). In addition, the Holy Spirit is equated with God: "you have lied to the Holy Spirit... You have lied not to man but to God" (Acts 5:3-4). Finally, Jesus is declared to be God: The apostle John informs us that "the Word was God" (John 1:1); the disciple Thomas cries out, "My Lord and my God" (John 20:28); and the book of Revelation equates Yahweh with Jesus by conflating the two into the same person: "Alpha and Omega... Yahweh,... Jesus" (Rev 1:8 compared with Rev. 22:13, 16). Thus, from the Old Testament we have a clear statement throughout that there is only one God, and from the New Testament we have further information that reveals that this one God is also three persons, Father, Son, and Holy Spirit, and that each of these persons have distinct roles within the one godhead. This may be a mystery, but it is not illogical.

In order to better understand how the Trinitarian statement of one in three and three in one can be considered logical, we can refer to the Law of Non-Contradiction, which states that something cannot be both true and false at the same time and in the same sense. The Trinity is not one essence and three essences at the same time; nor is it one person and three persons at the same time. Rather it is one essence and three persons at the same time. Therefore, it is not a contradiction to say that God is a Trinity, nor is it illogical.

Another way to understand the relationship between the three persons of the one God is to explore the Trinity as comprised of one "What" (nature/essence) and three "Whos" (persons). In this analogy, a triangle will be used in order to represent the Trinity. The three corners of the triangle correspond to the three persons in the Trinity, and the one triangle that these three corners make up (with their inter-linking lines) correspond to the one entity we call God.

Referring to the illustration below, we can observe that there is one "What" (essence) and three "Whos" (persons), the Father, Son and Holy

Spirit. Thus, when it is said that God is one essence in three persons, it can also be stated that He is one What and three Whos. Each person is distinct with a unique role in the relationship, but they all share the same common nature. Thus, as Norman Geisler puts it, "God is one in his substance but three in his relationships. The unity is in his essence (what God is), and the plurality is in God's persons (how he relates)."[539] In this way the *relationships* can be different (the Father is related to the Son as Father, and the Son is related to the Father as a Son), and their *functions* can be different (the Father sends the Spirit and the Spirit testifies of the Son (Jn. 14:26)), and yet they can still share the same essence. There is only one What.

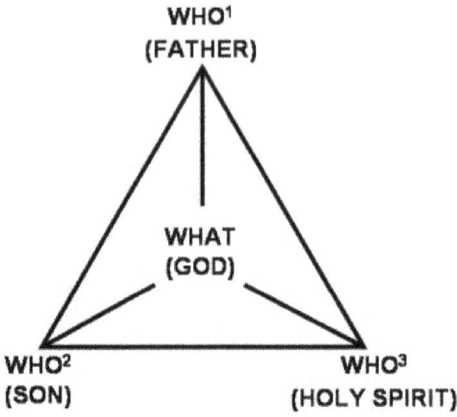

Furthermore, the existence of these eternal relationships between the Father, Son, and Spirit provide a basis for God's love for us. For if there had not been love between the Father, and the Son, and the Spirit from eternity past, how could God have loved us before the creation? How could God be love itself if there had not been a relationship within the Trinity? Perhaps this is why Ravi Zacharias says that, "Only in the Trinity is there Unity and Diversity in the Community of the Trinity."[540]

## Conclusions

When Muslims are confronted with the true teaching of the Christian church, they should understand that Christians do not believe in three gods; and they certainly do not believe that Mary was a god, and together with the Father had physical relations that produced Jesus, the son. Either the Qur'an is condemning an erroneous interpretation of the Christian understanding of the Trinity, or the author has purposely misrepresented

---

[539] Geisler, *Answering Islam*, 266.
[540] http://wonderful-words-of-life.blogspot.com/2012/07/trinity.html

the Orthodox Christian view of the Trinity in order to promote condemnation of Christianity. Whichever the case, this all indicates that the God of the Bible could not also be the God of the Qur'an.

## Did Jesus Die on the Cross?

### Christian Doctrine

The crucifixion and death of Jesus Christ on the cross is central to Christianity. If Jesus did not die on the cross, then Christians could not claim that Jesus resurrected from the dead. If Jesus did not rise from the dead, then we are all still in our sins and the "gospel" is not "good news." If Jesus did not rise from the dead, then, as Paul says,

**1 Corinthians 15:14, 17-19** English Standard Version (ESV)

[14] And if Christ has not been raised, then our preaching is in vain and your faith is in vain. [17] And if Christ has not been raised, your faith is futile and you are still in your sins. [18] Then those also who have fallen asleep in Christ have perished. [19] If in Christ we have hope in this life only, we are of all people most to be pitied.

All four gospels, the letters of Paul and the other New Testament writers, and the early Church Fathers give clear testimony to the death and resurrection of Jesus Christ. This is the central event in Christianity.

### Muslim Beliefs

Based on one verse, Muslims claim that Jesus did not die on the cross. Rather, they claim that it only "appeared" as if Jesus was crucified. Instead, Muslims believe that Allah took Jesus up into heaven where he will wait until the end times to return. After he returns and completes his mission, then he will die.

*"That they said (in boast), "We killed Christ Jesus the son of Mary, the Apostle of Allah"; but they killed him not, nor crucified him, but so it was made to appear to them, and those who differ therein are full of doubts, with no (certain) knowledge, but only conjecture to follow, for of a surety they killed him not: Nay, Allah raised him up unto Himself; and Allah is Exalted in Power, Wise"* (Surah 4:157-158)

Interpretations of this verse differ among Muslims. Some Muslims believe that someone was made to appear like Jesus and was crucified in his place. Other Muslims believe that Jesus did not actually die on the cross but merely "swooned" and later recovered in the tomb.

Some verses in the Qur'an, however, support the view that Jesus did die. From his cradle Jesus purportedly said to his mother, *"So peace is on me the day I was born, the day that I die, and the day that I shall be raised up to life (again)"* (Surah 19:33). Could this actually be used to support the view that the Qur'an supports the death and resurrection of Jesus?

Some will affirm the historicity of the crucifixion, but will then deny the resurrection, as many skeptics do today. For example, Docetism teaches that the body of Jesus died, but his soul could not die. This has been a popular interpretation by liberal Christian scholars today.[541] However, most Muslims today believe that someone else was crucified and Allah miraculously took Jesus up to heaven alive.

## Biblical Evaluation

The main problem for Muslims is that if the Qur'an has it wrong about the crucifixion of Jesus, then the Qur'an is not a divine book and Islam is not a true religion. On the other hand, if Jesus did not die on the cross and then rise from the dead three days later, as the Bible claims, then the Bible is not a divine book and Christianity is not a true religion. Thus, the stakes on both sides are very high!

As mentioned above, all four gospels, the letters of Paul and the other New Testament writers, and the early Church Fathers give clear testimony to the death and resurrection of Jesus Christ. This is the central event in Christianity. How can one ambiguous verse in the Qur'an hope to counter the weight of the historical evidence on the side of the crucifixion?

Gary Habermas, one of the world's experts on the resurrection, concludes from his survey of over 25,000 published works since 1975 that spoke of the crucifixion that all but "a handful" of scholars agree that Jesus Christ not only existed but that he died by crucifixion. Again, how can one obscure reference in the Qur'an hope to topple one of the clearest facts of ancient history?[542]

The bulk of the New Testament was written because Jesus Christ rose from the dead. If he did not die, then there would have been no need to write anything about his life and teachings. The Qur'an, therefore, is either wrong in its assessment of the death of Jesus or the majority of Muslims today have incorrectly understood Surah 4:157.

---

[541] John Shelby Spong, *Resurrection: Myth or Reality?* (HarperOne, 1995).

[542] Gary Habermas, "Resurrection Research from 1975 to the Present: What are Critical Scholars Saying?," *Journal for the Study of the Historical Jesus*, 3.2 (2005), 135-153.

## Building Bridges to Understand

From a historical point of view, the claim by Muslims that Jesus Christ was not crucified was made 600 years after the event and has no historical support from the first century. Perhaps one of the best ways to help Muslims understand the historicity of the resurrection of Jesus Christ would be to use Dr. Gary Habermas' "minimal facts" argument.[543] The five essential facts to relate are:

1. Jesus died by crucifixion. Most historians accept the fact that a man named Jesus Christ lived in the first century and died by crucifixion.

2. His disciples believed that He rose and appeared to them. Whether or not Jesus actually rose from the dead, his disciples were so persuaded of this fact that they spent the rest of their lives telling this story. None of them ever denied what they had witnessed first hand.

3. The church persecutor Paul was suddenly changed. The apostle Paul first tried to destroy the early church, but after his encounter with the risen Jesus Christ he became the chief evangelist for the church.

4. The skeptic James, brother of Jesus, was suddenly changed. Something transforming happened to James that turned him completely around so that he became one of the great leaders of the early church. Experiencing his half-brother, Jesus, resurrected from the dead could do this.

5. The tomb was empty. There have been many attempts to discount this fact, but they all fall far short of the simple explanation that Jesus, who had been crucified and dead, had risen from the dead and exited the tomb.

All Christians agree that Jesus Christ died on the cross. Even non-Christian historians are in overwhelming agreement about the historicity of Jesus' death on the cross. Therefore, the Qur'an is in error or the interpretation of Surah 4:157 by the majority of Muslims is in error. However, if Jesus did die on the cross and then rise from the dead three days later, as he said he would and the evidence supports this, then Christianity is true and Islam is false!

---

[543] Gary Habermas and Mike Licona, *The Case for the Resurrection* (Kregel, 2004).

## Balanced Apologetics

One thing we need to realize is that good Apologetics must take a balanced approach because both the irenic and polemic approaches are important tools. It is rather like a football game. Sometimes you are on the defense and sometimes you are on the offense, and you need to know when to take on those different roles. Good Apologetics flows between defending the faith and promoting the reasonableness of that faith. All of this takes place in the midst of a relationship; that is fundamental. There are three things to bear in mind when learning about Apologetics. First, you need to **understand** both what Muslims believe and what you yourself believe. Sometimes a deeper understanding will only come through controversy. For example, I have often come to understand a theological truth better through defending my beliefs than through merely reading doctrine or attending theology classes. When I have been asked questions I could not answer, I would first admit that it was a good question. Then, I would tell them that I would need some time to research the question before getting back to them with a good answer. This method not only provided a reason to get together again, but it also gave me a chance to search out a good answer as well as develop a way to explain it to my Muslim friend. In doing this, my faith has been refined in the fire and then fueled by a deeper knowledge. I have also gained more respect from my Muslim friends when I come back with a thoughtful answer to their question. The same result can be true for anyone who is willing to have an honest relationship with Muslims and do the theological work of searching out answers.

The second thing to bear in mind is that we need to learn to **defend** what we believe. This may be intimidating for some, but it can be exhilarating as well. It is also helpful because when we defend our faith, we help someone else understand the core beliefs of Christianity. Christians believe that Christianity IS true, and therefore they need to be able to defend it.

Thirdly, Christians also need to be able to **refute** what is in error. Sometimes this is the most important aspect of our conversation with Muslims. Too often these days Christians are pressured to acquiesce to views which Muslims promote, even when they are historically and factually erroneous because there is an expectation that accepting these views will support a peaceful co-existence. However, as we have seen in earlier chapters, this kind of cover-up often leads to the promotion of more egregious errors, which encourages Muslims to feed these errors to the media, and, in turn, there is even more pressure applied to the non-Muslims who reject these views. As Townsend warns, there is a very strong political and social undertow that seeks to disseminate a false history and theology of Islam in order to subvert Christianity and promote a government more favorable to Islam.[544] We need to resist this movement and identify the errors that promote these false views. On the other hand, we also need to use these Apologetic tools to reach Muslims for Christ.

Finally, If the ultimate goal of Apologetics is to understand what we believe, defend the Christian faith, and refute error so that Christ can be proclaimed and unbelievers may come to Him as the source of all Truth and the savior of the whole world, then we certainly need to be prepared to do this (1 Timothy 3:15).

**Study Questions:**

1. What are the three key words concerning Apologetics and how do they work together to prepare Christians to reach out to Muslims?

2. In each of the following doctrinal questions, first, explain what Christians believe about the doctrine, and then explain what Muslims believe. Next, evaluate the Muslim view through a biblical critique. Finally, explain how the biblical critique can be used in order to build a bridge with Islam. (You may want to make a chart in order to better organize your answers).

    a. How can God have a son?

    b. Has the Bible been changed?

    c. Do Christians worship three Gods?

    d. Did Jesus die on the cross?

---

[544] Peter Townsend, *Nothing to Do with Islam? Investigating the West's Most Dangerous Blind Spot* (Peter Townsend, 2016), 151-6.

# CHAPTER 17 What is God Doing in the Muslim World?

## Introduction

Islam seems to be on the move around the world, exerting its influence through terrorism and the spread of Sharia, as well as immigration and political persuasion. Some reports conclude that Muslims will outnumber Christians by the end of this century,[545] and other sources predict that Christianity will recede into obscurity as Islam rises in power and influence. However, Christian leaders around the world are pointing to revivals occurring in a number of developing nations, especially in the Global South, where millions are turning to Christ and churches are booming. In addition, unprecedented numbers of Muslims are converting to Christianity, with many reported instances of miracles as well as visions and dreams leading Muslims to Christ.

These are just some of the very exciting things going on in the Muslim world today that will be discussed in this chapter. As we approach this topic, however, it would be helpful to first have some background on what's happening and what people are thinking before we get into the big questions. We will first look at the issue of how Islam and Christianity as world religions today compare in size. Together, they make up the two largest religions in the world. They also make up more than half the population of the world at this point. In addition, we will look at which of these two religions is creating the most converts at this time. Are more people converting to Christianity, or are more turning to Islam today? What does that mean for Christians here in the West? Another area to consider is the reason that Christians themselves convert to Islam. If they were true Christians, could they turn from Christ and embrace Muhammad? We also want to understand how many Muslims have converted to Christianity and why. What are the bridges that ultimately lead Muslims to Christ, and how can these bridges inform our understanding of God's work today? What are the barriers that keep Muslims from becoming Christians, and what can be done to eradicate those barriers? These are all important questions for Christians to answer if they are truly interested in reaching out to Muslims.

---

[545] The Future of World Religions: Population Growth Projections, 2010-20150. Pew Research Center, April 2, 215.
http://www.pewforum.org/files/2015/03/PF_15.04.02_ProjectionsFullReport.pdf, 14.

## Growth and Conversion

First, we will consider the significant issue of which religion is the largest, and which is currently growing the fastest in the world today. Christianity has in fact been the largest world religion for some time. Since 1900, Christians have comprised approximately one-third of the world's population. These figures include Protestants, Catholics, Orthodox, and all other denominations and groups. Currently, these groups total about 2.2 billion people (31%). This number includes all people who self-identify as Christians and does not probe the depth of their faith. On the other hand, it is estimated that there are about 1.6 billion Muslims around the world today 23%).[546] However, in 1985 there were only about 600 million Muslims, so Islam has more than doubled in the last generation or two. It is, therefore, in terms of percentage and world-wide spread, the fastest growing religion in the world today.[547] In fact, forecasts for 2050 from the Pew Research Center conclude that the global Muslim population is expected to grow at a faster rate than the overall population.[548] Therefore, it is believed that the number of adherents to Islam will surpass those who follow Christianity beginning in 2070.

What is the reason for this rapid growth of Islam in the world today? Could the increase of Muslims in the world be due to Christians converting to Islam? According to various reports, it is estimated that around 20,000 to 30,000 Americans convert to Islam annually in the United States.[549,550] Most of these converts are African-Americans, and many of the remaining number are women who have married Muslim men. In Britain, it is estimated that around 5,000 people convert to Islam every year, and most of these are women.[551] In France, where there are an estimated six million Muslims, about 100,000 are thought to be converts.[552] According to the

---

[546] Ibid., 6.

[547] Ruth Gledhill, "Islam is world's fastest-growing religion, will equal Christianity by 2050" (*Christianity Today*, 2 April, 2015) Retrieved 7 May 2016.
https://www.christiantoday.com/article/islam-is-worlds-fastest-growing-religion-will-equal-christianity-by-2050/51321.htm.

[548] The Future of World Religions, 70. "Why Muslims are the world's fastest-growing religious group." www.pewresearch.org. Retrieved 5 May 2016.

[549] https://www.huffingtonpost.com/2011/08/24/post-911-islam-converts_n_935572.html

[550] http://standpointmag.co.uk/features-may-10-why-do-western-women-convert-julie-bindel-islam-female-conversion

[551] https://www.theguardian.com/world/2013/oct/11/islam-converts-british-women-prejudice. Retrieved July 1, 2018.

[552] https://www.nytimes.com/2013/02/04/world/europe/rise-of-islamic-converts-challenges-france.html

World Christian Encyclopedia, worldwide there are over 800,000 conversions to Islam from all other religions per year, including Christianity.[553]

## Reasons for Conversion

Why do Christians convert to Islam? This is another important issue to consider as we seek to understand the Muslim world today. *Christianity Today*, in its August 20, 1990 issue, listed the following main reasons.[554] First, Islam's doctrine is simple and rational, not involving complex doctrinal issues such as the Trinity. Second, many believe that in Islam all believers are equal, in spite of its extensive history as a slave trading culture. Additionally, Islam is seen as a practical religion which requires adherence to five simple pillars. Islam's lack of a priesthood is also appealing. Conversion to Islam does not require confession of sins or teach a need of salvation. It is a religion simply of good works and bad works, which is attractive for many. While adherents have no assurance of salvation, they nonetheless seem to prefer to feel their salvation is in their own hands. It may also be that certain ethnic or cultural groups find certain aspects of Islam to be particularly appealing; for instance, African-Americans may convert at least in part due to historical factors such as racism, segregation, and racial division.[555] For Anglo-Americans, Islam gives direction and discipline, which their own upbringing may lack. A number of white American converts have been driven to Islam by the degradation of the West, seeking instead an orderly religion that would lead to a higher way of living. Others have been attracted to Islam because conversion to Islam does not require confession of sins or the need of salvation. Unfortunately, some may have been drawn to Islam because they never really understood what true Christianity teaches, or they never had the gospel clearly explained to them.

On the other side of the equation, why do people convert to Islam? Put another way, shy is Islam a growing religion today? One factor in Islam's growth has been through conversion, but it turns out that this has actually had little permanent impact on the total Muslim population since the number of people who convert to or depart from Islam in any given period are roughly equal. Thus, the 2010 Pew Research Forum stated that "this report excludes the religious conversion as a direct factor from the

---

[553] http://www.bible.ca/global-religion-statistics-world-christian-encyclopedia.htm

[554] "Why Muslims are the world's fastest-growing religious group". www.pewresearch.org. Retrieved 5 May 2016.

[555] https://www.religion-online.org/article/turning-to-islam-african-american-conversion-stories/

projection of Muslim population growth."[556] Essentially, this means that the "back door" is apparently just as large as the "front door." According to Muslim scholars who have researched this phenomenon, from 50% to 70% of converts to Islam leave Islam within a few years, mostly because they find it difficult to fit into the new culture presented through the mosque.[557] Thus, those entering Islam from Christianity or secular worldviews often decide that Islam is not right for them after all.[558] If conversions are not the real reason for the growth of Islam, then what is?

Another factor of growth is simply fertility rates. A number of scholars say the primary reason for the present growth of Islam is that Muslim families generally have many children, and every child born into a Muslim family is considered a Muslim from birth. This is a matter of simple demographics. Eric Kaufman, a professor of politics at the University of London, is one of many who argues that the main reason why Islam is expanding is not because of conversion to Islam, but because Islam tends "to be 'pro-natal' and they have more children."[559]

Muslims have the highest birth rate in the world at an average of 3.1 per woman (2.7 in North America, 2.1 in Europe, and over 3.5 in Africa). In comparison, Christians come in second with an average birth rate of 2.7 per woman (2.0 in North America, 1.6 in Europe, and a greater fertility rate in Africa). Due to the overall Muslim growth in population, which is said to be twice the rate of the world's overall population growth because of general young age and a high fertility rate, research groups such as the Pew Research Center project that by the end of the century Islam will outgrow Christianity. The report states that in 2050, the two religions will be near parity, with Muslims numbered at 2.8 billion, or 30% of the population (from 23% at present), and Christians still having a slight advantage at 2.9 billion, or 31% of the population. However, the projection is that by 2070 the Muslim population will equal the Christian population, and by 2100 Muslims will reach 35% of the world's population while Christians will

---

[556] "The Future of the Global Muslim Population, Related Factors: Conversion", The Pew Forum on Religion and Public Life, 27 January 2011.

[557] https://imamluqman.wordpress.com/2010/01/13/seven-out-of-every-ten-converts-leave-islam-by-imam-luqman-ahmad/ (Retrieved 1/23/19).

[558] It is interesting to compare Islam to Mormonism in this regard. There are approximately 11 to 15 million Mormons worldwide, and this number has been consistent for many years. Many Christians become Mormons but eventually realize that Mormonism, in spite of its claims, is not true Christianity, and they eventually depart again.

[559] http://vancouversun.com/news/staff-blogs/think-religion-is-declining-look-at-who-is-going-forth-and-multiplying. Retrieved 7/1/2018.

number only around 34%.⁵⁶⁰ Of course, these projections are based on the present rate of births for the two religious groups, rather than conversion rates or any other factors. However, with the charts unclear due to limited and outdated figures, this is a precarious basis of prediction because there are already many parts of the world that have seen seriously declining birth rates. For example, there is a precipitous decline of birth rates in the non-Muslim areas of Europe, which is the main reason that many demographers predict that Islam will soon overwhelm Europe. However, the fertility rate worldwide is falling.⁵⁶¹ In fact, a new study by demographers Charles Westoff and Tomas Frejka suggest that the gap between Muslims and non-Muslims is shrinking and that the decline of the Muslim fertility rate may be taking place at a faster rate than among non-Muslims.⁵⁶² Since the projections made in the Pew Research Report of Muslims outnumbering Christians by the end of the century are based on past fertility rates of Muslims and these rates are already falling, perhaps a recalibration is in order.

Interestingly, in his book *How Civilizations Die and Why Islam is Dying Too*, Daniel Goldman recognizes the risks facing the non-Muslim areas of Europe and believes that when the fertility rate of a nation falls below replacement levels, its civilization eventually disappears. However, he also argues that Islam may be in the greatest danger of dying out. He states the following:

> Thanks to collapsing birth rates, much of Europe is on a path of willed self-extinction. The untold story is that birthrates in Muslim nations are declining faster than anywhere else and at a rate never before documented. Europe in its decline may have the resources to support an aging population, if at a terrible cultural and economic cost. But in the impoverished Islamic world an aging population means a civilization on the brink of total collapse, something Islamic terrorists know and fear.⁵⁶³

Thus, Goldman counters the Pew Research Center's demographic predictions. He posits that the fertility decline in the Islamic world is actually beginning to happen at a much more precipitous rate than that of the Western world due to the rapid exposure of Muslims to Western culture

---

⁵⁶⁰ The Future of World Religions: Population Growth Projections, 2010-20150. Pew Research Center, April 2, 215.
http://www.pewforum.org/files/2015/03/PF_15.04.02_ProjectionsFullReport.pdf, 14.

⁵⁶¹ David Goldman, *How Civilizations Die and Why Islam is Dying Too*, (Regnery, 2011), ix-xxiii.

⁵⁶² "Do Muslims Have More Children Than Other Women in Western Europe?". Population Reference Bureau. https://www.prb.org/muslimsineurope/ (Retrieved 8 May 2016).

⁵⁶³ Goldman, *How Civilizations Die and Why Islam is Dying Too*, 4.

with its education, technology and freedoms. He even argues that the increasing violence of Islam is due to in great part to this rapid implosion, and the "looming demographic collapse may encourage Islamic terrorists to 'go for broke.'"[564] If he is right, Islam will actually shrink in numbers in the decades to come, and Christianity will remain the largest world religion. However, if the Pew Research Center is right, Islam will become the largest world religion by 2070.

## Are Muslim and Christian Conversions the Same?

On the other hand, there may be a different perspective on how we should think about these theories and the reasons for the growth of a religion. This chapter started out by noting that Islam is on the move in the world today. However, it may be more accurate to say that God is on the move, and there are a number of Evangelicals who give testimony to several exciting worldwide movements that give credence to this perspective. One of the most exciting aspects of this movement is in regard to the number of Muslims converting to Christianity. There may be a large number of non-Muslims converting to Islam, as was noted above, but there are more people in the world converting to Christianity. This is an important point because there is a tremendous difference between conversions in Islam and in Christianity.

In Islam, every child born into a Muslim family, or at least to a Muslim father, is considered a Muslim by birth. Conversion, then, would only apply to those outside of Islam who make a conscious decision to say the Shahada and follow the words of the Qur'an and Muhammad. In Christian circles, however, there is a saying that "God has no grandchildren." This means that we are all individually responsible to God and when we are saved, we are adopted as his sons and daughters. In Christianity, at least in a basic sense, every man, woman, and child need to be "born from above" in order to be considered a true part of the family of God. Since conversion is part of becoming a true Christian for everyone, it makes sense that Christianity ranks first in net gains through conversion in the world today for those who come to Christ outside of a Christian background. According to the *World Christian Encyclopedia*, approximately 2.7 million people convert to Christianity annually from another religion, including from Islam.[565] This means that there are over 7,000 people a day, from all non-Christian backgrounds, turning to Christ in faith around the world.

---

[564] Ibid., bookjacket cover.

[565] David B. Barrett; George Thomas Kurian; Todd M. Johnson, eds. *World Christian Encyclopedia* (Oxford University Press, 2001), 360.

According to Miller and Johnstone, in their article "Believers in Christ from a Muslim Background," it is estimated that over 10 million Muslims converted to Christianity around the world between 1960 and 2010.[566] As we shall see, the conversion rate of Muslims turning to Christ since 2010 has continued to rise at a significant pace.

While some people from Christian backgrounds who convert to Islam may be rejected by their former friends, most new converts find acceptance by both their new Muslim *umma* as well as society in general. In contrast, Muslim converts to Christianity are far more likely to experience persecution from their Muslim friends and family members. In fact, Muslims who convert may face job loss, family ostracism, beatings, and even death for apostasy. The Hadith records Muhammad saying, "If somebody (a Muslim) discards his religion, kill him,"[567] and the Qur'an states clearly that those who turn away from Islam are apostate, and should be killed wherever they are found (Qur'an 4:89). This attitude is still prevalent in many places in the world today. For example, in one of the largest surveys conducted across the Muslim world, the Pew Research Center discovered that 76% of South-Asian Muslims and 56% of Egyptian Muslims believed that anyone who leaves Islam should be killed.[568] Bernard Lewis, a scholar on Islam, summarizes the apostasy issue this way:

> The penalty for apostasy in Islamic law is death. Islam is conceived as a polity, not just as a religious community. It follows therefore that apostasy is treason. It is a withdrawal, a denial of allegiance as well as of religious belief and loyalty. Any sustained and principled opposition to the existing regime or order almost inevitably involves such a withdrawal.[569]

Not all Muslim countries carry out death penalties for those accused of apostasy, but the punishment is often severe. Even those who do not face such threats still face the heartbreak of broken family relationships or other professional and educational penalties. For these reasons, many Muslims convert in secret and keep their new faith a secret from friends and family. They may still go to the mosque, but they pray to Jesus as God and study the Bible alone or in small groups of trusted friends. Fortunately,

---

[566] Duane Miller and Patrick Johnstone. "Believers in Christ from a Muslim Background: A Global Census." Interdisciplinary Journal of Research on Religion, Vol. 11 (2015), Article 10, 17.

[567] Sahih Bukhari (52:260).

[568] The Pew Forum, 30 April 2013, The World's Muslims: Religion, Politics and Society.

[569] Lewis, Bernard (1998-01-21). "Islamic Revolution." The New York Review of Books. https://www.nybooks.com/articles/1988/01/21/islamic-revolution/ (Retrieved 1/23/19).

despite the persecution and hardships, Muslims are continuing to turn to Christ in unprecedented numbers. It may even be that the harshness of a convert's circumstances discourages insincere converts or those who convert for merely social reasons, meaning that Muslim converts to Christianity will more likely take the decision seriously. This would lessen the number of converts who "slip" back to their previous faith, in contrast to those who convert to Islam looking for an easy religion but ultimately leave it in discouragement.

## A Fresh Wind: The Significance of Global Muslim Conversions

There are currently some very encouraging signs that the number of Muslim conversions to Christianity is growing in amazing ways. David Garrison, a missionary pioneer to the Muslim world with the Southern Baptist International Mission, writes in his compelling book, *A Wind in the House of Islam*, about the extensive interviews he has conducted with Muslim converts all over the world.[570] Garrison has worked among Muslim people groups for 30 years, studying many languages and traveling through dozens and dozens of countries. His focus has been on movements of Muslims to Christ, defining a "movement" as including 100 new church starts or 1000 baptisms occurring over a period of two decades. He notes that just within the last 20 years, movements to Christ among Muslims have taken place simultaneously in more than 70 separate locations in 29 nations. To put this in perspective, we need to realize that before the 19th century there were no voluntary movements of Muslims to Christ at all. In the 19th-century, there were two movements, one in Indonesia and one in Ethiopia. In the 20th-century, there were 11 additional movements. In the first years of the 21st-century alone there have been an additional 69 movements. In his remarkable summation, Garrison estimates that there have been between two and seven million converts to Christianity in the past twenty years, the numbers being prone to underestimates due to the severity of persecution in the Muslim world. Others actually estimate that there have been some 10 million, or even as many as 15 million, with up to 500,000 in Iran alone.[571] This means that more Muslims have come to Christ in the past 20 years than in the preceding fourteen hundred years!

---

[570] David Garrison, *A Wind in the House of Islam: How God is drawing Muslims around the world to faith in Jesus Christ* (Wigtake, 2014).

[571] Duane Miller and Patrick Johnstone. "Believers in Christ from a Muslim Background: A Global Census." Interdisciplinary Journal of Research on Religion, Vol. 11 (2015), Article 10, 17.

If this is the case, then where are these conversions taking place? Garrison has documented these movements occurring in what he calls the Nine Rooms in the House of Islam. While there are a number of Muslims turning to Christ in the West, Garrison focuses on the rest of the world and names the following nine areas where movements are taking place: North Africa, West Africa, East Africa, Arab World, Persian World, Turkestan, Western South Asia, Eastern South Asia, and Indo-Malaysia. These are very different regions, but it is the same Spirit that is moving across the land and doing something wonderful and powerful.

## Bridges for Muslims

How and why are these Muslim movements taking place today? What is the Lord using to bring hundreds of thousands of Muslims to Christ? Why is it happening now and not for the last 13 centuries? How can we be a part of it? In his book, David Garrison refers to ten discernable bridges that God is using to reach the Muslim world.[572] The first is faith, especially the faith of the missionaries who carry the gospel into the House of Islam, and the faith of the converts who often face persecution. Think about how many more doors could open up if more Christians lived a life of bold obedience and joined the ranks of those reaching out to Muslims. As Garrison says, "It is that higher call of faith, that biblical call, that leads the faithful to discipleship and service in the House of Islam today."[573] May there be many more servants of Christ willing to follow this path of faith.

The second bridge is prayer, the primary weapon in spiritual warfare and the primary strategy used when entering new territory. Ephesians 6:10-18 gives us a moving picture of what it means to confront the spiritual forces of evil in the world today, and we certainly need to have the full armor of God in place in order to stand firm against the strongholds that hold Muslims back from hearing and receiving the Gospel of Christ. Garrison comments that prayer is the "great unseen force that has both stimulated Christians to venture into the House of Islam and pierced the hearts of Muslims whom they encounter there."[574] The third bridge is Scripture, which is increasingly becoming available in local languages and is impacting the hearts of Muslims. It is revealing that in the Ephesians 6 passage mentioned above that the one offensive weapon, besides prayer, that is given to the Christian to fight against the forces of evil is the "sword of the Spirit, which is the Word of God" (Eph. 6:17). It is often the case that when Muslims finally get to the point of reading the Bible seriously, especially the

---

[572] Garrison, *A Wind in the House of Islam*, 240-249.
[573] Ibid., 240.
[574] Ibid., 241.

gospels, the Holy Spirit quickens their understanding, and they soon commit their lives to the Lord. This is why it is so important for Christians to make Bibles available to Muslim friends in their own heart language, for most Muslims have never read the Bible before.

The fourth bridge, the activity of the Holy Spirit, has become one of the most influential forces in bringing Muslims to Christ. The pervasive presence of the Holy Spirit is very powerful, and God is visiting Muslims through dreams, visions, and answered prayers in the name of Jesus. A number of researchers have concluded that a quarter to a third of all Muslim conversions over the past 20 years involve some type of dream, vision, or supernatural intervention by God. If there are between 10-15 million Muslims who have come to the Lord over this period of time, then that means that millions of Muslims have had these experiences that often lead them to seek the One who has revealed Himself to them. Dreams and visions are very much revered by Muslims, and they find them very meaningful. It seems that God has found a special way for the Holy Spirit to "blow" through the House of Islam.

The fifth bridge that Garrison mentions is the testimony of faithful Christian witnesses. There are also millions coming to Christ inside the Muslim world because of faithful Christian witnesses both within and without. The sixth bridge, Learning from the Body of Christ, and the seventh, which involves Communication, also impact many Muslims through new as well as traditional approaches such as translations of the Bible, Muslim-focused outreach of various types, contextualized witness,[575] the Internet, satellite television and radio broadcasts, prayer walks, and Quranic bridging. The eighth bridge involves allowing Muslims to discover the truth of the Bible through discussions as well as reading the Scriptures in a group setting. Garrison says that Muslims don't like to be told they are wrong, so it is often better to let them "discover" the truth through their own exploration. In this case, we always need to be ready to give an answer when they ask us to be part of the discovery process (1 Peter 3:15).

Interestingly enough, the ninth bridge involves Islam itself leading many to Christ. A professor friend of mine once said that Osama Bin Laden was one of the leading evangelists for Christianity. Why? Because there were so many who were repulsed by what he said and did, and they wanted nothing to do with that type of Islam. Islam, in fact, is often its own worst enemy. Due in part to the rejection of radical Islam today, more Muslims are ready to listen to the gospel. In addition, having the Qur'an in their own language actually turns some Muslims to Christ, because when

---

[575] "communicating in a manner that is clearly understood in the culture and worldview of those who are intended to hear it."

they read and truly understand the meaning and implications of the words, they realize that much of what they had learned from their Muslim leaders about the Qur'an is not accurate, nor does it offer them much hope for the future. For example, the Qur'an offers no assurance of salvation; salvation is found in Christ alone. When Muslims understand that Christianity offers something that Islam does not have, they are drawn in. Moreover, when Muslims are confronted with the many mistakes and changes in the Qur'an and the inaccuracies of their early history, they often begin to view Islam from a more critical position. They may also look at the life of Muhammad from their own sources, and they realize that he was not even qualified to be a prophet. In other words, accurate history, primary sources, and scholarly discussions on the problems of Islam and the Qur'an may open eyes and lead Muslims to the truth.

The last bridge concerns the role of indigenization. This takes place when new believers within a culture own and advance the gospel to their own people group, taking discipleship to deeper levels. There are some excellent indigenous Christian leaders today within the Muslim world, and we need to come alongside and help them. Outsiders and missionaries can take support roles, serving as encouragers, servant-leaders, trainers, and shadow pastors. In this way, the Holy Spirit can "lead them into all truth" (John 16:13).

## Dreams and Visions in the House of Islam

As mentioned earlier in the chapter, a number of researchers have concluded that over the past 20 years around a third of all Muslim conversions have involved some type of dream, vision, or supernatural intervention by God. Certainly, such a positive movement must be the result of God's Holy Spirit working in powerful ways to break down the spiritual walls that keep Muslims from accepting Christ. There are a number of Christians, however, who are still suspicious about this type of spiritual activity and feel that supernatural movements were no longer needed after the New Testament was put into circulation and God's revelation became available to all people. It must be pointed out, though, that there are many people today who remain outside of Christ and do not have access to God's Word, especially within the world of Islam. Perhaps God has decided it is time to do something amazing among Muslims. If this is the case, then at least Christians should be aware of this new wind blowing through the House of Islam.

One very helpful book dealing with the work of the Holy Spirit today is Jerry Trousdale's *Miraculous Movements*.[576] In this book Trousdale, the Director of International Ministries for CityTeam International, recounts the miraculous way that the Holy Spirit is preparing hundreds of thousands of Muslims in Africa to be transformed by the truth of Jesus Christ. Through dreams and visions, as well as the result of witnessing miracles, men and women are experiencing the power of the Holy Spirit in their lives, and many of these turn to Jesus Christ as their Lord and Savior.

Through his many interviews with former Muslim leaders, Trousdale has found that one of the main reasons that Muslims have been so open to these supernatural events is that they have become very disenchanted with Islam. He relates that,

> Inside Islam, disillusionment and discouragement are widespread and closely related to the Qur'anic teachings, Islamic cultural pressures, social mores, and so forth. The church of Jesus Christ is largely not aware that God Himself is working inside Islam, orchestrating events that are even now beginning to crack the foundations of Islam and prepare hearts to discover the loving God who sacrificed His Son that they might know Him.[577]

Thus, God is even using the negative features of Islam to prepare hearts so that they are open to witnessing the power of God in the world today. This clear movement of the Holy Spirit is very likely one of the reasons David Garrison has seen a burst of movements of Muslims toward Christ in the last two decades. There is indeed a revival in many parts of the Muslim world.

In regard to this unprecedented activity of the Holy Spirit in the Muslim world, Trousdale comments, "From first to last, these movements are about God doing what only God can do, and inviting His people to join Him in the process. He is taking the initiative so that, by the time Christians are on the scene, Jesus has already strategically prepared hearts to engage."[578] God is preparing Muslims through the activity of the Holy Spirit, but Christians are still very much involved in the process. As Trousdale realizes, God is opening the doors and now it is up to Christians to "learn how to cooperate with His work of invading the impossible with love."[579] This is our opportunity. This is the time.

---

[576] Jerry Trousdale, *Miraculous Movements: How hundreds of Thousands of Muslims Are Falling in Love with Jesus* (Thomas Nelson, 2012).

[577] Ibid., 71.

[578] Ibid., 73.

[579] Ibid., 73.

Chip Ingram, senior pastor of Ventura Christian Church, says this work of the Spirit is a "paradigm shifting movement of God" [580] that is turning the Muslim world upside down. Trousdale describes this movement in his book and explains how God is preparing the way.

> What is remarkable today is that, in a world where unnumbered Muslims have no access to the good news – no Bibles in their language, no churches, no known Christians, few or no Christian radio or television options in their language -- they are living and dying without any exposure to Christ. So God introduces Himself personally and gives birth to something in a Muslim man or woman's heart that causes him or her to begin a journey of discovering and obeying God, seeking to find followers of Jesus to help them complete that journey.[581]

Thus, one way that God has chosen to reveal himself to Muslims has been the movement of the Holy Spirit through the dreams and visions of Muslims. This supernatural work of God may be controversial for some, but Trousdale says that in his interviews with former Muslim leaders, "about 40 percent reported a dream or vision of Jesus that prompted them to begin a search to know more about Isa al Masih (Jesus the Messiah)."[582] Certainly, we should at least be open to something that God seems to be using to break down the walls and bring many Muslims to Himself. Finally, Trousdale concludes by reminding us that, "These dreams are dramatic evidence that the missionary God of the Bible is doing dramatic things to rescue Muslims from Islam. They often create questions in the heart of the dreamer, and Christians are needed to be there when the opportunity comes, to help the dreamer understand their meaning."[583] It is important to note that even though this is a movement begun by God, laborers are very much needed to reap the harvest.

There are other researchers who have studied this new wind in the House of Islam. In his article titled "When Muslims Dream of Jesus,"[584] Darren Carlson, founder, and president of Training Leaders International, recounts a study published by Dudley Woodberry in 2007 that listed reasons for converting to Christianity from 750 interviews with former Muslims. Among the expected reasons, such as "the love of God, a changing view of the Bible, and an attraction to Christians who loved other," one of

---

[580] Ibid., book cover
[581] Ibid., 133.
[582] Ibid., 133.
[583] Ibid., 134.
[584] Darren Carlson, "When Muslims Dream of Jesus," International Mission News, Lightstock, May 31, 2018.

the other main reasons was experiencing dreams and visions.[585] A study by Mission Frontiers magazine reported that around 25 percent of 600 Muslims converts experienced dreams that led to their conversions.[586] In his book, *Dreams and Visions: Is Jesus Awakening the Muslim World?* Tom Doyle says that "about one out of every three Muslim-background believers had a dream or vision prior to their salvation experience," though he also mentions that other researchers report a number closer to 25%.[587] This is still very significant, especially for Western Christians who generally discount or deny the need for the occurrence of dreams and visions in a religion with a clear Scriptural record. These cautions are justified in the cases of asylum seekers who use "borrowed" stories in order to claim a Christian conversion experience in order to seek favor in the application process, or others who may be waiting for a dream or vision before they will listen to the gospel or read the Bible. However, passages in the Bible, such as Joel 2:28. recount that a time will come when the LORD will pour out his Spirit through dreams and visions. There are those who say that dreams and visions could not be for today and therefore must be a ploy of Satan, but they need to read Matthew 12:22-36 where Jesus reminds us that Satan would not use miraculous means to honor Christ. Whether or not we believe that the Holy Spirit works today through dreams and visions, we must reconcile ourselves to the fact that between 25-33 % of Muslim converts to Christianity say that dreams and visions have had a significant role in leading them to Christ.

One of the more interesting angles to this phenomenon is that Muslims, especially Shia Muslims, are often very open to dreams and have support from their culture and the Qur'an for seeking answers to their needs through the interpretation of dreams. Thus, dreams about Jesus Christ are regarded as significant and even prophetic. Nabeel Qureshi was even guided by his Muslim mother, who believed that Allah spoke through dreams, to seek interpretations for his dreams which ultimately contributed to his conversion to Christ.

Darren Carlson, through his interviews, lists the following categories of dreams:

- Jesus speaking Scripture to them, even Scripture they had never heard before.

- Jesus telling people to do something.

---

[585] Ibid.

[586] Ibid.

[587] Tom Doyle, *Dreams and Visions: Is Jesus Awakening the Muslim World?* (Nashville, TN: Thomas Nelson, 2012), reviewed by Mark Kreitzer in *Global Missiology*, January 2015.

- A dream or vision that led to a feeling of being clean or at peace.
- A man in white physically appearing.[588]

One of the most widely reported visions is a man appearing in bright white clothes and using Scripture to witness to the person, such as "I am the way and the truth. No one comes to the Father except through me." He may tell them to "follow him" or "believe in him." He will also tell them that he is "Jesus, the Son of God," or even that he is the "Alpha and the Omega." One Iranian man at a refugee center recounted seeing a man dressed in white tell him to "stand up and follow me." When the Iranian man asked, "Who are you?" the man in white replied that he was the "Alpha and the Omega," and the "only way to heaven." Later, when the man was talking to an Iranian pastor, the pastor opened to the Book of Revelation and read to him the verse where Jesus identifies himself as the "Alpha and Omega." The man was convicted and asked how he could accept this Jesus. The pastor gladly led him in a prayer to accept the Lord and then gave him a Bible. Later, the man came back with 10 other men and said they would like to have Bibles as well.[589]

There are a number of other ways that Jesus reveals himself, but one of the more unique stories I have found regards the "God who walks on water." Carlson relates that during a crowded boat crossing of the Mediterranean Sea from Turkey to Athens, a 7-year old girl fell off the boat. The frantic parents rushed around the boat asking others to help find her. Suddenly, they found her on the other side of the boat, dry and claiming that a "man who walked on water" rescued her and put her back on the boat. The parents were overjoyed at finding their daughter but dismissed her story. When they arrived at the island of Lesbos, they met a Christian who, without knowing why, asked them if they wanted to know about a God who walked on water. They were astounded at his words and wanted to know more. The Christian turned to the Bible (Matt. 14:22-33) and read them the story of Jesus walking on the water. Amazed, they recounted the story of their daughter's rescue by the "man who walked on the water" and they all rejoiced.

Whatever we think of God using supernatural dreams, visions, and miracles to bring Muslims to Himself, there are millions of faithful former Muslims in the Kingdom today because these activities led them to seek the source of their experiences. This may be one of the more powerful ways that God is working in the House of Islam today, but there are still other ways that we can be a part of this movement.

---

[588] Carlson, "When Muslims Dream of Jesus."

[589] Carlson, "When Muslims Dream of Jesus."

# Barriers for Muslim Conversion

Garrison also tells us that we need to recognize that there are five barriers that may hinder these movements. The first is contentious Christians. When Christians are divided and at war amongst themselves, Muslims do not see Christ in them. Fear and hatred are barriers, so we need to remind people to critique Islam but love Muslims themselves. Another barrier is an attempt by Christians to imitate Islam. Islam is a highly legalistic religion that prescribes every aspect of life and conduct. Christians need to demonstrate true "freedom in Christ" and not bondage to the law. We also cannot afford to respond to Islamic violence in kind. In addition, we must recognize that we cannot overlook injustice to Jews, minorities, and other social groups. Injustice within Islam has turned some Muslims toward Christianity. Finally, we cannot respond in ignorance and apathy. Remember, "Radical Islam is not the problem; lukewarm Christianity is." Most Western Christians know little about Islam or the ways that God is at work in our world to reach Muslims. Many don't even care. We must always be asking ourselves, "How can I be a part of what God is doing? How can I contribute? How can I reach out to Muslims in love with the gospel of Truth?" These are exactly the subjects we will be dealing with in the next chapter.

**Study Questions:**

1. What is the main reason for the rapid growth of Islam today? How does it compare to the growth of Christianity? What are the projections for future growth? Do you agree with the Pew Research Center statistics or David Goldman's assessment? Why?

2. What are the main reasons for Christians converting to Islam?

3. Are Muslim and Christian Conversions the Same? What are the differences?

4. What are the indications that God is on the move today bringing many people to Christ? Why do you think this movement is not very widespread in America and Europe?

5. What are some of the main reasons that Muslims are converting to Christ?

6. How and why are the Muslim movements mentioned by David Garrison taking place today? Why are these movements happening now and not for the last 13 centuries?

7. What are some of the "bridges" that David Garrison mentions and how are they used to bring Muslims to Christ?

# CHAPTER 18 How Do You Reach Muslims with Both Truth and Love?

## Introduction

We have learned that within the last two decades, more Muslims have come to Christ than within the last 1400 years. That's something to think about! Why are they coming to Christ now? What is happening?

The walls are being broken down. God is moving! In a way, we need to be thankful for the immigrant situation because God is bringing Muslims to our doorstep, and we have many opportunities that we would not have had otherwise.

God makes it clear through his Word that he is very concerned about Muslims. He wants them to come to Him, and He's giving them, as well as us, many opportunities to engage with this movement of the Spirit. We need to keep that in mind. However, there's also another side. As we have seen through 1400 years of history, one of the ways that Islam first gains a foothold and then comes to dominate an area is through migration. The first great migration, called the Hijrah, was the migration into Palestine and Syria. Although Muslims started off as a minority in those areas, they eventually became the dominant force. Today there are over 50 countries (25% of all countries) with a Muslim majority, and Muslims want to retain forever any country that they have once ruled. This is the reason that the region of Palestine and Jerusalem, in particular, are such important issues today — Jerusalem once belonged to Islam and Muslims want it back. To lose these lands indicates defeat in their eyes, which is unacceptable. In order to win the world for Allah, Muslims need to hold on to every piece of land they conquer. Even the country of Spain, which was once in Muslim hands, is considered a lost possession, and some Muslims want it back.

Thus, there are two sides to the issue of immigration. On the one hand, there are many new opportunities. On the other hand, we face new dangers. Sweden is a case in point. It seems at present that Sweden will never again be the same. The percentage of Muslim immigrants has reached 8%,[590] and this minority has already changed Sweden in significant and negative ways, especially in regard to an increase in the number of

---

[590] Hackett, Conrad. "5 facts about the Muslim population in Europe." Pew Research/Fact Tank. Pew Research Center. Retrieved 12 December 2017. http://www.pewresearch.org/fact-tank/2017/11/29/5-facts-about-the-muslim-population-in-europe/

bombings and sexual crimes.[591] Sweden has been changed through the influence of Islam, perhaps permanently. It seems that much of Europe is also following in the footsteps of Sweden and other countries that have growing numbers of Muslim immigrants.[592]

We also need to keep in mind the population/percentage chart from an earlier chapter.[593] As the percentage of the number of Muslims rises in a country, there are predictable increases in the number of terrorist activities, sexual crimes, and demands for the rights of Muslims over the rights of the native citizens. We cannot afford to turn a blind eye to these statistics because they present very real dangers to the American way of life.

England has provided us with an example of the difficult situations that have developed due to the recent immigration and concentration of Muslims, especially in the London area. In reports of recent bomb attacks, the government has revealed that there are 3,000 Muslims who are being closely monitored and over 20,000 on their "watch list." However, the British don't have a sufficient police force to keep up with this.[594] A number of other countries in Europe, such as France, Germany, and Sweden, face similar scenarios.

We cannot allow the United States to follow the example of Europe. We need to break the mold. We need to bring Christianity to Islam, and break down that ancient wall that has existed for these past 1400 years. We must open our eyes to see the greatness of God's hand in what He is doing in the world today, and how we can be part of this wonderful opportunity. This is why it is imperative that we learn how to reach out to Muslims with the gospel. It is one of the best ways that we can be used by God to help breach the spiritual walls that keep Muslims out of the Kingdom of God. In this chapter, we will be looking at some ways that we can use to reach Muslims with the gospel. This must, of course, be done with both love and truth. Love alone leads to the results we see in Europe today—the trampling and overrunning of the rights and freedoms of the host nation. Clearly love is not enough; we must have a love that is rooted in truth. We must also have boldness that is rooted in love for the individual Muslim.

---

[591] https://www.commentarymagazine.com/foreign-policy/europe/invisible-crisis-europe-sweden-migrants/

[592] The Future of World Religions: Population Growth Projections, 2010-20150. Pew Research Center, April 2, 215. http://www.pewforum.org/files/2015/03/PF_15.04.02_ProjectionsFullReport.pdf, 50.

[593] Percentage chart on Muslim growth by Peter Hammond, "What Islam Isn't," FrontPageMagazine.com, Monday, April 21, 2008.

[594] BBC, 2017: http://www.bbc.co.uk/newsbeat/article/40158730/does-a-terror-watch-list-exist-in-the-uk-and-how-is-it-used-by-police (accessed 6/10/2018).

In order to do that, we need to face our fears, question Islam, build relationships, and preach the truth of the Gospel.

## Facing Our Fears

Let us first examine some of our fears. One of the greatest fears we face is that our own lack of knowledge will be exposed. How many Americans have a solid knowledge of the Qur'an, Muhammed, or the Hadith? We feel that we don't know enough, so we say nothing. Yes, it is important to be informed, and by reading this book you have made a good beginning. You will have found by now that the core beliefs of Islam, the five pillars, are in many ways simple to comprehend. This is something that many converts to Islam have found appealing. However, you have also come to understand that in many ways Islam is much more complex than the five pillars, and therefore demands that we search out the deeper issues more diligently. Remember that Muslims welcome questions about what they themselves believe. This is a wonderful way to break down barriers, and a great opportunity to in turn share what we ourselves believe. Often, in fact, Muslims will follow a discussion of their own beliefs with a question about what we as Christians believe. We need to, therefore, be prepared to explain our own beliefs.

Another aspect of the lack of knowledge that restrains our desire to talk about our faith is our inability to discuss difficult issues such as the Trinity and the inerrancy of the Bible. These certainly are intimidating issues, but there are good resources available to help us address them, including some of the earlier chapters in this book, which provide practical advice for Christians who do not have extensive theological training. Remember our guiding verse: "Always be prepared to give an answer to everyone who asks you to give the reason for the hope that you have, but do this with gentleness and respect" (I Peter 3:15). Also, remember that first-century converts to Christianity underwent extensive, in-depth theological training before they were baptized. Let this be an example to us of the importance of our own diligent study.

A second fear of confrontation for many Christians stems from the fact that most Muslims we know are so different from us. We don't know how to engage them, and so we fear that we will appear silly or ignorant. Certainly, Muslims are culturally different from us, whether they are from the Middle East or Indonesia or Europe, but we know other people from different cultures, and they have successfully contributed to the unique "melting pot" that has become America. People from other countries are fascinating to talk to and build relationships with, and it is generally true that when we show interest in them, they in turn will show interest in us as well. Let us use this natural curiosity to build relationships that will bridge the gap and provide opportunities to present the gospel.

Another fear that we naturally feel is the fear of terrorism. Since many terrorists are Muslims, how can we be assured that the one Muslim we happen to have coffee with or even invite into our home is a peaceful person? Admittedly, it is true that there are some Muslims who wish to bring harm to America and are part of a movement to gain more control in our government, our education, and our social fabric. We must, therefore, always be prudent in our outreach. It is also true that there have been plenty of Islam-inspired terrorist attacks in America, and our law enforcement agencies have been diligently working to prevent other attacks. However, Muslim terrorists – like the Somalis of Minneapolis that joined ISIS – and others involved in jihadist terrorism are still in a small minority. As of March 2018, there have been 409 Muslims charged with terrorist activities on American soil. A large proportion have been converts to Islam (31%), and most were U.S. born citizens (220), naturalized citizens (93) or permanent residents (55).[595]

Fortunately, most Muslims here in America are peaceful. America is a land of great opportunity, and most Muslims who come to our shores are simply seeking a chance at a better life or a better education. They simply want what we ourselves want – peace, economic success, and a good environment in which to raise their families. Readers who have gotten to know Muslims here in America will have experienced this. Therefore, we should not fear reaching out to our Muslim friends with the truth of the gospel, for this is the only thing that will give Muslims the chance to experience the true peace that only comes from knowing Jesus Christ.

## The Great Debate

In the debate on the best way to reach Muslims with the gospel, there are basically two camps. There are those who seek relationships with Muslims by promoting peace, and there are those who seek to win over Muslims by emphasizing the theological differences. The first group would be on the *irenic*, or peaceful, side, and the second group would tend toward the *polemical*, or confrontational side. Think of this as a way of reaching out with either love or truth.

On the "peace" side, people want to focus on the similarities between Christianity and Islam. They would tend to say that the God of Islam and the God of Christianity are the same. This irenic side deals with topics such

---

[595] Newamerica.org -- https://www.newamerica.org/in-depth/terrorism-in-america/part-i-overview-terrorism-cases-2001-today/ (accessed 6/18/2018).

as our shared "desire for 'god," or "giving financially to the poor," downplaying differences in beliefs even to the point where it borders on accepting heretical views for the sake of keeping the peace. Those on this "peaceful" side would thus prefer to err on the side of non-confrontation so that conversational opportunities remain open and Muslims not be offended and respond violently. Appeasement is usually advocated. The "polemic" side, however, focuses on the differences between Christianity and Islam, claiming a superiority of Christianity over Islam and ultimately arguing that Christianity is true while Islam is not. This confrontational side essentially seeks to critique Islam and refute error. It focuses on pursuing the truth rather than compromising doctrine and sees debate between Christians and Muslims as ideally removing obstacles in the Muslim's thinking toward Christianity. As we have learned, Apologetics is one approach that can successfully remove these barriers.

This was true in the life of Nabeel Qureshi, a man whose experience is a great testimony to the power of Apologetics. Apologetics helped him to work through and overcome many of the obstacles that held him back from making a decision for Christ, and this helped him to be more open to the gospel message later on. In the end, it is best to use both methods: open-hearted friendship seeks to encourage as well as critique. We need to seek peace as well as confrontation in love – to find a balance between Truth and Love. Following are some ways that this balance can be achieved, and a loving relationship can be established.

## What Can Be Done?

There are three things that we can all do: *question Islam, love Muslims, and preach the Gospel.*[596] Let us first look at the reason why we should question Islam, or, more specifically, help Muslims to question Islam. In Peter Townsend's book, *Nothing to Do With Islam?* he begins his response by admitting that "we have a problem with Islam."[597] In fact, he says the greatest problem is Islam itself because the main beliefs of Islam are diametrically opposed to the fundamental beliefs of Christianity (Trinity, deity of Christ, Crucifixion, and atonement by Christ alone). Therefore, Townsend says the first thing that must be done is to undermine belief in Islam because "… the core beliefs of Islam are part of the problem and … belief in it should, therefore, be questioned and undermined."[598] This is

---

[596] CHRISTIAN APOLOGETIC EVANGELISM: What Will You Say to a Muslim?

https://christianpublishinghouse.co/2018/02/24/christian-apologetic-evangelism-what-will-you-say-to-a-muslim/

[597] Townsend, *Nothing to Do with Islam?*, 141.

[598] Ibid., 142.

what we should do with any religion or philosophy that makes claims about what is true. We want to know whether it is true or not, so we question it. We certainly invite this practice in Christianity. When we teach students about theological issues, we should invite them to question the sources and the views that are presented. There are good ways to question beliefs, and researching answers help to solidify what we believe. We do not need to fear the truth, especially if it is on our side. This can give us greater confidence in what we believe.

Since jihad and terrorism are often linked to Islam, Townsend uses this association to explore the possibility of a new interpretation of Islam. He says, "It is possible to argue on the basis of this [Qur'an and Hadith] that physical jihad for the sake of Allah is not a fringe concern in terms of the core beliefs of Islam, but that it is, in many ways, central to it."[599] In his book, Townsend gives many examples of how physical jihad for the sake of Allah is indeed a core tenant of Islam and has been consistently taught by Muslim scholars over the last 1400 years. Earlier chapters in this book have also presented plenty of material demonstrating that violent jihad has always been part of the core of Islamic belief and practice.[600]

At the present time, Townsend wonders if moderate Muslims who are opposed to violent jihad and terrorism may be able to develop a form of "Islam Lite." In other words, would it be possible to create a more tolerant Islam by rejecting the violent passages in the Qur'an and the Hadith and form a religion that would line up more with the values of peace, love, and mutual understanding? There are some moderate Muslims who actually advocate this kind of Islam, such as Zudhi Jasser and Raheel Raza, who are on the advisory board of the Clarion Project, an organization that promotes a more moderate Islam.[601] They strive to bring about a type of reform within Islam that would promote peace and understanding by disregarding the verses in the Qur'an that support terrorism and jihad. This is an admirable goal. Townsend, however, believes that this will be impossible because it would mean rejecting three absolutely foundational ways of interpreting the Qur'an.

One of the ways of interpretation that would have to be abandoned would be the Law of Abrogation, which favors the later violent verses over the more peaceful earlier verses. This practice goes back all the way to Muhammad, and it is still supported by Muslim scholars as well as Muslim jihadists who interpret the meaning of the Qur'an through the lens of abrogation. Secondly, the normative interpretation of the Qur'an by the

---

[599] Ibid., 142.
[600] See Spencer, *The History of Jihad: From Muhammad to ISIS*.
[601] https://clarionproject.org/clarion-project-advisory-board/

early commentators opposes a peaceful Islam. Throughout the history of Islam, the main commentators have consistently promoted violent jihad in the way of Allah as one of the main ways to carry out Allah's mandate to dominate the world.[602] In his book, *The History of Jihad*, Robert Spencer says,

> ... there is no period since the beginning of Islam that was characterized by large-scale peaceful coexistence between Muslims and non-Muslims. There was no time when mainstream and dominant Islamic authorities taught the equality of non-Muslims with Muslims, or the obsolescence of jihad warfare. There was no Era of Good Feeling, no Golden Age of Tolerance, no Paradise of Proto-Multiculturalism. There has always been, with virtually no interruption, jihad, everywhere Muslims and non-Muslims have lived in close proximity with one another.[603]

In fact, a number of Muslim writers admit that without a strict interpretation of the Qur'an, especially in regard to the jihad verses, it is likely that Islam would not have been able to survive. Even today, popular imams such as Qaradawi argue that without the apostasy laws calling for death for those who turn away from Islam, it is possible that Islam would not have survived this long.[604] In other words, he is saying that there has to be a strict interpretation of the Qur'an as well as an active promotion of jihad in order for Islam to move forward. In addition, this authoritarian view of Islam all but closes the gates of *ijtihad*, which is the type of interpretation that the moderate Muslims promote.[605] This is why hardline jihadists often consider moderates to be heretics and unbelievers and therefore seek to kill them.

Thirdly, they would have to repudiate the example of Muhammad, since he was a warrior. He believed in and personally performed violent jihad. Even the accepted traditions record that he sent his men on over 70 raids and personally guided at least 28 of them.[606] Thus, Muhammad was very much involved in jihad while conquering Mecca and parts of Arabia, all through violent means.

---

[602] See Spencer, *The History of Jihad*. Also see William Wagner, *How Islam Plans to Change the World* (Grand Rapids, MI: Kregel, 2004).

[603] https://www.jihadwatch.org/2018/07/robert-spencer-the-history-of-jihad-is-the-crown-and-culmination-of-all-my-work

[604] Nonie Darwish, Gatestone Institute, February 5, 2013: https://www.gatestoneinstitute.org/3572/islam-apostasy-death

[605] see Reilley, *The Closing of the Muslim Mind*.

[606] Watt, *Muhammad at Medina* (Oxford: Clarendon Press, 1956), 339-343.

These are the reasons that Townsend says that "in the eyes of true believers, an Islam that does not seek to dominate will no longer be Islam at all."[607] In light of this, then, Townsend says it is of the utmost importance that Islam must be "critiqued, questioned, and undermined."[608] Ultimately, as we reach out to Muslims to bring them to the Lord, we need to demonstrate to them that Islam is not factual, and we need to present evidence to them that Christianity is. In this way, we may understand that undermining Islam is actually a loving thing to do.

We can see all this borne out in the life of Nabeel Qureshi. Why did he leave Islam? Among other reasons, his faith was undermined when he realized that Islam does not coincide with actual history, nor does its worldview provide a foundation for a successful culture. Qureshi wanted the truth, and through the loving witness of his Christian friends, he discovered the Truth in Jesus Christ. This is why we need to recognize that Townsend is putting forth an idea that is very important in reaching Muslims. Of course, we need to do this with "respect and gentleness," as the verse in 1 Peter 3:15 says, but we also need to help Muslims question their own beliefs in order to throw off the shackles of Islam and embrace the truth of Christianity.

## Undermine Islam in Order to Help Muslims Leave Islam

It may sound harsh, but Townsend firmly believes that "the best way to counter jihad ideology is to help Muslims leave Islam."[609] He says this is because we need to deal with the "root cause" of the violence promoted by Islamic terrorism (which is Islam itself). Attempts to thwart the attacks of radical Islamic jihadists are only dealing with the symptoms. So, what is the remedy? Let us look at this logically. If Islamic terrorism is based on Islamic beliefs, then if someone ceases to believe in Islam, they should no longer have a reason for carrying out terrorist attacks against non-Muslims. Therefore, the best way to deal with radical Islam is to help Muslims leave Islam.

Think back to 9/11, when nineteen Saudis hijacked planes plowed into buildings and killed thousands of innocent people. Why did they do this? Because of their Islamic beliefs. If they had not held such beliefs, would they have done these things? Probably not. There have been more than 33,000

---

[607] Townsend, *Nothing to Do with Islam?*, 144.
[608] Ibid., 144.
[609] Ibid., 145.

Islamic terrorist attacks around the world since 9/11.[610] Would any of these atrocities been carried out if these Muslim men and women did not have Muslim beliefs that promoted jihad as a way to please Allah and carry out his will? No, probably a few or none of them would have been perpetrated. So, what does this mean for us? The core of their reasoning is that they are Muslim, and they follow Islamic beliefs and have specifically pledged allegiance to Allah and jihad. If they were Christians, they presumably would not have done those things because they would not have had those motives. If they were Buddhists, they also would not have done those things. But, being Muslims, they did it because their Qur'an, their beliefs, and their leaders told them to do it, in order to dominate the world and subjugate Christians, Jews and others who do not call on the name of Allah. Thus, Islamic terrorism is clearly based on Islamic beliefs, as has been demonstrated earlier in this book.

Furthermore, when a Muslim terrorist turns away from Islam or becomes a Christian, he no longer has a desire to bring harm to Christians and Jews. After becoming a Christian, he sees the world in a totally different light. Beliefs are important. Ideas do have consequences. Daniel Shayesteh for example was a typical revolutionary in Iran who was taught to hate the infidel. He also believed that the Ayatollah Khomeini would usher in an Islamic theocracy that would bring prosperity and peace to Iran.[611] However, as he realized that Islamic sharia imposed by the new regime actually brought less freedom and more hardship, he rebelled and soon found himself facing a death sentence. He escaped and later, through some Christian friends, became a Christian. Now, like many former Muslims who have converted to Christianity, he has a new perspective:

> My family's life is changed now and our mind-set is different. We believe in Christ now. We have learned to not respond to the cruelty of Islamists in Iran as they responded to us and millions of other Iranians. We pray for Islamists every day that they might see the glory of loving Jesus and start respecting people regardless of race, nationality or belief.

It seems to be obvious that the root cause of a Muslim's desire to kill Christians and Jews is Islam itself: Islamic beliefs, jihad verses in the Qur'an, and Muhammad's commands in the Hadith. However, when Muslims turn their backs on these beliefs by leaving Islam, they have no further desire to bring harm to others. Once we see this direct connection, we should encourage Muslims to turn away from the root cause of their actions and

---

[610] Religion of Peace: https://www.thereligionofpeace.com/ (accessed June 8, 2018).

[611] Daniel Shayesteh, *The House I Left Behind: A journey from Islam to Christ* ( Talesh Books, 2012).

instead turn toward beliefs that bring true peace and freedom to the soul. Therefore, one of the best ways to deal with radical Islam is to help Muslims leave Islam.

So, then, how can this be done? Townsend says that in questioning Islam we need to look at four main ways that will help us do this effectively.[612] The first thing is to educate ourselves. We need to understand why the arguments made for the truth claims of Islam are incorrect, and we need to be able to counter the reasons that Muslims give for their beliefs. Secondly, we need to be able to discuss these arguments with Muslims. In other words, we need to be able to defend the truth and refute error. Studying these areas will give us confidence in what we believe and confidence in challenging our Muslim friends to think through the reasons for their own beliefs. This is where Apologetics comes in. Thirdly, we need to support the efforts of ex-Muslims as they help other Muslims leave Islam. Many times these former Muslims are the best ones to challenge the beliefs of Muslims because they have lived according to these beliefs all their lives. Finally, we need to remain vigilant and fight the censorship that tries to silence opponents of Islam. As we look across the pond to our Christian partners in England and Europe, we can see how censorship against Christians reaching out to Muslims has been devastating to the work of the gospel and destructive of the common freedoms that were so valiantly fought for in past wars. The obfuscation by political leaders, who have caved into the demands of Muslim activists, must be addressed and the truth must be heard, if for no other reason than good men need to stand up for what is right.

## Love Muslims

What else can be done? After questioning Islam, we need to love Muslims. These are people who are made in the image of God, and we need to help them come to know this God who loves them and wants them to be in his kingdom. Islam is the barrier that keeps them from knowing this God, and we have the opportunity to help them leave Islam and embrace the gospel of the One who can save them.

The key to reaching Muslims with the gospel is simple: relationships, relationships, relationships! Millions of Muslims are turning to Christ around the world today. Many come to Jesus Christ because he reveals himself to them in a dream or a vision.[613] Others come because they hear the Word of God preached through the internet or by satellite broadcasts. Through

---

[612] Townsend, *Nothing to Do with Islam*, 146-148.
[613] Trousdale, *Miraculous Movements*.

all these powerful witnesses of the Holy Spirit working in the lives of Muslims, Christians are needed to come alongside Muslims and lead them home. Relationships are essential to this movement of the Holy Spirit in the world today. Even in helping Muslims leave Islam, relationships are necessary to guide people through the various obstacles and answer questions that arise.

Let us look at several helpful books and ideas about building relationships with Muslims. One book is *Muslims, Christians, and Jesus*, by Carl Madieras.[614] He has some very helpful suggestions for building relationships. One suggestion is to visit mosques. Most are very welcoming to visitors who simply sit in the back and observe. This is a great way to meet Muslims. It is also a great place to ask questions about Islam in a way that will help you gain respect from the Muslims as well as build trust. Another way to reach out is to invite Muslim colleagues to meals. You may also be invited to attend one of their important feasts. It is not unusual when Muslims get to know you for them to invite you to join in on a celebration such as *Eid al Fitr*, at the close of Ramadan.

A particularly good way to get to know Muslims is to volunteer to teach English, which is always much appreciated. There are often programs in churches for teaching English to recent immigrants. This is an excellent way to meet Muslims who are hungry for friendships in a place that may seem hostile and lonely to them. There are also university programs that appreciate Americans getting together with international students in order to help them gain a better grasp of English. The relationships that often result from this type of outreach may have eternal rewards. Muslims love to talk about their religion, and they are often open to hearing you talk about your own beliefs. This can best be carried out around a meal or a cup of coffee. You can also help out with campus ministries if you live in a university town. Outreaches such as these often have lunches, dinners, and other opportunities in which to get involved. Many churches also have ministries to international students or prayer groups for Muslim outreach. If your church does not have an outreach ministry but does have international students in the area, encourage your church to get involved.

Bear in mind that relationships take a great deal of time, and you may not see results for years, only to have them suddenly appear. One well-known Christian writer and speaker became a believer after five years of Apologetics in the context of relationship. Indeed, results may come long after your relationship has ended.

---

[614] Carl Madearis, *Muslims, Christians, and Jesus: Gaining Understanding and Building Relationships* (Minneapolis: Bethany House, 2008).

Another book, *Reaching Muslims*, written by Nick Chatrath, is a helpful guide to building bridges.[615] He emphasizes the importance of building a true friendship, and he has many examples and ideas for how to do this. He encourages all who would reach out to cultivate a posture of welcome and acceptance. Pray for open hearts! Be truly interested in others. Actually, get to know some Muslims. Show love in action. Get engaged in politics and issues of social need (but do be well informed!). As you build actual relational bridges, seek to develop a true friendship. They want to know that you truly care about them as a person and not just someone that you are trying to convert to Christianity. Therefore, build trust, ask good questions, and be a good listener.

You also need to be prepared to give good answers, especially regarding theological questions. Read the gospels together—perhaps read a chapter a week in the gospel of John, discussing the chapter when you next meet. One of the ways that I have often brought up theological discussions with my Muslim friends is to challenge them when they express a view about Christianity that is not accurate, asking, "Do you want to know what Christians really believe about that?" This often piques their interest and it opens the door in a non-threatening way for you to explain in more detail what you believe as a Christian. It also may be appropriate to give your friend a good quality Bible. (They do judge a book by its cover.) Be sure to pray for your Muslim friends. Without the work of the Holy Spirit in their lives, your words will not be effective. In the end, as you challenge their beliefs about Islam, and seek to build a relationship with them, be sure that you are prepared to give them answers about your own beliefs. Perhaps the greatest thing you can do is to be prepared to share with your Muslim friends the gospel of Jesus Christ.

## What Can Be Done? Preach the Gospel

A third book that is a great resource is *The Gospel for Muslims* by Thabiti Anyabwile.[616] Anyabwile, a former Muslim himself, notes, "As a Christian you already know everything you need to know to effectively share the good news of Jesus Christ with Muslim people. The same message that saves us—the gospel—is the message that will eternally change our Muslim neighbors and friends."[617]

---

[615] Nick Chatrath, *Reaching Muslims: A One-Step Guide for Christians* (Oxford: Monarch Books, 2011).

[616] Thabiti Anyabwile, *The Gospel for Muslims: An Encouragement to Share Christ with Confidence* (Chicago: Moody, 2010).

[617] Ibid., 13.

So, we already have the answer. We already have the tools to reach out to Muslims. We know the gospel. We just need to share it with our Muslim friends. It is the same gospel that everyone needs to know, regardless of their faith or background.

Anyabwile is in line with many others who reach out to Muslims. They all agree that our direction in forming relationships needs to be toward the gospel—that is our goal and direction. Anyabwile goes on to say, "In my experience, Christians know the gospel. They simply lack confidence in its power."[618] The gospel is "the power of God for salvation to everyone who believes, to the Jew first and also to the Greek" (Romans 1:16)—and also to the Muslim! He distinguishes between Apologetics and evangelism, saying, "Apologetics is a helpful discipline, but it is not evangelism. The Gospel for Muslims is concerned not with defense but with a good offense, with getting the gospel out to others."[619] So we should have both a defense and an offense, but a purposeful offense — preaching the gospel. This again highlights how the best Apologetic approach is one that keeps a balance between the polemic and the peaceful in our conversations.

The ultimate goal, then, is to put all of these things together. One of the best books on Islam demonstrates how these approaches work together. The late Nabeel Qureshi, in his book *Seeking Allah, Finding Jesus*, reminds us to always be prepared to give an answer.[620] He himself was an example of this, always being ready to engage. As a great apologist who spoke in many settings, Nabeel was enamored with apologetics because that was what led him to the Lord, through the patient and loving ministry of faithful friends over a five-year period. After becoming a Christian, he was very concerned with reaching Muslims with the gospel that transformed his life. He realized that the best way to do this was through both Apologetics and Evangelism.

A major role of Apologetics is to show how something is false, while the gospel shows what is true. This is the ultimate way that we can show both Truth and Love. (Truth and Love in the Defense of the Gospel.) There will be true peace for everyone who believes in Jesus Christ as Lord and Savior. And this is what Nabeel found. Muslims want that true peace just as we do. We have the answer; now we need to find ways to get the answer to them.

In conclusion, there are three things that we need to always be prepared to do. First, we need to be prepared to *question Islam* in order

---

[618] Ibid., 13.
[619] Ibid., 14.
[620] Qureshi, *Seeking Allah, Finding Jesus*, 18.

to get Muslims to leave Islam. This opens the door. Then, we need to *love Muslims* and build relationships with them because they need to see the gospel lived out. This invites them into your world. It is also much easier to help your Muslim friend question Islam when they trust you and can observe Christ working in your life. Finally, you need to *share* with them *the Gospel* of Jesus Christ. Muslims need to know the good news! This is the bridge that leads them to Jesus Christ. Ultimately, this is the only thing that is going to truly set Muslims free.

These three things, as well as the message of this book, can be summed up in the verse that has guided us through this book:

**1 Peter 3:15** English Standard Version (ESV)

[15] but in your hearts honor Christ the Lord as holy, always being prepared to make a defense to anyone who asks you for a reason for the hope that is in you; yet do it with gentleness and respect,

**Study Questions:**

1. What are some of the fears Christians have about reaching out to Muslims with the gospel of Jesus Christ? How can these fears be overcome?
2. The "great debate" concerning how Christians reach out to Muslims revolves around seeking relationships (the irenic approach) or emphasizing theological differences (the polemical approach). What are the advantages and disadvantages of each side?
3. How can the relationship building emphasis and the theological emphasis work together in order to reach Muslims with both Truth and Love?
4. Why did Nabeel Qureshi leave Islam? What do you think are the main reasons Muslims leave Islam?
5. Peter Townsend believes that the best way to counter jihad ideology is to help Muslims leave Islam. What are his reasons for this approach? What are the four reasons Townsend gives that will help Christians lead Muslims away from Islam?
6. What are the best ways that you can reach out to Muslims with Love and Truth?

# Epilogue

This book has dealt with a number of areas — historical, theological, cultural, and evangelical. One of the main themes, however, has been that love and truth must accompany all efforts to understand and to explain the implications of these major apologetic points. It is the purpose of this book to present evidence and logical arguments in the spirit of truth – based on reality – and love towards others, which is based on and flows from God's love for us. Too often, the search for spiritual truth can be harsh because there is no love or respect for others, or it can go to the other extreme by having plenty of love but lacking intellectual courage, which then can end in heresy. We need both truth and love in balance so the truth of the gospel can lead to the love of Christ. At the end of this book, then, it is my hope that the evidence and arguments throughout have clearly been presented within this framework, and that the readers will ultimately come away with this idea of truth and love together.

The title of this book implies that it is written primarily for the Christian reader. That is because one important goal of this book has indeed been to enable Christians to understand Islam better. This is not only so that they can defend their beliefs in the Trinity, the deity of Christ, the resurrection, and the accuracy of the Scriptures, but so they can also refute errors that may lead to heresy.

However, the book has also been written for a non-Christian audience. For those who may not necessarily accept all the tenets of Christianity, the book has sought to present the recent arguments of a number of respected scholars, all of which reach significant conclusions concerning the historicity of Islam's origins. These conclusions include the arguments that Islam may have begun as a heretical interpretation of Judaism and Christianity, then as it solidified began to borrow holy writings from various sources for its nascent Qur'an and took the memory of a popular Arab religious leader to become the newly imagined founder of the faith. The scholars discussed here also argue that military success by these early believers enabled them to proclaim that Islam is the right path to Allah and their belief system is the most correct of all faiths, cementing the stray origins into a coherent narrative of Islam's beginnings. It is the intent of this book that all readers, especially non-Christians, will be able to use this evidence and the arguments around it to thoughtfully reconsider some of the more accepted narratives about Islam's origins and the central themes of its history.

Moreover, it is the author's hope that many Muslims will also read this book and find it to be a helpful guide in comparing Islam and Christianity. As the book presents different ideas about Islam, it is also hoped that Muslim readers will thoughtfully consider the evidences and arguments in order to seek the truth. For that reason, the book has sought to provide access to first-hand accounts that can shed light on what Muslims believe and why, as well as offer reasons for the faith that Christians have in the historicity of their own religious beliefs. Since, as the Law of Non-Contradiction reminds us, Islam and Christianity cannot both be true religions, we need to realize that only one may be true, or both may be false. While it can be a comforting and indeed a popular idea that both religions can be true, we must remember that logically Islam cannot be the successor to Christianity since the fundamental beliefs are diametrically opposed.

Therefore, it is the author's hope that at the end of this book, every reader will come away with something to reflect on, something to question or further research, and something to provide a new source of encouragement or faith.

### A Final Word: Former Muslims Who Chose a Different Path

At the close of this book, I want to leave readers with several real-life examples of Muslims who grappled with the evidences of both Islam and Christianity. Sometimes converts from Islam to Christianity can give us the clearest reasons for learning about Islam and reaching out to Muslims with truth and love.

### Karim Shamsi-Basha

One of these men is Karim Shamsi-Basha, who wrote in his book a message to his family:

> You don't have to be ashamed because I chose a different path. Just be at peace with the fact that this different path can actually lead to loving God instead of fearing Him. It can lead to God dwelling within you instead of being far from you. It can lead to a God who wants to commune and fellowship with you.[621]

This paragraph reveals several important points in Karim's life as a Muslim in contrast to his life in Christ. As a Muslim he placed his hope in doing enough good works to please Allah, whereas as a Christian he now places his hope in what Christ has done for him on the cross. As a Muslim

---

[621] Karim Shamsi-Basha, *Notes on Paul and Me: A Journey to and from the Damascus Road from Islam to Christ* (Vestavia Hills, Alabama: Solid Ground Christian Books, 2013) x.

he had feared Allah, whereas as a Christian his love for God grows deeper every day. As a Muslim, he only knew Allah as a distant God, whereas in Christianity he feels blessed to be able to have a relationship with the living God of the universe. Ultimately, Karim was drawn to the God of Christianity because he realized that it was the love of God that drew him in and saved him, and he wanted this love for his family members as well.

Overall, it seems that being awakened to the differences between Islam and Christianity gave him a way to contrast the God of Christianity and the God of Islam, as well as a number of other doctrinal issues that demonstrate that Islam and Christianity are not only dissimilar but are actually polar opposites. He wrote that some of the things that spoke to him about Christianity were fulfilled prophecies, the truth of the Bible, the fact of the resurrection, the miracles of Jesus (even in the Qur'an), his own physical healing through prayer, and God's unconditional love. He also gave testimony that Lee Strobel's book, *The Case for Christ*, helped him to see how apologetics could bolster his faith and answer many of the questions that he had about his faith. The greatest draw for Karim, however, was the love of God shown through the death of Christ on the cross for his sins, and the love of God that was displayed by other Christians.

### Nabeel Qureshi

Another former Muslim who made a great difference when he came to Christ was Nabeel Qureshi. Nabeel was a good friend of mine, and I admired him greatly. His death due to stomach cancer still saddens me, but I remind myself that Jesus Christ died around the same age and still had a tremendous influence on the world. I am glad that Nabeel was able to leave us some excellent books that sound the depths of his soul. I think his book, *Seeking Allah, Finding Jesus*, is the best general book on Islam from a Christian's perspective, perhaps because it was written by one who had also had a Muslim perspective.

Nabeel was devout in his Islamic beliefs and deeply wanted to honor and serve Allah. However, his world was rocked beyond measure when he began his friendship and dialogue with his good friend David Wood. Through these discussions, Nabeel tested his beliefs against the gospel of Jesus Christ and realized that the truth of Christianity was superior. David demonstrated the truth of the Scripture, but it was also the bond of this strong friendship that allowed Nabeel to trust David's words and open himself to the arguments. Nabeel said that his first year as a Christian was the most difficult time of his life. His family and friends turned away from him and every day was a struggle dealing with the emotional pain. However, he also realized that the Lord was very real in his life and was carrying him through the tough times. In his epilogue to his book, *Seeking*

*Allah, Finding Jesus*, Nabeel recounts why the joy of finding Jesus surpassed any suffering that he could ever encounter.

> But I will also honestly say that looking back on it eight years later, it was the most powerful time of my life. It shaped me, molded me, changed me into a disciple of Jesus. The Holy Spirit was my comforter. His word was my sustenance, and I would not give up that time for anything. The suffering is what transformed me into a true follower of Jesus. My life now, including my walk with God and my relationship with my wife, are truly blissful, far more wondrous than I could have ever imagined when I was a Muslim.
>
> All suffering is worth it to follow Jesus. He is that amazing. I pray that I will meet you someday, my dear friend, so we can rejoice and praise God together for our joys and our sufferings.[622]

Nabeel had come to Christ by embracing the truth of the gospel, but God used the love of his friend David Wood to reach a Muslim who was seeking the true God. As with Karim, it was the love of Christ that drew Nabeel to faith in Jesus Christ, but apologetics played a fundamental role in making clear paths to the rough places of their hearts. Truth and love in balance is what is needed for us all to reach out to our Muslim friends with the same truth of the gospel and the transformative love of Jesus Christ.

---

[622] Nabeel Qureshi, *Seeking Allah, Finding Jesus*, 287.

# Glossary for The Guide to Answering Islam

*Abrogation:* the belief that later revelations (Medinan surahs) sometimes contradicted the earlier ones (Meccan surahs). Therefore, the later revelations canceled and replaced the earlier ones. For example, Surah 9:5, often called the "sword verse," is said to nullify and replace 124 verses that called for tolerance, compassion, and peace (Q. 2:106, Q. 16:101, Q. 13:39)

*Adhan:* the Muslim call to prayer

*Ahl al-Kitab:* term meaning "people of the book," or perhaps "followers of an earlier revelation" (see Armstrong), usually referring to Jews and Christians

*Al Kitab*: the Book, the Qur'an

*Al-Qaeda, al-Qaida:* "The Base." A militant Sunni Islamist organization founded by Osama bin Laden in 1988

*Amir:* a governor or commander of a Muslim province; this title was common during the military rule of the Middle Period

*Ansar:* the Helpers; refers to the Medina clansmen who converted to Islam

*Arians*: Early non-Trinitarian heresy started by Arius in the 4th century, who said that Jesus Christ is the son of God, but that he did not always exist with the Father and therefore was a created being.

*Ash'arites:* a political-philosophical group that initially followed a middle road seeking to balance reason with revelation, but under the influence of al-Ghazali the synthesis between man's reason and God's will was rejected.

*Ayah*: (pl. *ayat*) in the context of the Qur'an, ayah means "verse," and is marked off by a sequential number.

*Basmallah/Bismillah*: the words of invocation which begin most surahs in the Qur'an – "**In the name of God**, the Compassionate, the Merciful."

*Bid'ah:* religious innovation, heretical doctrine, or heresy

*Burqa:* long drape or veil worn by women that covers the face and body, except for the eyes (except when a mesh screen is used to cover the eyes as well)

*Caliph (khalifa):* title for the head of the Islamic state. Originally the spiritual and political 'successor' to Muhammad; later took on a more strictly political meaning

*Caliphate:* the rule of the Caliph or Khalifa.

*Dabiq:* the key site in Muslim apocalyptic views where the great battle of Armageddon will take place, with the Muslims coming out victorious over the non-believers. It is also the name of the official magazine for ISIS, which promotes their views and serves as a major recruiting tool for their cause.

*Dar al-Harb:* the "House of War;" those outside the House or family of Islam

*Dar al-Islam:* the "House of Islam; the lands under Muslim rule.

*Da'wa:* the mission or practice of calling non-believers to Islam. Islamic evangelism.

*Dhimmi:* "People of the Book" or "protected ones" – Jews and Christians who enter into a contract with a Muslim government for protection and pay a head tax called the jizya. This is sometimes referred to the "third choice" given to non-Muslims under Muslim rule. The first two are "convert or be killed."

*Din/Deen:* the idea of faith or religion, specifically as affecting man's spiritual welfare

*Ebionites:* An early Jewish-Christian heresy that regarded Jesus Christ as the Messiah but did not accept his divinity or virgin birth. Their emphasis was on following Jewish laws and traditions. There are some references to the Ebionites living in Northwestern Arabia as late as 1000 AD.

*Fatwa:* legal declaration made by a qualified Muslim jurist on matters of Islamic law

*Fiqh:* study and application of Islamic law and jurisprudence

*Hadith:* term meaning "story," refers to the collection of the traditional sayings and doings of Muhammad not from the Qur'an but recorded by companions and family. Second highest authority after the Qur'an. These were collected and written down around 150 years after the death of Muhammad.

*Hajj:* the pilgrimage to Mecca; one of the five "pillars" of Islam, and a duty for every Muslim once in his or her lifetime (if able).

*Hajji:* one who has completed the Hajj to Mecca

*Hanifs:* pre-Islamic Arab monotheists

*Hijab:* a veil or headscarf worn by Muslim women; a customary practice of modesty which also marks a sense of pride in Muslim identity

*Hijaz:* the region of western Arabia, including both Mecca and Medina

*Hijra:* the emigration from Mecca to Yathrib (Medina) in 622 AD. This is the first year in the Islamic calendar.

*Iblis:* the devil or Satan (corruption of the Latin word *diabolus*)

*Ijtihad:* the "independent reasoning" or personal interpretation that a Muslim jurist uses to apply the sacred traditional law to contemporary circumstances; also an intellectual struggle over (or private opinion of) law and ethics

*Imam:* divinely inspired leader of the Muslim community

*Injil:* the gospels or New Testament, sent to Jesus by Allah and revised in the Qur'an

*Inshallah:* common Muslim phrase meaning "if God wills it"

*Intermediate Monotheism:* pre-Islamic belief in one God inspired by an Arabized mixture of Christian and Jewish beliefs, which later developed into the religion of Islam

*Isa:* the name used for Jesus in the Qur'an

*Islam:* "surrender" to the will of God

*Islamism:* a movement within Islam that primarily seeks the creation of an Islamic polity

*Isnad:* a chain of transmission that is supposed to validate a particular hadith. Since the hadith were first transmitted orally, this chain of transmission tries to name the people involved in order to provide a reputable link to the sources.

*Jahiliyyahh/Jayiliyya:* term meaning "The Time of Ignorance." This originally referenced Arabian history prior to Islam, but some Muslim fundamentalists today use the word to condemn a modern society that they believe has rejected God, even a society that claims to be Muslim.

*Jewish-Christianity:* First century Jews who followed Jesus as Messiah but rejected the idea that Jesus could also be God. It is possible that descendants of this group may have contributed to the formation of the intermediate monotheism that became Islam.

*Jibril , Jibril:* Gabriel, the angel that is said to have revealed the Qur'an to Muhammad

*Jihad:* holy war; to struggle to finish a task as well as one possibly can

*Jinn:* spiritual beings – demons or angels of Allah

*Jizyah:* the head tax paid by a *dhimmi* for protection under Muslim rule.

*Ka'aba:* the ancient sanctuary at Mecca that housed the tribal deities of the Hijaz before Muhammad cleansed them and rededicated the sanctuary to Allah alone.

*Kafir:* term for an unbeliever

*Kalam:* Islamic theology; the study of Islamic doctrine

*Kharijites:* secessionists, or "those who leave." This is the group that broke away from Ali and the early Shiites. They equated faith with works and insisted that in regard to the relationship between faith and works, there could be no middle ground. A Muslim was either a true believer or not a Muslim at all. It is believed that a Kharijite follower later assassinated Ali.

*Madrassa:* Islamic religious school, usually linked to a mosque

*Mahdi:* the "hidden Imam," a significant eschatological figure who is believed to be hidden until the Last Days, when he will bring about a new age of justice

*Al-Mahdi:* a messianic concept, usually held by various Shi'i sects, which differs from the traditional beliefs concerning the Mahdi and his role

*Masjid:* place of Muslim worship; a mosque

*Meccan Qur'an:* the chronologically earlier Surahs supposedly revealed to Muhammad before his emigration to Medina. They are generally short, and they emphasize, among other things, God as the creator of all, some principles for ethical living, and warnings about the judgment to come. These are generally arranged toward the end of the Qur'an even though they are believed to have been revealed to Muhammad before his emigration to Medina.

Theodor Nöldeke proposed a different chronological order, consisting of 90 surahs, as follows:

- First Meccan Period: from the first to the fifth year of Mohammed's mission

96, 74, 111, 106, 108, 104, 107, 102, 105, 92, 90, 94, 93, 97, 86, 91, 80, 68, 87, 95, 103, 85, 73, 101, 99, 82, 81, 53, 84, 100, 79, 77, 78, 88, 89, 75, 83, 69, 51, 52, 56, 70, 55, 112, 109, 113, 114, 1

- Second Meccan Period: the fifth and sixth year of his mission:

54, 37, 71, 76, 44, 50, 20, 26, 15, 19, 38, 36, 43, 72, 67, 23, 21, 25, 17, 27, 18

- Third Meccan Period: from the seventh year to Hijra:

32, 41, 45, 16, 30, 11, 14, 12, 40, 28, 39, 29, 31, 42, 10, 34, 35, 7, 46, 6, 13

*Medinan Qur'an:* The last 24 -30 Surahs of the Qur'an, believed to have been revealed in the last years of Muhammad's life when he lived in Medina. The scholar Nöldeke lists these particular surahs: 2, 98, 64, 62, 8, 47, 3, 61, 57, 4, 65, 59, 33, 63, 24, 58, 22, 48, 66, 60, 110, 49, 9, 5 (Surah 9, one of the last Surahs considered to be revealed, contains a number of verses on violent jihad). They deal with details governing a growing community, such as moral principles, legislation, warfare, and laws governing family, money and acts of worship. The vocabulary was simpler, and there was a greater focus on offensive jihad, longer verses and the treatment of non-Muslims.

*Monophysites*: Early Christians who opposed the concept of the hypostatic union, or the union of Christ's humanity and divinity in one hypostasis, or individual existence. Instead they believed that Christ had but a single nature with his human nature being absorbed into his divinity.

*Muhajirun:* migrants who went on the hijra

*Mujahadin:* Muslim militants; literally "those who wage jihad" (singular *mujahid*)

*Mu'minun:* "believers" in a pre-Islamic intermediate monotheism

*Murji'ites:* A faction which opposed the Kharijite position, believing that faith alone saved a person. The name means "those who defer," and it was given to them because they deferred final judgment to God, who was the only one who could ultimately decide who would be saved on the Last Day.

*Mu'tazilites:* "Those who separate themselves." These were the first to apply reason to their view of God's justice in man's freedom of will. They were opposed by the Ash'arites.

*Nabi:* a prophet

*Naskh:* the abrogation of one verse in the Qur'an by another verse

*Nazarenes*: Similar to the Ebionites, the Nazarenes were heretical Christians who rejected Jesus Christ as the Son of God. However, they accepted the virgin birth. Like the Ebionites, they considered themselves Jews, only used the Aramaic Gospel of the Hebrews, and followed the law of Moses.

*Nestorians:* Early Christians who opposed the concept of the hypostatic union, or the union of Christ's humanity and divinity in one hypostasis, or individual existence. Instead they believed that Christ had two somewhat distinct natures, human and divine. Opposite to Monophysitism.

*Paradise:* literally "garden" – the idea of a place of heavenly rest and delight for those who have lived according to Allah's will

*PBUH:* acronym for "peace be upon him," a phrase used exclusively for prophets

*Qadarites:* a group that believed that man must have free will and responsibility over his actions. Thus, they opposed the traditionalists who believed that in order for Allah to truly be sovereign that man could not have any free will, since this would limit the power of Allah.

*Qiblah:* the correct direction of prayer, oriented towards Mecca. This direction was originally towards Jerusalem, but Muhammad altered it later.

*Quryana:* Syriac for "Lectionary," which was composed of Biblical extracts, interspersed with hymns – created for use in Christian services.

*Ramadan:* the month of fasting and the ninth month of the year in the Muslim calendar

*Rashidun Caliphate:* the "rightly guided" Caliphs; the first four caliphs after Muhammad's death: Abu Bakr, Umar, Uthman, and Ali.

*Rasul:* a messenger

*Salam:* peace

*Salat:* ritual prayer performed five times a day at sunrise, noon, afternoon, sunset, and evening. One of the five "pillars" of Islam.

*Sawm:* fasting

*Shahada:* the Muslim creed or profession of faith: "There is no God but Allah, and Muhammad is God's messenger [prophet]."

*Shahid:* a martyr

*Shariah:* Islamic laws that have the Qur'an and Hadith as their primary source; means "straight path"

*Shirk:* to obscure the Oneness and unity of Allah in any way

*Sira:* biographical material on Muhammad

*Sunna:* the traditions of Muhammad composed of the hadith

*Surah (Sura):* a chapter in the Qur'an. There are 114 Surahs in the Qur'an. It has a similar *root* with the Hebrew word 'שורה' meaning a 'row'

*Tafsir:* commentaries on the Qur'an

*Taqiyyah:* cautionary dissimulation or lying about one's faith in a specially allowed situation

*Taurat or Tawrat:* the books of Moses

*Tawhid/Tauheed:* "making one;" refers to God's absolute unity and oneness.

*Ummah:* community of believers, often refers specifically to the one at Medina

*Zabur:* the Psalms

*Zakat:* term meaning "purity" – refers to the mandatory alms given by each Muslim to the community and distributed to the poor. One of the five "pillars" of Islam.

*Zoroastrianism:* An ancient monotheistic religion from the region of present-day Iran promoted by the prophet Zoroaster (also known as Zarathustra). Belief is in a supreme being named Ahura Mazda, or Wise Lord. It is possible that Zoroastrian beliefs in judgment after death, heaven and hell, and free will may have influenced Islam.

## Subject Index

Abassid, 163
Abrogate, 210, 252
Abrogated, 66, 211, 213, 283
Abrogation, 211, 213, 218, 315, 328
Ahl al-Kitab, 328
Ahmadiyyah, 188, 199
Ahmed, 43, 82, 159, 202, 349
Akbar, 251
Al-Andalus, 90, 92
Alawites, 190, 191
Al-Bukhari, 144, 202, 211
Al-Farabi, 82, 86
al-Faruqi, 153, 349
al-Ghazali, 70, 72, 73, 78, 84, 85, 86, 87, 101, 188, 328
al-Harb, 131, 217, 261, 329
Al-Ikhwan, 192
al-Khawarazmi, 84
Allah, 12, 13, 14, 15, 19, 20, 23, 24, 25, 26, 27, 28, 32, 33, 38, 40, 41, 42, 43, 44, 51, 53, 54, 55, 65, 66, 68, 69, 70, 71, 73, 74, 75, 76, 77, 78, 87, 93, 97, 98, 99, 100, 101, 102, 103, 104, 105, 107, 108, 109, 110, 111, 113, 115, 116, 119, 120, 121, 134, 137, 140, 141, 142, 143, 144, 145, 146, 147, 148, 149, 150, 152, 153, 154, 155, 156, 157, 158, 159, 160, 162, 163, 164, 165, 166, 167, 168, 170, 171, 172, 173, 176, 181, 183, 185, 187, 189, 191, 192, 197, 198, 201, 202, 203, 204, 206, 208, 209, 210, 211, 212, 213, 214, 215, 216, 217, 218, 219, 225, 227, 232, 234, 235, 243, 245, 247, 248, 249, 251, 253, 254, 255, 256, 258, 259, 262, 266, 268, 269, 270, 272, 273, 274, 276, 277, 281, 282, 284, 285, 286, 289, 290, 307, 310, 315, 316, 318, 322, 324, 325, 326, 327, 330, 331, 333, 354, 356, 357
Allahu, 251
al-Mahdi, 167
al-Malik, 32, 34, 35, 45, 49, 53, 55, 56, 59, 60, 65, 67, 71, 196
al-Masih, 164
Al-Mawdudi, 15
almsgiving, 148
al-Qaeda, 243, 244, 246
al-Qaida, 328
al-Tabari, 29, 39, 53, 145
al-Tirmidhi, 171
al-Zabayr, 59
Andalusia, 89
Andalusian, 84, 85, 89, 90, 351
antichrist, 164, 166, 173, 174, 175, 178, 179, 182
apologetic, 10, 12, 19, 20, 36, 50, 51, 56, 65, 68, 217, 218, 221, 237, 240, 261, 275, 314, 324
Apologetics, 8, 91, 275, 292, 293, 314, 319, 320, 322, 352
Aquinas, 232
Arab, 8, 14, 16, 34, 35, 36, 44, 55, 57, 58, 59, 60, 72, 80, 83, 84, 128, 129, 159, 192, 204, 225, 226, 228, 233, 236, 237, 245, 249, 272, 277, 302, 324, 329, 352, 353, 354
Arabia, 8, 12, 14, 16, 17, 18, 19, 21, 27, 47, 52, 55, 57, 60, 61,

62, 63, 64, 72, 79, 80, 128, 131, 136, 185, 191, 201, 267, 286, 316, 329, 330
Arabized, 47, 49, 56, 58, 60, 169, 330
Arabs, 12, 17, 24, 35, 47, 55, 56, 57, 58, 60, 64, 67, 80, 84, 89, 104, 105, 129, 163, 224, 226, 249
Aramaic, 40, 64, 172, 332, 353
archaeological, 19, 60, 63, 107, 282
archaeologist, 46, 63, 106
archaeology, 91, 280
archeological, 20, 28, 36, 46, 63, 83, 106
archeology, 91
Aristotle, 82, 83, 85, 236
Armageddon, 161, 247, 329
astrolabe, 82, 83
astronomer, 82
astronomers, 82
astronomy, 82
Ayatollah, 167, 318
Bagdad, 81
Baghdad, 80, 81, 83, 84, 212, 245
Baha'i, 189, 199
Baha'u'llah, 189
Bahira, 22
Basmallah, 328
Bid'ah, 328
Byzantine, 18, 19, 53, 54, 55, 58, 59, 81, 83, 84, 88, 129, 130, 203, 230, 249, 260
Byzantines, 129, 190, 230, 249
Byzantium, 80, 85
Caliph, 41, 43, 45, 53, 57, 167, 329
caliphate, 45, 53, 60, 80, 164, 192, 193, 247
caliphates, 80
caliphs, 53, 54, 63, 80, 91, 184, 185, 187, 196, 333

Charlemagne, 80, 81, 83, 85, 88, 354, 355
Christendom, 208, 227, 230
Christian, ii, iii, 8, 9, 10, 17, 19, 20, 22, 23, 28, 31, 32, 33, 34, 35, 37, 40, 46, 47, 48, 49, 50, 51, 52, 55, 56, 57, 58, 59, 65, 70, 71, 73, 74, 75, 76, 77, 78, 83, 84, 85, 88, 89, 90, 92, 94, 95, 97, 100, 101, 102, 103, 105, 106, 108, 110, 111, 112, 113, 114,115, 123, 124, 125, 126, 129, 130, 134, 136, 140, 141, 143, 147, 148, 149, 150, 151, 153, 155, 156, 157, 160, 162, 168, 172, 173, 175, 176, 177, 178, 180, 182, 188, 190, 193, 196, 197, 201, 203, 214, 216, 219, 221, 222, 223, 224, 225, 226, 227, 228, 229, 230, 231, 232, 233, 235, 236, 237, 239, 240, 241, 247, 248, 249, 250, 251, 254, 261, 263, 265, 266, 267, 268, 269, 271, 272, 273, 274, 275, 276, 277, 279, 283, 284, 286, 288, 289, 290, 291, 293, 294, 296, 297, 299, 300, 302, 303, 304, 306, 307, 308, 309, 317, 318, 319, 320, 321, 322, 324, 325, 326, 329, 330, 333, 349, 350, 352, 353, 355, 356, 357
Christianity, 8, 9, 10, 17, 18, 19, 28, 32, 33, 37, 50, 56, 57, 60, 65, 66, 71, 73, 74, 75, 76, 77, 89, 90, 92, 93, 94, 95, 97, 100, 102, 106, 109, 112, 114, 115, 124, 125, 129, 130, 136, 137, 140, 141, 142, 143, 147, 148, 150, 151, 152, 154, 155, 156, 159, 160, 161, 163, 165, 168, 169, 178, 180, 182, 191, 195, 197, 198, 199, 201, 208, 214, 220, 221, 223, 225, 226, 227,

228, 233, 235, 236, 240, 241,
249, 250, 257, 259, 260, 265,
268, 270, 272, 273, 275, 277,
285, 287, 289, 290, 291, 292,
293, 294, 295, 296, 297, 299,
300, 301, 303, 306, 309, 311,
312, 313, 314, 317, 318, 321,
324, 325, 326, 330, 349, 351,
353, 354, 356, 357, 358
Christians, 7, 8, 9, 10, 17, 18, 19,
20, 24, 36, 37, 40, 43, 50, 51,
54, 57, 61, 65, 66, 71, 72, 74,
75, 76, 77, 78, 80, 83, 84, 85,
89, 90, 91, 92, 94, 100, 102,
104, 105, 107, 108, 109, 110,
111, 112, 113, 114, 115, 116, 120,
122, 123, 124, 125, 126, 128,
129, 130, 135, 136, 137, 140,
142, 149, 150, 151, 152, 154,
155, 156, 159, 160, 161, 162,
163, 164, 165, 170, 172, 174,
175, 176, 178, 179, 180, 182,
188, 190, 192, 196, 197, 198,
202, 203, 207, 210, 213, 214,
217, 218, 219, 221, 222, 223,
224, 225, 226, 227, 228, 229,
233, 234, 235, 236, 237, 238,
239, 240, 241, 242, 249, 250,
254, 260, 261, 262, 265, 266,
267, 268, 269, 270, 271, 272,
273, 274, 275, 276, 277, 278,
279, 281, 284, 285, 286, 287,
288, 289, 291, 292, 293, 294,
295, 296, 297, 302, 304, 305,
306, 309, 312, 314, 318, 319,
320, 321, 322, 323, 324, 325,
326, 328, 329, 332, 333, 350,
351, 352, 354, 355, 356
Christoscale, 254
Church, 10, 18, 89, 94, 214, 222,
224, 231, 233, 236, 267, 283,
289, 290, 306, 352, 354

churches, 64, 83, 90, 123, 126,
129, 130, 238, 249, 250, 260,
279, 294, 306, 320
circumambulating, 20
circumambulation, 14
coercion, 9, 126, 127
coercive, 35
conquer, 19, 93, 158, 165, 174,
176, 205, 310
conquered, 53, 79, 83, 84, 85,
87, 94, 122, 182, 195, 210,
229, 237
conquering, 163, 208, 231, 235,
249, 316
conquest, 17, 54, 55, 65, 66, 67,
77, 88, 89, 90, 92, 136, 195,
201, 208, 210, 213, 219, 229,
230, 233, 235, 249
conquests, 79, 88, 91, 92, 95,
201, 203, 214, 236
conversion, 66, 77, 151, 163, 201,
211, 295, 296, 297, 298, 299,
307
conversions, 66, 68, 89, 296,
297, 299, 301, 302, 303, 304,
307
converted, 17, 27, 44, 52, 85, 90,
91, 124, 136, 210, 247, 270,
275, 294, 300, 318, 328
converting, 56, 93, 294, 295,
299, 306, 309
converts, 77, 125, 201, 294, 295,
296, 297, 300, 301, 302, 307,
312, 313, 325
corrupt, 15, 88, 160, 223, 224
corrupted, 14, 41, 43, 51, 60, 101,
105, 107, 115, 154, 169, 247,
279, 281, 282, 283
corruption, 42, 105, 112, 284,
330
corruptions, 44, 100
Crone, 18, 28, 29, 55, 56, 57, 62,
350
crusader, 230

crusaders, 222, 228, 229, 230, 231, 232, 233, 239
crusades, 222, 225, 230, 231, 237, 239
Crusades, 9, 77, 81, 84, 88, 129, 200, 204, 208, 221, 222, 223, 224, 225, 226, 227, 228, 230, 231, 232, 233, 234, 235, 236, 237, 238, 239, 240, 241, 250, 349, 352, 353, 354, 355, 356, 357
Dabiq, 161, 247, 249, 257, 258, 329
Dajjal, 163, 164, 166, 168, 172, 176, 177, 178, 182
Dala'il, 173
Damascus, 18, 35, 53, 55, 56, 80, 135, 166, 237, 278, 284, 325, 352, 355
'Dar-al-Salaam, 128
Dawah, 14, 29, 353
Deen, 192, 329
dhimma, 90, 123
dhimmi, 130, 260, 331
dhimmis, 90, 120, 123, 130, 140
Dhimmitude, 117, 122, 140, 208, 350
disobey, 109
Docetism, 290
Doctrina, 34
dreams, 23, 177, 226, 294, 303, 305, 306, 307, 308
Druze, 190
Ebionism, 17
Ebionites, 18, 329, 332
emigrants, 32
emigrated, 56
emigration, 24, 330, 331
epigraphic, 46
epigraphical, 64, 282
epigraphy, 33
eschatological, 170, 188, 331

eschatology, 161, 162, 163, 164, 166, 167, 168, 169, 170, 172, 177, 178, 182
eyewitness, 46, 56, 90, 91, 195
eyewitnesses, 35, 106
Fatimid, 191
Fatimids, 224
fatwa, 226, 232
Fernandez-Morera, 84, 85, 89, 351
fragment, 106
fragmentary, 36, 47, 48, 56, 60
fragmented, 49, 183
fragments, 46, 48, 49, 106, 107
Gabriel, 24, 25, 38, 41, 48, 107, 109, 113, 159, 282, 330, 351, 355
garden, 109, 141, 164, 333
gardens, 172
Gnosticism, 191
Goddess, 13, 286
Hadith, 13, 27, 28, 30, 31, 36, 40, 47, 53, 62, 66, 70, 93, 97, 98, 103, 116, 120, 121, 122, 135, 137, 140, 144, 145, 158, 161, 162, 163, 164, 168, 169, 172, 175, 181, 183, 184, 185, 187, 191, 202, 206, 208, 209, 210, 211, 212, 220, 235, 246, 261, 276, 282, 300, 312, 315, 318, 329, 333
hadiths, 149, 158, 206, 211
Hagarism, 47, 55, 56, 57, 350
Hajj, 99, 145, 329
heresies, 19, 65, 197
Heresy, 18, 35, 52, 56, 135
heretic, 86
heretical, 8, 17, 18, 19, 34, 35, 70, 86, 190, 192, 199, 249, 286, 314, 324, 328, 332
heretics, 94, 171, 188, 197, 316
hijab, 118, 265
hijabs, 133
Hijaz, 17, 61, 63, 64, 330, 331

Hijra, 330, 332
Hijrah, 24, 175, 247, 310
historical, 8, 9, 12, 15, 16, 19, 20, 21, 22, 27, 28, 29, 30, 31, 33, 34, 37, 40, 45, 46, 50, 51, 52, 56, 59, 60, 61, 62, 65, 67, 79, 82, 83, 90, 91, 105, 107, 116, 195, 196, 199, 207, 208, 210, 212, 218, 221, 223, 224, 227, 231, 244, 253, 262, 282, 290, 291, 296, 324
homosexuality, 138, 255
homosexuals, 138
houri, 171
houris, 169
Hudaybiyyah, 26, 30
Iblis, 108, 141, 142, 330
Ibn-e-Rushd, 82
idol, 12
idolaters, 210, 252
idolatrous, 12
idolatry, 12, 17, 268
idols, 14, 26, 277
ijtihad, 316
infidel, 54, 149, 155, 161, 166, 170, 194, 206, 228, 231, 244, 248, 259, 318
infidels, 69, 125, 128, 130, 146, 191, 203, 218, 247, 250, 251
Inquisition, 88
inquisitions, 90
inscription, 32, 33, 34
inscriptions, 28, 32, 33, 34, 36, 46, 47, 54, 59, 61
intolerance, 185, 193, 221, 222, 226, 227, 237
intolerant, 120, 191
invasion, 55, 89, 90, 201, 226, 236, 246
invasions, 56, 90
Ishaq, 26, 28, 29, 30, 83, 103, 209, 256, 352
Ishmaelites, 18, 32, 35, 56, 60, 135

Islam, ii, iii, 7, 8, 9, 10, 12, 13, 14, 15, 16, 17, 18, 19, 20, 21, 22, 23, 24, 27, 28, 29, 30, 31, 32, 33, 34, 35, 36, 37, 39, 40, 41, 43, 44, 45, 46, 48, 49, 50, 52, 53, 54, 55, 56, 57, 58, 59, 60, 61, 62, 63, 64, 65, 66, 67, 68, 70, 71, 73, 74, 75, 76, 77, 78, 79, 81, 82, 83, 84, 85, 87, 88, 89, 90, 91, 92, 93, 94, 95, 97, 98, 100, 101, 107, 108, 109, 110, 112, 113, 114, 115, 116, 117, 118, 119, 121, 122, 123, 124, 125, 126, 127, 129, 130, 131, 133, 135, 136, 137, 138, 139, 140, 141, 142, 143, 144, 146, 147, 148, 149, 150, 151, 152, 153, 154, 155, 156, 157, 158, 159, 160, 161, 162, 163, 164, 165, 166, 167, 168, 169, 170, 173, 174, 175, 176, 177, 178, 179, 180, 181, 182, 183, 184, 185, 187, 188, 189, 190, 191, 193, 194, 195, 196, 197, 198, 199, 201, 202, 203, 204, 205, 206, 207, 208, 209, 210, 211, 212, 213, 214, 215, 216, 217, 218, 220, 222, 223, 224, 225, 226, 227, 228, 229, 231, 234, 235, 236, 237, 242, 243, 244, 246, 247, 248, 249, 250, 251, 252, 253, 254, 257, 258, 259, 260, 261, 262, 263, 265, 266, 267, 268, 269, 271, 272, 273, 275, 276, 277, 282, 284, 288, 290, 291, 293, 294, 295, 296, 297, 298, 299, 300, 301, 302, 303, 304, 305, 306, 308, 309, 310, 311, 312, 313, 314, 315, 316, 317, 318, 319, 320, 321, 322, 323, 324, 325, 326, 328, 329, 330, 333, 334, 349, 350, 351, 352, 353, 354, 355, 356, 357, 358

Islamic, 8, 9, 12, 14, 15, 16, 17, 18, 19, 20, 21, 24, 29, 31, 32, 40, 41, 42, 44, 47, 48, 49, 53, 54, 55, 58, 59, 60, 62, 64, 65, 68, 69, 70, 71, 72, 73, 74, 76, 77, 79, 80, 81, 82, 83, 84, 85, 86, 87, 88, 89, 90, 92, 94, 95, 97, 98, 99, 100, 101, 107, 108, 111, 114, 116, 117, 118, 120, 121, 124, 125, 126, 128, 129, 130, 131, 135, 137, 139, 141, 147, 150, 151, 152, 153, 154, 156, 158, 159, 160, 161, 162, 163, 164, 165, 166, 168, 169, 170, 171, 172, 174, 175, 176, 177, 178, 179, 180, 181, 182, 184, 185, 187, 188, 190, 192, 193, 194, 195, 201, 202, 203, 204, 205, 206, 207, 208, 210, 212, 213, 215, 216, 218, 221, 223, 224, 225, 226, 234, 235, 236, 237, 239, 240, 242, 243, 244, 245, 246, 247, 248, 249, 251, 252, 255, 256, 257, 258, 259, 261, 262, 263, 267, 269, 276, 287, 298, 300, 305, 309, 315, 316, 317, 318, 326, 329, 330, 331, 332, 333, 349, 350, 351, 352, 353, 355, 358

Islamism, 72, 330

Islamist, 70, 72, 225, 226, 246, 328, 355

Islamists, 73, 160, 172, 215, 226, 246, 250, 318

Islamization, 160, 192, 349

Islamoscale, 252, 253, 255

Ismaili, 190

Ismailism, 191

Isnad, 330

Israel, 105, 127, 130, 160, 165, 167, 174, 177, 183, 189, 190, 213, 245, 246, 285, 287

Israelites, 104

Jahiliyyah, 12, 13, 14, 15, 16, 20, 21, 247, 352

Jahiliyyahh, 330

Jesus, 9, 10, 14, 17, 18, 21, 33, 34, 35, 36, 37, 38, 39, 40, 43, 50, 51, 56, 57, 60, 65, 66, 67, 76, 77, 93, 101, 102, 103, 104, 105, 108, 109, 112, 114, 115, 116, 135, 136, 137, 138, 139, 140, 151, 152, 155, 156, 157, 159, 162, 163, 164, 165, 166, 167, 168, 169, 170, 172, 174, 175, 176, 177, 178, 179, 180, 181, 182, 183, 189, 197, 198, 218, 219, 220, 231, 236, 239, 240, 247, 254, 257, 265, 266, 268, 270, 271, 272, 273, 274, 275, 276, 277, 278, 279, 281, 285, 286, 287, 288, 289, 290, 291, 293, 300, 301, 303, 305, 306, 307, 308, 313, 317, 318, 319, 320, 321, 322, 323, 326, 327, 328, 329, 330, 332, 351, 354, 357

Jewish, 8, 16, 17, 18, 19, 24, 25, 30, 33, 34, 35, 40, 46, 47, 48, 49, 50, 52, 55, 56, 57, 58, 65, 71, 84, 85, 89, 100, 104, 108, 112, 165, 196, 265, 281, 329, 330

Jewish-Christian, 19, 35

Jewish-Christianity, 18

Jibra'il, 330

jihad, 89, 137, 149, 155, 170, 171, 172, 192, 201, 202, 203, 204, 205, 206, 207, 208, 209, 210, 211, 212, 213, 214, 215, 216, 217, 218, 220, 226, 232, 234, 235, 237, 239, 241, 244, 247, 248, 251, 258, 260, 261, 315, 316, 317, 318, 323, 332

jihād, 202

jihadi, 244

jihadis, 257

jihadism, 246
Jihadists, 215
jinn, 107
jizya, 93, 120, 122, 130, 247, 253, 329
Jizyah, 54, 163, 165, 176, 212, 331
Judaism, 17, 18, 33, 57, 58, 60, 89, 94, 136, 169, 191, 195, 324, 351
Judeo-Christian, 57
Jurisprudance, 70
Ka'aba, 13, 14, 17, 20, 99, 331
Kaaba, 22, 24, 26
Kaaba shrine, 22
kafir, 146, 166, 252, 259
Kalam, 331, 357
Kalām, 70
Kathir, 211, 212
Khadija, 23
Khaldun, 29, 84, 159, 206, 352
Khalifa, 329
Kharajite, 53, 186
Kharajites, 195
Kharijite, 331, 332
Koran, 40, 47, 48, 50, 58, 61, 64, 137, 172, 352, 353
Kufic, 283
Lectionary, 333
legalism, 18, 34, 156, 188
legalistic, 188, 309
Liturgical, 141, 353
liturgy, 8, 47
love, 7, 10, 67, 74, 75, 76, 92, 102, 109, 111, 113, 136, 137, 138, 139, 151, 156, 157, 161, 180, 181, 182, 188, 189, 197, 198, 216, 220, 233, 234, 235, 236, 248, 260, 261, 262, 263, 266, 269, 270, 271, 288, 305, 306, 309, 311, 313, 314, 315, 319, 320, 321, 323, 324, 325, 326, 327
Luxemberg, 171, 172

Luxenberg, 40, 353
madhab, 185
Madhabs, 185, 187
Madhi, 163
Madrassa, 331
maghazi, 25
Mahdi, 158, 162, 163, 164, 165, 166, 167, 168, 172, 173, 174, 175, 176, 177, 178, 182, 187, 188, 189, 191, 192, 194, 247, 331, 352
Mahmed, 35
maiden, 171, 172
maidens, 164, 169, 170, 171
Makkah, 24
Mary, 40, 51, 57, 102, 108, 159, 169, 276, 277, 285, 286, 288, 289, 351
Masih, 306
Masjid, 24, 331
massacred, 252
massacres, 29, 128, 240
Mecca, 8, 16, 17, 22, 24, 25, 26, 41, 61, 62, 63, 64, 80, 98, 99, 163, 165, 170, 208, 209, 316, 329, 330, 331, 333, 357
Meccans, 25, 26, 29, 209
Medina, 17, 24, 25, 26, 29, 30, 35, 39, 44, 61, 63, 64, 175, 208, 209, 211, 316, 328, 330, 331, 332, 334, 349, 357
Medinan, 202, 328, 332
Melkites, 195
migrants, 311, 332
migration, 55, 126, 175, 310
migrations, 158
migratory, 55
Mohammad, 41, 224, 349
Mohammed, 58, 80, 81, 83, 85, 88, 331, 354, 355
monk, 22, 35, 123
monks, 35, 238
Monophysites, 18, 58, 195, 332
Monophysitism, 17, 333

monotheism, 12, 18, 19, 33, 35, 36, 55, 57, 58, 59, 60, 71, 97, 98, 101, 330, 332
monotheistic, 16, 18, 46, 48, 57, 58, 59, 60, 268, 334
monotheists, 284, 329
Mormonism, 297
Mormons, 297
mosque, 46, 69, 98, 131, 134, 183, 225, 261, 297, 300, 331
mosques, 63, 83, 90, 99, 126, 160, 259, 320
mu'minun, 56
Mu'tazilite, 69
Mu'tazilites, 69, 87, 111, 195, 332
Muawiya, 80
Muawiyah, 53, 55, 59, 186, 196
Muhajirun, 32, 332
Muhammad, 8, 12, 13, 14, 15, 16, 17, 18, 19, 20, 22, 23, 24, 25, 26, 27, 28, 29, 30, 31, 32, 33, 34, 35, 36, 37, 38, 39, 40, 41, 42, 43, 44, 45, 46, 48, 49, 51, 52, 53, 54, 55, 56, 57, 58, 59, 60, 61, 63, 64, 65, 66, 68, 70, 79, 80, 82, 83, 86, 87, 93, 97, 98, 99,103, 104, 105, 107, 108, 109, 110, 111, 113, 116, 120, 121, 122, 137, 144, 148, 149, 155, 158, 159, 162, 163, 164, 165, 166, 167, 170, 175, 183, 184, 185, 186, 187, 188, 189, 190, 191, 194, 196, 197, 199, 202, 203, 204, 205, 206, 207, 208, 209, 210, 211, 217, 218, 219, 220, 228, 235, 240, 243, 244, 246, 248, 249, 253, 254, 255, 256, 257, 259, 261, 262, 274, 276, 277, 278, 282, 283, 286, 294, 299, 300, 304, 315, 316, 318, 329, 330, 331, 332, 333, 349, 350, 352, 356, 357
Muhammed, 312
Mujahadin, 332

mujahid, 332
mujahideen, 251
mujahidin, 212
Murji'ites, 68, 78, 332
Muslim, 8, 9, 10, 12, 13, 14, 15, 16, 18, 19, 20, 21, 22, 25, 27, 28, 29, 30, 31, 32, 33, 34, 37, 38, 40, 41, 44, 46, 47, 50, 51, 52, 53, 55, 56, 59, 60, 61, 65, 66, 67, 68, 69, 70, 71, 72, 73, 75, 76, 77, 78, 80, 81, 82, 83, 84, 85, 86, 87, 88, 89, 90, 91, 92, 93, 94, 95, 97, 98, 99, 100, 101, 102, 103, 105, 107, 109, 110, 111, 112, 113, 114, 115, 116, 117, 118, 119, 120, 122, 123, 124, 125, 126, 127, 128, 130, 131, 132, 133, 134, 135, 136, 137, 140, 141, 142, 143, 144, 147, 150, 152, 153, 154, 156, 157, 158, 159, 160, 161, 162, 164, 165, 166, 167, 168, 169, 170, 172, 173, 174, 175, 176, 177, 178, 179, 180, 182, 183, 184, 187, 188, 189, 190, 191, 192, 193, 194, 195, 196, 197, 198, 199, 202, 203, 204, 205, 206, 207, 208, 210, 211, 212, 214, 215, 216, 217, 218, 219, 220, 221, 222, 223, 224, 225, 226, 227, 228, 229, 232, 234, 235, 236, 237, 238, 239, 241, 242, 243, 244, 245, 247, 248, 250, 251, 252, 253, 255, 256, 258, 261, 262, 265, 267, 269, 270, 271, 272, 274, 275, 276, 281, 282, 283, 285, 289, 292, 293, 294, 295, 296, 297, 298, 299, 300, 301, 302, 303, 304, 305, 306, 307, 309, 310, 311, 313, 314, 315, 316, 318, 319, 320, 321, 322, 323, 325, 326, 327, 328, 329, 330, 331, 332,

333, 334, 351, 353, 354, 355, 356, 357
Muslims, 7, 8, 9, 10, 12, 14, 15, 16, 18, 19, 20, 21, 22, 24, 25, 26, 27, 28, 31, 32, 34, 35, 36, 37, 38, 40, 41, 42, 43, 44, 50, 51, 52, 53, 54, 55, 56, 58, 66, 68, 70, 71, 72, 73, 74, 75, 76, 77, 78, 80, 81, 83, 84, 85, 87, 88, 89, 90, 91, 92, 93, 94, 95, 99, 100, 101, 102, 103, 105, 106, 107, 108, 109, 110, 111, 112, 113, 114, 115, 116, 117, 118, 119, 120, 121, 122, 123, 124, 125, 126, 127, 129, 130, 131, 132, 134, 135, 136, 137, 140, 141, 142, 143, 144, 145, 146, 147, 148, 149, 150, 152, 153, 154, 155, 156, 157, 158, 159, 160, 161, 162, 163, 164, 165, 166, 167, 168, 169, 170, 171, 172, 173, 176, 177, 178, 179, 181, 182, 183, 184, 185, 186, 187, 188, 189, 190, 191, 192, 193, 194, 195, 197, 198, 199, 201, 202, 203, 204, 205, 206, 207, 208, 209, 210, 211, 212, 213, 214, 215, 216, 217, 220, 221, 222, 223, 225, 226, 227, 228, 229, 230, 232, 234, 235, 237, 238, 239, 240, 241, 242, 243, 244, 245, 246, 247, 248, 249, 251, 252, 253, 254, 255, 257, 258, 259, 260, 261, 262, 263, 264, 265, 266, 267, 268, 269, 270, 271, 272, 273, 274, 275, 276, 277, 278, 279, 281, 282, 283, 285, 286, 288, 289, 290, 291, 292, 293, 294, 295, 296, 297, 298, 299, 300, 301, 302, 303, 304, 305, 306, 307, 308, 309, 310, 311, 312, 313, 314, 315, 316, 317, 318, 319, 320, 321, 322, 323, 325, 329, 332, 350, 351, 352, 353, 354, 355, 357
myths, 237
Nabataean, 63, 64
Nabataeans, 63, 64, 65
Nazoreans, 17, 57
neo-Platonic, 190
Neo-Platonism, 191
Neo-Revisionist, 44, 46
Nestorian, 22, 83
Nestorianism, 17
Nestorians, 18, 58, 195, 333
nonbelievers, 204
non-believers, 24, 66, 117, 128, 162, 176, 179, 203
non-believers, 207
non-believers, 209
non-believers, 210
non-believers, 234
non-believers, 248
non-believers, 259
non-believers, 329
non-believers, 329
non-Christian, 299
non-Muslim, 22, 55, 59, 68, 91, 118, 127, 133, 140, 158, 176, 191, 202, 251, 298
non-Muslims, 15, 28, 34, 37, 40, 52, 66, 90, 92, 93, 116, 120, 122, 124, 131, 132, 133, 136, 161, 162, 163, 165, 179, 188, 190, 204, 206, 208, 211, 216, 217, 227, 238, 242, 245, 247, 251, 252, 259, 262, 292, 298, 299, 316, 317
numismatic, 46
numismatics, 32, 33
obedience, 70, 72, 74, 76, 112, 148, 156, 234, 302
obedient, 134, 164
obey, 51, 241
obeyed, 141
obeying, 184, 216, 306

obligation, 73, 112, 159, 171, 206, 247, 258
obligations, 97, 98, 99, 147, 168, 215
obligatory, 14, 98, 99, 118, 248, 258
oral, 28, 31, 41, 43, 45, 47, 282
orally, 31, 32, 330
origin, 8, 32, 34, 36, 42, 44, 46, 49, 50, 52, 56, 60, 61, 64, 116, 141, 157, 199
orthodox, 8, 17, 18, 33, 47, 57, 80, 87, 185, 187, 191, 195, 198, 203, 207, 212, 286
orthodoxy, 74, 78, 92, 192, 196, 275
Ottoman, 79, 80, 81, 354
pact, 123
pact-umar, 123
pagan, 12, 13, 14, 15, 16, 17, 18, 19, 20, 55, 58
paganism, 12, 17, 18, 23, 169
pagans, 14, 66, 190, 232
Palestine, 56, 64, 128, 130, 203, 224, 228, 231, 310
papyri, 280
papyrus, 88, 106
parchment, 49, 88, 107
parchments, 49
PBUH, 183, 206, 333
peace, 24, 26, 27, 53, 79, 91, 92, 93, 120, 125, 127, 128, 129, 130, 131, 139, 154, 160, 165, 166, 167, 174, 179, 181, 188, 198, 201, 205, 209, 211, 214, 215, 216, 217, 218, 219, 220, 235, 239, 242, 243, 250, 252, 254, 260, 261, 262, 263, 289, 308, 313, 314, 315, 318, 319, 322, 325, 328, 333
peaceful, 26, 90, 92, 201, 209, 210, 211, 213, 217, 218, 221, 226, 227, 237, 240, 242, 292, 313, 314, 315, 316, 322

penalties, 300
penalty, 14, 124, 151, 152, 157, 300
Petra, 8, 17, 61, 62, 63, 64
pilgrim, 99, 234
pilgrimage, 14, 26, 32, 99, 165, 329
pilgrimages, 118, 186, 229, 238, 239
pilgrims, 227, 228, 229
pillage, 231
pillaging, 225
polemic, 292, 314, 322
polemical, 313, 323
polemicists, 129, 249
politically, 56, 71, 116, 120, 140, 160, 202, 248
polytheism, 123, 145
polytheists, 248, 256, 258
prayer, 10, 40, 53, 63, 66, 76, 93, 98, 115, 118, 123, 125, 131, 132, 148, 166, 170, 206, 211, 302, 303, 308, 320, 326, 328, 333
predestination, 69, 71, 78, 111
prophecies, 38, 104, 165, 326
prophecy, 38, 104, 105, 148, 161, 167, 188, 257
prophesied, 247
prophesies, 113
prophet, 18, 19, 22, 23, 25, 26, 29, 30, 31, 33, 34, 35, 37, 39, 43, 44, 52, 53, 54, 56, 58, 59, 63, 79, 97, 98, 101, 103, 104, 113, 116, 124, 137, 144, 149, 162, 165, 166, 175, 179, 182, 183, 184, 188, 189, 190, 191, 192, 212, 247, 249, 277, 304, 332, 333, 334
prophets, 14, 44, 59, 103, 105, 113, 148, 163, 165, 169, 179, 180, 248, 269, 282, 333
Qadarites, 195, 333
Qaeda, 196, 215, 244, 328

Qaradawi, 316
Qibla, 211
Qiblah, 333
Qur'an, 8, 12, 14, 18, 20, 21, 23, 28, 29, 31, 33, 35, 36, 37, 38, 39, 40, 41, 42, 43, 44, 45, 46, 47, 48, 49, 50, 51, 53, 54, 61, 62, 63, 64, 66, 67, 69, 70, 71, 72, 73, 75, 77, 78, 85, 86, 87, 89, 93, 94, 97, 98, 99, 100, 103, 104, 105, 107, 108, 111, 112, 113, 115, 116, 118, 121, 122, 134, 135, 137, 138, 140, 141, 143, 144, 145, 146, 147, 148, 149, 152, 157, 158, 161, 162, 164, 165, 168, 171, 172, 175, 179, 181, 183, 184, 185, 186, 188, 189, 191, 192, 195, 197, 199, 202, 204, 205, 206, 207, 208, 209, 210, 211, 212, 213, 214, 217, 218, 219, 220, 234, 243, 244, 246, 247, 249, 251, 252, 253, 254, 255, 256, 257, 259, 260, 261, 262, 267, 269, 272, 273, 276, 278, 279, 281, 282, 283, 285, 286, 287, 288, 289, 290, 291, 299, 300, 303, 307, 312, 315, 316, 318, 324, 326, 328, 329, 330, 331, 332, 333, 334, 351, 355
Qur'ān, 31
Qur'anic, 17, 45, 47, 49, 50, 63, 64, 99, 111, 133, 141, 187, 188, 203, 207, 212, 220, 246, 259, 269, 305, 351, 356
Quran, 109, 116, 159, 248, 258, 285
Quranic, 45, 46, 49, 303, 357
Quraysh, 22, 25, 26, 256
Qurayza, 26, 30, 256, 349, 352
Qureshi, 7, 116, 117, 140, 217, 218, 243, 261, 262, 265, 269, 273, 274, 307, 314, 317, 322, 323, 326, 327, 354
Quryana, 40, 333
Qutb, 15, 225, 251, 354
rabbi, 265
Rabbinic, 58
racial, 193, 296
racism, 296
radical, 9, 72, 125, 157, 172, 188, 214, 217, 220, 226, 238, 242, 252, 253, 258, 260, 261, 262, 303, 317, 319
radicalism, 9, 251
radicalization, 215
radically, 219, 259, 266
radicals, 125, 215
Ramadan, 99, 133, 145, 320, 333
rape, 119, 130, 133, 250
raped, 125
Rashidun, 80, 184, 185, 333
Rasul, 28, 38, 98, 333
reading, 99, 292, 302, 303, 312
readings, 40, 123, 283
recite, 23, 41
Reconquista, 89
reformation, 217, 218, 243
reformers, 207, 221, 222
relations, 26, 102, 184, 222, 225, 227, 276, 277, 286, 288
relationship, 37, 74, 75, 77, 92, 102, 111, 113, 142, 143, 151, 177, 187, 188, 198, 216, 217, 218, 219, 246, 259, 270, 278, 285, 287, 288, 292, 314, 320, 321, 323, 326, 327, 331
relationships, 10, 40, 136, 198, 209, 246, 262, 286, 288, 300, 312, 313, 319, 320, 322, 323
resurrected, 107, 109, 113, 163, 166, 273, 289, 291
resurrection, 57, 74, 86, 109, 148, 161, 162, 169, 180, 270, 272, 273, 289, 290, 291, 324, 326
revelation, 14, 20, 23, 24, 25, 36, 41, 42, 43, 44, 58, 60, 85, 86,

94, 99, 100, 103, 105, 107, 109, 122, 168, 179, 189, 254, 269, 278, 281, 282, 283, 304, 328
revelations, 12, 14, 20, 41, 45, 189, 190, 209, 210, 211, 276, 281, 284, 328
revenge, 231
revisionism, 223
revisionist, 45, 55, 56, 59, 67, 70, 71, 83, 84, 87, 116, 207, 208, 210, 212, 213
reward, 53, 55, 76, 103, 110, 147, 152, 156, 161, 169, 171, 172, 212, 237
rewarded, 109, 161, 171
rewards, 164, 320
Ridda, 52
righteous, 109, 110, 112, 143, 146, 148, 151, 152, 169, 240
righteousness, 76, 141, 154, 156, 189, 216, 227
ritual, 99, 100, 118, 189, 333
rituals, 26, 97, 99, 152, 153
Rock, 32, 33, 47, 54
Ryland, 283
sack, 222, 226
sacked, 81, 237
sacking, 230
Saladin, 225, 229
Salafi, 246
Salafism, 191
Salafist, 185, 246
Salam, 333
Salat, 98, 333
salvation, 50, 66, 67, 69, 75, 76, 108, 110, 111, 112, 113, 114, 117, 141, 142, 144, 146, 147, 148, 149, 150, 151, 152, 153, 154, 155, 156, 157, 177, 181, 196, 197, 232, 234, 261, 282, 296, 304, 307, 322
Samarquand, 283
Sana'a, 46, 61
Sawm, 99, 333

scale, 89, 181, 253, 254, 316
scales, 110, 147
scribe, 42, 279, 280
scribes, 27, 30, 41, 42, 43, 62, 280
scriptural, 20, 276
Scripture, iii, 42, 51, 137, 197, 210, 281, 282, 284, 302, 307, 308, 326
scriptures, 17, 40, 41, 42, 43, 44, 46, 50, 51, 60, 77, 100, 105, 108, 112, 189, 267, 269, 282
seven, 14, 99, 144, 145, 164, 165, 171, 174, 244, 297, 301
Seveners, 187, 190
Shahada, 32, 54, 98, 211, 299, 333
**Shahadah**, 98
shahid, 170
shariah, 117, 175
Shi'ah, 185
Shi'i, 195, 331
Shi'ism, 185, 195
Shi'ite, 194
Shi'ites, 186, 187
Shiites, 194, 331
Shirk, 144, 145, 277, 333
Sira, 27, 31, 36, 40, 121, 333
Sirat, 28, 38, 47, 163, 166
slaughter, 211, 240
slaughtering, 225
slave, 15, 112, 113, 119, 135, 139, 296
slavery, 14, 30, 119, 135
slaves, 14, 55, 90, 119, 135, 242, 256
Sufi, 29, 85, 187, 198, 199
Sufis, 187, 198
Sufism, 187, 191, 353
Suleyman, 81
Sunna, 333
sunnah, 116, 183, 184, 185, 186, 192, 251

Sunni, 53, 69, 80, 130, 162, 164, 167, 179, 184, 185, 186, 187, 188, 190, 191, 192, 194, 195, 196, 198, 199, 246, 249, 328, 350
Sunnis, 53, 162, 167, 185, 186, 194
Sunni-Shi'a, 195, 350
Sunni-Shia, 194, 195, 196, 199
Sura, 51, 99, 102, 118, 134, 137, 138, 139, 144, 203, 209, 210, 211, 212, 216, 253, 254, 267, 276, 281, 282, 334
Surah, 42, 43, 44, 48, 54, 66, 75, 76, 101, 104, 156, 159, 183, 251, 252, 273, 276, 277, 278, 282, 283, 285, 286, 289, 290, 291, 328, 332, 334
Surahs, 40, 44, 111, 331, 332, 334
Suras, 51, 144, 212
syncretism, 190, 191
syncretistic, 190
Tabari, 25, 53, 86, 173, 256
Tafsir, 40, 47, 145, 212, 334
Taliban, 196
Taqiyya, 179
taqiyyah, 181
Taurat, 105, 334
Tauret, 51, 281
Tawheed, 269
Tawhid, 101, 244, 270, 274, 334
Taymiyah, 146
Taymiyya, 190, 191, 203
terror, 128, 171, 225, 255, 256, 261, 311
terrorism, 73, 179, 193, 205, 207, 214, 215, 225, 240, 242, 243, 257, 259, 294, 313, 315, 317, 318
terrorist, 179, 191, 204, 224, 225, 243, 244, 246, 252, 263, 311, 313, 317, 318

terrorists, 171, 193, 207, 208, 213, 243, 245, 252, 257, 259, 260, 298, 299, 313
**Textual Criticism**, ii, iii
theocracy, 88, 130, 236, 261, 318
theocratic, 131, 137, 261
totalitarian, 85
tradition, 53, 56, 83, 98, 99, 118, 144, 145, 184, 217, 243, 267, 282
traditional, 8, 9, 12, 13, 15, 16, 17, 18, 19, 21, 22, 27, 28, 30, 31, 33, 34, 36, 37, 40, 41, 43, 44, 46, 47, 48, 49, 52, 53, 55, 56, 60, 61, 65, 67, 68, 79, 81, 87, 91, 99, 100, 116, 143, 163, 167, 171, 187, 192, 196, 202, 212, 246, 283, 303, 329, 330, 331
Traditionalist, 69
traditionalists, 69, 78, 111, 333
traditions, 22, 29, 36, 47, 48, 91, 118, 161, 164, 166, 167, 168, 169, 170, 171, 183, 184, 235, 262, 266, 316, 329, 333
Trinitarian, 268, 287, 328, 354
Trinity, 33, 38, 57, 97, 101, 102, 103, 104, 113, 114, 177, 261, 266, 270, 272, 273, 274, 276, 278, 282, 285, 286, 287, 288, 296, 312, 314, 324, 352
truth, 7, 8, 9, 10, 12, 14, 15, 20, 37, 40, 42, 48, 50, 51, 54, 61, 65, 66, 76, 92, 105, 115, 137, 159, 180, 181, 198, 209, 210, 217, 236, 240, 253, 258, 261, 262, 263, 285, 292, 303, 304, 305, 308, 311, 313, 314, 315, 317, 319, 324, 325, 326, 327
twelfth, 187, 224
Twelver, 167, 190, 195
Twelvers, 167, 187
tyranny, 167, 207
Umar, 41, 43, 52, 53, 123, 184, 333

Umayyad, 53, 58, 80, 186
*Umayyads*, 80, 349
Umma, 100, 183, 197
ummah, 27, 52
Uthman, 41, 42, 43, 45, 53, 60, 138, 184, 186, 283, 333
vengeance, 232
version, 19, 28, 29, 32, 41, 42, 43, 44, 45, 46, 49, 57, 60, 82, 100, 106, 143, 212, 226, 235, 267
versions, 32, 60, 163
violence, 73, 90, 127, 203, 205, 207, 211, 212, 213, 214, 215, 216, 218, 226, 231, 233, 235, 244, 252, 257, 262, 299, 309, 317
violent, 89, 90, 122, 203, 205, 207, 210, 211, 213, 218, 220, 246, 248, 251, 257, 259, 260, 262, 315, 316, 332
violently, 125, 154, 314
virgin, 38, 171, 172, 329, 332
virgins, 170, 171, 172
visions, 24, 170, 177, 294, 303, 305, 306, 307, 308
Wahab, 22
Wahabbism, 191

Wahhabi, 185, 194
Wahhabis, 191
Wahhabism, 191, 196, 246
Wahhbism, 191
Waraqah, 23
warfare, 13, 68, 83, 92, 128, 203, 206, 207, 208, 211, 214, 219, 233, 235, 236, 302, 316, 332
warrior, 25, 38, 107, 204, 207, 316
warriors, 43, 126, 201, 225, 230, 234, 240
wars, 52, 80, 163, 188, 194, 203, 224, 226, 227, 234, 319
war-torn, 27
worldview, 20, 73, 74, 84, 114, 115, 116, 117, 130, 155, 261, 303, 317
worldviews, 21, 297
Yahweh, 102, 268, 269, 270, 272, 273, 274, 287
Yathrib, 24, 330
zakat, 53, 66, 93, 99, 206, 211
Zakat, 99, 145, 334
ZamZam, 99
Zoroaster, 334
Zoroastrian, 46, 86, 90, 169, 334
Zoroastrianism, 18, 162, 169, 334

# Bibliography

Adang, Camilla, Maribel Fierro and Savine Schmidtke. *Ibn Hazm of Cordoba: The Life and Works of a Controversial Thinker.* Brill, 2013.

Al-Araby, Abdullah. *The Islamization of America: The Islamic Strategy and the Christian Response.* Booklocker.com, 2003.

Ali Dashti, *Twenty Three Years: A Study of the Prophetic Career of Mohammad.* New York: Routledge, 2008.

Al-Dawoody, Ahmed. *The Islamic Law of War: Justifications and Regulations.* Palgrave: Macmillan, 2011.

al-Faruqi, Isma'il. *Islam.* Nils: Argus Communications, 1984.

Andrea, Alfred and Andrew Holt. *The Seven Myths of the Crusades.* Indianapolis, Indiana: Hackett Publishing Co., 2015.

Arafat, W.N., *New Light on the Story of Banu Qurayza and the Jews of Medina.* Journal of the Royal Asiatic Society of Great Britain and Ireland, 1976.

Armstrong, Karen. *Islam: A Short History.* New York: Random House, 2002.

Aslan, Reza. *No God but God: The Origins, Evolution, and Future of Islam.* New York: Random House, 2006.

Austen, Ralph. African Economic History. Currey and Heinemann, 1987.

Barakat, Ahmad. *Muhammad and the Jews.* New Delhi: Vikas Publishing House, 1979.

Beck, Glenn. *It IS About Islam.* Simon and Schuster, 2015.

Berg, Herbert. *Routledge Handbook on Early Islam.* New York: Routledge, 2018.

Berkey, Jonathan. *The Formation of Islam: Religion and Society in the Near East, 600–1800.* Cambridge: Cambridge University Press, 2003.

Blankinship, Khalid Yahya. *The End of the Jihad State, the Reign of Hisham Ibn 'Abd-al Malik and the collapse of the Umayyads.* State University of New York Press, 1994.

Boa, Ken. *I'm Glad You Asked: In-Depth Answers to Difficult Questions about Christianity.* David C. Cook, 1995.

Bogle, Emory. *Islam: Origin and Belief.* Austin, University of Texas, 1998.

Bostom, Andrew. *The Legacy of Jihad: Islamic Holy War and the Fate of Non-Muslims.* New York: Prometheus, 2005.

Braswell, George. *Islam: Its Prophet, Peoples, Politics and Power.* Broadman & Holman, 1996.

Bufano, Michael. *A Reconsideration of the Sunni-Shi'a Divide in Early Islam.* Clemson University, 2008.

Caner, Ergun and Emir. *Unveiling Islam.* Grand Rapids: Kregel, 2002.

Caner, Ergun and Emir Caner. *Christian Jihad.* Grand Rapids: Kregel, 2004.

Carimokam, Sahaja. *Muhammad and the People of the Book.* Xlibris, 2010.

Catherwood, Christopher. Christians, *Muslims and Islamic Rage.* Grand Rapids: Zondervan, 2003.

Chatrath, Nick. *Reaching Muslims: A One-Step Guide for Christians.* Oxford: Monarch Books, 2011.

Cook, David. *Understanding Jihad.* University of California Press, 2005.

Crone, Patricia. *Slaves On Horses: The Evolution of the Islamic Polity.* Cambridge: Cambridge University Press, 1980.

Crone, Patricia, and Michael Cook. *Hagarism; The Making of the Islamic World.* Cambridge University Press, 1977.

Donner, Fred. *Muhammad and the Believers: At the Origins of Islam.* Cambridge, MA: Harvard University Press, 2010.

Donner, Fred. *Narratives of Islamic Origins: The Beginnings of Islamic Historical Writing.* New Jersey: The Darwin Press, 1998.

Durant, Will. *The Story of Civilization,* vol. 4, "The Age of Faith." New York: Simon and Schuster, 1950.

Durie, Mark. *The Third Choice: Islam, Dhimmitude and Freedom,* Deror Books, 2010.

Esposito, John. *Islam: The Straight Path*, 3rd. ed. Oxford: Oxford University Press, 1998.

Fernandez-Morera, Dario. *The Myth of the Andalusian Paradise: Muslims, Christians, and Jews under Islamic Rule in Medieval Spain.* Wilmington, Delaware: ISI Books, 2016.

Fregosi, Paul. *Jihad in the West: Muslim Conquests from the 7th to the 21st Centuries.* New York: Prometheus, 1998.

Gabriel, Mark. *Islam and Terrorism.* Lake Mary, FL: Frontline, 2002.

Garrison, David. *A Wind in the House of Islam: How God is drawing Muslims around the world to faith in Jesus Christ* (Wigtake, 2014).

Gauss, James. *Islam & Christianity: A Revealing Contrast.* Alachua, FL: Bridge-Logos, 2009.

Geisler, Norman, and Abdul Saleeb. *Answering Islam: The Crescent in Light of the Cross.* Grand Rapids, MI: Baker Books, 2002.

Ghazanfar, S.M. *Medieval Islamic Economic Thought: Filling the Great Gap in European Economics.* London: Routledge Curzon, 2003.

Gibbon, Edward. *The History of the Decline and Fall of the Roman Empire.* New York: Harcourt, Brace, 1960.

Gibson, Dan. *Qur'anic Geography: A Survey and Evaluation of the Geographical References in the Qur'an with Suggested Solutions for Various Problems and Issues.* Canada: Independent Scholars Press, 2011.

Gilchrist, John. *Jam' Al-Qur'an -- The Codification of the Qur'an Text: A Comprehensive Study of the Original Collection of the Qur'an Text and the Early Surviving Qur'an Manuscripts.* Mondeor, South Africa: Muslim Evangelism Resource Center of Southern Africa, 1989.

Gilliot, Claude. "Reconsidering the Authorship of the Qur'an: Is the Qur'an Partly the Fruit of a Progressive and Collective Work?" in *Towards a New Reading of the Qur'an.* Gabriel Said Reynolds, ed. Indiana: Notre Dame, 2005.

Glueck, Nelson. *Rivers in the Desert.* New York: Farrar, Strous and Cudahy, 1959.

Goldenberg, David, *The Curse of Ham, Race and Slavery in Early Judaism, Christianity, and Islam.* Princeton University Press, 2005.

Goldman, David. *How Civilizations Die and Why Islam is Dying Too.* Regnery, 2011.

Goldschmidt, Arthur. *A Concise History of the Middle East,* 11th ed. Boulder, CO: Westview Press, 2016.

Greear, J. D. *Breaking the Islam Code.* Harvest House, 2010.

Grudem, Wayne. *Bible Doctrine: Essential Teachings of the Christian Faith.* Zondervan, 1999.

Hanapi, Mohd Shukri. "From Jahiliyyah to Islamic Worldview: In a Search of an Islamic Educational Philosophy," International Journal of Humanities and Social Science, Vol. 3 No. 2 (January, 2013) 214-15.

Hillenbrand, Carole. *The Crusades: Islamic Perspectives.* Edinburgh: Edinburgh University Press, 1999.

Holland, Tom. *In the Shadow of the Sword: The Birth of Islam and the Rise of the Global Arab Empire.* New York: Doubleday, 2013.

Hoyland, Robert. *Seeing Islam as Others Saw It.* Princeton, NJ: Darwin Press, 1997.

Ibn Hisham 1/151-155; Rahmat-ul-lil'alameen 2/89, 90.

ibn Izzat, Muhammad and Muhammad Arif, *Al Mahdi and the End of Times.* Dar Al Taqwa Ltd., 1997.

Ibn Khaldun, *The Muqaddimah*, trans. by Franz Rosenthal. New York: Pantheon Books Inc., 1958.

Ibn Ishaq, Muhammad. *The Life of Muhammad*, ed. Alfred Guillaume. Karachi: Oxford University Press, 1955.

Ibn Warraq, ed. *The Quest for the Historical Muhammad.* NY: Prometheus Books, 2000.

Ibn Warraq, ed. *What the Koran Really Says: Language, Text, and Commentary.* New York: Prometheus Books, 2002.

Ibrahim, Raymond. *Crucified Again: Exposing Islam's New War on Christians.* D.C.: Regnery, 2013.

Janosik, Daniel. *John of Damascus, First Apologist to the Muslims: The Trinity and Christian Apologetics in the Early Islamic Period.* Eugene, Oregon: Pickwick Publications, 2016.

Janosik, Daniel. "The Real Story Behind the Massacre of the Banu Qurayza." CSIOF Occasional Papers, No. 3, 2012, 97-114.

Janosik, Daniel. "Is Islam a Religion of Peace," Christian Post, Feb. 3, 2015.

Janosik, Daniel. "Déjà vu All Over Again: The Christian Church's response to the First Islamic Invasion, and how it compares to the Church's response to Islam today," ETS Conference, San Diego, 2014.

Johns, Jeremy. "Archaeology and the History of Early Islam: The First Seventy Years." *Journal of the Economic and Social History of the Orient*, Vol. 46, 4, 2003, 411–36.

Kaltner, John. *Islam: What Non-Muslims Should Know*, Minneapolis: Fortress, 2003.

Karkkainen, Veli-Matti. *One with God: Salvation as a Deification and Justification*. Minnesota: Liturgical Press, 2004.

Kateregga, Badru and David Shenk, *Islam and Christianity: A Muslim and a Christian in Dialogue*. Herald Press, 2011.

Kotter, Bonifatius. *Die Schriften Des Johannes Von Damaskos*, II. NY: Walter De Gruyter, 1981.

Lester, Toby. "What Is the Koran?" Chap. in *What the Koran Really Says: Language, Text, and Commentary*. 107-128. New York: Prometheus Books, 2002.

Lewis, Bernard. *The Crisis of Islam: Holy War and Unholy Terror*. New York: Random House, 2004.

Lewis, Bernard. *From Babel to Dragomans: Interpreting the Middle East*. Oxford: Oxford University Press, 2004.

Lewis, Bernard. *What Went Wrong? Western Impact and Middle Eastern Response*. Oxford: Oxford University Press, 2002.

Lewis, Bernard. *Islam and the West*. New York: Oxford University Press, 1993.

Lewis, C. S. *Mere Christianity*. Harper One, 2015.

Lewis, David Levering. *God's Crucible: Islam and the Making of Europe, 570-1215*. New York: W.W. Norton, 2008.

Lings, Martin. *What is Sufism?* Cambridge: The Islamic Texts Society, 1993.

Luxenberg, Christoph. *The Syro-Aramaic Reading of the Koran: A Contribution to the Decoding of the Language of the Koran*. Berlin: Verlag Hans Schiler, 2007.

Maalouf, Amin. *The Crusades through Arab Eyes*, trans. John Rothschild. New York: Schocken Books, 1984.

Margoliuth, D.S. *Encyclopedia of Religion and Ethics*, volume 8, Ed. James Hastings. Edinburgh: T&T Clark, 1915.

Maududi, Abul A'la. *Towards Understanding Islam* (U.K.I.M Dawah Centre).

Macdonald, Duncan B. *Development of Muslim Theology, Jurisprudence and Constitutional Theory.* New York: Charles Scribner, 1903.

Madden, Thomas. *The Concise History of the Crusades*, Third edition. New York: Rowman & Littlefield, 2014.

Madearis, Carl. *Muslims, Christians, and Jesus: Gaining Understanding and Building* Relationships. Minneapolis: Bethany House, 2008.

McDermott, Gerald and Harold Netland, *A Trinitarian Theology of Religions: An Evangelical Proposal.* Oxford University Press, 2014.

Moucarry, Chawkat. *Faith to Faith: Christianity and Islam in Dialogue.* Inter-Varsity Press, 2001).

Nevo, Yehuda, and Judith Koren. *Crossroads to Islam: The Origins of the Arab Religion and the Arab State.* NY: Prometheus Books, 2003.

Ohlig, Karl-Heinz and Gerd-R. Puin, eds. *The Hidden Origins of Islam: New Research into its Early History.* NY: Prometheus Books, 2010.

Ohlig, Karl-Heinz, ed. *Early Islam: A Critical Reconstruction Based on Contemporary Sources.* NY: Prometheus Books, 2013.

Pirenne, Henri. *Mohammed and Charlemagne.* New York: Meridian Books, 1957.

Pratt, Douglas. *The Challenge of Islam: Encounters in Interfaith Dialogue.* Burlington, VT: Ashgate, 2005.

Pratt, Douglas. *The Church and Other Faiths: The World Council of Churches, the Vatican, and Interreligious Dialogue.* Peter Lang, 2010.

Quataert, Donald. *The Ottoman Empire, 1700-1922.* Cambridge University Press, 2005.

Queller, Donald E. and Thomas F. Madden. *The Fourth Crusade: The Conquest of Constantinople*, 2nd ed. University of Pennsylvania Press, 1999.

Qureshi, Nabeel. *Seeking Allah, Finding Jesus: A Devout Muslim Encounters Christianity.* Grand Rapids, MI: Zondervan, 2014.

Qureshi, Nabeel. *Answering Jihad: A Better Way Forward.* Grand Rapids, MI: Zondervan, 2016.

Qureshi, Nabeel. *No God But One: Allah or Jesus?* Grand Rapids, MI: Zondervan, 2016.

Qutb, Sayyid. *Milestones.* Birmingham, UK: Maktabah, 2006.

Rahman, Fazlur. *Islam*, 2nd edition. Chicago: University of Chicago, 1979.

Reilly, Robert. *The Closing of the Muslim Mind: How Intellectual Suicide Created the Modern Islamist Crisis.* Wilmington, Delaware: ISI Books, 2010.

Reynolds, Gabriel Said. *The Emergence of Islam: Classical Traditions in Contemporary Perspective.* Minneapolis: Fortress Press, 2012.

Reynolds, Gabriel Said, editor. *The Qur'an in Its Historical Context.* New York: Routledge, 2008.

Rhodes, Ron. *Reasoning from the Scriptures with Muslims.* Eugene, Oregon: Harvest House, 2002).

Richardson, Joel. *The Islamic Antichrist: The Shocking Truth about the Real Nature of the Beast.* Los Angeles: WND Books, 2009.

Riddell, Peter, and Peter Cotterell, *Islam in Context: Past, Present, and Future.* Grand Rapids, MI: Baker, 2003.

Riley-Smith, Jonathan. The Crusades: A Short History. Athlone Press, 2001.

Steven Runciman. *A History of the Crusades*, vol. 3. Cambridge: Cambridge University Press, 1951-54.

Sardar, Ziauddin, and Zafar Abbas Malik. *Introducing Islam.* Cambridge: Icon Books, 2001.

Scott, Emmet. *Mohammed & Charlemagne Revisited: The History of a Controversy.* Nashville, TN: New English Review, 2012.

Sekulow, Jay. *Rise of ISIS: A Threat We Can't Ignore.* Howard Books, 2014.

Shahid, Samuel. *The Last Trumpet.* Xulon Press, 2005.

Shamsi-Basha, Karim. *Paul and Me: A Journey to and from the Damascus Road From Islam to Christ.* Birmingham, AL: Solid Ground Christian Books, 2013.

Shayesteh, Daniel. *The House I Left Behind: A journey from Islam to Christ.* Talesh Books, 2012.

Small, Keith. *Textual Criticism and Qur'an Manuscripts.* Lexington Books, 2012.

Smith, Colin. *Christians and Moors in Spain.* Warminster: Aris & Phillips, 1988.

Smith, Jay. Six Muslim Beliefs (Iman) and a Christian's Response: http://www.debate.org.uk/debate-topics/theological/6belief/

Solomon, Sam and Atif Debs, *Not the Same God: Is the Qur'anic Allah the Lord God of the Bible? Wilberforce Publications, 2016.*

Spencer, Robert. *Did Muhammad Exist? An Inquiry into Islam's Obscure Origins.* Wilmington, Delaware: ISI Books, 2012.

Spencer, Robert. *The Complete Infidel's Guide to ISIS.* Regnery Publishing, 2015.

Spencer, Robert. *The Truth About Muhammad: Founder of the World's Most Intolerant Religion.* D.C.: Regnery, 2006.

Spencer, Robert. *The Politically Incorrect Guide to Islam (and the Crusades).* D.C.: Regnery, 2005.

Spencer, Robert. *Islam Unveiled: Disturbing Questions About the World's Fastest-Growing Faith*, San Francisco: Encounter Books, 2002.

Spencer, Robert. *Muslim Persecution of Christians.* Sherman Oaks: David Horowitz Freedom Center, 2011.

Spencer, Robert. *Not Peace but a Sword: The Great Chasm Between Christianity and Islam.* San Diego, Catholic Answers, 2013.

Spencer, Robert. *Stealth Jihad: How Radical Islam is Subverting America without Guns or Bombs.* Washington, D.C.: Regnery, 2008.

Spencer, Robert. *The History of Jihad: From Muhammad to ISIS.* New York: Post Hill Press, 2018.

Spong, John Shelby. *Resurrection: Myth or Reality?* HarperOne, 1995.

Stark, Rodney. *God's Battalions: The Case for the Crusades.* New York: Harper One, 2009.

Swartley, Keith, ed. *Encountering the World of Islam.* Littleton, CO: Biblica, 2005.

Sweetman, J.W. *Islam and Christian Theology: A Study of the Interpretation of Theological Ideas in the Two Religions.* Part I: Volume I. London: Lutterworth, 1955.

Tolan, John. *Saracens: Islam in the Medieval European Imagination.* Columbia University Press, 2002.

Townsend, Peter. *Questioning Islam: Tough Questions & Honest Answers About the Muslim Religion.* Peter Townsend, 2014.

Townsend, Peter. *Nothing to Do with Islam? Investigating the West's Most Dangerous Blind Spot.* Peter Townsend, 2016.

Townsend, Peter. *The Mecca Mystery: Probing the Black Hole at the Heart of Muslim History.* Peter Townsend 2018.

Trifkovic, Serge. *The Sword of the Prophet: Islam – History, Theology, Impact on the World.* Boston: Regina Orthodox Press, 2002.

Tritton, A.S. *Muslim Theology.* Connecticut: Hyperion, 1947.

Trousdale, Jerry. *Miraculous Movements: How hundreds of Thousands of Muslims Are Falling in Love with Jesus.* Thomas Nelson, 2012.

Tyerman, Christopher. *The Debate of the Crusades.* New York: Manchester University Press, 2011.

Volf, Miroslav. *Allah: A Christian Response.* Harper One, 2011.

Wagner, William. *How Islam Plans to Change the World.* Grand Rapids, MI: Kregel, 2004.

Walzer, Richard. *Greek into Arabic.* Oxford: Oxford University Press, 1962.

Wansbrough, John. *Quranic Studies: Sources and Methods of Scriptural Interpretation.* New York: Prometheus Books, 2004.

Warner, Bill. *Sharia Law for Non-Muslims*, Center for the Study of Political Islam, 2010.

Watt, W. Montgomery. *Muhammad at Medina.* Oxford: Clarendon Press, 1956.

Weidekopf, Steve. *The Glory of the Crusades.* El Cajon, California: Catholic Answers, 2014.

Wensinck, A.J. *The Muslim Creed: Its Genesis and Historical Development.* Cambridge: Cambridge University Press, 1932.

Wilken, Robert. "Christianity Face to Face with Islam." *First Things*, January 2009.

Williams, J. L. *A Christian Perspective on Islam.* Wake Forest, NC: Integrity Publishers, 2008.

Wolfson, Harry. *The Philosophy of the Kalam.* Cambridge, MA: Harvard University Press, 1976.

Wood, Graeme. "What ISIS Really Wants." *The Atlantic Monthly*, March, 2015.

Work, Telford. "Sharpening the Doctrine of God: Theology Between Orthodox Christianity and Early Islam," November 25, 2002. Orthodox Theology Group, American Academy of Religion, Unpublished manuscript.

Youssef, Michael. *Blindsided: The Radical Islamic Conquest*. Kobri, 2012.

www.ingramcontent.com/pod-product-compliance
Lightning Source LLC
Chambersburg PA
CBHW071108160426
43196CB00013B/2508